CW00701264

THE DEVELOPER'S GUIDE TO THE JAVA™ WEB SERVER™

CD-ROM includes trial version of Java™ Web Server™ v.1.1.3

THE DEVELOPER'S GUIDE TO THE JAVA™ WEB SERVER™

Building Effective and Scalable Server-Side Applications

Dan Woods
Larne Pekowsky
Tom Snee

ADDISON–WESLEY

An Imprint of Addison Wesley Longman, Inc.

Reading, Massachusetts • Harlow, England • Menlo Park, California
Berkeley, California • Don Mills, Ontario • Sydney
Bonn • Amsterdam • Tokyo • Mexico City

Many of the designations used by manufacturers and sellers to distinguish their products are claimed as trademarks. Where those designations appear in this book and Addison-Wesley was aware of a trademark claim, the designations have been printed in initial caps or all caps.

The authors and publisher have taken care in the preparation of this book, but make no expressed or implied warranty of any kind and assume no responsibility for errors or omissions. No liability is assumed for incidental or consequential damages in connection with or arising out of the use of the information or programs contained herein.

The publisher offers discounts on this book when ordered in quantity for special sales. For more information, please contact:

Corporate, Government, and Special Sales Group
Addison Wesley Longman, Inc.
One Jacob Way
Reading, Massachusetts 01867

Library of Congress Cataloging-in-Publication Data

Woods, Dan
    The developer's guide to the Java™ Web Server™ : building effective
and scalable server-side applications / Dan Woods, Larne Pekowsky,
Tom Snee.
        p.   cm.
    ISBN 0-201-37949-X
        1. Java (Computer program language)   2. Web servers.
3. Application software—Development.   I. Pekowsky, Larne.
II. Snee, Tom.   III. Title.
QA76.73.J38W662   1999
005.2'762--dc21   99–27336
                                                                    CIP

Copyright © 1999 by Addison Wesley Longman, Inc.

Screen shots are reproduced courtesy of Sun Microsystems, Inc.

All rights reserved. No part of this publication may be reproduced, stored in a retrieval system, or transmitted, in any form, or by any means, electronic, mechanical, photocopying, recording, or otherwise, without the prior consent of the publisher. Printed in the United States of America. Published simultaneously in Canada.

ISBN 0-201-37949-X
Text printed on recycled and acid-free paper.

2 3 4 5 6 7   MA   02 01 00 99

2nd Printing   August 1999

The authors would like to thank everyone on the Java Web Server team for all the assistance during the building of the Money.com site, as well as the many hours spent providing information and suggestions for this book.

For my parents, George and Sheila Woods
D.W.

For the Handlynx
L.P.

For my mother, Diane Preston, and father, Tom Snee, Sr.
T.S.

CONTENTS

FOREWORD

The Java Web Server was designed by developers for developers. This book was written by developers for developers using the Java Web Server. It gives you, the Java Web developer, a wealth of information, guidance, and support for writing Web-based, platform-independent applications.

Whether you are a seasoned Java programmer or just starting to look at Java as an alternative to writing Web applications, this book has something for you. The extensive code examples, from servlet writing, to templates, to session tracking, and more, will give developers at any level insight into the inner workings of the features that make the Java Web Server a solid development platform.

If you are a seasoned developer who has mastered servlet writing and more, please be sure to check out the chapters on internationalization, optimization, and communicating with external applications. These topics, along with threading, make up the majority of questions that get posted on the *jserv-interest* list. This book will save you a post (and time waiting) to get the answer.

Many books get a developer started with a programming model, then abandon them just as their application is up and running but far from being "real" or productized. Because the authors used the Java Web Server to build the *Money.com* site, you will be guided through the entire development process, dealing with issues such as debugging, performance, stress testing, security, logging, maintenance, and customization. Their first-hand experience will save you considerable time in designing and building your own Java application.

Enjoy and use the wisdom in the book, and enjoy the beauty of developing in Java.

Connie Weiss
Senior Engineering Manager
Sun Microsystems, Inc.
Java Software Division

PREFACE

This book was born of the excitement of using a fine piece of technology. The authors discovered the Java™ Web Server™, used it for a major project, and loved it so much that we wanted to share our experience with the world at large.

The Java Web Server is like an addictive drug. After one taste you want more. After a month of regular use, you are hooked. And it is never possible to forget the experience. If this technology has the same effect on readers as it had on the authors, then we can expect many more Java Web Server programming zealots in the next few years.

We hope that this book provides you with a guide to the "charms" of the Java Web Server, and that your experience is as satisfying as ours has been. The book is presented in five parts: Overview, A Guide to Administration and Features, Coding Techniques, Application Development Techniques, and Java Web Server Internals.

Part I, Overview, starts with a comparison of the Java Web Server and other application architectures for the Web (Chapter 1). After the case for the Java Web Server is presented, the chapter moves on to overviews of the Java Web Server and the Servlet API. Chapter 2 describes the sample applications presented in the book.

Part II, A Guide to Administration and Features, walks through each of the server's features in detail. The reader learns how to create servlets (Chapter 3), how to configure and manage them (Chapter 4), and how to use functions like templating (Chapter 5), Java Server Pages (Chapter 6), session tracking (Chapter 7), and internalization and localization (Chapter 8).

Part III, Coding Techniques, dives into the guts of coding applications properly to achieve maximum performance in the Java Web Server. First servlets and the Servlet API are dissected (Chapter 9), followed by recommendations for writing thread-safe code (Chapter 10).

The following chapters cover optimizing performance of the Java virtual machine™ (Chapter 11) and the Java Class Libraries (Chapter 12). The last three chapters in this part cover techniques for communicating with external applications (Chapters 13, 14, and 15). In these chapters, servlets that communicate through sockets, e-mail, JDBC, RMI and CORBA are described.

The focus of Part IV, Application Development Techniques, is designing, debugging, stress testing, and tuning the performance of applications. Chapters 16 through 19 contain battle-tested practical tips for development.

Part V, Java™ Web Server™ Internals, groups several topics together—security, customizing, logging, and building services based on the Java Server Infrastructure—which are based on the low-level constructs of the Java Web Server and are the most likely to change in future releases. Many of the classes discussed in Chapters 20 through 22 will eventually be replaced by new implementations.

The appendix, Developer Resources, identifies helpful resources, both written and available on the Internet.

Suggestions for Reading This Book

Those who are new to the Java Web Server and servlet programming, or those who prefer a top-down explanation, from the general to the specific, will probably want to read the book straight through. Those who prefer an explanation that starts from the inside of an application—the guts of the code[1]—and proceeds outward will probably find it more useful to read Part I, then jump to Part III, and then Part IV. These readers can refer to Part II as questions arise.

We hope that developers reading this book find, as we did, that the Java Web Server is the gateway to a world of rapid development for scalable applications.

---

[1]In order to make the code readable, sometimes it has been shown in a less-than-optimal fashion. Please see the companion CD for the optimized versions.

ACKNOWLEDGMENTS

The authors would like to thank the widely scattered group of people who helped take this book from an idea to the printing press. Kevin McKean, editor of Money.com, started the ball rolling when he bought into the idea of basing his site on the Java Web Server. The original Java Web Server developers— Connie Weiss, James Duncan Davidson, Jim Driscoll, and Rob Clark—all gave generously of their fine minds. The current team, led by Martin Knutson, continued that tradition.

Dan Okrent and Linda McCutcheon, pappa and mamma bear of Time Inc. New Media, provided moral support, a couple of plane tickets, and sage advice. Our technology reviewers made the book far more focused and, even more helpful, accurate. Jon Meyer, Elliotte Rusty Harold, Anders Kristensen, Evan Coyne Maloney, and Tim Lindholm were especially insightful and even nice about their corrections.

Dan Woods would like to thank his wife, Daniele Gerard, and children, Fiona and Eamon, for putting up with grumpy daddy after early morning writing sessions. Tom Snee would like to thank his friends for understanding his disappearance into the world of writing. Larne Pekowsky would like to thank Steve Byrne and The Blackdown Java-Linux Porting Team, for their rock-solid Linux port of the Java Development Kit, under which most of the sample code was developed.

Of course, we would not have a book if it were not for the driven women of Addison Wesley Longman. Mary T. O'Brien snared us, Elizabeth Spainhour brought us to heel, and Marilyn Rash beat the errors out. We thank you and all others who helped.

PART I

Overview

PART 1

Overview

CHAPTER 1

The Big Picture

The Web has grown up. Applications are no longer like cute 2-year-old children who are delightful to watch whatever they do. Today's Internet applications must deliver high performance to succeed. The Internet and Intranet have vaulted applications from the desktops of data entry clerks right onto the CEO's laptop. High performance in such situations is not a luxury. Data entry clerks live with the performance they are given. CEOs—and, more important, customers—will not. After a short childhood, Web applications have graduated from college and must now earn their keep.

The key question of this book is: What are the best methods for developing high-performance Web applications? The answer we provide and elucidate is that, in general, using the Servlet Application Programming Interface (API) via the Java Web Server (JWS) is the fastest and most productive way to write high-performance Web applications. We believe that the advantages of Java as a language, servlets as architecture, and the Java Web Server as an elegant implementation provide a compelling platform for strategic development.

We arrived at this conclusion through fighting the guerilla war of Internet development over the past five years. We tried almost every software development technique before we started using the JWS. Now we do not want to use anything else. We begin with a tour based on our experience. In this chapter we provide a quick overview of the state of the art of Web development and the strengths and weaknesses of each approach.

Introduction to the Java Web Server

The Java Web Server represents a tremendous step forward for developers who seek to create scalable, portable, reliable applications that integrate functionality from diverse sources. It is a pleasant surprise that after all the buzz about Java applets, all the bouncing heads, and all the focus on Java for Web browsers, the fulfillment of Java's promise as a programming language should come on the server side.

From our perspective, the Java Web Server belongs in the same category as the various application server products on the market. The Java Web Server provides a framework for the integration, management, and delivery of application services that has a perfect mix of structure and flexibility. Whether you call it an application server, middleware, or anything else, the Java Web Server provides just enough functionality glue to hold together heterogeneous collections of applications without getting in the way.

Application Development and the JWS

The Java Web Server starts with the Java programming language, of course, and all the benefits of Java accrue to the Java Web Server. More specifically, note the following.

- *Rapid development:* The elimination of pointers protects against suicidal behavior. Java programs can fail, but gone are the days of analyzing the mysteries of core dumps. Java's elegant implementation of object-oriented programming techniques makes coding a pleasure.
- *Portability:* Java's portability is most profoundly successful on the server side, chiefly because most server-side programs need not traverse the thorny ground of graphical user interface (GUI) programming. Programs on the server side really can be written once to run anywhere. Another often overlooked portability feature is that Java code can be written anywhere as well. Code can be written on laptops and deployed on mainframes, which speeds up development.
- *Integration with other applications through a network:* Connecting to socket-based or CORBA applications is made easy through the networking classes, and other services that are written in Java can be exposed through remote method invocation. As a last resort, the Java Native Interface allows a programmer to construct interfaces to just about any application programming interface (API).
- *Threaded programs:* Java's thread model eases the complex job of constructing multithreaded programs.

The most prominent strength of the Java Web Server is that it provides a three-layer container for applications. The outermost layer is the Java Server, which contains a service, which surrounds the Servlet API, which, in turn, surrounds the code for an application. This structure along with the myriad other Java libraries is the glue that holds together powerful sets of applications.

The JWS's Powerful Features

Moving beyond the benefits of the Java programming language, the Java Web Server also enables application development with the following powerful features.

- *Fast and scalable:* The servlet architecture is built from the ground up for scalability. Unlike the CGI interface to applications programs, under which programs must be loaded into memory each time they execute, Java servlets load once and then reside in memory, which greatly speeds execution. Servlets start out with the assumption that they will execute in a multithreaded environment. The server keeps a pool of threads ready to handle requests as they arrive. The execution speed of Java is already sufficient for all but the highest-performance applications. With the improvements in execution speed expected from the HotSpot Java virtual machine (JVM), execution speed will only get better.
- *Integration with the HTTP protocol:* The Java Web Server provides an extremely tight integration with HTTP requests. Parsing of HTML elements such as command-line arguments and form variables is performed via standard utility methods. Advanced HTML processing features such as server-side includes are also supported.
- *Security:* The Java Web Server provides an extensible and configurable implementation of users, groups, and access control lists for controlling use of files, directories, and servlets. The security system can be extended to manage authentication through custom databases.
- *Logging:* The Java Web Server allows log records to be written according to whatever format is required. Standard log formats of the WWW Consortium are supported and custom log files can be created to meet specific needs.
- *Templating and Java Server Pages:* Templating provides a model for a simple content management system that can be quite successful for many sites. With Java Server Pages (JSP), HTML files can be embedded with Java code to allow flexible presentation for applications. JSPs can interface with JavaBeans and also employ special tags to control page output with as little coding as possible. This technology provides tremendous opportunities for personalization and configurability.
- *Extensibility:* Any of the functions in this list can be extended or replaced with custom code.
- *Easy to configure and manage:* Configuration and management of the server primarily take place through a Web interface that can be accessed remotely.

First-Hand Experience with JWS

Our experiences while developing the Money.com Web site for *Money Magazine*, America's leading personal finance magazine, illustrate the benefits of the Java Web Server. We began development of a new version of the magazine's site with the existing site that garnered 2.5 million page views a week.

The charge was to take what existed—a site that had been developed over two years and contained myriad sources of financial information, as well as a collection of homegrown applications—and transform it into an even more gargantuan site by adding a large collection of proprietary information from Thomson Investors Network. We also had to allow for private labeling of the site for various financial providers. This meant that the site had to permit pages to be dynamically generated, that is, custom tailored at request time for the users of each financial provider. And these dynamic pages had to be created to allow the integration of the existing pages and applications.

The Java Web Server made it possible to integrate the existing and new functionality in a manner that was scalable, reliable, and high-performance. We launched the new version of Money.com on October 16, 1997, and it handled the 2.5 million page views without a hitch. At that time, the site was the largest site, by volume, served using the Java Web Server.

The development of the new site took about three months, mostly consumed by design and stress testing. Coding was by far the least time-consuming part, and we never, not once, had to look at a core dump. Since working on the magazine's site, the Java Web Server has found a home at hundreds of sites on and off the Web.

Web Development Techniques

To further our case for the Java Web Server, we will now examine the most popular alternative methods used for Web application development.

Perl Code Executed via CGI

The most rapid path to a prototype for many applications is through writing Perl code executed through the common gateway interface (CGI). Indeed, this method is so attractive that most Web developers cut their teeth on Perl and wrote their first Web projects in this pervasive language. Other interpreted scripting languages, such as TCL and Python, are also popular choices because of their power and speed of development.

Here we discuss Perl, although what we say applies to almost all similar languages. Despite their advantages for quick development and prototyping,

Perl and other interpreted scripting languages are not the right choice for scalable applications.

The CGI was introduced as an extension to the original NCSA server to allow programs to create dynamic Web pages—pages that are created when they are requested. Static pages exist in files that are served out when requested. Dynamic pages are created by executing a program that assembles the information needed for the page, formats the information in HTML, and then writes it out to the user's browser. Dynamic pages generally contain the contents of a database query or the output of a program.

CGI programs are simple to administer. Generally, all that must happen is that a Web server must be told that a certain directory is available to contain CGI programs. On many systems, this directory defaults to cgi-bin.

When a request for a CGI program arrives, the Web server starts the program specified in the URL in a separate process on the server. The arguments to the CGI program are passed in through the URL, the environment variables, or the standard input stream. Output is returned to the browser through the standard output stream, as shown in Figure 1.1.

The strength of this architecture is its simplicity. Once the CGI directory containing the binaries is placed in the Web server configuration file, programs may be executed from within that directory quite quickly. No configuration changes are needed to introduce new programs for execution. Once a program is copied into the proper directory and marked as an executable, it can start servicing requests.

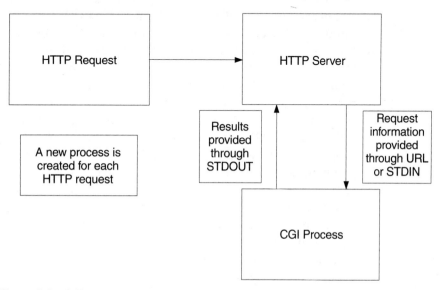

Figure 1.1   CGI application structure

The second major strength is the Perl language's ability to enable rapid development. Its regular expression features are perfect for many Web applications, which are frequently heavy manipulators of text. A wealth of public domain code exists for Perl, which allows a programmer to introduce all sorts of functionality from third parties, almost all of it free.

The problem with this development method is that it contains several performance bottlenecks. Each request creates a new process and loads its own copy of the program into memory. Creating a new process means setting up all the administrative overhead the operating system needs to keep track of a separate address space. This is a time-consuming and resource-intense operation. Once the new process is created, the flow of control must pass from the Web server to the CGI process and back again. This context switch is also a heavyweight operation that is best avoided in high-performance systems. With Perl code these problems are compounded because an interpreter must be loaded. At times of peak usage, the entire Web server can be bogged down as hundreds of Perl interpreters chug through the interpretation of their code.

Because CGI programs are loaded into memory for each request, no persistent connections to databases or other application services can be maintained. If a program wants to access some information in a Sybase or Oracle database, then the connection must be opened for each request, which can be a heavy-duty operation. Also, because the programs exist in memory for only the duration of the request, no state can be maintained in the program. Any persistent information—information that is maintained from request to request—must be written to a database or a file or preserved in the resulting page as arguments present in the URL or form variables. All these methods incur substantial overhead. As we said, databases must be established for each request. Writing to a file means that all requests become synchronized around access to that file, which can mean that all the Perl intepreters loaded to service the request must wait in single file for access. This is not the picture of a high-performance application.

Other problems with this structure stem from its simplicity. In most applications, the HTML statements delivered by CGI programs are embedded in the programs. This can make cooperation between a graphic design staff and a programming staff difficult. Simple changes to HTML may require a programmer. Also, if a lot of code is brought in from libraries, a huge amount of memory will be used for each instance of the Perl interpreter.

Improvement for the CGI application architecture can be achieved by writing code in C or C++ rather than in Perl. This makes the loading and execution of applications much faster. But the advantages of rapid development and easy debugging go flying out the window.

It is worth mentioning a variant on the CGI architecture called WINCGI, which was created in the O'Reilly server. In this CGI flavor, the input and output to a CGI program are contained in files. This technique, although popular with PC-DOS programmers, never caught on as widely as the next flavor we will discuss, FAST CGI.

FAST CGI

Significant improvement over the basic CGI architecture is available through the FAST CGI protocol, created by Open Market, Inc., and supported by the Apache Web Server. The fundamental idea of FAST CGI is to avoid reloading and initializing an application program for each request. In FAST CGI, applications execute as persistent daemons—programs that start up, initialize, and then wait for a request. A lightweight portion of the Web server accepts the CGI request, grabs any parameters passed, and opens a connection to the application daemon through a socket or a named pipe. The daemon program handles the request much faster than if it were running as a CGI because it does not have to load itself into memory each time. This allows persistent connections to databases or other application services to be maintained. The FAST CGI method does incur a context switch as the flow of control is passed from the Web server to the application daemon.

The FAST CGI protocol allows for load balancing across multiple daemons and for multiplexing many requests over a single socket connection to a multi-threaded daemon capable of simultaneously processing many requests. Unfortunately, in most implementations of FAST CGI, this architecture still remains single threaded through the daemon, which can be a major performance problem. The management of the named pipe or socket connection increases the complexity of the development and decreases reliability.

NSAPI

The Netscape Server Application Programming Interface (NSAPI) overcomes many of the performance problems inherent in CGI applications at the cost of rapid development. The NSAPI allows for the creation of server application functions (SAF), which essentially run as a part of the Web server in the same address space as Netscape's code. SAFs must be thread safe and must be written extremely carefully. If they crash, so does the server.

SAFs are written in C and are compiled into dynamic link libraries (DLLs). To install an SAF in a server, configuration files must be told where the DLL is so that it can be loaded at startup time. The server must be restarted to introduce a new SAF. After the server starts up with a new SAF, the SAF is invoked at the appropriate point in the processing of a request to perform its work.

Actually, the entire Netscape server is simply one long sequence of SAFs that are executed to perform various tasks involved in responding to an HTTP request. SAFs exist to initialize the server, authenticate users, translate file-names, check authorization, and process MIME types and errors. The most common type of SAF for an application is a service SAF that exists to send in-formation back to the requestor. Figure 1.2 shows how control flows through the various stages of the Netscape server. Each SAF is called in the same way with three arguments: a parameter block, which contains configuration infor-mation, the session, which contains variables that describe the TCP/IP connec-tion, and the request, which contains variables related to the current request.

Each Netscape server runs as a multithreaded process. For the versions of Netscape's server that run on the most popular platforms, each request is han-dled by a different thread. When the request arrives, it proceeds through the various SAFs that modify working variables, request headers, and response headers using NSAPI library routines. After each SAF executes, it returns a result code that the server uses to determine what to do next.

Once the service SAF gets control it starts the task of sending data in re-sponse to the HTTP request. Each SAF does much of its work with the NSAPI library functions that provide thread-safe and platform-independent versions of such commonly required application functions as IO, memory manage-ment, and thread management. NSAPI functions also exist to handle the HTTP protocol.

The basic structure of service SAFs is as follows: First the proper content type is placed in the response header, followed by any other required response headers. Then the HTTP response status is set and the start response function is called to send the HTTP response and headers. The bulk of the data is then sent using the NSAPI net_write routine. Calling net_write is the equivalent to pumping data out the STDOUT pipe in the CGI method.

As a programmer using NSAPI for applications, you get the thrill of, in effect, joining the Netscape server development team. The code for an applica-tion written in NSAPI executes right alongside the server code provided by Netscape. Application SAFs have the same rights and privileges as those that come with the server. This, of course, is a great blessing when it comes to per-formance. Applications in essence are an extension of the server. This structure is a deadly curse when it comes to reliability. If you make a mistake and acci-dentally synchronize your code so that only one thread can go through at a time or, even worse, cause a segment violation, the server and all others using it suffer the consequences.

As far as rapid development goes, NSAPI programs can be a tough slog. They must be developed in C, which is powerful and dangerous.

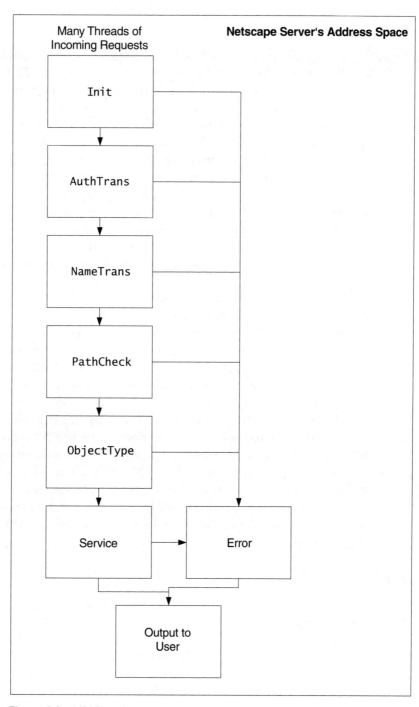

Figure 1.2 NSAPI application structure

Netscape WAI

Netscape recommends that developers who are starting afresh use the Web Application Interface (WAI) rather than the NSAPI. The WAI overcomes the most profound difficulty with NSAPI applications through the use of CORBA to manage the communication between the Web server and the application. In the WAI application structure, the application does not run in the same address space as the server. Rather, the incoming request is routed through the Object Request Broker (ORB) of the CORBA protocol to the application program that runs as a daemon in a separate address space. This architecture protects the server from badly written application code. If an application blows up, no harm is done to the server. On the other hand, running a WAI application in a separate daemon means that each request must undergo a context switch from the address space of the server to the address space of the WAI application and back again. WAI daemons are multithreaded, so many requests can be sent from the server to the WAI application at once.

The WAI technique does not allow the almost unlimited control over the processing of a request that NSAPI affords. It does, however, allow the application program to be written in a variety of languages, including Java and C++. Netscape provides a set of objects in C++ and Java to manage communication with the server. Starting with these objects, an application can be built to accept an incoming request from the server, process it, and return the resulting Web page.

One potential speedup to the WAI architecture is available. If the WAI application is written in C, the application can be run "in process," that is, as part of the Web server. In effect, an in-process WAI application runs as part of the server's address space, just like an NSAPI application. If a programmer is willing to take that risk, why not just write the application as an NSAPI application and avoid the WAI overhead? One reason is that an application written in WAI can rapidly be developed and tested out of process and then moved in process to increase performance.

ISAPI

The Internet Server Application Programming Interface (ISAPI) used to extend the functionality of the Microsoft Internet Information Server is similar to NSAPI in that it requires the extension to be packaged in a dynamically linked library. The programs used to extend the IIS are called ISAPI extensions or ISAPI filters. Extensions are programs that perform some application function. Filters are programs that are called for every request at predefined points. Filters are a great way to provide custom logging or authentication.

Application developers use extensions most. Extensions are almost always written in C++ with the Microsoft Foundation Classes, although they can be written in any language that can produce a DLL. Extensions are compiled into DLLs. Unlike NSAPI SAF functions, ISAPI extensions usually are loaded at the time of the first request.

At load time, the GetExtensionVersion function is called, which identifies the DLL to administrators, as well as any DLL functions to perform initialization. When a request for the DLL arrives, the HttpExtensionProc routine of the DLL is called and is passed. A parameter called the Extension Control Block retrieves information about the request, such as input parameters.

The broad structure of the ISAPI looks quite a bit like the NSAPI. Both techniques benefit from tight integration with the server, both require thread-safe code, and both run in the same address space as the server, all of which account for the performance benefits. The drawback of tight integration is that a poorly written ISAPI program can hobble or even crash the HTTP server. Using the Microsoft Transaction Server, ISAPI extensions can also run out of process, which subjects a request to a context switch but protects the server from being blown away by a bad extension.

Active Server Pages

Microsoft has an easier-to-use interface for application programmers, called Active Server Pages (ASPs), that provides an optimized environment for creating applications using scripting languages. Active Server Pages can be written in VB Script and JScript, which are provided by Microsoft, and Perl Script, which is provided by third-party vendors.

The environment in which Active Server Pages are executed is provided by an ISAPI extension. When a request for an ASP arrives at the server, it is routed to the ASP ISAPI extension, which then reads in the scripted pages and executes them. The ASP extension tries to improve performance of the scripted code by compiling it to a byte code, which is executed at a higher rate of speed than raw scripted code like Perl.

Active Server Pages have many features of the Java Web Server. The ASP architecture is based on a request/response sort of paradigm, with objects that encapsulate the request, response, session, and application. ASPs support templating and session tracking and are multithreaded. ASPs can be run in process or out of process using the Microsoft Transaction Server.

Active Server Pages allow for the rapid development of scripting languages, like Perl, with several performance enhancements. The byte code compilation improves performance of the scripted language, and the multithreaded implementation of the ASP extension avoids a context switch for each request. On the other hand, ASPs rely on the VB Script, which is less powerful than scripting languages like Perl and is of limited utility for large-scale applications.

The Java Web Server

The most profound difference between the previous approaches and the Java Web Server is the reliance on the Java language as the language for the extending server. Java frees us from worrying about access violations. It means that we have the rapid development of Perl and TCL and also the C++ ability to handle large applications. It means well-behaved code across platforms. It means that components can reside wherever it makes sense to us on the network.

For application developers, the Java Web Server is fast and safe. Extensions made to the server make it easy to track sessions and to combine servlets in chains of execution. JWS is modular and supports a component architecture, which makes it more suited to large applications.

Another striking difference between the Java Web Server and the other techniques discussed is its design. The other Web servers all started life as HTTP servers and were extended to allow for application programming. The Java Web Server, however, was conceived from the start as a way to deliver applications. The JWS does, of course, perform all the functions of a traditional Web server, but the delivery of applications is the main reason for the Java Web Server's existence. In fact, many parts of the JWS that perform standard system functions are servlets just like any other. This means that extending the functionality of the server is just like writing an application.

The final difference is that the Java Server and the Servlet API are not bound tightly to the HTTP protocol. The Java Web Server is an implementation of a server for the HTTP protocol that uses the Java Server Infrastructure (JSI) to provide a gateway to the Servlet API. The Servlet API is a general-purpose method for creating applications that fall under the request/response paradigm. Because the JSI and Servlet API are general-purpose application-building techniques not designed only for HTTP, they are the perfect foundation for integration of diverse application services. Legacy applications can be made to speak UDP or TCP/IP and can be front-ended by the Java Web Server, which can combine and integrate many services.

The first step in creating an application with the Java Web Server is to write a servlet. Servlets are the foundation of the JWS. They are just like any other Java program except for the fact that they are extensions of servlet classes that provide the glue to connect an application with the Web server. To execute a servlet, it first must be compiled and placed into the `Servlets` directory of the Java Web Server or in another directory that is in the classpath. Figure 1.3 shows the general structure of the Java Web Server.

In the general structure of a Java server, some sort of service is bound to an incoming port using TCP/IP or some other protocol. The service then maps the incoming requests to the memory-resident instances of the servlets' classes that

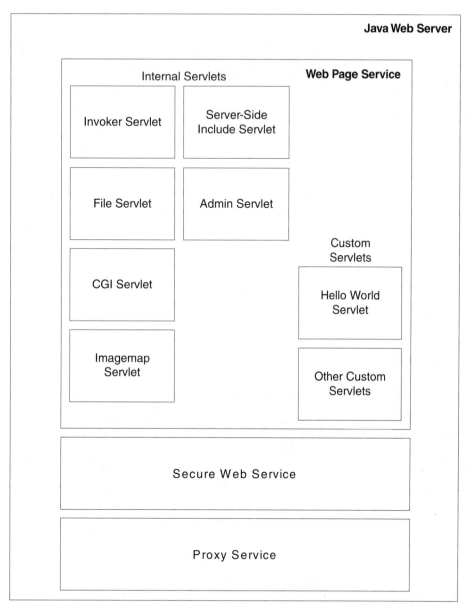

Figure 1.3   Structure of the Java Web Server

it dispatches. In the Java Web Server, the Web Service or the Secure Web Service accepts requests and then dispatches them to servlets. The servlet is chosen either because it is explicitly named in the request or because of an alias that maps a URL to a servlet.

The service() method of the servlet designated to handle the request is then invoked. The service method has two parameters, a request object and a response object. In the JWS, the servlet for HTTP requests is a subclass of the GenericServlet class called HttpServlet. The request and response objects are also subclassed to HttpServletRequest and HttpServletResponse. The HTTP versions of these objects have special members and functions to help handle the details of the HTTP protocol. Functions exist to read form data, get HTTP headers, set the type of output, specify the protocol return code, and perform many other tasks.

Once the service method has been called, the flow of execution proceeds as it does for most HTTP applications. Arguments are read either from the query string or from an input stream, some sort of application function is performed, HTTP header information is set, and then the content is written to an output stream. Listing 1.1 shows some sample code that illustrates what the "Hello World" program looks like as a servlet.

Listing 1.1   HelloWorldServlet.java, the "Hello World" servlet.

```
import java.io.*;
import javax.servlet.*;
import javax.servlet.http.*;

public class HelloWorldServlet extends HttpServlet {

    public void doGet (HttpServletRequest req,
                       HttpServletResponse res)
       throws ServletException, IOException
    {
      res.setContentType("text/html");

      ServletOutputStream out = res.getOutputStream();
      out.println("<html>");
      out.println("<head><title>Hello World</title></head>");
      out.println("<body>");
      out.println("<h1>Hello World</h1>");
      out.println("</body></html>");
    }

    public String getServletInfo() {
      return "Create a page that says <i>Hello World</i>"
              + " and send it back";
    }
}
```

The Java Web Server also has a set of internal servlets used to perform common Web server functions. The Invoker servlet loads servlets into the Web server. The File servlet reads and sends out plain HTML files. The CGI servlet invokes programs through the CGI gateway. The Server-Side Include servlet processes requests for includes from HTML files, and the Imagemap servlet routes clicks on image maps to the appropriate URL.

Servlets stay resident, like NSAPI and ISAPI programs. The code implementing a servlet must be thread safe and ideally should take advantage of a multithreaded architecture to increase the speed of processing. Servlets are as tightly bound to the Web server as are NSAPI and ISAPI, and their performance is almost as fast, suffering only because the Java virtual machines and compilers have not yet caught up with C++. Ballpark estimates put the performance of the JWS for static content at about 70 to 80 percent of that of commercial servers. The HotSpot compiler should significantly improve the performance of Java.

Because servlets are programmed in Java, they cannot trash the Web server, although, to be frank, it is possible to write servlets improperly and slow the Web server down through poor coding practices. Teaching ways to avoid such practices is the mission of this book. Servlets are simple in architecture, like CGI programs, and allow for rapid development through Java and through the utility methods provided by the HTTP versions of the servlet classes.

The Java Web Server, in short, offers the tight integration and speed of execution of the ISAPI and/or NSAPI architectures with the simplicity and the rapid development of the CGI. We find that these benefits are more profound in practice than in theory: implementing in Java takes one-third to one-fifth of the coding and debugging time of using C++, based on the author's experience. Table 1.1 summarizes the benefits and drawbacks of each method.

Overview of the Java Web Server

We will now take a whirlwind tour of the Java Web Server and the Servlet API. This explanation is far from exhaustive. It is provided as a quick once-over so that as we progress through the book each part of the Java server is already in perspective.

Configuration and Administration

Configuration of the Java Web Server takes place through a Web interface that is constructed of Java applets that communicate with a supporting administrative server (Figure 1.4). The interface allows for the manipulation of the key parameters that control the execution of the server. The JWS has three services available after installation: a Web Service, a Secure Web Service that uses a Secure Sockets Layer (SSL), and a Proxy Service that allows for caching of pages. Through the interface an administrator can start, stop, and restart services. An administrator can change the port from which the server accepts

Table 1.1 Comparison of Application Development Methods

Application Method	Server to Application Handoff	Application Persistence	Code Execution	Server Memory Safety	Languages	Threading Support
Perl/CGI	New process created for each request; heavyweight context switch between processes	No separate daemon; application program is reloaded and initialized for each request	Interpreted for scripting languages	Server protected in separate daemon; interpreted languages don't allow direct memory manipulation	Perl, Python, Java, C, C++—almost any language	Single threaded
Fast CGI	Heavyweight context switch	Separate application daemon loaded once and reused for each request	Language dependent; multiple languages supported	Server protected by separate daemon	Any language —usually Perl, C, or C++	Single threaded in most implementations
NSAPI/ISAPI	Application can run in process without context switch	Application becomes part of the Web server	Compiled code	Server vulnerable to application	C or C++ with MFC	Multithreaded
WAI	Generally run in separate daemon, which requires context switch	Separate application daemon	Compiled code	Server protected by separate daemon	C, C++, Java	Multithreaded
Active Server Pages	Can be run in process without context switch or as a daemon with context switch	Application can become part of the Web server or separate daemon	Byte code interpretation	In process, server protected by scripted code; out of process, protected by separate daemon	VB Script, JScript, Perl Script	Multithreaded
Java Web Server	No context switch	Application becomes part of the Web server	Byte code interpretation	Server protected by Java language	Java	Multithreaded

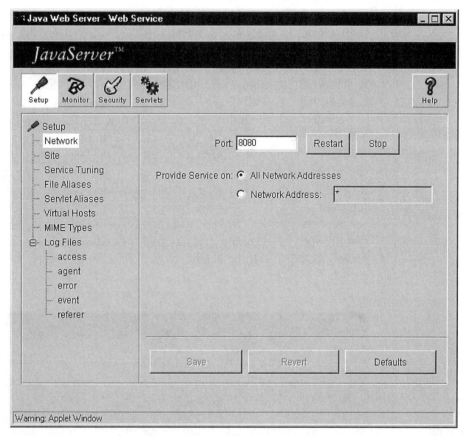

Figure 1.4 The Java Web Server administration tool

requests as well as ports to which administrative connections are made. The administration interface can change network parameters, such as which interface card to listen on, and site parameters, such as the location of the root directory. Aliases for files or for servlets can be constructed. Tuning parameters can be set for servlets—for example, cache size, minimum and maximum number of threads, and keep-alive settings such as maxium connections and timeouts. Standard Web parameters, such as the mapping of MIME types to file extensions and the location and behavior of log files, can also be set.

Loading and Invoking Servlets

Servlets are the core of the Java Web Server (we survey their internal structure in Chapter 9). Here we talk about how servlets can be loaded, executed, and administered.

Servlets are simply Java classfiles that employ the Servlet API to do their work. In the JWS, servlets can be loaded from the `<service_root>/servlets` directory or from a remote location. (`<service_root>` is a placeholder for whichever directory contains the installation of the Java Web Server.) It is important to note that the `Servlets` directory does not appear in the CLASSPATH.

Servlets can be added and configured with the administration interface. The Add interface allows servlets to be loaded into the server so that they are ready for execution as soon as a request arrives. The Configure interface allows the details of a servlet to be changed. Properties for each servlet that are accessible to the servlet when it is first loaded can be set in the Configure interface.

Servlets can be invoked in a variety of ways (Figure 1.5). A URL can directly specify a classfile that has been placed in an appropriate place in the server's CLASSPATH. If the "Hello World" class we examined earlier were placed

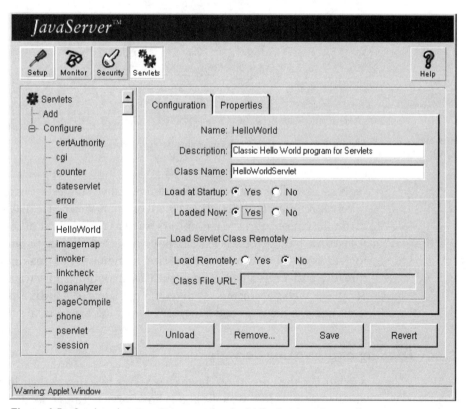

Figure 1.5   Servlet administration screen for the JWS administration tool

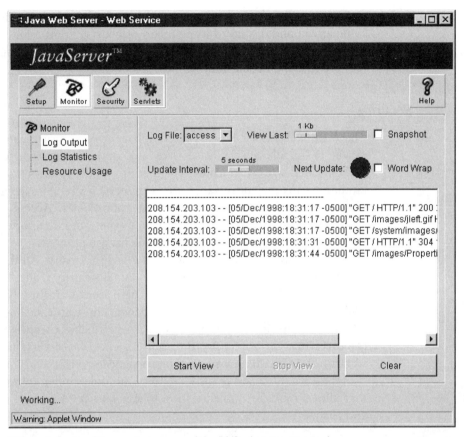

Figure 1.6 Log File monitor screen of the JWS administration tool

in the `<service_root>/servlets` directory and then loaded into the server through the administration tool, it could be invoked with the URL

http://<your_machine_name>:8080/servlet/HelloWorld

(The port number 8080 is the default port for incoming requests after the JWS is installed.) Servlets can also be executed by requesting a URL that is an alias for the servlet, by calling them from server-side includes or even by other servlets calling each other as part of a filter chain.

Monitoring

The administration interface allows the log files to be examined in a variety of ways (Figure 1.6). Through a log file viewer an administrator can control how much of the log file will be displayed, the width of the log entry, and the frequency with which the display will be refreshed. Log file data can also be summarized and displayed using tables or charts. Another interface shows the memory and handler threads used by a service as well as the number of requests that are arriving during varying intervals of time.

Security

The Java Web Server has a full complement of security features plus a few others to handle special cases like SSL and servlets loaded remotely but authenticated with certificates. The security model follows a standard pattern familiar to anyone conversant with Web servers. Users are assigned to groups. Groups and users are placed on access control lists. Access control lists are associated with resources—that is, files, servlets, and directories, as well as the permissions that users and groups on the list are granted.

A Java-specific security feature is the security realm. All the users, groups, and access control lists are contained within a security realm. Different realms are used for different types of security. There are realms for UNIX and NT that both interact with operating-system–dependent features. There is a default realm for controlling example servlets. A certificate realm is used to protect resources that are served by the secure sockets layer version of the JWS. A servlet manager realm exists to support signed servlets.

The Java Web Server also supports multiple cipher suites, a part of SSL that allows multiple authentication schemes to be employed between servers and clients.

Templates

Templating and JSPs are powerful tools for Web developers. These features are techniques for creating HTML pages, and they provide a key methodology for content management and application development.

Templating is a feature that allows a global structure to be applied to a set of HTML documents. When a set of pages are set to be served by the TemplateServlet, which replaces the default FileServlet, certain substitutions are made when those pages are served. The FileServlet is the internal servlet that is used to serve out plain HTML files. Each page served by templating can have the HEAD and BODY tags controlled by a default template file, named default.html. When it is being served, the document is carved into two pieces, the portion between the beginning and ending HEAD tags and the portion between the beginning and ending <BODY> tags. Each portion is extracted and placed within the HEAD and BODY tags of the default template and then served. In this way, if the default template file is changed, the change will occur in all files served by templating. Further customization can occur through the use of definition files, which associate specific values to be substituted for variables in the template files. A definition file provides a set of values for the directory in which it resides and all subdirectories.

Listing 1.2 is a set of files that show how a `default.html` file and some test files would be combined to produce an output page.

Listing 1.2   The JWS template pages.

default.html
```
<HEAD>
<subst data="HEAD"/>
</HEAD>
<BODY BGCOLOR="#FFFFFF">
<H1>A templated page!</H1>
<subst data="BODY"/>
<HR>
<FONT SIZE="-1">This page comes to you courtesy
of the Java Web Server</FONT>
</BODY>
</HTML>
```

test1.html
```
<html>
<head>
<title>Hello world!</title>
</head>
<body>
Hello world!
</body>
</html>
```

test2.html
```
<html>
<head>
<title>Hello again, world!</title>
</head>
<body>
Hello again, world!
</body>
</html>
```

Here's what the end user gets when requesting `test1`.

```
<!-- Java Web Server Template:
     public_html/template/tests/default.template -->
<HEAD>
<title>Hello world!</title>
</HEAD>
```

```
<BODY BGCOLOR="#FFFFFF">
<H1>A templated page!</H1>
Hello world!
<HR>
<FONT SIZE="-1">This page comes to you courtesy
of the Java Web Server</FONT>
</BODY>
</HTML>
```

To use this example:

1. Use the administration tool to assign an alias, perhaps /templates, to the template servlet.

2. The <server_root>/public_html/template directory should have come with the Web server. Create a subdirectory, perhaps tests, to contain default.template, test1.html, and test2.html.

3. You can now see the pages at

   http://<your machine>:8080/templates/tests/test1.html and *test2.html*

4. Make a change to the default template. Instantly, the change is reflected in both pages!

Java Server Pages

Java Server Pages, which allow Java code to be embedded within an HTML file, is, perhaps, after the Servlet API, the most powerful feature provided for Web developers in the Java Web Server. To use a JSP, a developer creates a file that is part HTML and part Java code. Such a file is stored in a filename with the extension *.jsp. The hybrid HTML/Java file is then compiled and turned into a servlet, which lets the embedded code control the output of the HTML. There is almost no limit to the kinds of pages that can be produced with this technique. Java Server Pages are a godsend for developers who seek an elegant way to integrate application functionality and HTML display. Java Server Pages also provide pages similar enough to HTML that designers can modify the HTML they contain without the help of a programmer. Listing 1.3 is a Java Server Page that implements the "Hello World" example.

Listing 1.3   A simple Java Server Page.

```
<java type="import"> java.util.* </java>
<java type="import"> java.text.* </java>
<html>
<head>
   <title>Page-compiled Hello World</title>
</head>
<body>
Hello world!   The local time is
```

```
<java>
Date theDate   = new Date();
StringBuffer sb = new StringBuffer();
DateFormat   tf = DateFormat.getTimeInstance(DateFormat.LONG);
out.println(tf.format(theDate));
</java>
</body>
</html>
```

Session Tracking

Session tracking is a feature of the Java Web Server that allows developers to capture and preserve an application's state across HTTP requests. As most developers discover soon after they start programming Web applications, preserving state in a stateless protocol can be quite annoying. URLs, cookies, form variables, or databases all have significant drawbacks for storing state.

Session tracking is a lightweight method of storing an arbitrary amount of information between requests. Users are identified from request to request via a unique session identifier that is stored in a cookie in their browser or embedded in the URL. The advantage of this recognition scheme is that it does not require users to register to identify themselves. They can have an anonymous identity. When a user makes his first request, a session object is created and the application stores whatever it desires within the session object. As subsequent requests are made, the information in the session object is read and updated by the application. The application code is dramatically simplified because it does not have to jump through the hoops required by form variables, URL rewriting, or database access.

Session tracking has extensive configurability to allow the server administrator to control the behavior of the session objects created. The maximum amount of session objects that can be in memory at once, the time-out period, the location of the swap directory for session objects, and a variety of characteristics of the cookies are among the parameters that can be changed. Session tracking is the key to implementing personalized services.

Listing 1.4 is a simple example of session tracking that adds a counter to the HelloWorld servlet.

Listing 1.4 Hellocounter.java, a simple session tracking servlet.

```
import java.io.*;
import javax.servlet.*;
import javax.servlet.http.*;
public class hellocounter extends HttpServlet {
  public void doGet (HttpServletRequest request,
                     HttpServletResponse response)
      throws ServletException, IOException
```

```
        {
              // Get the Session object. This will set a cookie in the browser,
              // if it is not already present.
              HttpSession session = request.getSession(true);

              // Get the count from the session.
              Integer count = (Integer) session.getValue("hello.counter");

              // If this session does not have a count yet, provide one,
              // otherwise increment it.
              if (count == null) {
                count = new Integer(1);
              } else {
                count = new Integer(count.intValue() + 1);
              }

              // Save the new value.
              session.putValue("hello.counter", count);

              // Send out the page!
              response.setStatus(HttpServletResponse.SC_OK);
              response.setContentType("text/html");

              ServletOutputStream out = response.getOutputStream();

              out.println("<html>");
              out.println("<head>");
              out.println("   <title>Session Tracking Test</title>");
              out.println("</head>");

              out.println("<body>");
              out.println("<h1>Hello world!</h1>");
              out.println("You have greeted the world " + count +
                      ((count == 1) ? " time" : "times"));
              out.println("</body></html>");
        }
    }
```

Java Server Infrastructure

The Java Server Infrastructure is a set of APIs that are used to build Java servers and services. For example, the JWS is built using the Java Server Infrastructure. The idea of the JSI is that just as servlets will be able to execute with any Web server that supports servlets, eventually services will be able to run within any platform that supports them. APIs exist for Web-based administration, security, HTTP support, sandboxes, servlets, servlet beans, SSL, page compilation, and session tracking.

The most prominent advantage of the Java Server Infrastructure for developers is its capacity to transcend the world of Web servers and bring information through diverse protocols to servlets for processing. The Java Web Server is tightly bound to the HTTP protocol transmitted using the TCP/IP protocol. JSI services can implement any protocol. Endpoint classes provide an abstraction of the network interface, which allows traffic from many different protocols to be handled and passed on to services. The chapters on Java Server Infrastructure cover various aspects of the JSI.

 NOTE: When reading or using this material, it is important to note that Sun has not committed to preserving the classes at this level in future versions of the JWS. In fact, Sun has suggested that it may move to reimplement parts of the Java Web Server that now use the JSI using the Java ServerSpaces technology. We feel, however, that the material on the JSI allows developers to extend the JWS in ways that are important with respect to logging, security, or special-purpose servers, so we have kept this material in this book.

Overview of the Servlet API

Now we switch from the Webmaster's view of the Java Web Server to the programmer's view. We will dive into servlets in order to give readers an idea of what life is like for a servlet programmer.

What Are Servlets?

A servlet is the extension of the applet concept to the server. Applets were introduced when Java first arrived on the Internet to show how the Web could deliver applications as well as HTML files. Applets woke up Web pages with animation and attractive interfaces. They also carried with them the platform independence and the rapid development of Java. Servlets should have a similar effect on server-side programming. Through intelligent use of the servlet architecture, programmers will finally have a chance at realizing the long-promised benefits of object-oriented languages: rapid development, code reuse, and repurposable implementations.

Servlets are programs that do their work by extending a set of Java interfaces called the Servlet Application Programming Interface. The Servlet API is an approach to writing applications that assumes that some sort of request for information will be received by a program that will generate a response. Sun calls this model the request/response paradigm.

Although we feel that the JWS is the most attractive way to develop and deploy servlets, it is important to point out that the servlet architecture is being adopted by most server platforms. At the time of this writing, almost all popular Web servers support servlets or have plans to do so.

Another way of looking at servlets is as a thin layer for managing the communication between an application program and the outside world. The job of the service and servlet layers is to grab an incoming request, parse the input into a well-understood form, provide methods for reading and writing the input data, accept output data from the application, and pass the output data to the ultimate destination.

The Servlet API is specified as a collection of five Java interfaces. The structure of the interfaces is shown in Figure 1.7. The boxes shown in the figure

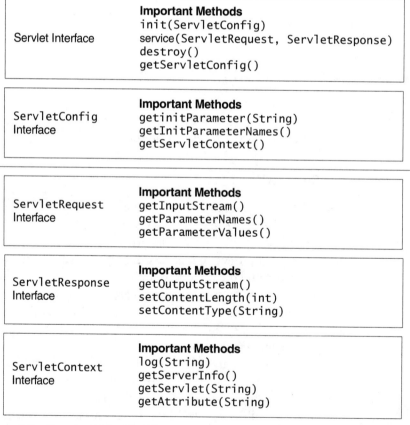

Figure 1.7   Overview of Servlet API

illustrate the important methods of each interface and how the interfaces are connected. The box marked `GenericServlet` is there to show that the `GenericServlet` class implements the `Servlet` and the `ServletConfig` interfaces. The `GenericServlet` class is the fundamental application class for servlets. Almost all servlets are subclasses of this class or its descendants.

The `Servlet` interface contains the methods that are used to do the work of the application: `init()`, `service()`, and `destroy()`. The `init()` method is called when the servlet is loaded; it is not called for each request. The `init()` method is the spot where a servlet gets ready to perform its work. This method has one argument, the `ServletConfig` object, which provides access to configuration and system parameters. This is the method in which configuration parameters are read, pools of resources set up, connections to databases established, and other such tasks performed. The `init()` method is guaranteed to be single threaded.

The `service()` method is where each request is transformed into a response. This method must be written to be thread safe because each request that arrives at the JWS is handled by a different thread. Two arguments are passed when the `service()` method is invoked, a `ServletRequest` object and `ServletResponse` object. The job of the `service()` method is to use the `ServletRequest` object to figure out what to do, do it, and then send the result back to the user through the `ServletResponse` object.

The `destroy()` method is called when the servlet is unloaded. It is the place to undo all the initialization done in the `init()` method. It is important to point out that an application program should never call the `init()` or `destroy()` methods directly. This can cause unpredictable and potentially damaging behavior.

The `ServletConfig` interface is the gateway to configuration parameters and other system information. Its three methods are `getInitParameter (String)`, which retrieves the value of a single initialization parameter, `getInitParameterNames()`, which retrieves an enumeration of all initialization parameters, and `getServletContext`, which returns the `ServletContext` object. Initialization parameters are those that are set in the property screen of the `Configure` section of the `Servlet` portion of the administration tool.

The `ServletRequest` interface encapsulates incoming requests. This object is implemented by the JWS to pass on all relevant information about a request to the application. Incoming data is passed to the application in two ways, through parameters and through streams. The `getParameterNames()` and `getParameterValues(String)` methods give the `service()` method access to parameters. `getInputStream()` gives the `service()` method the ability to read the incoming data that is provided via a stream. This method and its counterpart `ServletResponse` are subclassed and enhanced to meet the needs of HTTP. We discuss the enhancements in the following section.

The `ServletResponse` interface routes the output of a `service()` method back to its destination. The `setContentLength(int)` and `setContentType (String)` allow the output stream to be described. The `getOutputStream()` method lets the `service()` method grab the output stream so that it can write out the results of the request. Again, this interface is significantly enhanced for HTTP in the `HttpServletResponse` interface.

The `ServletContext` interface meets the need to talk to other parts of the system. The `log(String)` method writes information to a log. The `getServer-Info()` method returns information about the server that is running the servlet. The `getAttribute(String)` method returns attribute values of the server. The `getServlet(String)` method returns a reference to the servlet object of the name specified.

Knowing something about the main points of the Servlet API should clarify the tasks of the Java Web Server—or any server written to support servlets. When a request comes in over the network, the server must create a `ServletRequest` object, map the request to a servlet, load the servlet if it is not loaded, create a `ServletResponse` object, and then call the `service()` method of the servlet being invoked. Obviously, the reality is much more complex, but this is an accurate high-level view of the tasks of the server.

Servlets for the HTTP Protocol

The previous section discussed the structure of a generic servlet, one that is not designed for any specific protocol like HTTP. The existence of a level of encapsulation above HTTP has advantages for server developers who can write servers that handle traffic from any protocol and pass requests on to servlets. Web programmers, of course, use the interface that is designed specifically for HTTP. The `javax.servlet.http` package extends the servlet, request, and response interfaces to make them more friendly to the Web. The HTTP versions of these three interfaces all work fundamentally the same as the generic versions. The difference is that these versions are adorned with methods to handle the specifics of HTTP. The three most important parts of the HTTP-specific classes and interfaces are `HttpServlet`, `HttpServletResponse`, and `HttpServletRequest`.

The `HttpServlet` class extends the `GenericServlet` class to handle the different types of requests that come in over the Web. This class is used differently from the `GenericServlet` class in that programmers should not override the `service()` method to get the work of an application done. Instead, a `doGet()` method handles `GET` requests, a `doPost()` method handles `POST` requests. Methods named `doPut()`, `doDelete()`, `doOptions()`, and `getLastModified()` support those parts of the HTTP protocol. Each of the methods takes an

HttpServletRequest object and an HttpServletResponse object as arguments, just as the service() method does. All have default implementations that return an HTTP BAD_REQUEST error.

The HttpServletRequest class adds a trove of useful accessor methods to the generic ServletRequest interface. In addition to all the methods in ServletRequest, HttpServletRequest adds methods to get the cookies, header field values, request method, and query string of the incoming HTTP request. Another class, HttpUtils, has methods to parse the data in the input stream for a POST request or the arguments in the query string passed in a GET request.

The HttpServletResponse class is the mirror image of the HttpServlet-Request class. The response object has methods to set what the request object gets. Methods in this class set cookies and header values, send error or redirect messages, and encode URLs to contain session IDs if cookies are not supported in the browser sending the request.

Methods to handle use of persistent sessions exist in all HTTP versions of the servlet interface. These methods interact with the cookies being sent with the request to connect the servlet with the appropriate session object if session tracking is in use.

Conclusion

In this chapter we have made the case for the Java Web Server compared to other Web application development choices currently available. We have also presented a summary of the features available through the JWS. It is our hope that this chapter and the detailed explanations that follow offer the reader the same sense of excitement we had when we first came upon this wonderful technology.

CHAPTER 2

Introduction to the Sample Applications

Throughout the text, we refer to two sample applications, the full source code for which is available on the accompanying CD-ROM. Both applications were chosen for the way in which they illustrate common techniques that occur frequently in real-world applications, and both lend themselves well to servlets.

Project Plan Archive

Most developers begin a new programming project by writing a project plan. Good for most developers! Unfortunately, they almost always end a programming project with an outdated, inaccurate project plan.

Overview

Design changes and schedule rearrangements always occur during development, but few people have the discipline to go back to the plans and bring them up to date. We cannot count on future generations of programmers to have any more discipline than the current lot, so the project plan problem should not be treated as a people problem. Project plans should just be made easier to maintain.

Many a coding shop has ended up with a homegrown project management application. Ideally, it gives a simple interface for multiple concurrent project updates from clients on different platforms. Sounds like a job for servlets! The first sample application, a Java Web Server (JWS) project management system, uses a set of architecture-independent classes to model an archive of project plans and a relatively thin servlet to manage the archive.

The project plan archive application is designed to serve as the central repository of information about numerous projects. In addition to handling simple time lines and resource scheduling, it also interacts with electronic mail and directory services to relate the mail traffic about the project to the ongoing status of the project.

Object Model

One of the root objects of this application is the task. A task can be opened and closed. It has a name, description, and type. Projects are tasks (see Listing 2.1) that can themselves contain other tasks, for example, milestones to reach (see Listing 2.2), bugs to fix (see Listing 2.3), and topics (issues) to address (see Listing 2.4).

Listing 2.1   Task.java.

```java
package com.awl.cseng.jws.project;


import java.util.Date;


/**
 * Abstract superclass of all project tasks. Has properties
 * Opened (Date opened), Closed (Date closed), Due (Date due),
 * Name, Description, and Type (to be used by subclasses).
 */
public abstract class Task implements java.io.Serializable
{
    protected Date   opened, closed,      due;
    protected String name,   description, type;


    public    Task() { setOpened(new Date()); }


    protected void   setOpened(Date d)     { opened = d; }
    public    Date   getOpened()           { return opened; }

    protected void   setClosed(Date d)     { closed = d; }
    public    Date   getClosed()           { return closed; }

    public    void   setDue(Date d)        { due = d; }
    public    Date   getDue()              { return due; }

    public    void   setName(String s)     { name = s; }
    public    String getName()             { return name; }
```

```
public     void    setDescription(String s){ description = s; }
public     String  getDescription()         { return description; }

public     void    setType(String s)        { type = s; }
public     String  getType()                { return type; }

/**
 * Close this task, using the current date as the closing date.
 */
public void close() { setClosed(new Date()); }
}
```

Listing 2.2 `Milestone.java.`

```java
package com.awl.cseng.jws.project;


/**
 * A project milestone to be reached.
 */
public class Milestone extends Task
implements java.io.Serializable
{
  public Milestone() { type = "Milestone"; }
}
```

Listing 2.3 `Bug.java.`

```java
package com.awl.cseng.jws.project;

/**
 * A project bug to be tracked.
 */
public class Bug extends Task implements java.io.Serializable
{
  public Bug() { type = "Bug"; }
}
```

Listing 2.4 `Topic.java.`

```java
package com.awl.cseng.jws.project;


/**
 * A project issue to be discussed.
 */
public class Topic extends Task implements java.io.Serializable
{
  public Topic() { type = "Topic"; }
}
```

Milestones, bugs, and topics don't need to add anything to our notion of a generic task. Projects, however, need to be able to contain other tasks (see Listing 2.5).

Listing 2.5 `Project.java.`

```java
package com.awl.cseng.jws.project;


import java.util.Hashtable;
import java.util.Enumeration;


/**
 * A task that can have subtasks.
 */
public class Project extends Task implements java.io.Serializable
{
   protected Hashtable subTasks = new Hashtable();

   public Project() { type = "Project"; }

   public Task getSubTask(String s) {
      return (Task)subTasks.get(s);
   }

   public Enumeration getSubTasks() {
      return subTasks.elements();
   }

   public Enumeration getSubTaskNames() {
      return subTasks.keys();
   }

   /**
    * Silently fails if this project is already closed.
    */
   public void addSubTask(Task t)   {
      if ( this.getClosed() == null ) {
         subTasks.put(t.getName(), t);
      }
   }

   /**
    * Silently fails if this project is already closed.
    */
   public void removeSubTask(Task t) {
      if ( this.getClosed() == null ) {
         subTasks.remove(t.getName());
      }
   }
}
```

Notice that these classes don't depend on any of the Standard Java Extensions (javax.* packages). They can be instantiated and manipulated in any Java environment—an applet, an application, or even a servlet. Before we rush off and start using them, though, let's look at some helper classes that make it easier to assemble and use them.

The first is a set of literal strings that all pieces of the sample application can use to communicate with each other. Anyone who has worked with Web programming knows how annoying it can be to keep HTML form parameters in synch with CGI code. With these constants, code that generates HTML forms is guaranteed to use the same strings as the code that processes those forms. They are in an interface so that classes that want to use them can implement that interface to use their short names—for example, PROJECT instead of ArchiveConstants.PROJECT (see Listing 2.6). If they were in a class, other classes would have to refer to the constants by their long names.

Listing 2.6 ArchiveConstants.

```java
package com.awl.cseng.jws.project;


/**
 * Encapsulates String constants used by an archive of project
 * plans. These strings can be used in HTML forms for HTTP
 * archives, as email Subject headers for EmailArchives, or as
 * column names in a database table for DatabaseArchives.
 *
 * @see Archive
 * @see EmailArchive
 * @see DatabaseArchive
 */
public interface ArchiveConstants {
  public static final String ACTION = "ACTION";
  public static final String OPEN   = "OPEN";
  public static final String UPDATE = "UPDATE";
  public static final String CLOSE  = "CLOSE";

  public static final String TYPE      = "TYPE";
  public static final String MILESTONE = "MILESTONE";
  public static final String TOPIC     = "TOPIC";
  public static final String BUG       = "BUG";
  public static final String PROJECT   = "PROJECT";

  public static final String PROJECT_NAME = "PROJECT_NAME";
  public static final String NAME         = "NAME";
  public static final String DESCRIPTION  = "DESCRIPTION";
  public static final String DUE_DATE     = "DUE_DATE";
  public static final String OPEN_DATE    = "OPEN_DATE";
  public static final String CLOSE_DATE   = "CLOSE_DATE";
}
```

The second helper class is the Archive class (see Listing 2.7), which contains multiple projects.

Listing 2.7   Archive.java.

```java
package com.awl.cseng.jws.project;


import java.util.*;
import java.text.*;


/**
 * An archive of evolving project plans.
 */
public class Archive extends Task
implements java.io.Serializable, ArchiveConstants {
  // instance field
  protected Hashtable projects;


  // constructor
  public Archive() {
    projects = new Hashtable();
  }


  // instance methods
  public void      addProject(Project p)     {
    projects.put(p.getName(), p);
  }

  public void      removeProject(Project p) {
    projects.remove(p.getName());
  }

  public Project    getProject(String s)     {
    return (Project)projects.get(s);
  }

  public Enumeration getProjects()           {
    return projects.elements();
  }

  public Enumeration getProjectNames()      {
    return projects.keys();
  }


  /**
   * Updates an archive with a command stored in a Hashtable.
   * For instance,
```

```
 *  <CODE>
 *  Hashtable cmd = new Hashtable();
 *  cmd.put(ArchiveConstants.ACTION, ArchiveConstants.OPEN);
 *  cmd.put(ArchiveConstants.TYPE, ArchiveConstants.PROJECT);
 *  cmd.put(ArchiveConstants.NAME, "New Project Name");
 *  cmd.put(ArchiveConstants.DUE_DATE, "12/15/98");
 *  Archive archive = new Archive();
 *  archive.update(command);
 *  </CODE>
 *  creates an empty archive and then instructs it to create
 *  a new Project named "New Project Name" due to complete on
 *  12/15/98.
 *
 *  @param ht - Keyed by string constants in ArchiveConstants.
 *  @see ArchiveConstants#PROJECT_NAME
 *  @see ArchiveConstants#NAME
 *  @see ArchiveConstants#DESCRIPTION
 *  @see ArchiveConstants#OPEN_DATE
 *  @see ArchiveConstants#DUE_DATE
 *  @see ArchiveConstants#CLOSE_DATE
 *  @see ArchiveConstants#TYPE
 *  @see ArchiveConstants#PROJECT
 *  @see ArchiveConstants#MILESTONE
 *  @see ArchiveConstants#BUG
 *  @see ArchiveConstants#TOPIC
 *  @see ArchiveConstants#ACTION
 *  @see ArchiveConstants#OPEN
 *  @see ArchiveConstants#UPDATE
 *  @see ArchiveConstants#CLOSE
 */
public void update(Hashtable ht) {
  String projectName = extractParameter(ht, PROJECT_NAME);
  String name        = extractParameter(ht, NAME);
  String description = extractParameter(ht, DESCRIPTION);
  String action      = extractParameter(ht, ACTION);
  String type        = extractParameter(ht, TYPE);
  Date   openDate    = getDate(ht, OPEN_DATE);
  Date   dueDate     = getDate(ht, DUE_DATE);
  Date   closeDate   = getDate(ht, CLOSE_DATE);

  if ( action.equalsIgnoreCase(OPEN) ) {
    if ( type.equalsIgnoreCase(PROJECT) ) {
      Project project = new Project();
      project.setName(name);
      project.setDescription(description);
      project.setDue(dueDate);
      addProject(project);
    } else if ( projectName == null ) {
      throw new IllegalArgumentException(
                                "Project name not specified");
    } else {
      Task t;
```

```
      Project project = getProject(projectName);
      if ( project == null ) {
        throw new IllegalArgumentException(
                                  "Cannot find project "
                                  + projectName);
      }

      if ( type.equalsIgnoreCase(MILESTONE) ) {
        t = new Milestone();
      } else if ( type.equalsIgnoreCase(BUG) ) {
        t = new Bug();
      } else if ( type.equalsIgnoreCase(TOPIC) ) {
        t = new Topic();
      } else {
        throw new IllegalArgumentException("Unknown task: "
                                          + type);
      }
      t.setName(name);
      t.setDescription(description);
      t.setDue(dueDate);
      project.addSubTask(t);
    }
} else if ( action.equalsIgnoreCase(UPDATE) ) {
  Task t;
  if ( type.equalsIgnoreCase(PROJECT) ) {
    t = getProject(projectName);
  } else {
    t = getProject(projectName).getSubTask(name);
  }
  t.setName(name);
  t.setDescription(description);
  t.setOpened(openDate);
  t.setDue(dueDate);
  t.setClosed(closeDate);
} else if ( action.equalsIgnoreCase(CLOSE) ) {
  Project project = getProject(projectName);
  if ( project == null ) {
    throw new IllegalArgumentException("Cannot find project "
                                      + projectName);
  }
  if ( type.equalsIgnoreCase(PROJECT) ) {
    project.close();
  } else {
    Task t = project.getSubTask(name);
    if ( t != null ) {
      t.close();
    } else {
      throw new IllegalArgumentException("Cannot find "
                                        + name
                                        + " in project "
                                        + project.getName());
    }
  }
}
```

```java
    } else {
      throw new IllegalArgumentException("Unknown action: "
                                         + action);
    }
  }


  /**
   * Convenience method for extracting a String from a
   * Hashtable that stores Strings and/or arrays of Strings.
   * Throws ClassCastException if the value of ht indexed by
   * paramName is neither a String nor an array of Strings.
   */
  protected String extractParameter(Hashtable ht,
                                     String paramName) {
    String param = null;
    Object o = ht.get(paramName);
    if ( o instanceof java.lang.String ) {
      param = (String)o;
    } else {
      String[] paramArray = (String[])ht.get(paramName);
      if ( paramArray != null
      &&   paramArray.length > 0
      &&   paramArray[0] != null ) {
        param = paramArray[0].trim();
      }
    }
    return param;
  }


  /**
   * Returns null on bad input.
   */
  protected Date getDate(Hashtable ht, String dateType) {
    DateFormat shortFmt, mediumFmt, longFmt;
    Date date = null;

    String dateString = extractParameter(ht, dateType);

    try {
      shortFmt = DateFormat.getDateInstance(DateFormat.SHORT);
      date     = shortFmt.parse(dateString);
    } catch (ParseException e1) {
      try {
        mediumFmt = DateFormat.getDateInstance(
                                          DateFormat.MEDIUM);
        date      = mediumFmt.parse(dateString);
      } catch (ParseException e2) {
        try {
          longFmt = DateFormat.getDateInstance(DateFormat.LONG);
          date    = longFmt.parse(dateString);
```

```
        } catch (ParseException e3) {
          // No more formats to try . . .
          return null;
        }
      }
    }

  return date;
  }
}
```

Applications that have a GUI interface will probably use constructors to instantiate projects and other tasks and then use Archive's addProject() and getProject() methods to manipulate them. Applications that will use these methods with an HTML interface, on the other hand, will probably need to use the update() method, since that uses raw strings. Listing 2.8 is an example.

Listing 2.8   ManageServlet.java.

```java
package com.awl.cseng.jws.project;


import javax.servlet.*;
import javax.servlet.http.*;
import java.util.*;
import java.io.*;


/**
 * Allows users to manage project plans via HTML forms.
 *
 * @see Project
 */
public class ManageServlet extends HttpServlet
implements ArchiveConstants {
  // constant
  public static final String ARCHIVE_PATH
                                    = "SerializedArchivePath";


  // instance data members
  Archive archive;
  String  archivePath;


  // Servlet API methods
  /**
   * Requires initialization parameter whose name is defined by
   * ARCHIVE_PATH. This parameter is the location of a
   * serialized Archive object. If one does not exist, it will
   * be created when the servlet is shut down.
```

```
  *
  * @see Archive
  * @see #ARCHIVE_PATH
  */
public void init(ServletConfig conf)
throws ServletException {
  super.init(conf);

  try {
    archivePath = conf.getInitParameter(ARCHIVE_PATH);
    if ( archivePath == null ) {
      archive = new Archive();
    } else {
      FileInputStream    fileInput
                              = new FileInputStream(archivePath);
      ObjectInputStream objInput
                              = new ObjectInputStream(fileInput);
      archive = (Archive)objInput.readObject();
      objInput.close();
    }
  } catch (Exception e) {
    log("init(): " + e.getLocalizedMessage());
  } finally {
    if ( archive == null ) archive = new Archive();
  }
}


/**
 * Writes the updated archive object back to the file from
 * whence it came.
 */
public void destroy() {
  try {
    FileOutputStream    fileOutput
                              = new FileOutputStream(archivePath);
    ObjectOutputStream objOutput
                              = new ObjectOutputStream(fileOutput);
    objOutput.writeObject(archive);
    objOutput.close();
  } catch (IOException e) {
    log("destroy(): " + e.getLocalizedMessage());
  } finally {
    archive = null;
  }
}


/**
 * Updates the archive and then prints the same output as
 * doGet().
 *
```

```
 * @see #doGet
 */
public void doPost(HttpServletRequest req,
            HttpServletResponse resp) {
  try {
    int len = req.getContentLength();
    if (len > 0) {
      Hashtable ht = HttpUtils.parsePostData(len,
                                    req.getInputStream());
      archive.update(ht);
    }
  } catch (IOException e) {
    log("ProjMgmtServlet.doPost() caught " + e);
  }
  doGet(req, resp);
}


/**
 * Prints an HTML page displaying the current state of all
 * projects in the archive, followed by an HTML form for
 * updating the archive.
 */
public void doGet(HttpServletRequest req,
                HttpServletResponse resp) {
  resp.setStatus(HttpServletResponse.SC_OK);
  resp.setContentType("text/html");
  try {
    ServletOutputStream out = resp.getOutputStream();

    out.println("<HTML>");
    out.println("<HEAD>");
    out.println("<TITLE>Message Archive</TITLE>");
    out.println("</HEAD>");
    out.println("<BODY>");

    printArchive(out);

    printArchiveUpdateForm(out);

    out.println("</BODY>");
    out.println("</HTML>");

    out.close();
  } catch (IOException e) {
    log("ProjMgmtServlet.doGet() caught " + e);
  }
}


// implementation methods
/**
```

```
 * Writes a chunk of HTML displaying the current state of all
 * projects in the archive to the ServletOutputStream.
 */
void printArchive(ServletOutputStream out)
throws IOException {
  if (archive == null) {
    out.println("<H1>No Archive Available</H1>");
  } else {
    out.println("<H1>Archive</H1>");
    Enumeration projects = archive.getProjects();
    while(projects.hasMoreElements()) {
      Project proj = (Project)projects.nextElement();
      out.println("<H2>Project " + proj.getName() + "</H2>");
      out.println("<P>" + proj.getDescription() + "</P>");
      Date projectClosed = proj.getClosed();
      if ( projectClosed != null ) {
        out.println("Closed " + projectClosed);
      } else {
        out.println("Due " + proj.getDue());
      }

      Enumeration subtasks = proj.getSubTasks();
      while (subtasks.hasMoreElements()) {
        Task t = (Task)subtasks.nextElement();
        out.println("<H3>"
                      + t.getType()
                      + " "
                      + t.getName()
                      + "</H3>");
        out.println("<P>" + t.getDescription() + "</P>");
        Date taskClosed = t.getClosed();
        if ( taskClosed != null ) {
          out.println("Closed " + taskClosed);
        } else {
          out.println("Due " + t.getDue());
        }
      }
    }
  }
}


/**
 * Writes an HTML form for updating the archive.
 */
void printArchiveUpdateForm(ServletOutputStream out)
throws IOException {
  out.println("<FORM METHOD=\"POST\">");
  out.println("<TABLE>");
  out.println("<TR VALIGN=\"BOTTOM\">");
  out.println("\t<TH>Action</TH>");
  out.println("\t<TH>Type</TH>");
```

```
out.println("\t<TH>Project </TH>");
out.println("\t<TH>Name</TH>");
out.println("\t<TH>Description</TH>");
out.println("\t<TH>Deadline</TH>");
out.println("</TR>");

out.println("<TR VALIGN=\"TOP\">");
out.println("\t<TD>");
out.println("\t\t<INPUT TYPE=\"RADIO\" CHECKED NAME=\""
          + ACTION
          + "\"" VALUE=\""
          + OPEN
          + "\">open");
out.println("\t\t<INPUT TYPE=\"RADIO\" NAME=\""
          + ACTION
          + "\" VALUE=\""
          + UPDATE
          + "\">update");
out.println("\t\t<INPUT TYPE=\"RADIO\" NAME=\""
          + ACTION
          + "\" VALUE=\""
          + CLOSE
          + "\">close");
out.println("\t</TD>");

out.println("\t<TD>");
out.println("\t\t<INPUT TYPE=\"RADIO\" CHECKED NAME=\""
          + TYPE
          + "\" VALUE=\""
          + MILESTONE
          + "\">milestone");
out.println("\t\t<INPUT TYPE=\"RADIO\" NAME=\""
          + TYPE
          + "\" VALUE=\""
          + BUG
          + "\">bug");
out.println("\t\t<INPUT TYPE=\"RADIO\" NAME=\""
          + TYPE
          + "\" VALUE=\""
          + TOPIC
          + "\">topic");
out.println("\t\t<INPUT TYPE=\"RADIO\" NAME=\""
          + TYPE
          + "\" VALUE=\""
          + PROJECT
          + "\">project");
out.println("\t</TD>");

out.println("\t<TD>");
Enumeration projects = archive.getProjects();
out.println("\t\t<SELECT NAME=\"" + PROJECT_NAME + "\">");
```

```
      while (projects.hasMoreElements()) {
        Project p = (Project)projects.nextElement();
        out.println("\t\t<OPTION>" + p.getName());
      }
      out.println("\t\t<OPTION VALUE=\"\">&lt;NEW_PROJECT&gt;");
      out.println("\t\t</SELECT>");
      out.println("\t</TD>");

      out.println("\t<TD>");
      out.println("\t\t<INPUT TYPE=\"TEXT\" NAME=\""
                  + NAME + "\">");
      out.println("\t</TD>");

      out.println("\t<TD>");
      out.println("\t\t<INPUT TYPE=\"TEXT\" NAME=\""
                  + DESCRIPTION + "\">");
      out.println("\t</TD>");

      out.println("\t<TD>");
      out.println("\t\t<INPUT TYPE=\"TEXT\" NAME=\""
                  + DUE_DATE + "\">");
      out.println("\t</TD>");

      out.println("</TR>");
      out.println("</TABLE>");
      out.println("<INPUT TYPE=\"SUBMIT\" VALUE=\"SUBMIT\">");
      out.println("</FORM>");
  }
}
```

ManageServlet's doPost() method simply bundles up the form parameters into a hashtable of string arrays and sends them to the archive via update(). That method interprets the strings as commands to open new projects or close bugs.

Simple Gaming Engine

Our second sample application is a simple, yet hopefully useful, game engine. A game consists of one or more questions, and each question may be one of three types. Multiple-choice questions give players a list of possible answers; when one is selected, the game issues a response commenting on the choice (one answer may also be designated as the right one). Scored questions are like multiple choice, except that there is a score associated with each answer instead of a response. Finally, there are open questions that do not have a fixed set of responses, allowing users to answer any way they want. The answers are then tallied and the top ten presented. This is useful for survey types of questions, such as "Who is your favorite musician?"

A game is completely specified by the servlet parameters, so game designers do not have to be programmers. To keep the parameters straight, we use a simple naming convention. Questions are named `question0`, `question1`, and so on. Parameters relating to a question have names that start with the question name and a dot.

Each question has a parameter that indicates what kind of question it is. This parameter is called, not surprisingly, `question_name.type`, and it may be either multiple, scored, or open. Each question also has an associated text, which is the actual question to present to the user. This parameter is called `question_name.text`.

Open questions have only these two parameters. Multiple and scored questions also have one or more possible answers. These are named `question_name.answer0`, `question_name.answer1`, and so on. Finally, scored questions also have scores, which are named `question_name.score0`, `question_name.score1`, with the numbers corresponding to the numbers in the answers. Likewise, multiple-choice questions have responses called `question_name.response0`, and so on. Finally, multiple-questions may also have a parameter called `question_name.rightAnswer`, whose value should be a number corresponding to an answer number.

Listing 2.9 shows the parameters that define a simple game about servlets. The detailed code for this application is introduced in Chapter 9.

Listing 2.9   Game parameters.

```
name=Servlet Game
question0.type=open
question0.text=What do you like best about servlets?
question1.type=multiple
question1.text=What is the signature for HttpServlet.service()?
question1.answer0=service(Cheese,Squid)
question1.response0=Uh, you must live in an interesting world...
question1.answer1=service(ServletRequest,ServletResponse)
question1.response1=Close, but you can be more specific
question1.answer2=service(HttpServletRequest,HttpServletResponse)
question1.response2=Right!
question1.rightAnswer=2
question2.type=scored
question2.text=What are some of the benefits of servlets?
question2.answer0=Softens hands while you do dishes
question2.score0=0
question2.answer1=speed of execution and speed of development
question2.score1=10
question2.answer2=cross-platform
question2.score2=8
```

Conclusion

We use these servlets to demonstrate server-side Java functionality or optimization techniques. Each chapter has its own lightweight examples, but certain chapters refer to these more realistic applications. All sample application code can be found in electronic form in the CD-ROM accompanying this book.

PART 2

A Guide to Administration and Features

CHAPTER 3

Administrator's Guide to the Java Web Server

If Chapter 1 was a look at the blueprints of the Java Web Server, this chapter is a room-by-room walkthrough of the completed house. We attempt to cover each of the topics a developer encounters in creating servlets to implement applications and in configuring and managing the Java Web Server (JWS). After reading this chapter, it should be possible to immediately jump into writing simple servlets. The goal of this chapter is to provide the frequently unexplained context for understanding the Java Web Server: a detailed explanation of all the parts of the JWS, how they fit together, and how to use them.

We start with an overview of what is created during the installation of the Java Web Server. We examine the directory structure that contains the components of the server as well as explain how to start the HTTP service on Sun Solaris and Windows NT, the two officially JavaSoft-supported platforms for the Java Web Server.

We then move to a discussion of issues related to writing servlets in the section on creating servlets. We explain how to create servlets, compile them, place them in appropriate directory structures, and load them into the server. We also discuss how to map servlets to URLs, how to use aliases, how to restart servlets, and how to remove them once they are no longer necessary.

The Java Web Server Directory Structure

During installation of the Java Web Server, a server root directory must be chosen. This directory, referred to generically as <server_root>, has subdirectories that contain the Java class files that make up the server, binary executables of the Java Runtime Environment (JRE), sample programs, documentation, logs, and other components. On most systems the `<server_root>` directory starts out as `JavaWebServer1.1`. Of course, the version number at the end of the directory name changes from version to version. After installation, the JWS has a directory structure that looks like the one in Figure 3.1. Here is an explanation of each subdirectory.

- `admin`: This directory contains the files that make up all the Java-based administration applications.
- `bin`: This directory contains the executables for the Java Web Server. The executable in the file named `httpd` can be executed to start the JWS. We cover how to automatically start the server during a system boot in the next section of this chapter. Sun provides various C language source files that start the server in different configurations. A C file exists to start the server with the JRE supplied with the distribution or with the Java Development Kit (JDK) and a variety of other ways. On UNIX systems, a shell script to start the servers is provided.
- `cgi-bin`: This directory contains CGI programs that can be executed through the CGI servlet.
- `jre`: This directory contains the Java Runtime Environment distributed with the Java Web Server. The JRE is the minimum standard Java platform for running Java programs. It contains the Java virtual machine (JVM), Java core classes, and supporting files. Although the JWS distribution comes with the JRE, if the JDK is installed elsewhere it is possible to use the other installation by setting the `JDK_HOME` environment variable. If there are any concerns about disk space, users may not want a separate JRE for each Java product they use.
- `lib`: This directory contains the "JAR," meaning Java archive, and library files that contain the code to support the Java Web Server, the Java Server Infrastructure (JSI), and other components. After JDK 1.1 the Servlet API has become part of the `javax` libraries.
- `logs`: This directory contains the log files generated by the JWS and the administration services. This directory can be changed in the administration tool.
- `properties`: This directory contains files that specify the properties of the various services and servlets that come with the Java Web Server distribution. Properties are the initial arguments passed to a servlet or service when it starts up. They are used to contain values that should not be hard coded into the source code, like directory names, account names, and passwords to application services.

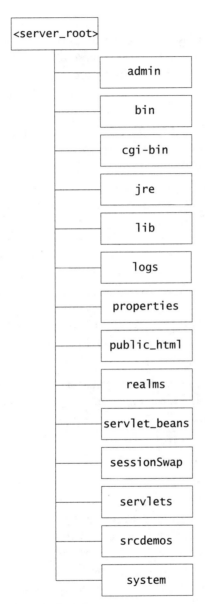

Figure 3.1   Directory structure of the JWS

- public_html: This directory is the default document root for the Java Web Server. It contains HTML files that demonstrate some of the sample servlets provided in the distribution. Servlets that echo form input, send mail, and check links are demonstrated, as well as pages that have other features like server-side includes.

- `realms`: This directory contains the access control lists (ACLs) and Group and Encrypted password files to support the various security realms offered by the Java Web Server. These files should be edited or changed only through the administration tool, not with a text editor.
- `servlet_beans`: This directory contains sample servlet beans code.
- `sessionSwap`: This directory contains the persistent serialized objects stored when session tracking is used. Session objects that have exceeded their in-memory time limits are written here until a user returns to resume the session.
- `servlets`: This directory contains all the sample servlets provided with the JWS. Class files loaded from this directory are loaded with a different method than class files in other directories. The details are dicussed in the creating servlets section. It may be a bad idea to put servlets created to support custom applications for a site in this directory. For a detailed explanation, see the discussion at the end of this chapter.
- `srcdemos`: This directory contains source code for sample applications that demonstrate useful techniques for implementing servlets. Programs are provided to show how to communicate between applets and servlets, to show how to use JDBC, RMI, or CORBA, and to illustrate other general-purpose applications.
- `system`: This directory contains documentation for servlets, error pages for the HTML protocol, and shared html and graphic files.

Installing the Java Web Server

The Java Web Server is started by executing the `httpd` program that is supplied with the distribution in the `<server_root>/bin` directory.

On UNIX systems, a script to execute the Java `httpd` program should be put into the `/etc/init.d/` script that runs at boot time. The instructions that come with the UNIX distribution give a full explanation of how to construct a proper startup script. To stop the JWS, enter the administration tool, which is explained in detail later in this chapter, and shut down the service.

On NT systems, the installation program asks the user if the JWS should be installed as a service. If the user answers yes, then the Java Web Server is started automatically at boot time. To stop the JWS, enter the Services program of the Windows NT Control Panel. The Java Web Server can be started and stopped easily from there. Once installation is complete and the Java Web Server has been started, enter this URL: *http://<YOURMACHINE>:8080/* The page in Figure 3.2 comes up, welcoming you to the Java Web Server.

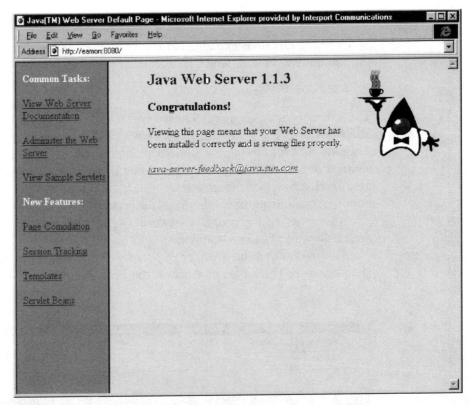

Figure 3.2 Default Java Web Server home page

NOTE: This URL assumes that the name of the computer running the Java Web Server is substituted for <YOURMACHINE> and that the default port setting of 8080 has not been changed. This port could be changed to the normal HTTP port of 80 in the administration tool.

One great way to test the Web server's functionality and learn about servlets is to run the Snoop servlet, which displays a wealth of information about servlets and the server. To run the Snoop servlet, enter this URL:

HTTP://<machine_name>/servlet/SnoopServlet

Snoop is similar to the printenv scripts found at many sites that print out all the environment variables.

Running the Administration Tool

Many of the functions explained in this chapter use the interfaces supplied by
the administration tool, which is invoked with the following URL:

http://<YOURMACHINE>:9090/

The screen shown in Figure 3.3 then appears and requests a correct login name
and password. The default login name with administrator privileges is `admin`.
The password for this login is `admin`. Creating a new administrator account and
shutting down access to the default account should be one of the first priorities
after installation. (See the section on security in Chapter 4 for a detailed explanation of creating another administrator account.)

After entering the proper password and pressing the Log In button, the
screen shown in Figure 3.4 appears.

This page shows the structure of Java servers, of which the Java Web Server
is an instance. The server, in this case the Java Web Server, handles the traffic

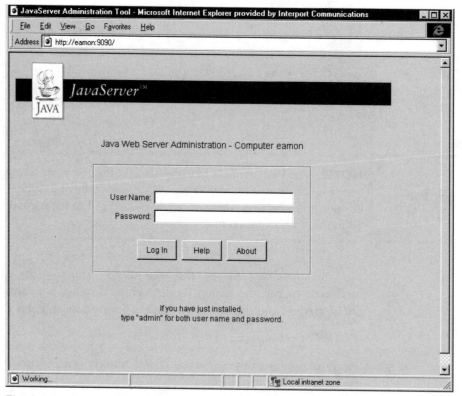

Figure 3.3   Java Web Server login screen

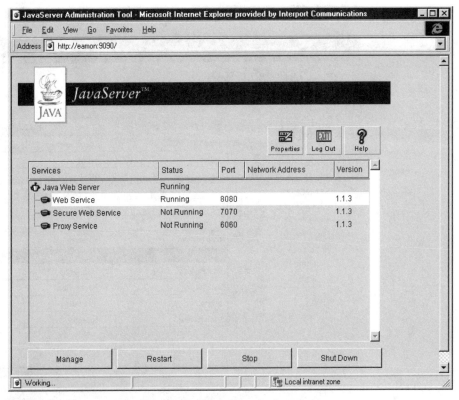

Figure 3.4 Services page of the JWS administration tool

from a network or other source of requests. A Java server can pass that traffic to a set of services that process the requests in some way. In the case of the JWS, three services are provided: a Web Service for HTTP requests, a secure Web Service for HTTP requests made through the secure sockets layer, and a proxy service for caching and redirecting HTTP traffic.

To enter the administration tool interface for the Web page service, either double click on the line labeled Web Service or single click on it and then click on the Manage button at the bottom of the screen. After the administration tool for the Web Service has been invoked, the screen shown in Figure 3.5 will appear. As the screen shot shows, the administration tool has four major branches off its home page represented in the toolbar at the top of the screen by the buttons labeled Setup, Monitor, Security, and Servlets. The functions available under each of these portions of the administration interface are explained in detail in Chapter 4. In this chapter, we explain just enough of the administration interface to enable us to create a servlet and give it an alias.

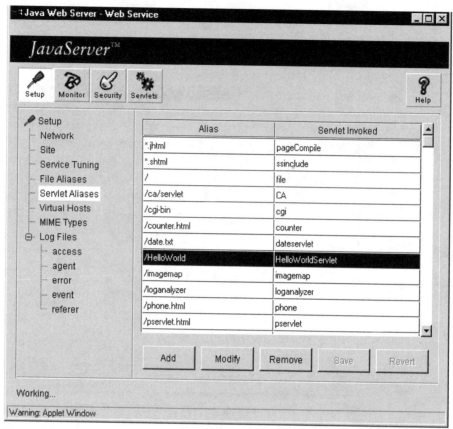

Figure 3.5   Setup screen of the JWS administration tool

Servlets

So far we have looked at the Java Web Server from the administrator's point of view. We have examined the knobs and controls that can adjust the behavior of the server. This next section takes us inside the black box and provides a programmer's overview of servlets.

Creating Servlets

Creating a servlet is easy. The inevitable HelloWorldServlet, the friendly handshake of every new language, shows the way. This servlet is provided as part as of the JWS distribution and is located in the Servlets directory. Here is the source straight from Sun; this program code shown in Listing 3.1 is available in the distribution in the file <server_root>/servlets/ HelloWorldServlet.java.

Listing 3.1   `HelloWorldServlet.java`, the "Hello World" program for servlets.

```
import java.io.*;
import javax.servlet.*;
import javax.servlet.http.*;

public class HelloWorldServlet extends HttpServlet {

    public void doGet (HttpServletRequest req,
                       HttpServletResponse res)
       throws ServletException, IOException
    {
       res.setContentType("text/html");

       ServletOutputStream out = res.getOutputStream();
       out.println("<html>");
       out.println("<head><title>Hello World</title></head>");
       out.println("<body>");
       out.println("<h1>Hello World</h1>");
       out.println("</body></html>");
    }

    public String getServletInfo() {
       return "Create a page that says <i>Hello World</i>"
              + " and send it back";
    }
}
```

As you examine Listing 3.1, notice how the `HelloWorldServlet` extends the `HttpServlet` class, as will almost all servlets. The `doGet()` method is overridden in the class to perform the work. The `doGet()` method has a request object that describes the request coming in and a response object that provides the methods used to respond to the request. Notice the `getServletInfo()` method implemented at the end. This method allows the administration tool and other development programs to interrogate the servlet to produce a better display. This method parallels the `getAppletInfo()` method found in client-side applet programming. We discuss the details of the "Hello World" servlet in Chapter 1 and we get deep into the structure of servlets in Chapter 9 on servlets and the Servlet API. For now, however, we will take for granted that we have a servlet to play with. The source for the `HelloWorldServlet` resides in a file named `<server_root>/servlets/HelloWorldServlet.java`. This point brings up an element of confusion in the JWS. Although in the distribution directory the `Servlets` directory is specfied in the plural form, "servlets," when a servlet is invoked, the URL contains the singular form of the word. The URL to invoke the `HelloWorldServlet` is

HTTP://<your machine>:8080/servlet/HelloWorldServlet

Such is life.

Compiling Servlets

If we want to run the HelloWorldServlet, we must first make sure that we have compiled the source file into a Java class file. Servlets are compiled just like any other Java program; the only complication is including the proper Java archive (*.jar) files in the class path so that all the proper classes are available to the compiler. For the compiler, use the same class path that is used when the Java Web Server is run in production.

This avoids any confusion that might be caused by having a different search order and different versions of JDK in each situation. Look at the class path of the startup script for a well-formed example of a class path. If the proper class path is not in place, then something like the following message will appear:

```
Can't find class sun/tools/javac/Main
```

Invoking and Loading Servlets

Once a class file has been compiled for a class and placed in the <server_root>/servlets directory, it is ready to be invoked. If there are any initial arguments for the servlet that will be accessed in the init() method through the getInitParameter() method of the ServletConfig object. Initial arguments should be placed in keyword=value format in a file with the same name as the class file of the servlet and the .initArgs extension. Although one can invoke servlets after they are put in the Servlets directory, it is good programming style to use the administrative tool to provide another name that can be used to refer to the servlet that is not the same as the class file of the servlet. This is accomplished through the servlets portion of the administration interface, which is invoked by pressing the Servlets button shown on the screen in Figure 3.5. Always referring to the servlet by its name allows the underlying class file to be changed to introduce new versions without overwriting the old versions. This makes backing out of a change quite easy.

The servlet administration interface looks like the screen in Figure 3.6. To add the HelloWorldServlet to the list of active servlets, enter the name HelloWorld in the Servlet Name box and HelloWorldServlet in the Servlet Class box. Click the Add button, and then "HelloWorld" will show up in the list of servlets under Configure on the left side of the screen.

The Bean Servlet part of the screen, located just below the Servlet Name and Class boxes, is used when servlet beans are being added to the Java Web Server. Beans are packaged servlets that are designed to be easy to sell, distribute, and use with third-party Integrated Development Environments (IDEs). We cover this topic more thoroughly in the section on writing servlets in Chapter 9.

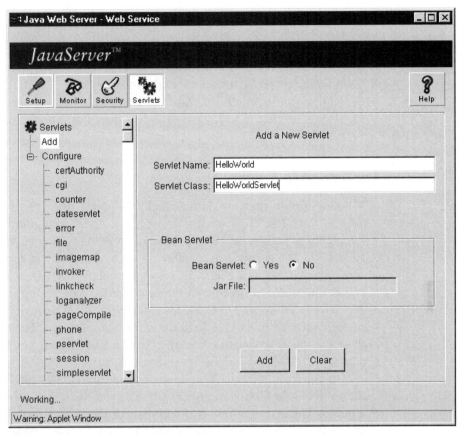

Figure 3.6 Screen for adding a new servlet in the JWS administration tool

Now that the `HelloWorldServlet` class has been added to the Web server, it can be executed in a couple of ways. The most basic method is to use the name of the servlet class file. To execute the `HelloWorldServlet` this way, first start up a Web browser and then enter this URL:

http://<YOURMACHINE>:8080/servlet/HelloWorldServlet

If everything is working correctly, the friendly and comforting "HelloWorld" text will appear in the browser window. So far, so good. Now recall that when the servlet was registered with the server, we entered the servlet name as `HelloWorld`. This name can also be used to invoke the servlet. The URL would look like this:

http://<YOURMACHINE>:8080/servlet/HelloWorld

Once again, if everything is working properly, "HelloWorld" should appear on the browser screen.

Both URLs assume, of course, that the name of the computer running the Java Web Server is substituted for <YOURMACHINE> and that the default port setting of 8080 has not been changed. When the JWS gets either of these URLs, it first determines if a servlet with that class name or servlet name is loaded. If a "Not Found (404)" error appears when the servlet is executed, it could be that the servlet was not compiled and that no class file exists in the <server_root>/servlets directory. The Java Web Server does not automatically compile the *.java file.

Loading Servlets in Advance

While servlets cannot be automatically compiled, they can be marked to be automatically loaded at startup through the servlet configuration interface. As we explained earlier, the JWS is nice enough to load a servlet when it is invoked via a URL. While this is acceptable for many purposes, it does mean that the first time a servlet is invoked, its response time is worse than it will be in subsequent invocations because of the time needed to load the servlet into memory. A more polite way to run a Java Web Server that provides more consistent performance for users is to load the servlets in advance. The downside is that the server takes longer to come up and start handling requests. This is usually a price worth paying.

To enter the interface that enables advance loading, click on the name of the servlet in the Configure list (Figure 3.6) and the screen shown in Figure 3.7 appears. The screen allows a description of the servlet to be entered and the class name to be changed. Clicking the Yes radio button in the Load at Startup line causes the servlet to be automatically loaded when the Java Web Server is started. Clicking Yes on the Loaded Now line loads the servlet into memory. The Load button at the bottom of the screen can also load a servlet. After the servlet has been loaded, the Load button changes to Unload, which will unload the servlet if clicked. The Save and Revert buttons are used to perform those functions for the values entered in the text boxes. Save enters the changes made and Revert restores the state of the servlet properties to those that existed before the edit.

The Properties screen is the second card in the servlet Configuration screen. Properties are values that are passed to the servlet at initialization. The properties exist to contain configuration parameters of a servlet that should not reside in the source code. The properties of the dbdemo servlet illustrate this perfectly. The Properties screen allows the password, user name, and other values to be set. We cover the proper use of properties more thoroughly in the section on writing servlets in Chapter 9. In any event, properties don't make much sense for HelloWorldServlet.

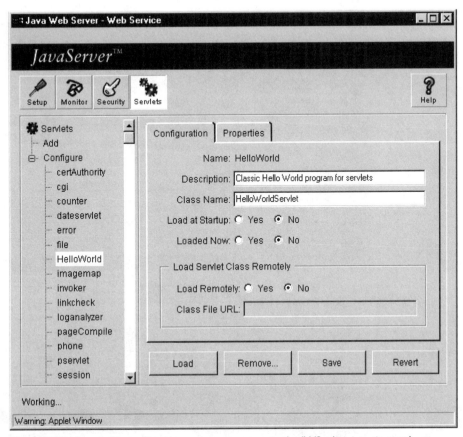

Figure 3.7 Screen for configuring servlet parameters in the JWS administration tool

In fact, `HelloWorldServlet` is kind of an awkward name, and even if the "HelloWorld" servlet name is used to invoke the servlet, there is no reason for a user invoking a Web Service to know a servlet is being executed. It certainly would be preferable to invoke the servlet with a URL like

http://<YOURMACHINE>:8080/HelloWorld

This is possible through a servlet alias, which can be assigned through the Setup portion of the administration tool.

To access the Servlet Alias feature, click on the Setup button at the top of the administration tool and then click on the Servlet Aliases entry in the list. The screen shown in Figure 3.8 will be displayed. To create a new alias, click the Add button and a blank line appears to contain the wildcard pattern for the alias that will permit the servlet to be invoked for a matching URL. In our case, we will enter /HelloWorld as the alias and HelloWorld as the name of

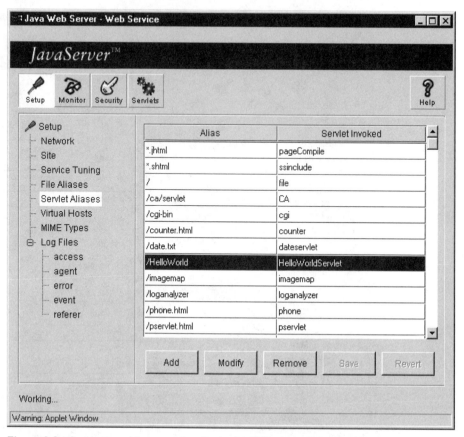

Figure 3.8   Screen for adding a servlet alias in the JWS administration tool

the servlet to be invoked. Press the Save button and the alias goes into effect. The preferable URL mentioned now works to invoke the HelloWorldServlet.

Notice that the list of alias wildcard patterns is filled with both entries like /HelloWorld, which specify specific directories and file names to be mapped to servlets, and entries like *.jsp, which map all files with a given extension to a particular servlet. It is probably better to enter the name of the servlet rather than the class file when specifying servlets in the administration interface, although both will work. Entering the servlet name provides an extra level of indirection as mentioned earlier.

To edit a servlet alias, simply click on the line that displays the alias and then click the Modify button. One can then change the values for the alias or the servlet and then click Save. Changes can be undone before the Save button is clicked by clicking the Revert button. This restores the values before the Edit button was clicked. A servlet alias can be deleted by clicking on the line that represents it and then clicking on the Remove button. This removes only the alias, not the servlet.

Where Should Servlets Live?

Where should we put the many servlets that will do our important work? It is tempting to put servlets in the <server_root>/servlets directory. This, indeed, is where the HelloWorldServlet lives. If it is good enough for Sun's sample code, why shouldn't it be good enough for our custom code? There are several reasons against putting custom servlets in the Servlets directory. Explaining them should illuminate some subtleties of how the JWS loads and executes servlets and allows them to interact.

The reason the location of a servlet is such an issue is that a special class loader is used to load servlets that reside in the <server_root>/servlets directory. This class loader has a nice feature. It monitors the class file and automatically reloads a servlet if the class file is newer than the one loaded into memory.[1] When classes are loaded from anywhere besides the servlets directory, the class loader provided with the JDK or JRE is used, and it does not automatically reload servlets. Unfortunately, while the special class loader is smart enough to automatically reload the servlet class itself, it is not smart enough to reload other classes it depends on.

For example, if an application has MyServlet.class that uses MySupport.class and both classes are updated, the new MyServlet.class is loaded but the old MySupport.class remains in memory. Also, if your servlet is somehow loaded by the default class loader, then you will have two copies of the class within the virtual machine (VM), each with its own static variables, and an instance of one cannot cast an instance of the other to its own class. The reason is that when loaders are operating within a VM, each loader keeps its own static variables. Classes that are identical except for the fact that they have been loaded with different loaders are considered separate classes by the VM.

Another problem with the special loader is that it is unable to load files that use the Java Native Interface, which is used to integrate non-Java languages with Java. Of course, the best course is to avoid the use of the Java Native Interface, but unfortunately this is not always possible. This problem is expected to be fixed in JDK 1.2.

Because of the potential for confusion, it is almost always better to shun the <server_root>/servlets directory, even though it can be convenient for development. This means that when new servlets are compiled, the server must be

---

[1]Details on the workings of the Java class loader can be found in the JDK documentation or Sun's *The Java Programming Language* reference book.

restarted. Manually unloading and loading the servlet again with the administration tool does not result in the recompiled servlet being loaded, because unloading a servlet does not remove the class file from memory. But this is not such a huge problem and is preferable to getting into the hard-to-find bugs that could be caused when using the special loader. We put our classes in a directory that we create after installation called <server_root>/classes. This directory is already present in the Java Web Server's class path in the distributed startup scripts, although the directory is not created during installation.

Another tip for avoiding trouble: Do not put your class files in a .jar or .zip file outside the <server_root>/lib directory. If you do, then the .jar or .zip file has to be added to the Java Web Server's class path. JAR files in the lib are automatically added to the class path by the shell script that starts the server. Notice here that we are not saying that the directories in which the .jar or .zip files reside must be in the class path. The filenames of the .jar and .zip files themselves must be in the class path if they are not in the lib directory.

Conclusion

In this chapter we provide the information a programmer needs for getting the Java Web Server up and running and to start writing simple servlets. The rest of the book builds from this foundation and delves deeper into the features, administration, and techniques for writing successful applications for the JWS.

CHAPTER 4

Configuring and Managing the Java Web Server

The administration tool of the Java Web Server is a refreshing advance beyond current servers on UNIX and Windows NT because it allows remote control of the server through a graphical user interface. The typical complaint about UNIX-based Web servers is that the servers may be remotely administered only through a command line or through a bare-bones Web interface with limited functionality. A command-line interface can be hard to use and requires sophistication in a system administrator.

The Web interfaces currently available do not allow complete administration or monitoring of all-important aspects of the server. The common complaint about NT servers is that the graphic administration interface is fine, a full-blown graphical user interface (GUI) that is easy to use, but it cannot be used remotely.

The Java Web Server (JWS) overcomes both problems by providing a Java applet-based graphical user interface for administration that can be accessed remotely through a Web browser. Using applets as the foundation for the administration interface combines the ease of use of the NT-style rich GUI interface with remote access. Among the nicer features of the administration tool is a monitor interface that provides a set of viewers for the server's log files.

In this chapter we get into the details of the administration tool. We walk through each screen of the interface and explain how it interacts with the Java Web Server to control the behavior of the server. If the JWS were a car, this chapter would be the equivalent of the part of the owner's manual that explains how each portion of the dashboard works.

Administration Basics

The administration interface of the Java Web Server starts out assigned to port 9090. To access the interface, you must enter the following URL into a Java-enabled browser or applet viewer:

http://<your_machine_name>:9090/

(Of course, you substitute the name of your machine for <your_machine_name>.) If the JWS is installed properly and is up and running, the first screen that will appear is the login screen we explained in Chapter 3. Remember that the default administration account is admin with a password of admin.

When setting up a server for development or production, one of the first steps after installation should be to change the administration tool's password. (See the section on security later in this chapter for detailed instructions on granting a user administrative privileges.) It is also recommended that the administration port be changed from the default of 9090 to another value. Failing to change the password or administrative port is like leaving the keys in the dashboard of a brand-new Range Rover with the doors unlocked.

After logging in to the Java Web Server, we can now go over each part of its dashboard and learn how to drive the server at maximum comfort and speed. First, however, we will lift the hood of the JWS to examine just how the administration tool does its work. The first thing to understand is that there are three important parts that work together to allow administration of the Java Web Server. The first is the Java Web Server itself, which is listening for requests on port 8080 by default. The next is another server called the Administration Server, which sits alongside the JWS.

The Administration Server is listening for requests on port 9090 by default. The final part of the Administration Server is the administration tool, which is a Java applet that talks to the Administration Server and to the JWS to get the work done. The result of this structure is a three-way conversation between the Administration Server, the Java Web Server, and the administration applet. How does the Java Web Server get requests to perform administration functions? It would certainly be a bad idea for administration requests that start and shut down the server to come over the same connection as HTTP traffic. Instead, the JWS listens for administration requests on a different port, called the internal port, which can be set by using the screens that allow the properties of a service to be managed. The default internal port is 9091, and both the Administration Server and the administration tool applet talk to the Java Web Server through this port.

Another important point to understand about the Java Web Server is that the information controlled by the administration tool is contained in a set of files in the directories in <server_root>/properties and <server_root>/realm. The administration tool is in essence an editor for these files. Almost all of the administration of the Java Web Server can be done through the administration tool, although there are some functions that can be performed only by editing the text files. Given that the JWS reads and writes administrative files, it is vital that the server run under a user account that permits these files to be changed.

Figure 4.1 on the next page shows the structure of the administration interface and what options are available at each level. As the diagram shows, the administration tool has four main sections.

1. Setup controls the basic parameters of the server such as the port on which requests are received, the default root directory for HTML files, file and servlet aliases, and other such parameters.
2. Monitor displays the data in log files and is equivalent to using the UNIX "more" utility to view a log file.
3. Security allows users, groups, access control lists, and resources to be associated with one another to control access.
4. Servlets controls the loading, unloading, and parameters passed to servlets. We covered most of the Servlet administration interface in Chapter 3 and will go into greater detail in Chapter 9 about servlet intervals.

Before we examine the administration tool sections and the associated interface screens, we take a quick look at the highest-level interface, the service screen that controls a few key parameters at the level of the service, the highest-level structure in the Java Server Infrastructure (JSI) architecture. Each major piece of functionality provided by the Java Web Server is packaged as a service, one for the Web, one for the Web over SSL, and one for the proxy service. We examine the interface for the Web service.

Service Interface

After logging in to the administration tool, the screen shown in Figure 4.2 appears, which allows an administrator to choose to manage any one of the various services available in the Java Web Server. Notice the three buttons at the top right of the screen: Properties, Logout, and Help. Logout is pretty straightforward: it is the way out of the administration tool. Help is also a no-brainer: it launches a Web browser to display the documentation about managing services. The Help button found on subsequent screens launches a browser that points to relevant documentation.

Press the Properties button and the screen in Figure 4.3 appears, which allows manipulation of some fundamental parameters of the Web Service. The

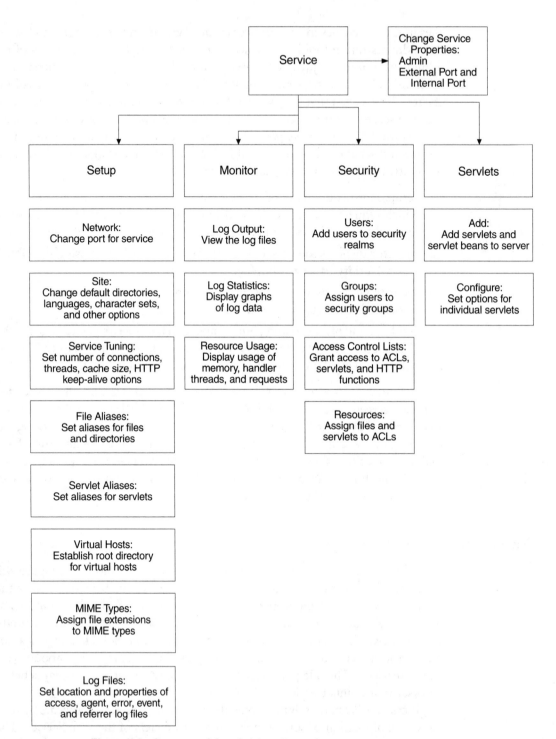

Figure 4.1   Structure of the administration tool

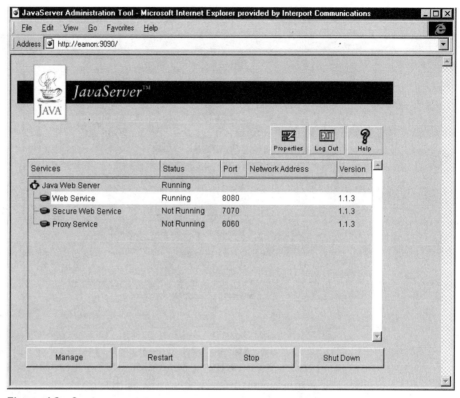

Figure 4.2 Services screen

three tabs at the top of the screen allow access to three cards. The Admin Password card allows the password for the admin account to be changed. This is one of the first duties of all right-thinking system administrators. The External Port card allows the administrator to set a new port for external access to the administration tool. External access means access over the Internet from another machine. The Internal Port card allows the port over which the administration server and the administration applet talk to the JWS to be changed. This port starts out as 9091.

NOTE: External access to the administration interface can be turned off by editing the file <server_root>/properties/server/adminserver/adminServices/ endpoint.properties and changing the endpoint.main.interface from * to localhost or <your_machine>.

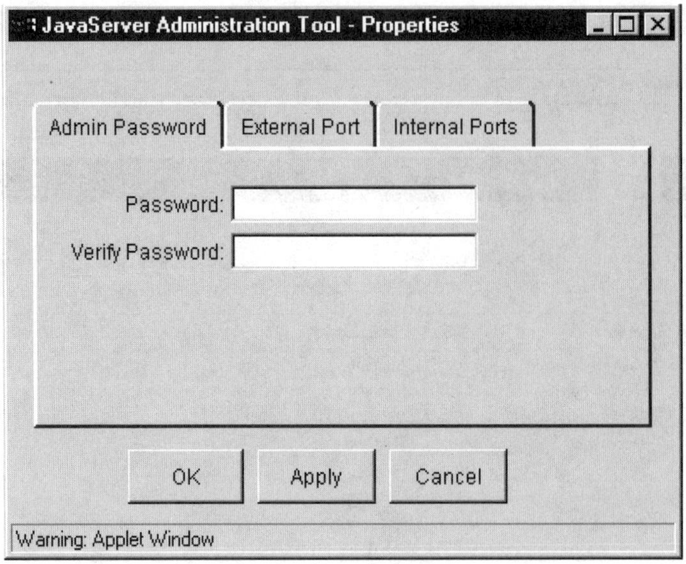

Figure 4.3   Administration tool Properties screen

The most secure way to administer the Java Web Server is to disallow any access through the external port. This method takes away the possibility for remote administration of the server. All administration must take place from a browser running on the same machine as the server.

Let us turn our attention back to the first service screen, specifically the buttons at the bottom: Manage, Start/Restart, Stop, and Shut Down. These buttons act on whichever of the services is highlighted on the screen. Click on the different services and notice how the number of active buttons changes depending on whether the service is active or not. When a service is running, the Start button becomes Restart. When a service is stopped, the Stop button becomes inactive.

The Start/Restart button starts the highlighted server or service running. If the server or service is running when this function is requested, then it is shut down before being started again. Even though the administration tool shows only one server present after a default installation, it is possible to administer multiple servers, each with its own set of services, through the administration tool.

The Stop button stops a server or service. The Shut Down button stops all services and the JWS itself. The Manage button is the gateway to the rest of the administration tool. Notice how the Manage button becomes inactive when the Server line of the screen is highlighted. Only services can be managed. It is also possible to enter the administration tool for a service by double clicking on the line containing the service.

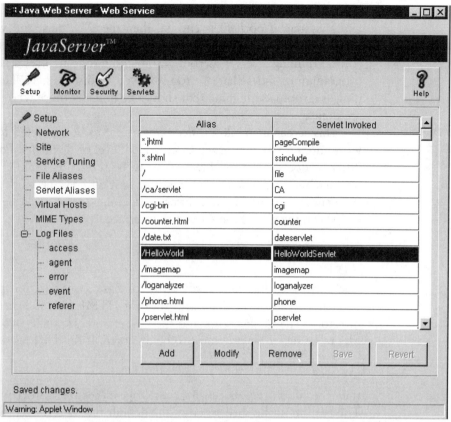

Figure 4.4 Setup screen

Once the administration tool for a service is launched, the screen in Figure 4.4 appears. The four buttons at the top of the screen allow access to the four sections of a service's administration tool. We will start with Setup.

Setup

The Setup interface is the workhorse of the administration tool; it provides most of the crucial functionality. Most of the functions Web server administrators typically use are found here. Each of the screens discussed is accessible by clicking on the word in the tree diagram at the left of the screen.

Network

The Network screen allows the default port for a service to be set. The port for the Java Web Server starts out as 8080. Most of the time the right setting for this port is 80, the standard port for incoming HTTP traffic. Note that on a UNIX system if port 80 is chosen, then the JWS must run with root access because only processes that have root access can listen to ports below 1024. Of course, running a server as root is something that involves a variety of system programming issues that are too involved to discuss here. Let's just say running as a root is something that should be done by those who know what they are doing.

This screen also allows incoming traffic to be restricted to a specific network interface, which provides an added level of flexibility. For example, two different document root directories can be served by running two servers on one machine and assigning each server to a different network interface with a different IP address. Then a different document root could be assigned to the traffic coming across each network interface.

Site

The Site screen has four cards on it for basic configuration parameters. The Contents card sets the document root for HTML files and the CGI-BIN script directory. The FileServlet and the CgiServlet use these two settings to find files to be served or programs to be executed. If this URL were entered

> *http://<your_machine>/mydoc/goodfile.html*

then the file in the <document_root>/mydoc/goodfile.html would be served. The bottom of the card specifies the default file to be served when a URL has only a directory name. The default setting is "index.html," which means that if the URL

> *http://<your_machine_name>:8080/system/*

were entered, the file served would be the same as if the URL

> *http://<your_machine_name>:8080/system/index.html*

had been requested.

The Java Web Server allows many such file names to be specified so that "welcome.html" could be the second default. If multiple files are specified they are searched for in the order in which they appear in the interface. This means that if a directory had an index.html file and a welcome.html file, index.html would be served for a URL without a file name if it appeared before welcome.html in the Contents card.

The next two cards, Languages and Character Sets, allow these internationalization options to be specified. The HTTP 1.1 protocol allows HTML to specify the language of a document and to specify the desired language of a reply. Recent browsers, like Netscape 4.0, actually implement these tags, but we recommend avoiding this functionality until its use is more widely accepted in the Internet community. Using them now will probably result in confusion because too much cooperation between the browser and server is required for language-specific tags to work properly. Note that this functionality is different from making a servlet amenable to internationalization, which we cover in a later chapter.

The leftmost card, Options, allows Security and Servlet chains to be enabled or disabled and directory listings to be provided when a directory is specified that does not contain a welcome file like `welcome.html` or `index.html`.

The button labeled "Remove all archived files" is used to clear out the files that have been logically deleted by `Put` and `Delete` requests. HTTP 1.1 `Put` and `Delete` requests are required to archive copies of files that are replaced or deleted. The files go into a holding area similar to the Recycle Bin on a Windows 95 desktop. This button allows the Recycle Bin to be emptied so that it does not become too large.

Session Tracking

Session tracking was removed from the administration tool of the Java Web Server in version 1.1.1. In order to manage the properties of session tracking, an administrator must now edit the following Properties file:

```
<server_root>/properties/server/javaWebserver/server.properties
```

Note that this properties file is now at the server level instead of at the service level as it was when there was an administration tool interface.

The excerpt from the `server.properties` file (see Listing 4.1) shows the values that can be changed to tune the behavior of session tracking. We cover the meaning of each of these settings in Chapter 7. Note that because administration is done through a Properties file, it is one of the few features of JWS administration that does not take effect right away. When any session tracking parameters are set, the server must be restarted for the parameter changes to take effect.

Listing 4.1 Server.properties excerpt.

```
#
# Properties for session tracking
#
enable.sessions=true
enable.urlrewriting=true
enable.cookies=true
enable.protocolswitchrewriting=true
```

```
session.inavalidationinterval=10000
session.swapinterval=10000
session.persistence=true
session.swapdirectory=sessionSwap
session.maxresidents=1024
session.invalidationtime=1800000

session.cookie.name=jwssessionid
session.cookie.comment=Java Web Server Session Tracking Cookie
#session.cookie.domain
#session.cookie.maxage
#session.cookie.path
#session.cookie.secure
```

Service Tuning

The Service Tuning screen (Figure 4.5) contains the parameters that are most likely to have a profound impact on the way the JWS performs. This screen controls the size of the thread pool used by various parts of the server as well as the settings for HTTP 1.1's Keep Alive feature that allows one TCP/IP connection to handle many HTTP requests.

The first card on this screen is the General settings for connections, which include the number of HTTP requests that can simultaneously be made to a service. A slider allows the administrator to set capacity for connections in the service and the size of the memory cache. The thread capacity is misnamed because in reality it controls not threads but rather the maximum number of concurrent client connections allowed for a service. After the maximum number of connections is reached, further connections are refused. Memory Cache is used to set the size of each entry in the service's memory cache. If this parameter is set to zero, then the cache is disabled. Memory Cache is used to store static HTML and images.

The second card of the Service Tuning screen controls the number of handler threads for the service. These threads are the ones that carry a request through the methods of the servlet that handles the request. The minimum setting for handler threads ranges from 0 to 100 with a default value of 10. The maximum also has a 0 to 100 range with a default value of 50. The time-out value has a range from 0 to 360 seconds with a default of 300 seconds, or 5 minutes.

These settings affect the behavior of the Web Service of the JWS as follows. When the service starts up it creates the number of threads set by the minimum setting for Handler Threads. It is a good idea to create these threads in advance and to keep them around in a pool because it avoids incurring the thread creation overhead at the time of each request. As requests arrive, the threads are dispatched to handle them. If the number of simultaneous

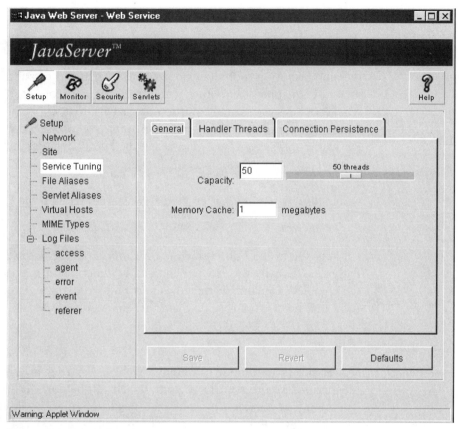

Figure 4.5   Service Tuning screen

requests grows beyond the minimum number of handler threads, then the server starts creating more up to the maximum specified. Threads that become idle are shut down after the number of seconds specified in the time-out parameter has passed. These settings are crucial to good performance of the Java Web Server. The most efficient settings for these parameters are determined through experimentation.

In general, the maximum number of threads should be larger than the maximum number of connections. This means that the number of connections governs the capacity for simultaneous requests and overflow is dealt with by refusing new connections. If the number of connections is larger than the number of threads, poor performance will result when the maximum number of threads is reached because requests for use of the threads queue up when the maximum is reached, which could mean a long wait for a response.

File Aliases

File aliases are familiar territory for most Web administrators. They allow one URL to be mapped to another. In the Java Web Server, the File Alias screen in the administration tool allows one file to be mapped to another or one directory to be mapped to another. The screen has two columns: Alias Pathname, which contains the filename portion of the URL that will be mapped to the Full Pathname, and Full Pathname. For example, if jwsdoc were put in the Alias Pathname and system/doc were put in the Full Pathname, then the URL

http://<your_machine_name>:8080/jwsdoc/index.html

would display the file that previously was accessed with the URL

http://<your_machine_name>:8080/system/doc/index.html

Any file in the Full Pathname directory could be accessed with the Alias Pathname. Usually this is what is desired. Sometimes it makes sense to specify the complete filename in the Alias and Full Pathnames. This results in a File Alias that points to a specific file rather than a directory.

Servlet Aliases

Servlet aliases are unique to the Java Web Server. They are similar to setting a file alias to execute a CGI program, which can be done in other Web servers. The Alias for a servlet is just like the Alias Pathname in a file alias. It identifies the URL that will invoke the servlet identified in the Servlet Invoked field. The servlet name rather than the class file name should be specified so that it will be possible to change the underlying class name without affecting the alias.

The Servlet Aliases administration interface can also be used to specify what is known as a servlet chain to an alias. A servlet chain is a sequence of servlets assigned to handle a request in which the output from the first servlet becomes the input to the next. To assign a servlet chain to an alias one must simply specify the servlets that are part of the chain, separated by commas with no spaces. Remember that for any servlet chain to work, servlet chaining must be enabled on the Options card of the Site Administration screen explained earlier. We discuss servlet chaining more fully in Chapter 9.

Virtual Hosts

Virtual hosts are a part of the HTTP 1.1 protocol that allows a browser to tell a Web server which host it thinks it is talking to. This allows the server handling the request to do something with that information, such as serve a different version of the site. In the Java Web Server virtual hosts are used to allow different document roots to be served by the File servlet depending on the value of the HTTP 1.1 Host: header field. Servlets are not affected by virtual host functionality. Of course, servlets can react to the value of the Host header for specific application needs.

A typical scenario for the use of virtual hosts is that two domain names, say www.ann.com and www.arbor.com, point to the same IP address. www.ann.com has a site associated with it in the <server_root>/public_html directory, the www.arbor.com site is in the <server_root>/arbor/public_html directory. The www.ann.com site is made the primary site by using the Site screen of the administration tool to set <server_root>/public_html as the document root directory for the Web Page service. The www.arbor.com site is made a virtual host with the Virtual Hosts screen. www.arbor.com is entered in the Host column and <server_root>/arbor/public_html is entered in the Document Root column.

If a user comes to the site with the www.ann.com host, File Servlet uses the information specified in the Site screen to serve pages from the <server_root>/public_html directory. If the user comes to the site with the www.arbor.com host, then File Servlet uses the information in the Virtual Host screen to serve pages from the <server_root>/arbor/public_html directory.

MIME Types

MIME types are the way servers talk to browsers to let them know what kind of data is being returned as a result of a request. When files are being sent to a server from a browser in a PUT request, the browser uses a MIME type to let the server know what kind of file is on the way. A feature unique to the JWS is the way MIME types can also be used to create servlet chains, as we explain later (see Chapter 9).

The MIME-Types screen of the administration tool has two columns: Extension and Type/Subtype. The Extension column contains the file extension that would be affixed to files of a certain type. The Type/Subtype column contains the designation of the major and minor type. The major type is a general description of what kind of file this is. Text, image, application, and video are examples of major types. Minor types are specific descriptions of what kind of text, image, and so on, is associated with the file extension. gif and jpeg are examples of minor types that identify specific types of images.

NOTE: The extension entries for jpeg images have three different spellings. This is designed to make the MIME-type definition as robust as possible to catch misspellings and odd spellings. (Currently, MIME extensions are case sensitive but they will be case insensitive in future versions.)

MIME types can be used to create servlet filter chains, as we explain in more detail in Chapter 9. A servlet chain is a sequence of servlets that work together to process some request. The output of one servlet becomes the input of the next. One way to create these chains is through the Servlet Aliases screen, which allows several servlets to be specified to handle the request of one alias. These chains also can be created through MIME types because of the Java Web Server's ability to assign all files of a certain MIME type to a servlet. Any file of that MIME type is processed through the assigned servlet as part of a servlet filter chain on its way out of the server.

Filter chains, another name for servlet chains associated with MIME types, cannot be created through the administration tool. Instead, a configuration file must be edited to assign the servlet to the MIME type. The file to be edited is `<server_root>/properties/process/javaserver/Webpageservice/mime-servlets.properties`. Remember that for any servlet chain to work, servlet chaining must be enabled on the Options card of the Site administration screen.

Log Files

The basic aspects of log files are managed through the five parts of the Log Files tree of the administration tool. The access log, agent log, error log, event log, and referer log are all managed through separate screens. The access log keeps a record of incoming requests from browsers and contains information such as the date of the request, the remote host and the remote user, and other request-related data. The agent log contains the user agent headers sent by browsers to identify themselves to the servers. The error log lists internal server errors. The event log contains a record of events such as startup and shutdown for the server and other detailed information about the behavior of servlets. Finally, the referrer log has the referrer header that shows from which page a given request for a page may have come.

The log management screens are all similar except for the description of the log files and the dropdown box displaying which messages are being captured. The Log Files access screen is shown in Figure 4.6. The common parts of the screen are the description, the Log To setting, and the File Name, Rollover File Size, and Buffer Size settings. The Which Messages setting changes for each screen. Description simply provides an expanded explanation of the log file. Log To allows the destination file type to be selected. Log files can be rolling files that are renamed when they are full. When a log file first fills up, it is renamed to `<logfilename>.1` and a new file of `<logfilename>` is created. When that file fills up, the renaming ripples through the existing files so that the current log file becomes `<logfilename>.1` and `<logfilename>.1` becomes `<logfilename>.2`, and so on. This renaming goes on until `<logfilename>.9`, which

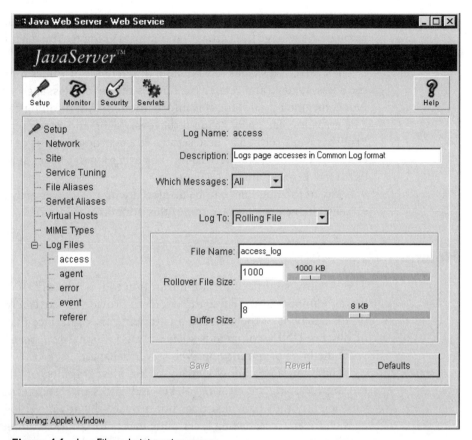

Figure 4.6   Log Files administration screen

is deleted instead of being renamed. The consequence of this scheme is that the amount of disk space that can be occupied by rolling log files is ten times the maximum rolling log file size.

Single files are like traditional log files that just grow and grow. Files can be avoided altogether by selecting the Standard Output or Error Output values of the Log To setting. If these values are chosen, then the log file output is written to the standard output or standard error output streams. On NT, they go nowhere because these streams are not visible in a Java Web Server service.

The box below the Log To entry changes based on the value selected for Log To. If Rolling File is selected, then the box displays the values shown in Figure 4.6. File Name is the name of the Rolling File. Rollover File Size is the maximum size of the file in kilobytes. Buffer Size is the size of the internal memory buffer to which the log records are written before they are written to the log file on disk. If Log To is set to Single File, then only the File Name appears in the box. If Standard Output or Error Output is selected, then the box has no settings. A message indicating that output is going to Standard Output or Error Output is displayed instead.

The Which Messages setting has a different set of values for each screen. For the access, agent, and referer log screens the Which Messages settings are either None, meaning do not log this information, or All, meaning capture it in a log. The error log has None, Major Problems, Major and Minor Problems, and All Problems as its settings. These settings are text descriptions of the four levels of errors used in the Java Web Server. The event log has None, Start/Stop Events, Detailed Events, and All Events.

Any of the Log Files can be displayed with the viewer provided by Monitor screens, the next section examines this administration tool.

Monitor

The Monitor section of the administration tool is a breath of fresh air for Web server administrators. These three screens provide an extremely useful window on the behavior of the server in an attractive user interface that takes the place of obscure UNIX commands such as "tail logfile | more" or other awkward methods of monitoring Web server behavior.

These interfaces allow viewing of log files, graphing of statistics based on the log files, and monitoring of key indicators of resource usage. While the functionality thus provided does not displace the advanced log analysis packages on the market, having it certainly makes for a more complete server. If the administration tool is the dashboard of the JWS, the monitoring interface is the speedometer.

Log Output

The Log Output screen is shown in Figure 4.7. It is designed to be an easy way to look at the various log files of the Java Web Server. The Log File box allows the log file to be displayed. The access, agent, error, event, and referrer logs are all available for display. The View Last slider sets how much of the log file is shown in the text window at the bottom of the screen. If the Snapshot box is checked, then the log file is displayed. If the Snapshot box is not checked, then the log file constantly will be redisplayed with the frequency set by the Update Interval setting, which can range from 1 to 15 seconds. If the Word Wrap box is checked, then the log file entries are wrapped around so that the entire line appears on one screen.

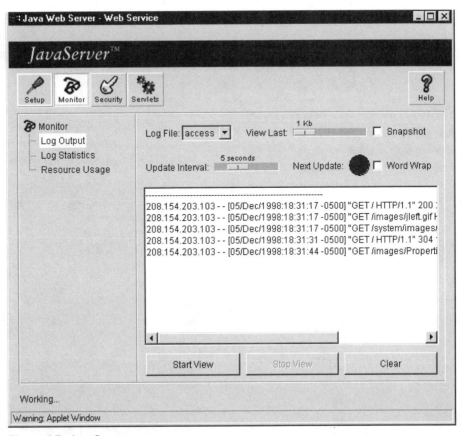

Figure 4.7   Log Output screen

Log Statistics

The Log Statistics screen provides a statistical snapshot of log file usage. The quantity displayed is the number of requests to the server, also known as "hits." The hits can be displayed sorted by time of day, in eight 3-hour intervals, or by domain name, `.com`, `.edu`, and so on. The scope of the display can be set to Day, which means the previous 24-hour period, Week, Month, or All. Information can be displayed as a pie chart, a bar chart, or a table. The pie chart is shown in Figure 4.8.

Resource Usage

The Resource Usage screen shown in Figure 4.9 displays the values for key variables of the Java Web Server. The Memory values show the total memory available to the JWS and the amount available for the service being monitored.

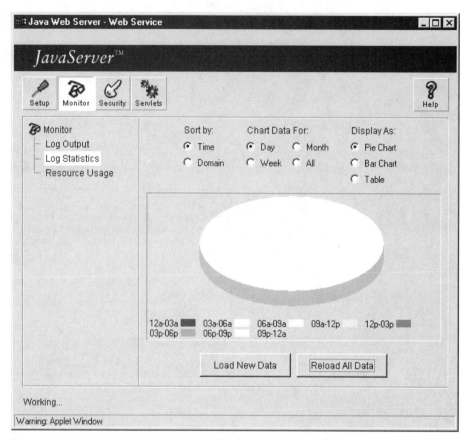

Figure 4.8   Log Statistics screen

The Handler Threads column shows the total handler threads active and how many are free to handle new requests. The Requests column shows how many requests arrived during the last interval and the number of those requests that were GETs. The Update Interval controls the size of the sampling interval.

Security

Security in the Java Web Server is a difficult issue. The confusion comes from the fact that the JWS is designed to be platform independent, but security systems are one of the most platform-dependent features of operating systems. The Java Web Server's approach to sorting out this complicated problem is to introduce the concept of a security realm, which is basically a container for a space of users, groups, and access control lists that control access to resources.

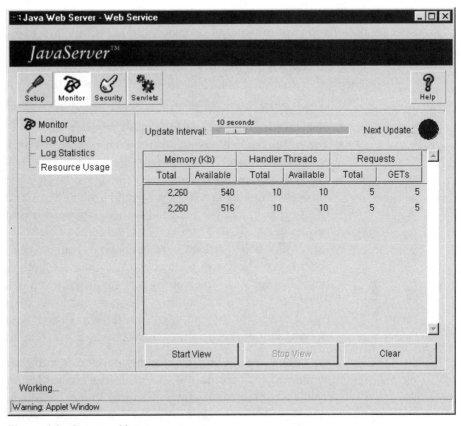

Figure 4.9 Resource Usage screen

Like the rest of the administration screens of the JWS, the Security screens are in effect editors for the underlying files that contain the settings. But unlike the rest of the interfaces, which allow a Web developer to do his or her work without ever editing the files by hand, effective security administration requires an understanding of how to edit the files.

For example, the only way to create another admin user is to reach into the underlying files and perform some administrative surgery. The first step is to create the user that you want to be an administrator in one of the security realms of the Java Web Server. For the sake of this example, we create the user and assign a password in the default realm. The next step is to use a text editor to edit the file in the `<server_root>/realms/data/defaultRealm/keyfile` directory and copy out the entry for the user you have assigned. Then edit the `<server_root>/realms/data/adminRealm/keyfile` file and add the copied entry to the bottom of the file. This user will now be an administrative user.

As the Java Web Server matures, less and less of the work will have to be performed with the kind of configuration file editing just explained. Before we start to explain the Security administration screens in detail, we must understand exactly what a security realm is and how it is used to provide security. There are five security realms in the Java Web Server: the default realm, the certificate realm, the servlet manager realm, the UNIX realm, and the NT realm.

- The *default* realm is used for sample applications.
- The *certificate* realm is used for SSL client authentication. The principal identified for SSL has to have a certificate.
- The *servlet manager* realm is used for signed servlets that are loaded remotely. The servlet manager realm allows a Webmaster to specify a rule so that if a servlet is signed with a certificate, it has a certain set of permissions.
- The *UNIX* and *NT* realms are designed to bring in the authentication provided on the native platforms. Unfortunately, both realms only bring in a subset of the security scheme provided on each platform. The *UNIX* realm, for example, allows a user to see all the users specified to access the system on which the JWS is running. It fails, however, to bring any of the groups of users provided in UNIX into the realm.

These realms are used for controlling user access to the server. The admin realm mentioned earlier controls administrative access. The internal structure of the realms is explained in detail in Chapter 20. Each realm has its own space of users, groups, and access control lists. Each of these realms within each service shares the same space of resources. When a request for a resource is made it is assumed by default to be granted. If the resource—a file or servlet for example—is associated with an access control list (ACL), then the method of obtaining the user name specified on the access control list is employed. Once the user name is obtained and a valid password is entered, then the requested type of access to the resource is compared with the type of access specified in the access control list. Access can be granted to everyone or can be restricted to a set of users or groups of users. If the access is allowed by the ACL to the user, it is granted. If it is not, then it is denied.

Given this background, we now proceed to show how the screens of the Java Web Server Security interface can be used to manage access to resources.

Users

The Users screen starts out, as all the Security screens do, with the choice of the realm that will be administered. Choosing the realm changes the nature of the screens that are displayed. For users the story is pretty simple for all of the realms. Users are added with the Add button at the bottom of the screen and are deleted with the Remove button. For certain realms, a Change Password button is present, which allows a password to be modified. Users may not be added in the UNIX or NT realms; instead, the user lists are read in from the operating system security system.

Groups

The Groups screen has the choice of realm at the top, followed by an interface for adding and deleting groups that is just like the interface for adding and deleting users. Below that is a box that shows the users in the realm who are associated with each group. This list of users has either been explicitly created in the JWS or has been brought in from the underlying native platform security system as in the NT and UNIX realms. The Add and Remove buttons below the Members and Nonmembers columns allow users to be included in or excluded from a group.

Access Control Lists

After choosing a realm in the access control list, the Webmaster must specify a set of permissions to be granted a selected user or group in that realm. ACLs can be created or deleted like users or groups. Users and groups are then added and deleted from each ACL and also granted permission to perform certain activities. The permissions that can be granted change from realm to realm. Generally, they are the permission to GET or POST a file, load a servlet, write a file with an HTTP PUT, or listen to a socket. Once a realm and a user or group have been chosen, then a tree diagram is displayed that shows which permissions have been granted to each user or group.

Resources

Resources are what is being protected on the Java Web Server. The Resources screen allows resources to be identified and then associated with an ACL in a particular realm. The Resources screen also allows the authentication scheme for that resource to be specified. The choices are Basic, nonencrypted HTTP authorization in which the password is transferred in an unprotected fashion; Digest, an MD5 hash mechanism not generally supported by most other Web servers or by browsers other than HotJava; and SSL authentication, available only in the SSL service.

Servlets

The servlets interface was covered in Chapter 1 and will be covered more thoroughly in Chapter 9. To summarize, the Servlets screen allows servlets to be added to the JWS so that they can be associated with a name, loaded automatically, and assigned startup parameters. Servlets can be explicitly loaded, unloaded, and of course deleted from the server.

Conclusion

Almost every single aspect of the Java Web Server can be controlled through the administration applet, which can be run from anywhere. Commands issued through the applet immediately update the running server and change its underlying configuration files. The administration applet makes the Java Web Server easier to administer than most other servers, especially those that must be rebooted before configuration changes can take effect.

CHAPTER 5

HTML Templates

As any veteran of the Web site development business knows from bitter experience, the key to designing and maintaining a flexible Web site at the lowest possible cost is clever use of templates. The key benefit of templating is that it allows the appearance of hundreds of pages to be changed in one fell swoop with little effort.

In general, templates are any method for publishing Web pages that allows the presentation of the content to be separated from the storage of the content. This can be as simple as having an entire site stored in well-formed HTML files in which comments or other indicators delimit the content in the files. A Perl script easily can process such files and rewrite them to change navigational information as well as headers and footers. Templating systems can be as complex as any advanced database application. In many systems templating is implemented by retrieving the data stored in a database with a language that mixes HTML, conditional logic, and looping statements to allow complete control over dynamically created pages.

The complexity of the HTML template system provided in the Java Web Server (JWS) is between those of the two examples with respect to functionality. HTML templates are a little more powerful and flexible than using Perl to reformat static HTML files but are not as powerful as using a hybrid HTML/programming language that in effect turns each page into a program. Java Server Pages (JSP), which we describe in Chapter 6, are an excellent implementation of a hybrid language.

The HTML templating mechanism relies on three powerful ideas: basing template substitution on the existing structure of HTML documents, using definitions files based on Java parameter files, and inheritance. These concepts are combined in a way designed to bring great joy to Web programmers everywhere.

How the JWS Templates Use Normal HTML Files

HTML templating in the JWS starts with a file named `default.template` as the base template for all pages. This is a file that is meant to control the presentation of existing HTML files in a manner illustrated by the diagram in Figure 5.1.

The basic idea of HTML templating is that the `default.template` file is the shell that is filled in with the information from what we will call the content page, that is, the page that is specified in the URL. If a URL that is controlled by the HTML templating mechanism is invoked, for example `gaynor.html`, it is combined with the information in `default.template` to produce the final page. The way the two pages are combined is illustrated in Figure 5.1. The `default.template` file is read—and cached in memory for later use—and the two `<SUBST>` tags are located. The SUBST tags in the `default.template` file act

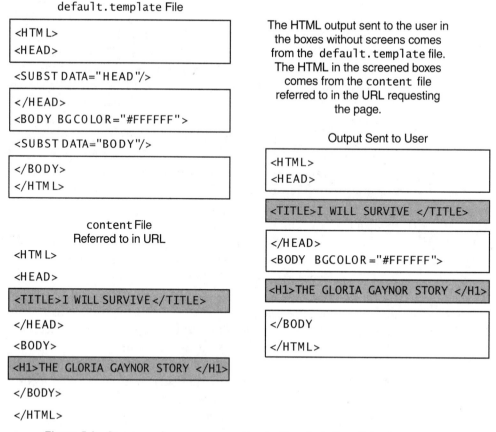

Figure 5.1   Structure of a page processed by the `TemplateServlet`

as placeholders for the information contained in the content file. The part of the content file that is located between the beginning and ending HEAD tags replaces the <SUBST DATA="HEAD"/> tag. The part of the content between the beginning and ending BODY tags replaces the <SUBST DATA="BODY"/> tag. The resultant HTML that is served to the user contains parts of both the default.template file and the file specified in the URL. (The SUBST tags are written in an abbreviated form. They can also be written <SUBST>BODY</SUBST>.)

Note that unlike many forms of templating, the Java Web Server does not require the underlying content file to be marked up with placeholders indicating where various elements should be inserted. Rather, the HTML file is parsed into the head and body section, which exists in all well-formed HTML files, and then those elements are inserted into a master template file.

So what bit of trickery is responsible for all of this magical combining? The magician in this case is the TemplateServlet servlet. This servlet is installed automatically after installation of the JWS with an alias of "template." We refer to the servlet by its alias name.

Files that are to be served with HTML templating must be mapped to the template servlet through the Servlet Aliases functionality (see Chapter 4). This servlet performs all the parsing and substitution mentioned in the previous paragraph each time the file is served. Be careful about using templating for the highest-volume pages because even though the default.template files and the default.definitions files covered later are cached, the template servlet does not cache the pages it creates. Rather, the whole process of parsing and substitution is repeated each time the page is served. For most pages this is not a problem, but be careful! We explore methods of testing how well a servlet handles a given load and suggest methods for improving performance using caching and other techniques in Chapter 11, which is about improving the performance of applications.

Generally, the servlet alias set up to map a set of URLs to the template servlet specifies that an entire directory be served by HTML templating. This means that any subdirectories in that directory also are served by the template servlet. If it makes sense, a single file can be specified to be served by the template servlet while others in the directory remain served by the default file servlet.

Definitions Files

The second powerful idea employed in HTML templates is that of the definitions file, named default.definitions. This file is used as a method of storing additional data that can be included in the template file. The definitions file holds keyword/value pairs. The keywords of these pairs can be included in a template file using the SUBST tag. Then, when the page is displayed, the value part of the pair is substituted in the output HTML. One useful application of this technique would be to introduce a table structure to each page that contains a column of left-hand navigation HTML. The diagram in Figure 5.2 shows how the substitution process would work with a definitions file.

As the diagram shows, the template servlet looks for keywords beyond HEAD and BODY in the default.definitions file. The values assigned to these

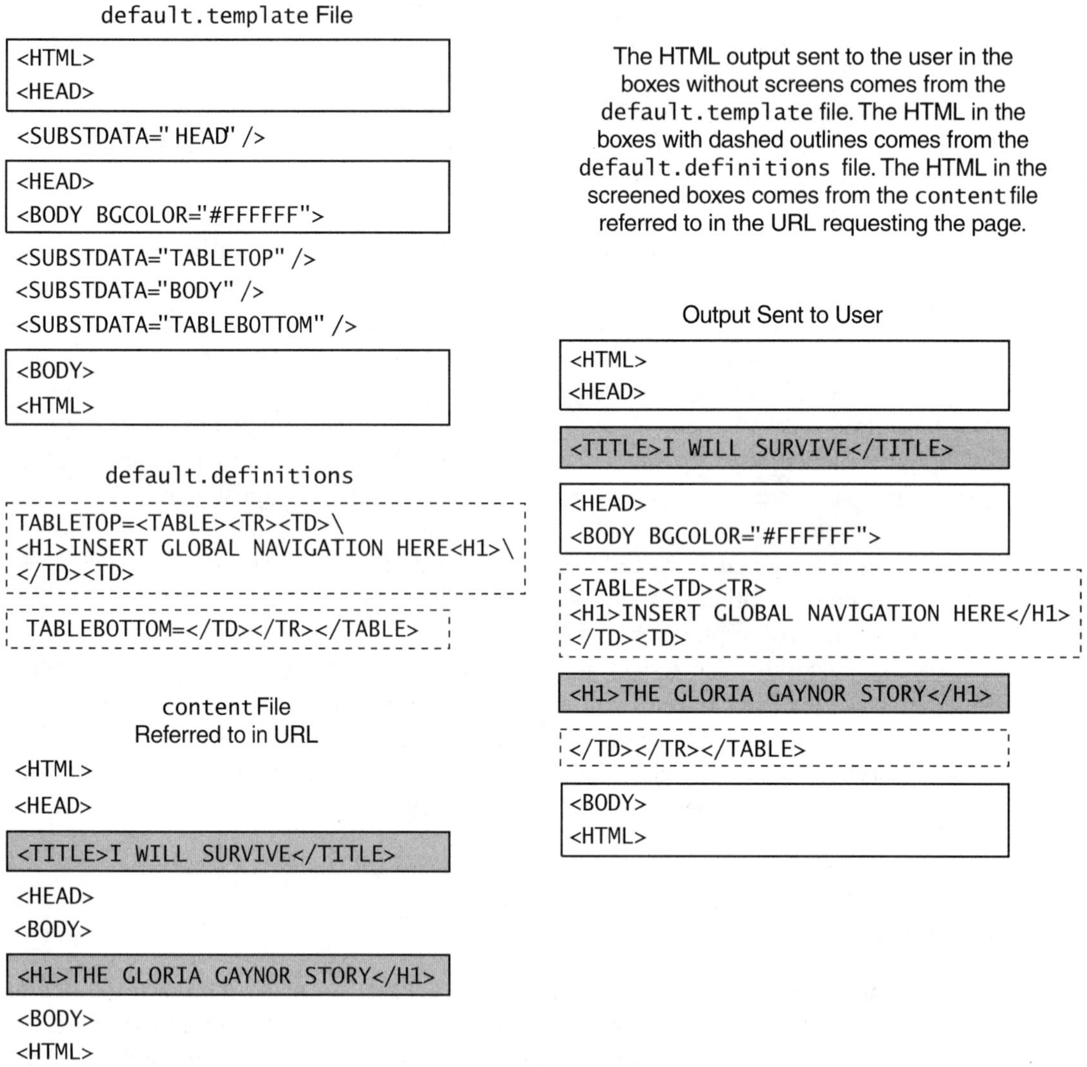

default.template File

```
<HTML>
<HEAD>
```

```
<SUBSTDATA=" HEAD' />
```

```
<HEAD>
<BODY BGCOLOR="#FFFFFF">
```

```
<SUBSTDATA="TABLETOP" />
<SUBSTDATA="BODY" />
<SUBSTDATA="TABLEBOTTOM" />
```

```
<BODY>
<HTML>
```

The HTML output sent to the user in the boxes without screens comes from the default.template file. The HTML in the boxes with dashed outlines comes from the default.definitions file. The HTML in the screened boxes comes from the content file referred to in the URL requesting the page.

default.definitions

```
TABLETOP=<TABLE><TR><TD>\
<H1>INSERT GLOBAL NAVIGATION HERE<H1>\
</TD><TD>
```

```
TABLEBOTTOM=</TD></TR></TABLE>
```

content File
Referred to in URL

```
<HTML>
<HEAD>
```

```
<TITLE>I WILL SURVIVE</TITLE>
```

```
<HEAD>
<BODY>
```

```
<H1>THE GLORIA GAYNOR STORY</H1>
```

```
<BODY>
<HTML>
```

Output Sent to User

```
<HTML>
<HEAD>
```

```
<TITLE>I WILL SURVIVE</TITLE>
```

```
<HEAD>
<BODY BGCOLOR="#FFFFFF">
```

```
<TABLE><TD><TR>
<H1>INSERT GLOBAL NAVIGATION HERE</H1>
</TD><TD>
```

```
<H1>THE GLORIA GAYNOR STORY</H1>
```

```
</TD></TR></TABLE>
```

```
<BODY>
<HTML>
```

Figure 5.2   Structure of a page served by the TemplateServlet that uses a definitions file

keywords are then substituted for the keywords in the HTML served to the users. As many tags as desired may be inserted into the default.definitions file. Definitions files are Java properties files, which allow comments introduced with # and lines to be continued if the last character on them is a \. Another important point to remember is that the substitution mechanism works only in the default.template file. If SUBST tags are placed in the content file, they are ignored.

Careful readers will notice that even with all the definitions, the content stays in two chunks represented by the HEAD and BODY SUBST tags. So why use a definitions file at all? Couldn't the information in the keyword/value pairs of the default.definitions file simply be included in the default.template file? The answer is that the default.definitions file would be useless without the third fundamental idea of HTML templates: inheritance.

Inheritance

Inheritance in HTML templates means that any subdirectory inherits the default.template and default.definitions file of its parent directory. If a base directory of a tree has a default.template file and a default.definitions file, then these files apply to all files in the base directory and all files in all subdirectories. The inheritance occurs for all subdirectories in a directory tree. If a subdirectory has a default.template file or a default.definitions file, then these files replace or modify the parent directory's files for the subdirectory and all its descendants.

There is one important difference between how inheritance works for template files and how it works for definition files. For template files, inheritance means that all subsequent directories inherit the template file of its parent. If a new template file is placed in a subdirectory, then that file replaces the inherited template file completely and is applied to all descendent subdirectories. For definitions files, inheritance is more powerful and more like the inheritance present in object-oriented programming languages. The definitions files in a parent directory apply to all descendant directories, just like template files. Unlike template files, definitions files can add or override values that exist in the parent. This means that if a certain directory needs to change only one keyword/value pair of its parent's definition file, then its definition file needs to contain only the keyword/value pair that is being overridden. All other keyword/value pairs descend from the parent and are applied to pages as if they were also included in the file. This type of inheritance provides a tremendous amount of flexibility and ease of use.

Now it becomes clear that the definitions file actually has a purpose. It can differentiate templating for subdirectories by providing alternate keyword/value pairs. One `default.template` can be modified by the values in different `default.definitions` files. A useful application of this technique would be to provide global and local navigation for different subdirectories of a Web site. By global navigation, we mean a way to traverse between the major sections of a Web site, like the chapters in a book. By local navigation we mean navigating within one section. To run these examples, the directories must first be copied from the CD that accompanies this book onto the document root directory of your Java Web Server installation.

The fantasy Web site we will use is called Automotive Records. It has a Disco and a Heavy Metal subsidiary. The template and definitions files shown in Listing 5.1, which reside in the base directory of the Automotive Records site, provide the basis for our example.

Listing 5.1   Sample template, definitions, and HTML files.

File: [JWS Document Root]/AutomotiveRecords/`default.template`

```
<html>
   <head>
     <title>Global Navigation with JWS Templates</title>
     <subst data="HEAD"/>
   </head>
   <BODY>
   <subst data="TABLETOP"/>
   <subst data="LOCALNAV"/>
   <subst data="GLOBALNAV"/>
   <subst data="TABLETOPEND"/>
   <subst data="BODY"/>
   <subst data="TABLEBOTTOM"/>
   </body>
</html>
```

File: [JWS Document root]/AutomotiveRecords/`default.definitions`

```
#
# TABLETOP is the HTML for the top of the table
#
TABLETOP=<table border=0 cellspacing=0 cellpadding=0>\
<tr><td width=150 align=left valign=top><P>
#
# TABLETOPEND is the HTML that separates the navigation
#              from the content
#
TABLETOPEND=</p></td>\
<!-- Gutter -->\
<td width=50><p></p></td>\
<!-- Main Content -->\
<td valign=top>
```

```
#
# TABLEBOTTOM closes out the bottom of the table
#
TABLEBOTTOM=</td></tr></table>
#
# GLOBALNAV is the HTML For navigation between sections of the site
#
GLOBALNAV=<!-- Global Navigation -->\
<h4><font color="#FFFFFF">AR Labels</font></h4>\
<p><a href="/AutomotiveRecords/disco">Disco Divas</a></p>\
<p><a href="/AutomotiveRecords/headbang">Heavy Metal</a></p>\
<p><a href="/AutomotiveRecords/">AR Home Page</a></p>
```

File: [JWS Document Root]/AutomotiveRecords/index.html

```
<html>
<head>
<title>Automotive Records Home Page</title>
</head>
<body>
<h1>Greetings from Automotive Records!</h1>
<p>
<h3>Your one stop shop for Disco and Heavy Metal</h3>
</body>
</html>
```

Let us assume that the Automotive Records site has two main sections that are stored in two different subdirectories. The Disco division is stored in the disco subdirectory and the Heavy Metal division is stored in the headbang subdirectory.

The default.definitions file in Listing 5.2 could be placed in the disco subdirectory.

Listing 5.2 Sample default.definitions file.

File: [JWS Document root]/AutomotiveRecords/Disco/default.definitions
File Contents:

```
#
# LOCALNAV contains the local navigation for the
#           Disco Divas section
#
LOCALNAV=<!-- Local Navigation -->\
<h4><font color="#FFFFFF">Disco Divas:</font></h4>\
<p><a href="gaynor.html">Gloria Gaynor</a></p>\
<p><a href="summer.html">Donna Summer</a></p>\
<p><a href="stansfield.html">Lisa Stansfield</a></p>
```

A couple of things stand out in the files in Listing 5.2. First, in the `default.template` file there is a keyword for `LOCALNAV`. When the `index.html` file is served out of the `AutomotiveRecords` directory, this keyword is not filled in because it does not appear in the `default.definitions` file for that directory. If a keyword is referred to in a `SUBST` tag in a template but not found, the tag is simply ignored.

But in the `disco` subdirectory, the definitions file contains an entry for `LOCALNAV`, the value of which then appears in the right-side table cell for each of the files in the `disco` directory. The links in the `LOCALNAV` HTML allow the user to move from file to file within the `disco` directory. In the `headbang` subdirectory the `default.definitions` file contains the links to the files in it. When one of these files is served, the local navigation links are shown with each file.

In these examples, we have focused on using templating to create different navigation based on tables. Even more flexiblity can be obtained by using HTML frames that are served with HTML templates. With this technique the frameset becomes the master template and the URLs referenced within become subtemplates that are served with HTML templating. There is no reason that the frameset itself cannot be a HTML template.

Template Filters

Once the concept of templates sinks into the brain, it does not take long for the idea of using templates with servlets to occur. Wouldn't it be great to format the output of a servlet using templates? The good news is that the JWS allows servlets to be formatted with templates through the `TemplateFilter`.

The way this works illustrates the power of MIME types and servlet chaining as a general technique. Here is an overview.

1. Make sure that servlet chaining is turned on. This parameter can be set on the options card on the Site section of the Setup portion of the administration tool.

2. Add a MIME type to the following Properties file:

   `<SERVER_ROOT>/properties/server/javaWebserver/Webpageservice/`
   `mimeservlets.properties`

   For this example we added the following entry to the MIME servlets file:

   `java-internal/templated-servlet=templatefilter`

   This entry means that all content that is set to the "`java-internal/templated-servlet`" MIME type will be sent to the Template Filter servlet.

3. Create the servlet that will have its output formatted by the template filter. In order for the servlet to work, it should set ContentType("java-internal/templated-servlet"). This will ensure that the output of the servlet is sent to the template filter, which was assigned to process this mime type in step 2.

4. Create an alias for the servlet under a directory that is assigned to the TemplateServlet. This alias will be used to find the template and default definitions files that will be applied to the template filter.

To recap, what happens is that the servlet is referenced by an alias that corresponds to a directory served by the TemplateServlet. The servlet pumps its output to a MIME type that is processed by the template filter. The template filter takes the output, looks in the directory specified by the alias, and uses the templates or definitions files found there to format the output.

Listing 5.3 shows a simple servlet that produces output that could be processed by the Template Filter servlet if the steps in our example are followed. The servlet could be set to any alias under the AutomotiveRecords directory and the output would be formatted just like the HTML files that reside in those directories.

Listing 5.3   Feedback.java servlet for use with the template filter.

```
import javax.servlet.*;
import javax.servlet.http.*;
import java.io.*;

/**
 * Feedback - allows customers to give comments or
 * suggestions to the Webmaster at Automotive Records.
 * Feedback will be appended to a file. The servlet output
 * will contain the same global navigation as every other page,
 * thanks to the template filter.
 */
public class Feedback extends HttpServlet {
  public void doGet(HttpServletRequest req,
                    HttpServletResponse res)
        throws IOException
  {
    handleFeedback(req,res);
  }

  public void doPost(HttpServletRequest req,
                    HttpServletResponse res)
        throws IOException
  {
    handleFeedback(req,res);
  }
```

```
public void handleFeedback(HttpServletRequest req,
                           HttpServletResponse res)
      throws IOException
{
  // Set the content type to java-internal/templated-servlet,
  // or whatever was used in mimeservlets.properties.  This
  // will cause the output to be sent through the
  // template filter
  res.setContentType("java-internal/templated-servlet");

  res.setStatus(res.SC_OK);
  PrintWriter out = res.getWriter();

  // If the user has provided feedback, we save it and print
  // a 'thank you' page.  If not, we send them a form to
  // fill out
  String values[] = req.getParameterValues("feedback");

  if(values == null || values.length < 1) {
    // We do not have the submission, send the form
    out.println("<HTML>");
    out.println("<HEAD>");
    out.println("<TITLE>Automotive Feedback</TITLE>");
    out.println("</HEAD>");

    out.println("<BODY>");
    out.println("We at Automotive Records value your opinion");
    out.println("Please leave your comment or suggestion below");
    out.println("<FORM ACTION=\"" + req.getRequestURI() + "\" "
                + "METHOD=\"POST\">");
    out.println("<TEXTAREA NAME=\"feedback\" COLS=\"50\" "
                + ROWS=\"10\">");
    out.println("</TEXTAREA><P>");
    out.println("<INPUT TYPE=\"SUBMIT\" NAME=\"Send it!\" "
                + VALUE=\"Send it!\">");
    out.println("</FORM>");
    out.println("</BODY>");
    out.println("</HTML>");
  } else {
    // We do have something from the user, save it, and send a
    // thank you message
    out.println("<HTML>");
    out.println("<HEAD>");
    out.println("<TITLE>Thanks!</TITLE>");
    out.println("</HEAD>");

    out.println("<BODY>");

    try {
      // Append this to the feedback file.  Note that this is
      // not safe! If multiple users send feedback at the
      // same time, it may be randomly mixed in the file.
      FileWriter f = new FileWriter("feedback.txt",true);
```

```
            PrintWriter p = new PrintWriter(f);
            p.println(values[0]);
            p.println();
            p.close();

            out.println("Thank you!  Your comment has been sent!");
        } catch (Exception e) {
            // Something went awry.  Oops.
            out.println("Sorry, an error occurred.");
            out.println("Please try again later");
        }
        out.println("</BODY>");
        out.println("</HTML>");
    }
  }
}
```

Conclusion

Templates and the template filter are powerful general-purpose mechanisms that solve many of the problems that arise in the management of a typical Web site. These solutions allow the proper separation of global aspects of the site and individual HTML files. With these tools, a Web developer can spend time making the applications and HTML pages better rather than on tedious tasks such as reformatting hundreds of HTML files with a Perl program.

CHAPTER 6

Java Server Pages

Unlike almost every other Web server, the Java Web Server, from its conception, was designed as a platform for application development. The servlet architecture provides the fundamental structure of the programs that execute within the Java Web Server. Java Server Pages take the servlet architecture and elegantly link it to HTML, the presentation layer for the Web. The result is a technique that dramatically speeds development and simplifies program maintenance. Except for the servlet architecture itself, we consider Java Server Pages the most beneficial feature of the Java Web Server for Web developers.

In Chapter 5, on HTML Templates in the Java Web Server (JWS), we stressed that experience teaches that the best way to manage a large amount of HTML is to separate navigational elements—headers and footers and the like—from the content of the HTML pages. This separation of presentation from content allows a site to adapt quickly to changing business and editorial needs. Large changes to the way the site looks do not require manual editing of every page on the site.

Java Server Pages extend the separation of presentation and content to application programs. With the Java Server Pages (JSP) architecture, servlets or JavaBeans can contain all the program logic that creates or assembles information. JSP can be used to format the output of programs in either of these categories. JSP is quite flexible. JSP can be in control and call Beans or other Java objects to perform a task and then format the output. In another model, servlets can be invoked directly with a URL, do their work, and then call JSP to format the output. Both methods separate the programming from the presentation quite effectively. JSP also allows Java code and HTML to be mixed together in almost any way for almost any purpose without regard to separating presentation and content.

The rewards of separation can be significant. One profound benefit is that it provides a simple and well-defined way for a programming staff to work with a design and HTML production staff. JSP allows programmers to be responsible for maintaining the servlets and beans and for communicating to the design staff how the programs work. The design staff can be responsible for presenting the output of the servlets and beans. A simple change to an HTML page does not mean that the programming staff must be involved. A change to a program does not require designers. In practice, implementing the separation and providing the rigorous documentation of programs that it requires is difficult. The JSP architecture does not guarantee success, but it certainly provides a powerful enabling technique.

The history of Java Server Pages is worth mentioning to provide an understanding of how the technique evolved and to grant credit to the pioneers of the technology. Java Server Pages has its roots in a technique called Page Compilation that was licensed in May of 1997 by Sun Microsystems from the Art Technology Group, the developers of the Dynamo Web Server, which, like the JWS, was developed entirely in Java. Page Compilation was released as a feature of the 1.1 Java Web Server. During the summer of 1998, Sun released a specification for Java Server Pages to improve Page Compilation, extend its functionality, adapt some of its features to emerging industry practice, and provide better integration with the JavaBeans architecture.

The new specification, which is what this chapter discusses, changed the name of the Page Compilation feature to JSP. Java Server Pages now has its own version numbers, and release 1.0 is expected in 1999. JSP will be released first in version 1.2 of the Java Web Server. The Running JSP section at the end of this chapter explains the differences between Java Server Pages and Page Compilation.

Structure of Java Server Pages

How does Java Server Pages work? A simple way into the subject is to discuss how pages would be written without Java Server Pages. Let's say we wanted to write a "Hello World" application that printed the date the page was generated. The servlet in Listing 6.1 would do the job quite nicely.

Listing 6.1   "Hello World" without Java Server Pages.

```
import java.util.Date;
import java.text.*;
import java.io.*;
import javax.servlet.*;
```

```
import javax.servlet.http.*;

public class HelloWorldDate extends HttpServlet {
  public void service(HttpServletRequest req,
                      HttpServletResponse res)
      throws ServletException, IOException
  {
    // Set header for output
    res.setContentType("text/html");
    res.setStatus(res.SC_OK);
    ServletOutputStream out = res.getOutputStream();

    DateFormat df = DateFormat.getDateTimeInstance();

    out.println("<HTML>");
    out.println("<HEAD><TITLE>Hello World Date</TITLE></HEAD>");
    out.println("<BODY>");
    out.println("<H1>Hello World on " +
        df.format(new Date()) +
        "</H1>");
    out.println("</BODY>");
    out.println("</HTML>");
    out.close();
  }
}
```

This servlet has a familiar feeling to an experienced Web programmer. Most of the code is dedicated to printing out HTML statements. A small portion does the work desired, in this case getting the time the page was served and adding it to the HTML. This program has familiar problems as well. If a simple HTML change is required, a programmer must make the change. Design and HTML experts are generally not comfortable changing statements in a program's source code. In order for them to make the change, they need to know not only how to change the program but also how to compile it. The bottom line is that this program is really a lot more like an HTML file than a program. Why not make it look a lot more like an HTML file? That's exactly what the JSP implementation of this program does (Listing 6.2).

Listing 6.2 "Hello World" with Java Server Pages.

```
<%@ import="java.util.Date" %>
<%@ import="java.text.*" %>

<HTML>
<HEAD><TITLE>Hello World Date</TITLE></HEAD>
<BODY>
<% DateFormat df = DateFormat.getDateTimeInstance(); %>
<H1>Hello World on <% out.println(df.format(new Date())); %> </H1>
</BODY>
</HTML>
```

This file looks a lot more like an HTML file than a program. Clearly, it has program-like elements: the import directive at the beginning and the Java code enclosed in <% %> brackets. But to a designer or HTML coder, it is much more familiar than the program in Listing 6.1. Because it is fundamentally an HTML file, a JSP can be edited with commonly used WYSIWYG HTML editors. To a programmer, it is also a much easier file to write. The tedious repetition of out.println statements is avoided at the expense of encapsulating all Java statements inside the <% %> brackets.

But how would a JSP file ever properly be served to the user? If the JSP page in Listing 6.2 were put in file named HelloWorldDate.html and served through the Java Web Server, it would not work properly. The code between the <% %> brackets would never be compiled and executed. Clearly, the only way Java code can be executed is if it is compiled and run from a class file or some other file containing the object code. If the page in Listing 6.2 were put in a file named HelloWorldDate.java, it would not compile. All the HTML statements are illegal to a Java compiler. The <% %> brackets are also not a part of Java.

The only thing that can make a page like this come alive is some sort of translator that reads in the HTML and Java statements and translates them into a program that looks like Listing 6.1. That is exactly what the JspServlet does. An oversimplified way to think of JspServlet is as a translator that converts the HTML-like format of Listing 6.2 into a program that looks like Listing 6.1. In essence, the JspServlet takes the HTML statements and puts them in out.println() statements in the resulting servlet.

NOTE: This is a gross but fundamentally accurate oversimplification. However, as we will discuss in a bit, it can be quite useful to think of the HTML statements in a JSP page as if they were all enclosed in out.println() statements.

All of the Java code enclosed in <% %> brackets is simply moved to the servlet file, which contains the Java source code produced by the translation. The translated servlet file is then compiled and run when a user requests the JSP page. Because the JSP is compiled behind the scenes, a designer can change a page and test it without knowing anything about running a compiler. So to recap, a JSP file is one that is written in HTML with embedded Java code or other special statements enclosed in <% %> brackets.

How does this all work in practice? Java Server Pages files have *.jsp extensions. The JWS comes installed with a servlet alias rule that maps all files with *.jsp extensions to the JspServlet. When a user makes a request for a JSP, the JspServlet looks to see if the JSP has been compiled. If the page has already been compiled, the JspServlet looks to see if the JSP file has changed since it was last compiled. If it has, then it is recompiled. If the class file of the JSP does not need to be compiled, then it is executed by invoking the service method, and the resulting HTML is served to the user. Obviously, if the JSP page must be compiled before it is executed, then it takes much longer to serve the page. But most of the time, the JSP will be compiled already, which makes the response quite speedy. Figure 6.1 shows the steps that the `JspServlet` goes through to execute a JSP page.

In subsequent sections, we examine the implications of this structure and the choices available to the user in a variety of dimensions, such as where the translated and compiled servlets reside; how to use other Java programs, such as JavaBeans; how to use JSP to format the output of a servlet; and how to derive JSP from custom classes.

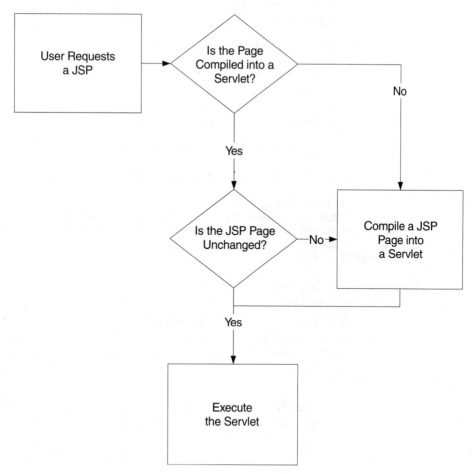

Figure 6.1 JSP `JspServlet` structure

Coding for Java Server Pages

Coding Java in JSP is a pretty straightforward business once a few concepts are understood. First a bit of terminology: Sun has taken to using the name `scriptlets` for the code within a JSP that is enclosed in `<% %>` brackets. The code within `<%@ %>` brackets in Listing 6.2 that contained the import statement is called a *directive*. (We cover the various uses of directives in a later section.)

The most important distinction to keep in mind when coding a JSP page is that the statements inside the `<% %>` tags are in the world of Java while those outside them are in the world of HTML. This can be easily illustrated by examining how comments can be inserted in a JSP file. In Listing 6.3, HTML comments and Java comments are both added to the `HelloWorldDate.jsp` file in Listing 6.2. If the HTML comment were placed within the `<% %>` brackets, the page would not compile. If the Java comment were moved outside the `<% %>` brackets, the comment would be displayed in the resulting HTML.

Listing 6.3   "Hello World" with comments.

```
<%@ import="java.util.Date" %>
<%@ import="java.text.*" %>

<HTML>
<HEAD><TITLE>Hello World Date</TITLE></HEAD>
<BODY>
<!-- Say Hello to the World and tell the date -->

<% DateFormat df = DateFormat.getDateTimeInstance(); %>

<H1>Hello World on <%
// Use the DateFormat class from the text library
out.println(df.format(new Date())); %> </H1>
</BODY>
</HTML>
```

Now that we are getting the hang of how Java Server Pages work, we address the issues that come up when real programming is attempted. The goal of the following discussion about various aspects of writing JSP pages is to establish a detailed understanding of how the `JspServlet` translates the JSP page into a servlet. Once this is understood, most of the issues involved in coding JSPs become no-brainers.

How does the translation work? An oversimplified but accurate view of the process is that the `JspServlet` starts with an empty shell of the service method of a class that extends `HttpServlet`. The `JspServlet` reads the JSP file and then takes each chunk of HTML outside the `<% %>` brackets and places it inside an `out.println()` statement. The Java statements within the `<% %>` brackets are simply copied into the file. The `<% %>` brackets themselves are not copied into the servlet file. This means that the servlet file created from Listing 6.3 looks a lot like the Java program in Listing 6.1. With that in mind, we move on to several issues that arise when coding JSP.

Declaring Variables in JSP

Our discussion will begin with variable declarations. Let's rewrite the HelloWorldDate.jsp to use a variable, as shown in the following code.

```
<%@ import="java.util.Date" %>
<%@ import="java.text.*" %>

<HTML>
<HEAD><TITLE>Hello World Date</TITLE></HEAD>
<BODY>
<% DateFormat df = DateFormat.getDateTimeInstance(); %>

<% String myDate = df.format(new Date()); %>

<H1>Hello World on <% out.println(myDate); %> </H1>
</BODY>
</HTML>
```

So far, so good. The variable would show up in the source code of the resulting servlet as a declaration. The variable's scope in this situation would extend to all Java code in all subsequent sections of the file enclosed in <% %> brackets. That means that if we wanted to add a statement later in the file, as in the following version of the HelloWorldData.jsp, use of the myDate variable would be allowed and it would have the same value.

```
<%@ import="java.util.Date" %>
<%@ import="java.text.*" %>

<HTML>
<HEAD><TITLE>Hello World Date</TITLE></HEAD>
<BODY>
<% DateFormat df = DateFormat.getDateTimeInstance(); %>

<% String myDate = df.format(new Date()); %>

<H1>Hello World on <% out.println(myDate); %> </H1>

<HR>
<i>This page printed on <% out.println(myDate); %>
                        for your pleasure </i>

</BODY>
</HTML>
```

As many variables as needed can be declared in a JSP page, just like in a Java program. The same rules apply, as well. The following code would produce an error.

```
<%@ import="java.util.Date" %>
<%@ import="java.text.*" %>

<HTML>
<HEAD><TITLE>Hello World Date</TITLE></HEAD>
<BODY>
<% DateFormat df = DateFormat.getDateTimeInstance(); %>

<% String myDate = df.format(new Date()); %>

<H1>Hello World on <% out.println(myDate); %> </H1>

<HR>
<% String myDate = df.format(new Date()); %>
<i>This page printed on <% out.println(myDate); %>
                             for your pleasure </i>

</BODY>
</HTML>
```

The reason this JSP page would fail is that the translated servlet produced by the JspServlet would look something like Listing 6.4 in our oversimplified translation model.

Listing 6.4   JSP "Hello World" with declaration problem.

```
import java.util.Date;
import java.text.*;
import java.io.*;
import javax.servlet.*;
import javax.servlet.http.*;

public class HelloWorldDate6 extends HttpServlet {
  public void service(HttpServletRequest req,
                      HttpServletResponse res)
       throws ServletException, IOException
  {
    // Set header for output
    res.setContentType("text/html");

    ServletOutputStream out = res.getOutputStream();

    out.println("<HTML>");
    out.println("<HEAD><TITLE>Hello World Date</TITLE></HEAD>");
    out.println("<BODY>");

    DateFormat df = DateFormat.getDateTimeInstance();
```

```
        String myDate = df.format(new Date());

        out.println("<H1>Hello World on ");
        out.println(myDate);
        out.println("</H1>");
        out.println("<HR>");

        String myDate = df.format(new Date());

        out.println("<i> This page printed on ");
        out.println(myDate);
        out.println("for your pleasure </i>");
        out.println("</BODY>");
        out.println("</HTML>");
        out.close();
    }
}
```

Clearly, the problem with this program is that the mydate variable is declared twice, which does not sit well with the Java compiler. Of course, this double declaration problem could be dealt with by adding curly brackets to the code so that each declaration is in its own scope. The rewritten JSP page in Listing 6.5 illustrates the use of such a technique.

Listing 6.5 JSP "Hello World" with variable declaration problem solved.

```
<%@ import="java.util.Date" %>
<%@ import="java.text.*" %>

<% DateFormat df = DateFormat.getDateTimeInstance(); %>


<HTML>
<HEAD><TITLE>Hello World Date</TITLE></HEAD>
<BODY>

<% { %>
<% String myDate = df.format(new Date()); %>

<H1>Hello World on <% out.println(myDate); %> </H1>
<% } %>

<HR>

<% { %>
<% String myDate = df.format(new Date()); %>
<i>This page printed on <% out.println(myDate); %>
                        for your pleasure </i>
<% } %>

</BODY>
</HTML>
```

The curly brackets save the day in this situation. Curly brackets are also essential when using flow-of-control statements such as if then else, or case or looping statements such as while or for.

Using if then *and Looping Statements in JSP*

In all the examples we have shown so far, all the HTML would be presented to the user as output. We have yet to see how flow-of-control statements such as if then else or while or for loops can control which HTML statements are presented to the user. Clearly, JSP would not be worth much as a programming tool if this were impossible. So how is it done?

It is with respect to the use of flow-of-control statements that it is most useful to think of the HTML statements in a JSP file as enclosed in out.println() statements. With this in mind, it becomes clear that if a set of HTML statements is placed within curly braces and the curly braces are used in an if then else statement, they will be executed only if certain conditions are true. Listing 6.6 shows how to conditionally include certain statements in a JSP file.

Listing 6.6   Conditional statements in a JSP.

```
<%@ import="java.util.*" %>
<%@ import="java.text.*" %>

<% Calendar now = Calendar.getInstance(); %>
<% int hourNow  = now.get(Calendar.HOUR); %>

<% DateFormat df = DateFormat.getDateTimeInstance(); %>
<% String myDate = df.format(new Date()); %>

<HTML>
<HEAD><TITLE>Hello World Date</TITLE></HEAD>
<BODY>
<H1>Hello World on <% out.println(myDate); %> </H1>

<H2> <% if (hourNow < 12) { %>
Good Morning
<% } else if (hourNow >= 12 && hourNow < 6 ) { %>
Good Afternoon
<% } else { %>
Good Evening
<% } %>
</H2>
</BODY>
</HTML>
```

Because each of the greetings "Good Morning," "Good Afternoon," and "Good Evening" is in essence embedded in an out.println() statement that is in turn in one of three blocks of an `if` `then` `else` statement, it is easy to see how the output from this JSP file will have only one greeting in it. The resulting code will look like Listing 6.7, using our oversimplified model.

Listing 6.7 Compiled servlet for conditional statement in a JSP.

```
import java.util.Date;
import java.text.*;
import java.io.*;
import javax.servlet.*;
import javax.servlet.http.*;

public class HelloWorldDate6 extends HttpServlet {
  public void service(HttpServletRequest req,
                      HttpServletResponse res)
      throws ServletException, IOException
  {
    // Set header for output
    res.setContentType("text/html");

    ServletOutputStream out = res.getOutputStream();

Calendar now = Calendar.getInstance();
int hourNow  = now.get(Calendar.HOUR);

DateFormat df = DateFormat.getDateTimeInstance();
String myDate = df.format(new Date());
out.println("<HTML>");
out.println("<HEAD><TITLE>Hello World Date</TITLE></HEAD>");
out.println("<BODY>");
out.print("<H1>Hello World on ");
out.print(mydate);
out.println("</H1>");
out.println("<H2>");
if (hourNow < 12) {
out.println("Good Morning ");
} else if ( hourNow >= 12 && hourNow < 6 ) {
out.println("Good Afternoon ");
} else {
out.println("Good Evening ");
}
out.println("</H2>");
out.println("</BODY>");
out.println("</HTML>");
}
}
```

The same principle holds for looping statements, which can be used to repetitively produce HTML. Listing 6.8 shows a program that loops through the list of parameters and prints each of them.

Listing 6.8   Looping statement in a JSP.

```
<%@ import="java.util.*" %>
<HTML>
<HEAD>
   <TITLE>Example 1: looping in JSPs</TITLE>
</HEAD>
<BODY>
<%
String queryString = request.getQueryString();
if(queryString == null) {
%>
   There was no query string provided!
   <%
} else {
Hashtable queryValues = HttpUtils.parseQueryString(queryString);
Enumeration e         = queryValues.keys();
%>
Here are the values you provided:
<UL>
<%
while(e.hasMoreElements()) {
   String key    = (String) e.nextElement();
   String values[] = (String[]) queryValues.get(key);
%>
<LI> <% out.println(key); %>
<!-- Each value in the query string may have multiple values. So,
      we have an inner loop to print each -->
<UL>
<%
for(int i=0;i<values.length;i++) {
%>
<LI> <%out.println(values[i]); %>
<% } %>
</UL>
<% } // This closes the loop over the ennumeration %>
<% } // This closes the 'else' clause %>
</UL>
</BODY>
</HTML>
```

Expressions in Java Server Pages

Avoiding tedium should be a goal of any programming system. In the listings in this chapter, the value of the variable mydate is embedded in an HTML state-ments in the following manner:

```
<H1>Hello World On <% out.print(myDate) %></H1>
```

This is fine but a bit clunky, given how frequently in JSP files one needs to in-sert the value of a variable. JSP of course does have a mechanism that provides a shorthand way to get this job done. The shorthand for inserting the value of expressions into HTML uses the <%= %> tag. Using the expression tag, the preceding statement would look like this:

```
<H1>Hello World On <%= myDate %></H1>
```

It is important to point out that this expression tag, unlike expressions used in the previous versions of Java Server Pages, works everywhere in a JSP file, including between double quotation marks. It is perfectly fine to put the value of a variable named coolurl in a quoted portion of an HTML statement:

```
<A HREF="<%=coolURL%>">Cool Site of the Book</A>
```

In the PageCompilation implementation, an expression in a statement like the one in this example would have required the variable to be enclosed in back quotes.

Printing HTML from Java Statements

Given the power of a JSP page, it is tempting to think that the days of having HTML between the parentheses in an out.println() statement are over for good. This is not the case, however. Instances do arise in which the sensible thing to do is print out some HTML with Java code. Because doing so makes a JSP page more difficult to maintain, printing HTML from Java should be done as infrequently as possible.

It is also important to understand that HTML printed from Java statements goes directly to the browser. No processing takes place to recognize server-side includes with the servlet tag. For example, a servlet tag written as follows would be sent directly to the requesting browser:

```
out.println("<servlet>getheader(req.getparm(\"<=%userid%>\"))
</servlet>");
```

It would result in the servlet tag not being executed. A servlet tag written as follows would be executed:

```
<servlet>getheader(req.getparm("<%=userid%>")</servlet>
```

The reason the <servlet> tag would not be executed if placed inside an out.println() statement is that it would never get seen by the preprocessor. For HTML in servlets, the preprocessing is done at compile time. The compiled code contains statements that make sure that the <servlet> tag is executed. The println() statement is executed after the compilation at runtime. At runtime in a JSP page, all the output goes directly to the browser and is not examined for servlet tags.

Other Coding Topics

A few more topics need to be mentioned to provide a full understanding of Java Server Pages. The first is the existence of a set of predefined variables that are available to every JSP page. So far we have discussed out.println() assuming that the out object was magically available. The good news is that the out variable is automatically declared along with three other variables: in, request, and response. (A variable called data is also declared for JSP internal purposes.) These four variables are always declared because they are fundamental to the processing of a JSP page.

- The request variable is the incoming request object. It is an instance of the javax.servlet.http.HttpServletRequest class.
- The response variable is the outgoing response object. It is defined by javax.servlet.http.HttpServletResponse.
- The in variable is the input stream that may be present if the request is an HTTP POST. This stream, an instance of the java.io.BufferedReader class, is contained in the request object.
- The out variable is the output stream that is contained in the response object. It is an instance of the java.io.PrintWriter class.

All these variables exist only as a matter of convenience. In servlet programming, one of the first tasks is to place the input and output streams in their own variables to simplify coding. In Chapter 9, we outline in great detail the methods that are available in the request and response objects. Remember that it is possible to use the predefined variables to invoke these methods. One useful technique is to redirect the user to an error page if something major is wrong. The following code fragment shows how easy this is.

```
<%@ import="java.util.*" %>
<%
String uri         = request.getRequestURI();
String queryString = request.getQueryString();
if(queryString == null || queryString.equals("")) {
%>
<HTML>
<HEAD>
  <TITLE>JSP with redirect</TITLE>
</HEAD>
<BODY>
<P>
```

This JSP page allows the user to go to a different site. Normally this would be done directly by an href, but that does not allow us to keep track of whom we are sending to which other site. So instead, we send the user back to this page, log which page they are really going to, and then issue a redirect that sends them where they really want to go (Listing 6.9).

Listing 6.9 JSP with an HTTP redirect.

```
</P>
<P>
Which of these two fine Java sites would you like to go to?
</P>
<A HREF="<%=uri%>?choice=1">Javasoft</A><br>
<A HREF="<%=uri%>?choice=2">Gamelan</A>
</BODY>
</HTML>
<%
} else {
// If the user hasn't made a selection, we come here
Hashtable queryValues = HttpUtils.parseQueryString(queryString);
String values[]       = (String[]) queryValues.get("choice");
if(values == null || values.length < 0) {
    log("User did not make a valid choice");
    response.sendRedirect(uri);
    return;
}
if(values[0].equals("0")) {
    log("Sent user to Javasoft");
    response.sendRedirect("http://www.javasoft.com");
} else if(values[0].equals("1")) {
    log("Sent user to Gamelon");
    response.sendRedirect("http://www.developer.com");
} else {
    log("User did not make a valid choice");
    response.sendRedirect(uri);
}
}
%>
```

Another useful thing to know about JSP is how to catch the IOException that occurs when the Stop button on the browser is pressed. When that happens, the game is over as far as the delivery of that page goes, and it makes sense to stop processing as soon as that exception is recognized. Exceptions that can occur during the course of coding, like dividing by zero, are handled as they are in all Java programs with the try catch blocks. In Java Server Pages it is no different.

It pays to remember that catching a Stop requires that the entire servlet reside within a try catch block. We should also remember that the exception will be recognized only at the time of the write to the output stream. As a matter of efficiency, the output stream of the JSP page will try to buffer all material written from a page so that it all can be written at once. This means that there is generally no opportunity to discover that the Stop button has been pressed until the entire page has been written out. In certain cases, when a key resource is being tied up by a page, for example, it may be desirable to find out several times during the construction of the output if the Stop button has been pressed. To do this, the out.flush() method must be called so that the buffered output is actually written to the browser so that the Stop interruption can be recognized. The example program in Listing 6.10 computes prime numbers and allows the user to interrupt after he or she has seen enough.

Listing 6.10 JSP that can catch Reset interrupts.

```
<%@ import="java.math.*"%>
<%@ import="java.util.*"%>

<SCRIPT runat="server">
BigInteger zero       = BigInteger.valueOf(0L);
BigInteger one        = BigInteger.valueOf(1L);
BigInteger n          = BigInteger.valueOf(2L);
BigInteger primes[]   = new BigInteger[100];
BigInteger lastPrime  = null;
int numPrimes         = 0;

public BigInteger nextPrime() {
  boolean maybePrime = true;
  int i;

  while(true) {
    maybePrime = true;
    for(i=0;i<numPrimes && maybePrime;i++) {
      maybePrime = !n.remainder(primes[i]).equals(zero);
    }

    if(maybePrime) {
      if(numPrimes == primes.length) {
        BigInteger newPrimes[] = new BigInteger[primes.length
                                    + 100];
        System.arraycopy(primes,0,newPrimes,0,primes.length);
        primes = newPrimes;
      }

      primes[numPrimes++] = n;
      n = n.add(one);
      return(primes[numPrimes-1]);
    }

    n = n.add(one);
  }
}
</SCRIPT>

<% if(request.getQueryString() != null) { %>
<HTML>
<HEAD><TITLE>Prime Adiministraors screen</TITLE></HEAD>
<BODY>
```

```
The last user gave up after seeing <%= lastPrime %>
</BODY>
</HTML>

<% } else { %>

<% BigInteger aPrime = null; %>
<% boolean didBreak  = false; %>

<% try { %>
<HTML>
<HEAD><TITLE>Prime Numbers</TITLE></HEAD>

<BODY>

Here are all the prime numbers. I bet you get tired of seeing them
before I get tired of generating them!<P>

<%
   while(!didBreak) {
      lastPrime = nextPrime();
      out.println(lastPrime);
      out.println("<BR>");
      out.flush();
   }
} catch (IOException IOe) {
   didBreak  = true;
   lastPrime = aPrime;
}
%>

<% } // This closes the else clause %>
```

Note that if the out.flush() method were not called, the exception would be caught only at the end of the JSP page or whenever the buffer was full enough to write.

Running JSP and Catching Compile and Execution Errors

So far we have focused on how to write JSP pages . Now we switch to the topic of how JSP pages are invoked and how to catch compile-time and runtime errors. As we mentioned earlier, the Java Web Server comes with a default servlet alias that maps all files with a *.jsp alias to the JspServlet. This means that any URL with a *.jsp extension that arrives at the server will be handed to the JspServlet for processing. If the underlying JSP file does not exist in the directory specified by the URL, then the JspServlet returns an error. It also means that the JspServlet plays by certain rules. It expects to find the *.jsp file in the directory specified in the URL. If different behavior is required, then multiple levels of aliasing may be required. To map the URL *http://mysite.com/myApp*

to a JSP page, we would have to first map the URL to a JSP file, which then would be mapped to a the `JspServlet` through the default rule.

Invoking a JSP page directly with a URL is only half the story. JSP pages can also be invoked by other servlets to format their output. The way this works is that the servlet is invoked by whatever means necessary. The servlet does the work it is designed to do and is left with some output that needs to be sent back to the requesting browser. Instead of sending this output to the browser directly, which would require that the servlet contain the HTML and other such formatting information, two APIs have been created, `HttpServiceRequest` and `HttpServiceResponse`, which allow the output to be inserted into a request object and to have a JSP invoked to convert that request object into an HTML page for the user. Details about how to use these APIs appear in the supplement to this chapter that is available on the Web (see the conclusion to this chapter for the URL).

Now that we are about to delve into debugging—a serious topic that does not permit the kind of oversimplification we have so far employed—we must explain a few more aspects of how Java Server Pages work.

The first oversimplification to correct is that the HTML statements in a JSP page are translated to a the underlying servlet by encapsulating them in `out.println()` statements. This is a powerful way to sort out certain issues, but the truth is just a little more complex. The way the translation process works is that instead of copying each line into the servlet file, the JSP file is opened and each chunk of HTML that resides between pairs of `<% %>` tags is read in and written out to the output file. This means that several lines of HTML may be read in and written out with one statement rather than having one `out.println()` statement for each line.

The other oversimplification is that the translation is done as straightforwardly as we have described. For example, we have assumed that an expression is translated into an `out.print()` statement. This also is not always the case. In this situation and in many others, optimizations are introduced to make the code perform as fast as possible. The result of all of this is that the code may appear more complex than we have so far shown. Listing 6.11 shows what the first JSP in this chapter actually looks like when translated to a servlet.

Listing 6.11   Servlet that results from JSP compilation.

```
package pagecompile;

import java.io.*;
import java.util.*;
import javax.servlet.*;
import javax.servlet.http.*;
import java.beans.Beans;
import com.sun.server.http.pagecompile.ParamsHttpServletRequest;
```

```
import com.sun.server.http.pagecompile.ServletUtil;
import com.sun.server.http.pagecompile.filecache.CharFileData;
import com.sun.server.http.pagecompile.NCSAUtil;

import java.util.Date;
import java.text.*;

public class _HelloWorldDate_xjsp extends
javax.servlet.http.HttpServlet {
    private static final String sources[] = new String[] {
        "/JavaWebServer1.1.1/public_html/HelloWorldDate.jsp",
    };
    private static final long lastModified[] = {
        905614776000L,
    };

    public void service(HttpServletRequest request,
                        HttpServletResponse response)
                        throws IOException, ServletException
    {
        PrintWriter out = response.getWriter();
        CharFileData data[] = new CharFileData[sources.length];
        try {
            for (int i = 0 ; i < data.length ; i++)
            data[i] = ServletUtil.getJHtmlSource(this,
                            sources[i],
                            "8859_1",
                            lastModified[i]);
        } catch (Exception ex) {
            ex.printStackTrace();
            throw new ServletException("fileData");
        }
        // com.sun.server.http.pagecompile.jsp.CharArrayChunk
                        /JavaWebServer1.1.1/
                        public_html/HelloWorldDate.jsp 2,0-
                        /JavaWebServer1.1.1/
                        public_html/HelloWorldDate.jsp 2,1
        data[0].writeChars(30, 1, out);
        // com.sun.server.http.pagecompile.jsp.CharArrayChunk
                        /JavaWebServer1.1.1/
                        public_html/HelloWorldDate.jsp 3,0-
                        /JavaWebServer1.1.1/
                        public_html/HelloWorldDate.jsp 7,1
        data[0].writeChars(58, 61, out);
        // com.sun.server.http.pagecompile.jsp.ScriptletChunk
                        /JavaWebServer1.1.1
                        /public_html/HelloWorldDate.jsp 7,1-
                        /JavaWebServer1.1.1/public_html/
                        HelloWorldDate.jsp 8,0
                DateFormat df = DateFormat.getDateTimeInstance();
```

```
// com.sun.server.http.pagecompile.jsp.CharArrayChunk
                /JavaWebServer1.1.1/
                public_html/HelloWorldDate.jsp 8,0-
                /JavaWebServer1.1.1/
                public_html/HelloWorldDate.jsp 8,20
     data[0].writeChars(174, 20, out);
// com.sun.server.http.pagecompile.jsp.ScriptletChunk
                /JavaWebServer1.1.1/
                public_html/HelloWorldDate.jsp 8,20-
                /JavaWebServer1.1.1/
                public_html/HelloWorldDate.jsp 8,61
            out.println(df.format(new Date()));
// com.sun.server.http.pagecompile.jsp.CharArrayChunk
                /JavaWebServer1.1.1/
                public_html/HelloWorldDate.jsp 8,61-
                /JavaWebServer1.1.1/
                public_html/HelloWorldDate.jsp 11,0
     data[0].writeChars(235, 23, out);
    }
}
```

A couple of things become clear after examining this code. The first is
that the translated Java source file is a lot less like the original JSP file than our
examples have led us to believe. Finding one's way around a translated source
file is far from trivial in a long page. Fortunately, the translation process places
comments in the source file that indicate from where in the original JSP file the
Java code was extracted.

Why would we want to know this? For debugging, of course. When a JSP
page is first executed, it is compiled. If any errors occur, they are reported to
the user through the browser. The messages look like this:

```
/JavaWebServer1.1.1/pagecompile/_HelloWorldDate5_xjsp.java
:56: Variable 'myDate' is already defined in this method.
            String myDate = df.format(new Date());
                   ^
```

The message comes from the Java compiler, which reports, as best it can,
where the problem showed up. Anyone familiar with compilers knows that the
line numbers reported can sometimes bear no relationship to the line on which
the mistake occurred. A missing semicolon can cause an error at another location in the file and a missing declaration won't be found until the undeclared
variable is used. Also, one mistake can cause a cascade of compiler error messages. These points hold for the Java compiler as well, and the messages that
are displayed on the screen show these characteristics. This means that if a
small error, like a missing semicolon, is fixed, then many other error messages
may disappear.

A close look at the error message in the example shows that each error message has a line number associated with it that refers to the line in the Java source code file of the translated JSP file. Where is this file? So far we have spoken about this file in rather vague terms without pinpointing where it exists and how it can be examined. Let's clear this up.

The location of the Java source code for JSP files is controlled by the workingDir property of the JspServlet. This defaults to the `<Server_root>/page_compilation` directory. The directory structure in this directory mirrors the `<document_root>`—usually `public_html`—directory for each JSP page that has been compiled. The mirroring is not exact. In the page compilation directory, all directory names and filenames are prefixed with an underscore _. The page compilation directory starts out empty but then is filled in with just as many subdirectories as are needed to store the JSP pages that have been compiled. The directories are not created until the JSP pages have been compiled.

The Java source code files for the servlets are named by prefixing an underscore to the name of the JSP page. The JSP page named `<document_root>/appdir/bonushonus.jsp` would have an associated Java source code file named `<server_root>/<page_compilation_directory>/_appdir/_bonushonus.java`.

To find what went wrong when the compilation error occurred, first look at the message and find the line number of the error. Next go to the associated servlet file in the page compilation directory and look for that line. Figure out what the error is, but do not correct it in the translated Java source file. It will do no good to make any corrections there because that file is overwritten each time the JSP file is compiled. Near that line that contains the error, usually right before it, should be a comment telling from which line numbers in the JSP file the Java code was extracted. Go to the JSP file to that line number, correct the error, and then reinvoke the servlet to see if the change worked.

In the future, as Sun works with the creators of Integrated Development Environments (IDEs), this debugging cycle will be much easier.

Compile errors are, of course, only part of the story when it comes to debugging. A whole new sort of error pops up at runtime while a program is doing its work. The classic runtime error is the divide-by-zero exception. I have always enjoyed dividing by zero; I'm not sure why it is such a problem for computers and mathematicians. The following code shows a program guaranteed to go sour.

```
<html>
<head><title>Divide By Zero </title></head>
<body>
<%int zero = 0; %>
<h1>Fourteen divided by zero equals: <%=14/zero%></h1>
</body>
</html>
```

When this program is executed, the following message appears on the screen of the browser that requested the JSP.

```
500 Internal Server Error
The servlet named "pageCompile", at the requested URL
http://dwoods:8080/JSPExamples/DivideByZero.jsp
reported this exception:
/ by zero
The administrator of this Web server should resolve this problem.
```

This kind of message can ruin your day, unless you understand how to fix such problems. The first stop for a runtime exception is the stack trace. Because servlets run in the Web server, the stack trace is dumped to the error log, which is located in the following file:

```
<server_root>/logs/javaWebserver/Webpageservice/error_log
```

This log can be viewed either by going to the log file in the file system or using the monitor interface of the administration tool. The stack trace identifies where the problem occurred and how the program got to that point.

A look in the error log after the exception tells the line of code on which the exception was thrown. Listing 6.12 shows the stack trace from the DivideByZero.jsp file.

Listing 6.12   Stack trace for divide-by-zero exception.

```
Stack Trace:
[Tue Jul 28 06:57:40 EDT 1998] Exception in servlet pageCompile
[Tue Jul 28 06:57:40 EDT 1998] java.lang.ArithmeticException: /
                               by zero
java.lang.ArithmeticException: / by zero
   at pagecompile._JSPExamples._DivideByZero.service(_DivideByZero
           .java:33)
   at javax.servlet.http.HttpServlet.service(HttpServlet.java:588)
   at com.sun.server.Webserver.pagecompile.JspServlet.doService(
                                   JspServlet.java:557)
   at com.sun.server.Webserver.pagecompile.JspServlet.doGet(
                                   JspServlet.java:358)
   at javax.servlet.http.HttpServlet.service(HttpServlet.java:499)
   at javax.servlet.http.HttpServlet.service(HttpServlet.java:588)
   at com.sun.server.ServletState.callService(ServletState.java:204)
   at com.sun.server.ServletManager.callServletService(
                       ServletManager.java:940)
   at com.sun.server.Webserver.HttpServiceHandler.handleRequest(
                               HttpServiceHandler.java:455)
   at com.sun.server.Webserver.HttpServiceHandler.handleRequest(
                               HttpServiceHandler.java:212)
   at com.sun.server.HandlerThread.run(HandlerThread.java:154)
```

The fourth line (the sixth line here) of the stack trace in this listing, the first line that begins with at, indicates where the exception occurred. Specifically, the stack trace says that the exception was thrown at line

```
at pagecompile._JSPExamples._DivideByZero.service(
_DivideByZero.java:33).
```

In English, this line says that the exception occurred in the method page-compile._JSPExamples._DivideByZero.service on line 33 of the _DivideBy-Zero.java file. Listing 6.13 shows that file, and a close look confirms that line 33 is where the nasty divide-by-zero took place.

Listing 6.13 Compiled servlet for divide-by-zero JSP.

```
package pagecompile._JSPExamples;

import java.io.*;
import java.util.*;
import javax.servlet.*;
import javax.servlet.http.*;
import com.sun.server.Webserver.pagecompile.filecache.*;
import com.sun.server.Webserver.pagecompile.
                            ParamsHttpServletRequest;
import com.sun.server.Webserver.pagecompile.*;

public class _DivideByZero
extends HttpServlet{

//----------------------
   static {
   }

   //--------------- The service method
   public void service (HttpServletRequest request,
                    HttpServletResponse response)
      throws ServletException, IOException
   {
     ServletOutputStream out = response.getOutputStream ();
     ByteFileData __fileData = null;
     try {
        __fileData = (ByteFileData) ServletUtil.getJHtmlSource(this,
        \\DivideByZero.jhtml", null, 901623420000L);
        if (__fileData == null) throw new ServletException(
           "FileChanged" );

        /*** lines: 1-4 */
        __fileData.writeBytes (0, 61, out);
int zero = 0;        /*** lines: 4-5 */
        __fileData.writeBytes (87, 39, out);
        out.print(ServletUtil.toString(14/zero));
        /*** lines: 5-7 */
```

```
    __fileData.writeBytes (157, 23, out);
  }
  finally {
    if (__fileData != null) __fileData.close();
  }
 }
}
```

Remember, never try to fix anything in this translated servlet file. It makes no sense, because changes are just overwritten. The way to fix errors is by changing code in the JSP file. Use the comments in the translated servlet file to find the right place in the JSP file.

Conclusion

Java Server Pages is becoming a much more powerful technology. Soon programmers will be able to encapsulate functionality for use by those who do not know how to write code in elegant ways. At this point it would be natural to turn to the more advanced features of Java Server Pages.

Unfortunately, we must stop without such an explanation. As of the time of this writing, the specification for the next version of Java Server Pages is not yet final, and we cannot in good faith explain a technology that is a moving target. The updated specification will be available on the JavaSoft site.

We trust that the information in this book's chapter, plus the updates that will soon be available on the Web, will provide you with a good introduction to a powerful technology.

CHAPTER 7

Session Tracking

One of the great challenges of Web application development is adapting the HTTP protocol to the needs of everyday applications. As a display mechanism, HTML does a fine job, but in keeping track of what a user has been doing from page to page, HTTP and HTML fall short. The biggest problem is how to manage the state of an application in the stateless HTTP protocol. The session tracking feature of the Java Web Server is aimed squarely at solving the state management problem.

Session tracking provides a system for a programmer to create objects that are associated with an individual user and store information in them that is available to a servlet or a set of cooperating servlets across page requests. This feature is another example of how the Java Web Server (JWS) was built from the ground up as a tool for application development.

Before we dive into the details of how session objects work, we need to clarify a few concepts that are essential to a lucid explanation of session tracking. The basic problem for many applications in HTTP is that the protocol deals with only one request at a time. When a user enters information that must be used by subsequent requests, the developer has to choose from several methods of storing that information for use in the subsequent requests. The choices follow.

Client-Side State

Saving the state of a program on the client side means that each page sent back to the user contains the information required for the next step in the transaction. When a user takes an action on that page, the *state* information is also sent to the server. The methods described in the following sections all preserve state on the client in different ways.

URL Encoding

The programmer can rewrite each URL on the page that is produced so that when any link is clicked the saved information is available to the program processing the HTTP GET request. This method works when each subsequent page is dynamically created with a program that uses the GET method. The problem is that if a link is traversed to a place that does not participate in the URL encoding process, all the information is lost. The other difficulty is that if lots of URLs must be encoded, there are many opportunities for mistakes, and the URLs can grow to absurd lengths.

Form Variables

The programmer can put the stored information in form variables. Hidden form variables are an especially popular place to put information that must be saved from request to request. In this method, each subsequent request must be a form submission and must produce a page that contains a form so that the variables containing the state can be preserved. This method has the same problems as the URL encoding method: if a page that is not participating in the scheme is visited, then the state is lost. Also, normal HTML links cannot be used. Every page must be a form with some sort of Submit button.

Cookies

Cookies are the best method of client-side state preservation for most purposes. Cookies are pieces of information that are written from the server to the browser and stored in a file controlled by the browser. The browser returns the cookies to the server that wrote them in the HTTP header. The program can then read the information out of this header and rewrite it if necessary. Cookies are a much nicer way of storing information on the client side because they do not rely on the user taking a certain path through a set of pages.

Once a cookie is written, it is presented to the server each time a request is made from the browser. Although cookies solve many of the problems associated with URL encoding and form variables, they suffer from one major difficulty. Browsers have a way of allowing cookies to be turned off so that a server's attempt to write a cookie to the browser is rejected. This means that any scheme to preserve state using cookies will work only if a user has cookies turned on. Another drawback is that cookies should not be used to store a huge amount of information. By design the maximum amount of information that can be stored is 4 kilobytes and too many cookies or too much information is a bad idea because the cookies or information is transferred in the header along with every request.

Server-Side State

A user does not have to be identified or reveal an identity for client-side state to be preserved. The only thing that must be stored in the client-side techniques is the information itself, not a unique identifier of the user. If the state is being kept on the server side, then the user must somehow be identified from request to request so that information that is stored on the server side can be retrieved. URL encoding, form variables, and cookies all can be used to preserve some sort of identifier. HTTP authentication in which a user identifies himself or herself with a password is another method of identification. It is important to point out that there is no such thing as pure server-side state—the client side must always cooperate by providing some sort of identifier.

Once a user is identified in some way, information can be associated with the user by using the unique identifier as a key into a database or a file or an array stored in memory. When a user arrives, the information associated with the user is looked up and used by a program. Any new information is then written to the database so that it can be retrieved on any subsequent request. In order for server-side state to be effective, a cache of some kind must be placed in front of the database so that each page request does not require a database access.

Sessions and Session Tracking's API Description

A *session* on the Web usually refers to the time a person is sitting at the computer using a particular Web site. In a stateless protocol the definition of a session is a matter of interpretation. Each request could be a session, for it is impossible to know if another request will follow. There is no logging on or off to formally indicate the beginning or ending of a session. The common definition of a session on the Web is a period of time. A session starts when the first request from a particular user is received and ends when the time period elapses. In the Java Web Server, this time period is set with the `sessionInvalidationTime` parameter. The time limit default is 30 minutes

Now that we have covered all the general issues involved in session tracking, we can explain how the JWS helps programmers with state management. When a user of the Java Web Server has session tracking turned on, he is assigned a unique session ID when the session object is first created. This ID uniquely identifies the user and associates the user with the session object that is created for him or her by the session tracking system. It is important to point out that identifying users does not involve knowledge about them; they are not asked questions in a dialog box. All the Java Web Server does is come up with a unique identification string and write it to the user's cookie so that the user can be identified on return requests.

The center of the session tracking system is an HttpSession object. The HttpSession object is created for the user if it does not already exist when the getSession method of the HttpServletRequest object is called. It is important that the session object is retrieved before data is sent back to the user. This is because the cookie containing the unique identifier for the user is not obtained until getSession has been called. The ID must be put in the header before any data is sent so that the data finds its way to the user. If the ID is put in after data has been sent, the cookie is never written to the user's browser because the header is sent only once, just prior to the first output.

Once the session object has been retrieved, the putValue(), getValue(), and removeValue() methods are used to access data in the session object. The session object points to an HttpSessionContext object that contains a list of all current HttpSession objects. When an object is added to the session object, the object being added may be notified that this has taken place if the object being added implements the HttpSessionBindingListener interface. Figure 7.1 outlines the structure of the session tracking system.

Now that we have set the scene, we move on to some examples that illustrate the session tracking structure and bring out some of the subtleties of implementing session tracking.

API Description

Session tracking's biggest fans will undoubtedly be programmers who have implemented systems that preserve state using traditional methods. The way session tracking is implemented in the Java Web Server takes care of most of the tedious details and leaves the programmer to work on making the application serve its purpose.

Session tracking's ease of use does not excuse the programmer from paying attention to a few important details. The most important one is the naming of the session objects (see Table 7.1). As shown in all the examples, session objects are identified by a naming convention of <servletname>.<variablename>. This convention avoids possible collisions between two servlets using the same variable name. The collision could occur because session objects for the whole server are stored in the same name space.

All session objects are identified by a combination of the name and unique identifier. If two different servlets used the same name, then they would share the same object. While this may be the desired behavior, it is certainly not behavior we want to happen by accident. The naming convention ensures that accidents won't happen. If session objects are going to be shared across servlets, it probably makes sense to use a common prefix, such as globaldata.variablename or something similar, that indicates the special nature of the shared session object.

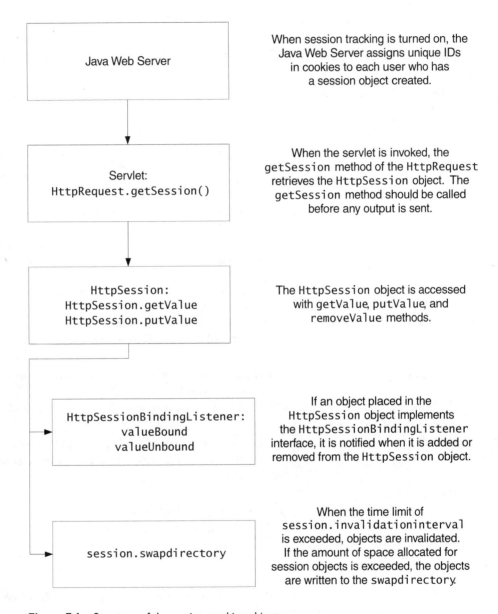

Figure 7.1   Structure of the session tracking objects

The next detail to keep in mind while coding with session objects is that grabbing the session object with the HttpServletRequest.getSession should be done before any output is sent in response to the request. This must be done so that the unique identifier is added to the headers before they are written to the users. This rule bears repetition, because failing to live by it means that session tracking will not work.

Table 7.1   Session Tracking Classes and Methods Using Session Objects

Method	Description
`HttpServletRequest`	
`getSession(Boolean create)`	Retrieves the session object. Creates a new session object if create parameter is true
`HttpSession`	
`getCreationTime()`	Returns time at which a session was created
`getId()`	Returns the identifier assigned to the session
`getLastAccessedTime()`	Returns the last time a client sent a request with the identifier connected with this session
`getValue(String)`	Returns the object associated with the variable name passed to this method
`getValueNames()`	Returns an array of variable names in this session object
`invalidate()`	Causes this representation of the session to be invalidated and removed from its context
`isNew()`	A session is new if it has been created but has not yet been associated with a client
`putValue(String, Object)`	Binds an object to a variable name
`removeValue(String)`	Removes the object bound to the variable name passed in
`HttpSessionBindingListener`	
`valueBound()`	Called when an object that has implemented this interface is added to a session object
`valueUnbound()`	Called when an object is removed from the session object
`HttpSessionBindingEvent`	
`getName()`	Returns the name to which the object is being bound or unbound
`getSession()`	Returns the session into which the session is being bound or unbound
`HttpServletResponse`	
`encodeUrl()`	Adds an ID tag to a URL if needed
`encodeRedirectUrl()`	Adds an ID tag to a redirect URL if needed

A final detail to remember is that the way the session object works—using the `putValue` method to associate a name and a stored object, a `getValue()` method to retrieve the object associated with the name, and the `removeValue()` method to delete a variable—is based on the `java.util.Dictionary` class.

The example program in Listing 7.1 provides a simple demonstration of the use of session objects. Note that this program will not work unless session tracking is turned on in the server that is executing the servlet. The program accepts a request from a user and prints out the number of times that the user has visited the servlet during the session by using a countervariable that is stored in the session object. The servlet also produces an HTML form that allows the user to make text comments that are then stored in an array that is also stored in the session object import java.util.*;.

Listing 7.1   Example1.java, a simple servlet that does session tracking.

```java
import java.io.*;
import javax.servlet.*;
import javax.servlet.http.*;
public class Example1 extends HttpServlet {
    public void doGet(HttpServletRequest req,
                      HttpServletResponse res)
        throws ServletException,IOException
    {
        ServletOutputStream out = res.getOutputStream();
        HttpSession session = req.getSession(true);
        Integer visitCount   =
            (Integer) session.getValue("example1.visitCount");
        Vector   statements  =
            (Vector)  session.getValue("example1.statements");

        if(visitCount == null)
            visitCount = new Integer(0);
        if(statements == null) {
            statements = new Vector(10);
            session.putValue("example1.statements",statements);
        }

        String values[] = req.getParameterValues("statement");
        if(values != null && values.length > 0)
            statements.addElement(values[0]);

        res.setContentType("text/html");
        res.setStatus(res.SC_OK);

        out.println("<HTML>");
        out.println("<HEAD>");
        out.println("<TITLE>Session tracking</TITLE>");
        out.println("</HEAD>");

        out.println("<BODY>");

        out.println("<P>");
        out.println("You have been here " +
                    visitCount.intValue() +
                    " times before, during this session");
        out.println("</P>");

        session.putValue("example1.visitCount",
                    new Integer(visitCount.intValue() + 1));

        if(statements.size() > 0) {
```

```
                    out.print("<P>Here is what you have said on ");
                    out.println("previous occasions:</P>");
                    out.println("<UL>");
                    for(int i=0;i<statements.size();i++) {
                        out.println("<LI>" + statements.elementAt(i));
                    }
                    out.println("</UL>");
                }

            out.println("<P>Want to add a comment?</P>");
            out.println("<FORM ACTION=" + req.getRequestURI() +
                        " METHOD=GET>");

            out.println("<INPUT TYPE=TEXT NAME=statement>");
            out.println("<INPUT TYPE=SUBMIT " +
                        "VALUE=Add this comment>");
            out.println("</FORM>");

            out.println("</BODY>");
            out.println("</HTML>");
        }
    }
```

NOTE: The HTML message says, "You have been here X times before during this session." The reason it says "during this session" is that the session objects are deleted when a session exceeds its time limit. The information in a session object is not persistent across sessions unless the programmer arranges for the values to be stored when the object expires or is invalidated and retrieved when the user comes back again (we present an example of this later). Session objects are like a convenient scratchpad for applications. Without help from a programmer, they do not provide storage beyond the life of the session.

Using Session Objects with a Sequence of Servlets

Some interesting issues arise when session objects are shared among servlets. As we mentioned earlier, shared session objects should be named in such a way that no collisions can accidentally occur. Another issue that needs to be addressed when sharing session objects across servlets is enforcing a certain order for the servlets. If an application is composed of three servlets that must be executed in order, then a user who visits the second or third servlet before she or he has visited the first servlet should be redirected to the first servlet.

One feature of the session object that makes enforced sequencing easier is the isNew() method, which returns true if the session object was just created when it was retrieved by the getSession() method. Another feature of session objects that helps in certain situations is that if you request an object from a variable name that does not exist, a null object is returned.

The example application in Listings 7.2, 7.3, and 7.4 uses these methods to enforce a sequence among the three servlets. Example2Intro must be the first servlet, followed by Example2Page1, and then Example2Page2. If page 1 or page 2 is requested first, the user is redirected to the first servlet. This technique can be applied to enforce all kinds of rules and dependencies among servlets.

Listing 7.2 Example2Intro.java, a servlet to ensure that pages are seen in order.

```java
import java.io.*;
import javax.servlet.*;
import javax.servlet.http.*;
public class Example2Intro extends HttpServlet {
    public void doGet(HttpServletRequest req,
                      HttpServletResponse res)
        throws ServletException,IOException
    {
        // Get the directory this was called from, and assume
        // that the next two pages are here as well
        String uri = req.getRequestURI();
        int pos    = uri.lastIndexOf('/');
        if(pos != -1) uri = uri.substring(0,pos+1);

        // Obtain or create a session for this user
        HttpSession session = req.getSession(true);

        // Print out the introductory comments
        ServletOutputStream out = res.getOutputStream();
        res.setContentType("text/html");
        res.setStatus(res.SC_OK);

        out.println("<HTML>");
        out.println("<HEAD>");
        out.println("<TITLE>Session example 2</TITLE>");
        out.println("</HEAD>");

        out.println("<BODY>");
        out.println("<P>");
        out.println("Welcome to another session tracking ");
        out.println("example!  This one uses session ");
        out.println("tracking to ensure that a set of pages ");
        out.println("are visted in the correct order");
        out.println("</P>");

        // Determine what the user has already seen
        Boolean seenIntro =
            (Boolean) session.getValue("example2.seenIntro");
        Boolean seenPage1 =
            (Boolean) session.getValue("example2.seenPage1");
        Boolean seenPage2 =
            (Boolean) session.getValue("example2.seenPage2");
```

```
        out.println("<P>");

        if(seenPage2 != null &&
          seenPage2.equals(Boolean.TRUE))
    {
            out.println("You have already seen both pages, ");
            out.println("you may revist either ");
            out.println("<A HREF=" +
                    uri +
                    "Example2Page1>Page 1</A> or");

            out.println("<A HREF=" +
                    uri +
                        "Example2Page2>Page 2</A> now.");
        } else if(seenPage1 != null &&
                seenPage1.equals(Boolean.TRUE))
    {
            out.println("You have already seen page 1, ");
            out.println("you may either revisit ");
            out.println("<A HREF=" +
                    uri +
                        "Example2Page1>Page 1</A> or " +
                    " proceed to ");
            out.println("<A HREF=" +
                    uri +
                    "Example2Page2>Page 2</A>.");
        } else {
            out.println("Now, please proceed to ");
            out.println("<A HREF=" +
                    uri +
                    "Example2Page1>Page 1</A>.");
        }
        out.println("</P>");

        out.println("</BODY>");
        out.println("</HTML>");
        out.close();

        // Indicate that the user has seen the intro
        session.putValue("example2.seenIntro",Boolean.TRUE);
    }
}
```

Listing 7.3   `Example2Page1.java`, the first servlet ordered by `Example2Intro`.

```
import java.io.*;
import javax.servlet.*;
import javax.servlet.http.*;
public class Example2Page1 extends HttpServlet {
    public void doGet(HttpServletRequest req,
                    HttpServletResponse res)
        throws ServletException,IOException
    {
```

```
// Get the directory this was called from,
// and assume that the other pages are here as well
String uri = req.getRequestURI();
int pos    = uri.lastIndexOf('/');
if(pos != -1) uri = uri.substring(0,pos+1);

// Obtain or create a session for this user
HttpSession session = req.getSession(true);

// If the session is new, the user must not
// have been through the introduction yet
if(session.isNew()) {
    res.sendRedirect(uri + "Example2Intro");
    return;
}

// The session might exist from some other servlet,
// but the user may not have seen the intro anyway. This is
// actually a sufficient check; the isNew in this
// case is redundant.

Boolean seenIntro =
    (Boolean) session.getValue("example2.seenIntro");

if(seenIntro == null || seenIntro.equals(Boolean.FALSE))
{
    res.sendRedirect(uri + "Example2Intro");
    return;
}

// The user has seen the intro, so let the user see
// this page
ServletOutputStream out = res.getOutputStream();
res.setContentType("text/html");
res.setStatus(res.SC_OK);

out.println("<HTML>");
out.println("<HEAD>");
out.println("<TITLE>Session example 2</TITLE>");
out.println("</HEAD>");

out.println("<BODY>");
out.println("<P>");

out.println("Welcome to page one of this example.  ");
out.println("You were only able to get here because ");
out.println("you've already been through the ");
out.println("introduction.");
out.println("</P>");

out.println("<P>");
out.println("You can now proceed to ");
out.println("<A HREF=" +
```

```
                            uri +
                            "Example2Page2>Page 2</A>.");
                out.println("</P>");

                out.println("</BODY>");
                out.println("</HTML>");

                // Indicate that the user has seen page 1
                session.putValue("example2.seenPage1"
                                 Boolean.TRUE);
        }
}
```

Listing 7.4   Example2Page2.java, the second servlet ordered by Example2Intro.

```
import java.io.*;
import javax.servlet.*;
import javax.servlet.http.*;
public class Example2Page2 extends HttpServlet {
    public void doGet(HttpServletRequest req,
                      HttpServletResponse res)
        throws ServletException,IOException
    {
        // Get the directory this was called from,
        // and assume that the next two pages are here as well
        String uri = req.getRequestURI();
        int pos    = uri.lastIndexOf('/');
        if(pos != -1) uri = uri.substring(0,pos+1);

        // Obtain or create a session for this user
        HttpSession session = req.getSession(true);

        // If the user hasn't seen the intro, send the user there
        Boolean seenIntro =
            (Boolean) session.getValue("example2.seenIntro");

        if(seenIntro == null ||
           seenIntro.equals(Boolean.FALSE))
        {
            res.sendRedirect(uri + "Example2Intro");
            return;
        }

        // If the user has seen the intro but not page 1, send
        // the user there
        Boolean seenPage1 =
            (Boolean) session.getValue("example2.seenPage1");

        if(seenPage1 == null ||
           seenPage1.equals(Boolean.FALSE))
        {
            res.sendRedirect(uri + "Example2Page1");
            return;
```

```
        }

        // The user has seen page1 and so is ready to see
        // the arcane knowledge hidden on page 2
        ServletOutputStream out = res.getOutputStream();
        res.setContentType("text/html");
        res.setStatus(res.SC_OK);

        out.println("<HTML>");
        out.println("<HEAD>");
        out.println("<TITLE>Session example 2</TITLE>");
        out.println("</HEAD>");

        out.println("<BODY>");

        out.println("<P>v);
        out.println("Welcome to the last page of the tour!");
        out.println("</P>");

        out.println("</BODY>");
        out.println("</HTML>");

        // Indicate that the user has seen page 2
        session.putValue("example2.seenPage2",Boolean.TRUE);
    }
}
```

Using Session Tracking without Cookies

As mentioned at the beginning of the chapter, cookies are a tremendously helpful mechanism. But because they involve the server writing information to the browser and because they can be used to keep track of a user's behavior, browser manufacturers always allow a user to turn off cookies. Some browsers do not support cookies at all. If cookies are turned off or unsupported, where does that leave session tracking, which relies on cookies? The answer is that session tracking must return to the roots of state management techniques. When cookies are turned off, the unique identifier that is stored in them is encoded in the URLs that make up the application.

The way this works is that each link on every page returned to the user must be encoded with the session ID information. This means that in Listings 7.2, 7.3, and 7.4, instead of code that looks like this

```
out.println("<A HREF=\"" + uri + "Example2Page1\">Page 1</A> or");
```

we would have to write

```
String myURL =  response.encodeUrl(uri + "Example2Page1");
out.println("<A HREF=\"" + myURL + \">Page 1</A> or");
```

Redirects are handled by a different encoding routine because different rules are applied to determine if rewriting is needed for redirects. Instead of writing

```
response.sendRedirect(uri + "Example2Intro");
```

we would write

```
String myURL = uri + "Example2Intro");
Response.sendRedirect(response.encodeRedirectUrl(myURL));
```

Both of these methods add a tag at the end of the URL that has the session ID. After encoding, a URL would look like this:

```
<A HREF="/Servlet/MyApp/Example2Intro;$sessionid$DA32242SSGE2">
```

It is important to point out that the encoding routines do not do a thing if they detect that the underlying browser is accepting cookies. If that is true, URLs are not changed a bit. Listing 7.5 is rewritten to employ URL rewriting.

Listing 7.5   Example1.java, a servlet that does session tracking without cookies.

```
import java.util.*;
import java.io.*;
import javax.servlet.*;
import javax.servlet.http.*;
public class Example1 extends HttpServlet {
    public void doGet(HttpServletRequest req,
                      HttpServletResponse res)
        throws ServletException,IOException
    {
        ServletOutputStream out = res.getOutputStream();
        HttpSession session = req.getSession(true);
        Integer visitCount  =
            (Integer) session.getValue("example1.visitCount");
        Vector statements   =
            (Vector)  session.getValue("example1.statements");

        if(visitCount == null)
            visitCount = new Integer(0);

        if(statements == null) {
            statements = new Vector(10);
            session.putValue("example1.statements",statements);
        }

        String values[] = req.getParameterValues("statement");
        if(values != null && values.length > 0)
            statements.addElement(values[0]);

        res.setContentType("text/html");
```

```
        res.setStatus(res.SC_OK);

        out.println("<HTML>");
        out.println("<HEAD>");
        out.println("<TITLE>Session tracking</TITLE>");
        out.println("</HEAD>");

        out.println("<BODY>");

        out.println("<P>");
        out.println("You have been here " +
                    visitCount.intValue() +
                    " times before, during this session");
        out.println("</P>");

        session.putValue("example1.visitCount",
                    new Integer(visitCount.intValue() + 1));

        if(statements.size() > 0) {
            out.println("<P>Here is what you have said on ");
            out.println("previous occasions:</P>");
            out.println("<UL>");
            for(int i=0;i<statements.size();i++) {
                out.println("<LI>" + statements.elementAt(i));
            }
            out.println("</UL>");
        }

        out.println("<P>Want to add a comment?</P>");
        out.println("<FORM ACTION=" +
                    res.encodeUrl(req.getRequestURI()) +
                    " METHOD=GET>");
        out.println("<INPUT TYPE=TEXT NAME=statement>");
        out.println("<INPUT TYPE=SUBMIT " +
                    "VALUE=Add this comment>");
        out.println("</FORM>");

        out.println("</BODY>");
        out.println("</HTML>");
    }
}
```

While it is great that session tracking is so resourceful that it can work with browsers that do not support cookies, it is important to point out that URL rewriting can work only if the application is a closed system of URLs. This means that for things to work properly, every page that is delivered must be either a servlet or a Java Server Pages (JSP). If there are plain HTML pages in the application, it is advisable to compile them as Java Server Pages so that URL rewriting takes place automatically.

Using Session Tracking with JSP

Session tracking and Java Server Pages work together to make things a bit easier on the programmer. In normal use of session objects, every URL must be encoded explicitly. With Java Sever Pages, all URLs that are in the HTML portion of the document are encoded automatically, if that is required. URLs that are within the Java coding section of the JSP must still be explicitly encoded. For certain applications that use a lot of static URLs to refer to different parts of the application, this feature can be a great benefit.

Using Session Listener

We have explained how session tracking can be used as a scratchpad that lasts for the duration of a session. To be truly useful for a wider range of applications, information must be able to be stored persistently across sessions. Although session objects have no facility for persistence—except perhaps for their ability to be swapped out when memory becomes full—the Http-SessionBindingListener interface provides the technique that allows session information to be stored persistently.

The HttpSessionBindingListener interface is not part of the HttpSession object. The listener interface is rather part of the objects that are stored in session objects. When the HttpSession.putValue and HttpSession.removeValue routines are called, the objects being stored are examined. If the methods in the HttpSessionBindingListener.valueBound and HttpSessionBindingListener. valueUnbound are implemented, the methods are invoked.

These methods provide a way to populate an object that is stored in the session object at the time of storage and to store the data in it at the time the session time limit expires, that is, when the session object is invalidated. In Listings 7.6 and 7.7, the Example3 servlet implements a login mechanism that extracts information from a database using the Persistent-SessionData object, which implements the HttpSessionBindingListener interface. The PersistentSessionObject uses its initializeSession() method to retrieve the data and the valueUnbound() method to store it back into the database.

Listing 7.6   Example3.java, a servlet that stores session data persistently.

```
import java.io.*;
import java.sql.*;
import javax.servlet.*;
import javax.servlet.http.*;
public class Example3 extends HttpServlet {
    public void service(HttpServletRequest req,
                        HttpServletResponse res)
        throws IOException
```

```
    {
        res.setContentType("text/html");
        res.setStatus(res.SC_OK);
        ServletOutputStream out = res.getOutputStream();

        // Get a session for this user
        HttpSession session = req.getSession(true);

        // If it's new, make the user log in
        if(session.isNew()) {
            sendLogin(out,req.getRequestURI());
            return;
        }

        // If we're logging in, set the username and initialize
        String values[] = req.getParameterValues("username");
        if(values != null && values.length != 0) {
            session.putValue("username",values[0]);
            PersistentSessionData.initializeSession(session);
        }

        PersistentSessionData obj =
(PersistentSessionData) session.getValue("example3.numVisits");
        Integer numVisits = new Integer(0);

        if(obj != null) numVisits = (Integer) obj.getObject();

        out.println("<HTML>");
        out.println("<HEAD>");
        out.println("<TITLE>");
        out.println("Persistent session tracking");
        out.println("</TITLE>");
        out.println("</HEAD>");

        out.println("<BODY>");

        out.println("<P>");
        out.println("You have been here " +
                    numVisits.intValue() +
                    " times before!");
        out.println("</P>");

        out.close();

        // Update the count.  It's now a little more complex,
        // because we need to store the persistent version
        session.putValue("example3.numVisits",
                    new PersistentSessionData(
                        new Integer(numVisits.intValue() + 1)));
    }

    private void sendLogin(ServletOutputStream out, String uri)
        throws IOException
```

```
        {
            out.println("<HTML>");
            out.println("<HEAD>");
            out.println("<TITLE>Please log in</TITLE>");
            out.println("</HEAD>");
            out.println("<BODY>");
            out.println("<FORM ACTION=" +
                        uri +
                        " METHOD=GET>");
        out.println("What is your username?");
        out.println("<INPUT TYPE=TEXT NAME=username>");
        out.println("<INPUT TYPE=SUBMIT VALUE=Log in>");
        out.println("</FORM>");
        out.println("</BODY>");
        out.println("</HTML>");
        }
}
```

Listing 7.7   PersistentSessionData.java, a class that implements HttpSessionBindingListener to save session data to a database.

```
import java.io.*;
import java.sql.*;
import javax.servlet.*;
import javax.servlet.http.*;
public class PersistentSessionData
    implements HttpSessionBindingListener
{
    private static String dbUrl    = "jdbc:postgresql:testdb";
    private static String dbuser   = "dbuser";
    private static String dbpasswd = "dbuser";
    private static Connection dbConnection = null;

    private Serializable object;

    public Serializable getObject() {return object;}

    /**
     * Initialize a session by pulling all the persistent data
     * out of the database and loading it into the session.
     * This assumes that the session will already contain a
     * username to use as an index to the database.
     */
    public static void initializeSession(HttpSession session) {
        String username = (String) session.getValue("username");

        if(username == null) return;

        try {
            // If the connection to the database has not yet
            // been established, do so now
            if(dbConnection == null) initDB();
```

```java
        // Get all the persistent objects this
        // user owns out of the database
        Statement statement =
            dbConnection.createStatement();

        ResultSet rs = statement.executeQuery(
                "select valuename,valuedata " +
                " from session " +
                " where username = '" + username + "'");

        if(rs == null) return;

        // Go through the data, build objects
        // from the serialized data,
        // and place them in the session
        String valueName;
        byte   valueData[];
        ObjectInputStream inStream;
        Serializable object;

        while(rs.next()) {
            valueName = new String(
                        rs.getBytes("valuename")).trim();
            valueData = rs.getBytes("valuedata");

            // Decode the value data
            byte data2[] = new byte[valueData.length/2];
            for(int i=0;i<valueData.length/2;i++) {
                int tmp = ((valueData[i*2]-'A')*16 +
                        (valueData[i*2+1]-'A'));
                if(tmp > 127) tmp -= 255;
                data2[i] = (byte) tmp;
            }

            // Convert the bytes back into an object
            inStream  = new ObjectInputStream(
                        new ByteArrayInputStream(data2));
            object = (Serializable) inStream.readObject();

            session.putValue(valueName,
                    new PersistentSessionData(object));
        }

        rs.close();
        statement.close();
    } catch (Exception exc) {
        exc.printStackTrace(System.err);
    }
    // Also set a special flag to indicate that this session
    // has been initialized.  This is the only way to do
    // this kind of check, because by this point isNew is
    // false, and there is no way to know whether a
    // session has no values because it hasn't yet been
```

```
        // initialized or because it just has no values
        session.putValue("didInitialize",Boolean.TRUE);
}

/**
 * The constructor takes a serializable object to wrap
 */
public PersistentSessionData(Serializable object) {
    // If the connection to the database has not yet been
    // established, do so now

    try {
        if(dbConnection == null) initDB();
    } catch (Exception e) {
        e.printStackTrace(System.err);
    }

    this.object = object;
}

/**
 * We don't need to do anything special when we're bound to
 * a session, but we still must provide the method
 */
public void valueBound(HttpSessionBindingEvent e) {
}

/**
 * When the value is unbound, we place it in the database
 * and associate it with the user indicated in the session
 */
public void valueUnbound(HttpSessionBindingEvent e) {
    // Get the session and name from the event
    String valuename     = e.getName();
    HttpSession session = e.getSession();
    String username     =
        (String) session.getValue("username");

    if(username == null) return;

    try {
        // Remove any previous instance of ourselves from
        // the database
        Statement statement =
            dbConnection.createStatement();

        statement.executeUpdate(
        "delete from session where username='" + username +
        "' and valuename = '" + valuename + "'");

        // Serialize the object
        ByteArrayOutputStream out =
            new ByteArrayOutputStream();
```

```
        ObjectOutputStream oout    =
            new ObjectOutputStream(out);

        oout.writeObject(object);
        byte data[] = out.toByteArray();

        // Some databases might not be able to store
        // arbitrary binary data, so we convert it into hex
        // format for storing
        byte data2[] = new byte[data.length * 2];

        for(int i=0;i<data.length;i++) {
            int tmp = (int) data[i];
            if(tmp < 0) tmp += 255;

            data2[i*2]   = (byte) (tmp/16 + 'A');
            data2[i*2+1] = (byte) (tmp%16 + 'A');
        }

        // Insert the information into the database
        statement.executeUpdate(
                    "insert into session values('" +
                    username              + "','" +
                    valuename             + "','" +
                    new String(data2) + "')");

        statement.close();
    } catch (Exception exc) {
        exc.printStackTrace(System.err);
    }
}

public static void initDB()
    throws ClassNotFoundException, SQLException
{
    // Load the driver
    Class.forName("postgresql.Driver");

    // Connect to database
    dbConnection = DriverManager.getConnection(dbUrl,
                                        dbuser,
                                        dbpasswd);
}
}
```

We have mentioned the fact that session objects are swapped. Here is how the system works in detail. Session swapping happens only when the number of active sessions specified by the session.maxresidents parameter is exceeded. session.maxresidents defaults to 1024. If the hardware that is executing the Java Web Server has sufficient memory, it is possible to push this number higher. Any adjustment, however, should be based on careful monitoring of the behavior of the server. When the `session.maxresidents` threshold is exceeded, the session objects that are the least recently used are swapped to disk using serialization. If the objects within a session tracking object are not serializable, then those objects are not swapped out and the goal of swapping—to reduce the amount of memory used—is not achieved. The best policy is to always make objects stored in session objects serializable. When swapping occurs, the serialized objects are written to the directory specified in the `session.swapdirectory` parameter, which defaults to `sessionSwap`. The server checks to see if the swap threshold has been exceeded according to the interval specified by `session.swapinterval`, which defaults to 10 seconds.

Sessions expire after the invalidation time limit has been exceeded. This interval is set by the `session.invalidationtime` parameter, which defaults to 30 minutes. The `session.invalidationinterval` parameter, which defaults to 10 seconds, determines how frequently the server checks to see whether session objects have exceeded their time limits.

If the JWS is shut down, sessions are saved and restored on startup if the `session.persistence` parameter is true. Objects that are not serializable are lost on startup, but those that are serializable are restored. If the `session.persistence` parameter is false, then all session information is lost when the Java Web Server is shut down.

Parameters also exist to control the details of the cookies that are written to the browser and other details of URL rewriting.

To manage the properties of session tracking, the administrator must edit the following properties file:

```
<server_root>/properties/server/javaWebserver/server.properties
```

Note that this properties file is now at the server level instead of at the service level as it was when session tracking was configured through the administration tool interface.

Listing 7.8, an excerpt from the `server.properties` file, shows the values that can be changed to tune the behavior of session tracking. Note that because it is done through a properties file, session tracking control is one of the few features of Java Web Server administration that does not take effect right away. When any session tracking parameters are set, the server must be restarted for the parameter changes to take effect. Table 7.2 explains each setting available to the administrator.

Listing 7.8   `server.properties`, a properties file that controls session tracking.

```
#
# Properties for session tracking
#
enable.sessions=true
```

```
enable.urlrewriting=true
enable.cookies=true
enable.protocolswitchrewriting=true

session.inavalidationinterval=10000
session.swapinterval=10000
session.persistence=true
session.swapdirectory=sessionSwap
session.maxresidents=1024
session.invalidationtime=1800000

session.cookie.name=jwssessionid
session.cookie.comment=Java Web Server Session Tracking Cookie
#session.cookie.domain
#session.cookie.maxage
#session.cookie.path
#session.cookie.secure
```

Conclusion

Session tracking is a breakthrough technology of the Java Web Server. It provides a general solution to a class of problems that had previously been solvable only through a significant coding effort or cumbersome techniques. In this chapter we have shown how to employ session tracking in a variety of situations that will arise in many applications. Our belief is that session tracking is an excellent example of the kind of functionality that will eventually become as standard as libraries for text manipulation or input/output.

CHAPTER 8

Internationalization and Localization

Internationalization is a set of techniques that allow programs to be easily adapted for use in different countries. Localization, a related topic, refers to adapting a program to operate properly in different locations. The fundamental idea of both internationalization and localization is to allow a program to encapsulate as much country-specific or location-specific information as possible in some external set of objects or files so that changing the program for a new country or locale involves only creating new versions of the external files.

The most important thing to keep in mind about these techniques is that they are simply enabling methods for good programming principles of information hiding and modular design. There is no way to "turn on" internationalization so that your program automatically can adapt to new countries. Rather, the internationalization techniques allow a program to be designed from the beginning to quickly adapt to new countries. In other words, internationalization is a tool; it does not provide the desired effect unless it is used properly.

Because internationalization and localization require more work—in some cases a considerable amount—a programmer should carefully consider whether a program will actually be used in another country or location before employing these techniques. For commercial products, it is almost certainly worth the trouble to take the time to write programs for export. But for most applications the choice is less obvious. In any event, however, the education of a Java programmer is not complete without a solid understanding of these techniques. (A couple of abbreviations seen all the time: i18n for Internationalization (because there are 18 letters between i and the last n) and l10n for Localization.)

Other programming systems have concepts similar to internationalization and localization. The Mac has resource forks. Windows has resource-only .dlls. The X-Windows system has resource files managed by xrdb. In Java, an individual object that has different values in different locales is called a *re-source*. A group of such resources is called a *resource bundle*, or just a bundle. In concrete terms, a resource bundle is a class that extends the abstract class `java.util.ResourceBundle`.

Internationalization API Overview

There is no servlet-specific i18n API; i18n is a fundamental part of the Java programming language. Table 8.1 is a quick overview of the relevant classes and methods. All these classes share a common idea. The idea is that a locale is specified either explicitly in the call to one of the classes or implicitly as a global default. Then, when the class does its work, the locale-specific information is looked up and used. A locale in Java is defined by a country code, a language code, and, optionally, a region. Resources are defined by resource names. The full specification of a resource is the resource name, language code, and country code. Resources are stored either in class files or in property files; both are named with the following pattern:

```
<resourcename>_<languagecode>_<countrycode>_<variant>.<extension>
```

The extension is either `class` or `property`.

The language code is two lowercase letters. A complete list is available at

http://www.ics.uci.edu/pub/ietf/http/related/iso639.txt

Table 8.1   Internationalization Classes

Java Class Name	Description
`java.util.Locale`	Class that names a particular place.
`java.util.ResourceBundle`	Collection of properties specific to one location or country.
`java.util.ListResourceBundle`	Implementation of `ResourceBundle` that stores properties in a class.
`java.util.PropertyResourceBundle`	Implementation of `ResourceBundle` that stores properties in a text file.
`java.text.Format`	Way of abstracting the presentation of some kind of data from the value of the data.
`java.text.DateFormat`	Subclass of `Format` that abstracts the representation of the data from the format of the data.
`java.text.NumberFormat`	Subclass of `Format` that abstracts the representation of a number from the format of the number.

The second parameter is a country, which is two uppercase letters. A complete list of these can be found at

http://www.chemie.fu-berlin.de/diverse/doc/ISO_3166.html

The third parameter is an optional variant. Variants have no predefined meanings. They are application specific. Variant codes could be used by an application to distinguish between dialects of U.S. English: Southern, Midwestern, and Boston, for example. For the United Sates, the country code is US and the language code is en.

Within the bundle, each of the values are identified by keywords that are used in the call to extract information from the bundle. A title of a Web page, for example, might be stored with the keyword `title`. In the class file, `title` would be used as a key into a hash table. In a properties file, `title` would be the keyword of the `keyword/value` pair.

The way this plays out in Java code is that when a request for a bundle is made, a locale object is either explicitly specified or implicitly retrieved from the system default locale. The bundle being retrieved is named in the request and the locale information is used to add the country code and language code so that the proper bundle can be found. All items subject to i18n or l10n must be stored in a resource bundle. The class path is searched for the bundle, and if it is found it is used.

The things that are internationalized are mostly strings and dates. In programs with a GUI, graphics and other arbitrary objects may have versions for different languages. The class or property files that contain these bundles must be in the class path.

So, for the most part, the programmer writing code for the Java Web Server will employ i18n and l10n in exactly the same way as when writing Java code for any environment. Strings, dates, and other objects that would change from country to country or locale to locale must be identified and stored in bundles. These bundles must be created and named properly, and the code should allow the right bundle to be specified at compile time or runtime.

The `java.io.Writer` class is the Java Web Server class that must be addressed to properly handle i18n. Servlets should call `HttpServletResponse.getWriter()` instead of `HttpServletResponse.getOutputStream()`. Note that `getWriter()` does not take a locale argument. It handles l10n only for the locale the Web server is in (or the default locale, if it has been changed), whereas the other classes can localize for any locale on the fly.

The default locale is another important aspect of internationalization. The default locale is set at startup time for the Java virtual machine (JVM). There is a native method in the `System` class called `initProperties()`, which is called by the JVM soon after startup. This native method sets a group of system properties, including `user.region` and `user.language`. Locale has a static initializer that gets these properties and builds a locale from them. This can be overridden on the command line:

```
java -Duser.region=JP -Duser.language=jp myProgram
```

will make `myProgram` behave as if it were run in Japan. There seems to be no global properties file where this can be changed.

Sample Programs

The following sample programs are brief examples of how to write servlets that use i18n and l10n techniques. For further study of these issues and more complex examples, see the tutorials on the `java.sun.com` Web site or textbooks on Java programming. The examples that we present cover the following coding topics:

- Example 1: Resource bundle stored in a class file
- Example 2: Resource bundle stored in a property file
- Example 3: Localizing dates
- Example 4: Compound messages
- Example 5: Multilocale servlets

Example 1: Resource Bundle Stored in a Class File

This example (Listing 8.1) prints a simple Web page with various properties stored in a `ResourceBundle` named `"SampleBundle1"`. The items stored in the bundle include text that is included in the HTML of the page and a `Point` object to illustrate that more than text can be stored.

Listing 8.1 `LocalizedServlet1.java`, a simple servlet that does internationalization.

```
import javax.servlet.*;
import javax.servlet.http.*;
import java.util.*;
import java.io.*;
import java.awt.Point;
public class LocalizedServlet1 extends HttpServlet {
  public void doGet(HttpServletRequest req,
                    HttpServletResponse res)
      throws ServletException,IOException
  {
    ResourceBundle bundle;
    // Try to get the resource bundle
    try {
      bundle     = ResourceBundle.getBundle("SampleBundle1");
    } catch (Exception e) {
      throw new UnavailableException(this,
```

```
                    "Could not load resources");
      }
      PrintWriter out = res.getWriter();
      res.setStatus(res.SC_OK);
      res.setContentType("text/html");
      out.println("<HTML>");
      out.println("<HEAD>");
      out.println("<TITLE>" +
                  bundle.getString("title") +
                  "</TITLE>");
      out.println("<BODY BGCOLOR=" +
                  bundle.getString("bgcolor") + ">");
      out.println("<H1>" + bundle.getString("title") + "</H1>");
      out.println(bundle.getString("welcome"));
      out.println("<P>");
      out.print(bundle.getString("intro"));
      Point p = (Point) bundle.getObject("location");
      out.println(p.x + ", " + p.y);
      out.println("</BODY>");
      out.println("</HTML>");
  }
}
```

When ResourceBundle.getBundle("SampleBundle1") is called several things happen. First, the default locale is looked up. As mentioned earlier, locales are specified by either two or three parameters. Once the locale is found, the search for the bundle begins. Bundles may reside anywhere in the class path. For a bundle named Foo and a locale with a language code of xx and country code of YY, getBundle() will first look for Foo_xx_YY.class, then Foo_xx.class, then Foo.class. If it does not find a class for the bundle, it will start looking for properties files, starting with Foo_xx_YY.properties, Foo_xx.properties, and Foo.properties. Listing 8.2 shows an English bundle for our servlet that we would store in a file named SampleBundle1_en_US.java that would be compiled into SampleBundle1.en.US.class.

Listing 8.2 SampleBundle1.java, a list-based resource bundle.

```
import java.awt.Point;
import java.util.*;
public class SampleBundle1 extends ListResourceBundle {
  public Object[][] getContents() {
    return contents;
  }
  static final Object[][] contents = {
    {"title",    "A Localized Servlet"},
    {"bgcolor",  "#FFFFFF"},
    {"welcome",  "Hi, welcome to the servlet."},
    {"intro",    "You are located at: "},
    {"location", new Point(123,324)}
  };
}
```

Note that it is possible to store objects of any type in a ListResource-Bundle. Although we have called this simply SampleBundle1.java, it is more properly called SampleBundle1_en_US.java, but assuming that the servlet is run in the United States, either name should do.

So far, so good. We have separated the logic from the elements that may vary between locales. Now, if we were to run this servlet on a Web server in Germany, we would just need to provide a new bundle, which would look like Listing 8.3.

Listing 8.3   SampleBundle1_de.java, a sample bundle localized for Germany.

```
import java.awt.Point;
import java.util.*;
public class SampleBundle1_de extends ListResourceBundle {
  public Object[][] getContents() {
    return contents;
  }
  static final Object[][] contents = {
    {"title",    "Ein Beschr\U00E4nktes Servlet"},
    {"bgcolor",  "#ffffff"},
    {"welcome",  "Hallo, willkommen zum Servlet."},
    {"intro",    "Sie werden lokalisiert an: "},
    {"location", new Point(87,374)}
  };
}
```

This bundle would be named SampleBundle_de_DE.class. Note the \U00E4 in the title string. This is an escape code representing the unicode character ä. A full list of unicode character codes is available from

http://www.unicode.org

Now, if we wanted to run the servlet in the United States and provide service for users in Germany, we would just need to replace the call by:

```
bundle = BundleBundle.getBundle("SampleBundle1");
```

which gets the bundle for the current default locale with

```
bundle = BundleBundle.getBundle("SampleBundle1",Locale.GERMANY);
```

If in the future the servlet needed to be used in France, Italy, or anywhere else, it would just be necessary for a translator to create new bundles and the programmer to change the locale in the getBundle() call.

Of course, another way to get the same result without changing the code would be to change the default locale for the entire Web server to Germany. This would affect not only this servlet but all servlets, logging, and all programs using internationalization. It is important to realize how much effort it takes to internationalize a program. The internationalization routines make it easier; they do not make it effortless.

Example 2: Resource Bundle in a Property File

Although `ListResourceBundles` allow any object to be stored, 90 percent of the time a servlet needs to customize only `Strings`. In fact, `ListResourceBundles` are primarily of interest to programmers writing applications that use the graphic objects from the Abstract Window Toolkit or the SWING toolkit, where it is often useful to put whole widgets that control graphic display into the bundle.

`PropertyResourceBundles` are much easier to work with than `List-ResourceBundles`, although a servlet uses them in the same way. If the following lines

```
out.print(bundle.getString("intro"));
Point p = (Point) bundle.getObject("location");
out.println(p.x + ", " + p.y);
```

were removed from our servlet, it would be possible to replace `Sample-Bundle1.java` with the properties file in Listing 8.4.

Listing 8.4 `SampleBundle1.properties`, a properties file for internationalization.

```
title=A Localized Servlet
bgcolor=#FFFFFF
welcome=Hi, welcome to the servlet.
```

Properties files may be thought of as a serialized `PropertyResourceBundle`, although the underlying classes do not treat them that way. It does mean, however, that they must reside somewhere in the class path. The properties file in Listing 8.4 should be called `SampleBundle1.properties`, or more exactly `SampleBundle1_en_US.properties`.

To create a version of the servlet for Italy, it would be necessary just to create `SampleBundle1_it_IT.properties` with Italian text and again replace

```
bundle = BundleBundle.getBundle"SampleBundle2");
```

with this:

```
bundle = BundleBundle.getBundle("SampleBundle2",Locale.ITALY);
```

Example 3: Localizing Dates

Bundles work well for storing changeable strings but are not suitable for many other i18n-related tasks. For example, consider printing dates. In the United

States, the convention is mm/dd/yy, but elsewhere in the world it is dd/mm/yy, dd/mm/yyyy, or one of many, many other variations. Clearly it is impractical to try to create a bundle containing every possible date! A programmer could check the current locale by hand and write code to do the correct formatting, but Javasoft has already done all that hard work and put the results in the java.text package. Date formats are specified in the default locale information or in a locale object explicitly passed to a DateFormat object.

The java.text.DateFormat class is a convenient way to render dates and times. Listing 8.5 is an example that illustrates how this class can be used for internationalization.

Listing 8.5   LocalizedServlet2.java, a servlet that localizes dates.

```
import javax.servlet.*;
import javax.servlet.http.*;
import java.util.*;
import java.io.*;
import java.text.*;
public class LocalizedServlet2 extends HttpServlet {
   public void doGet(HttpServletRequest req,
                     HttpServletResponse res)
        throws ServletException,IOException
   {
     ResourceBundle bundle;
     Locale locale = Locale.getDefault();
     // Try to get the resource bundle
     try {
        bundle = ResourceBundle.getBundle("SampleBundle2",locale);
     } catch (Exception e) {
        throw new UnavailableException(this,
                   "Could not load resources");
     }
     PrintWriter out = res.getWriter();
     res.setStatus(res.SC_OK);
     res.setContentType("text/html");
     out.println("<HTML>");
     out.println("<HEAD>");
     out.println("<TITLE>" +
                   bundle.getString("title") +
                   "</TITLE>");
     out.println("<BODY>");
     out.println(bundle.getString("message1"));
     DateFormat df = DateFormat.getDateTimeInstance(
                        DateFormat.SHORT,
                        DateFormat.SHORT,
                        locale);
     out.println(df.format(new Date()));
     out.println(bundle.getString("message2"));
     out.println("</BODY>");
     out.println("</HTML>");
   }
}
```

Listing 8.6 SampleBundle2.properties, a bundle used with a localized date servlet.

```
title=Another Localized servlet
message1=It is now
message2=in this Web Server's home town
```

Note that getDateTimeInstance takes a Locale, so we have created one at the top. Although the formatting classes and ResourceBundles can work independently, they are often found together. Listing 8.6 is the bundle used by this servlet. Again, it is simple to make this work for people in Italy. Just replace Locale.getDefault() with Locale.ITALY, and create SampleBundle2_it.properties (Listing 8.7).

Listing 8.7 SampleBundle2.properties, a bundle used with a localized date servlet for Italian.

```
title=Un altro localizzato servlet
message1=\U00C8 ora
message2=nella citt\U00E0 natale di questo server di Web
```

There are many other useful classes in the java.text package that do such things as formatting numbers and monetary values, both of which also vary widely between locations.

Example 4: Compound Messages

As Example 3 showed, it is quite easy to mix resources with localized dates and times. However, there is still one potential problem. The servlet assumes that the message will always consist of a first portion, then the date, then a remaining portion. For languages with different grammars, this may not be true. It may be necessary for the date to be the first or last portion of a grammatically correct sentence.

This would seem to imply that programmers need to write complex code to determine grammatical order and print out resources and dates or other elements in different orders. JavaSoft has once again done all this tedious work: properties contain what are called compound messages. Listing 8.8 shows a resource bundle that contains such a property.

Listing 8.8 SampleBundle3.properties, a bundle with compound messages.

```
title=A resource with a compound message
message=It is now {0,time,short} on {0,date,short} \
in this Web server's home town.
```

The elements in curly braces may be thought of as directives that will be filled in automatically. A directive like this contains two or three portions. The first is a number, 0 in this case, that indicates where the value will come from. When the message is rendered, an array of objects are passed in. The zero here refers to the index in that array. The second portion of the directive indicates what kind of value should be generated, and the third portion, if present, indicates how it should be presented.

Listing 8.9 shows a servlet that can use this bundle. First the array is constructed. We have only one element, a Date object, which will be used to render both the time and the date. Then we construct a MessageFormat object and tell it which locale to use. Finally, we get the property from the bundle and have MessageFormat() render it.

Listing 8.9 LocalizedServlet3.java, a servlet that handles compound messages.

```java
import javax.servlet.*;
import javax.servlet.http.*;
import java.util.*;
import java.io.*;
import java.text.*;
public class LocalizedServlet3 extends HttpServlet {
  public void doGet(HttpServletRequest req,
                    HttpServletResponse res)
      throws ServletException,IOException
  {
    ResourceBundle bundle;
    Locale locale = Locale.getDefault();
    // Try to get the resource bundle
    try {
      bundle = ResourceBundle.getBundle("SampleBundle3",locale);
    } catch (Exception e) {
      throw new UnavailableException(this,
                  "Could not load resources");
    }
    PrintWriter out = res.getWriter();
    res.setStatus(res.SC_OK);
    res.setContentType("text/html"");
    out.println("<HTML>");
    out.println("<HEAD>");
    out.println("<TITLE>" +
                bundle.getString("title") +
                "</TITLE>");
    out.println("<BODY>");
    Object messageArgs[] = {
      new Date()
    };
    MessageFormat format = new MessageFormat("");
    format.setLocale(locale);
    format.applyPattern(bundle.getString("message"));

    out.println(format.format(messageArgs));
    out.println("</BODY>");
    out.println("</HTML>");
  }
}
```

This has completely isolated the presentation of messages from the program logic. As the servlet needs to handle more locales, a language expert can simply create properties files completely defining the text, without needing to touch the servlet code at all beyond changing the locale at the top. Here is the compound message in Italian:

```
message=\u00C8 ora {0,time,short} sopra {0,date,short} nella\
citt\u00E0 natale di questo server di Web
```

Example 5: Multilocale Servlets

The first four example servlets have handled only a single locale. This may be fine for many applications, but it is not hard to make a servlet handle many locales at once. One way to do this is to accept parameters specifying what locale should be used. Listing 8.10 shows a modified version of Example 4 that does just that.

Listing 8.10   LocalizedServlet4.java, a servlet that works for many locales.

```
import javax.servlet.*;
import javax.servlet.http.*;
import java.util.*;
import java.io.*;
import java.text.*;
public class LocalizedServlet4 extends HttpServlet {
  public void doGet(HttpServletRequest req,
                    HttpServletResponse res)
       throws ServletException,IOException
  {
    ResourceBundle bundle;
    String language = "en";
    String country  = "US";
    String values[];
    values = req.getParameterValues("language");
    if(values != null && values.length > 0)
      language = values[0];
    values = req.getParameterValues("country");
    if(values != null && values.length > 0)
      country = values[0];
    Locale l = new Locale(language,country);
    // Try to get the resource bundle
    try {
      bundle = ResourceBundle.getBundle("SampleBundle3",l);
    } catch (Exception e) {
      throw new UnavailableException(this,
            "Could not load resources");
    }
    PrintWriter out = res.getWriter();
    res.setStatus(res.SC_OK);
    res.setContentType("text/html");
```

```
        out.println("<HTML>");
        out.println("<HEAD>");
        out.println("<TITLE>" +
                    bundle.getString("title") +
                    "</TITLE>");
        out.println("<BODY>");
        Object messageArgs[] = {
          new Date()
        };
        MessageFormat format = new MessageFormat("");
        format.setLocale(1);
        format.applyPattern(bundle.getString("message"));


        out.println(format.format(messageArgs));
        out.println("</BODY>");
        out.println("</HTML>");
    }
}
```

Once this code is compiled and installed, an index page could be created that links to LocalizedServlet4?language=en&country=US for U.S. users and LocalizedServlet4?language=it&country=IT for users in Italy.

It is even possible to automatically detect where a user is and instantly configure the servlet for them. This can be done by checking the full domain name of the user's location, as shown in Listing 8.11.

Listing 8.11   LocalizedServlet5.java, a servlet that automatically detects a user's locale.

```
import javax.servlet.*;
import javax.servlet.http.*;
import java.util.*;
import java.io.*;
import java.text.*;
public class LocalizedServlet5 extends HttpServlet {
    public void doGet(HttpServletRequest req,
                      HttpServletResponse res)
        throws ServletException,IOException
    {
        ResourceBundle bundle;
        Locale locale;
        String remoteHost = req.getRemoteHost();
        int    pos        = remoteHost.lastIndexOf('.');
        String domain     = remoteHost.substring((pos == -1) ?
                            0 : pos+1);
        if(domain.equals(".fr")) locale = Locale.FRANCE;
        else if(domain.equals(".de")) locale = Locale.GERMANY;
        else if(domain.equals(".it")) locale = Locale.ITALY;
        else locale = Locale.US;

        // Try to get the resource bundle
```

```
    try {
      bundle = ResourceBundle.getBundle("SampleBundle3",locale);
    } catch (Exception e) {
      throw new UnavailableException(this,
                "Could not load resources");
    }
    PrintWriter out = res.getWriter();
    res.setStatus(res.SC_OK);
    res.setContentType("text/html");
    out.println("<HTML>");
    out.println("<HEAD>");
    out.println("<TITLE>" +
                bundle.getString("title") +
                "</TITLE>");
    out.println("<BODY>");
    Object messageArgs[] = {
      new Date()
    };
    MessageFormat format = new MessageFormat("");
    format.setLocale(locale);
    format.applyPattern(bundle.getString("message"));


    out.println(format.format(messageArgs));
    out.println("</BODY>");
    out.println("</HTML>");
  }
}
```

Unfortunately, looking up the domain name is very time consuming, so it should not be done in a high-performance servlet. In addition, it would not support, for example, U.S. tourists in France who might be visiting a site to look up restaurants and would prefer to read the information in English. Generally, it is better to let the user select which localized version to see, as we did in Example 5, Listing 8.10.

Conclusion

In this chapter we have demonstrated the power of internationalization and localization. While these techniques are part of the Java programming language and not unique to the Java Web Server, we have tried to show how they can be applied when writing servlets. Using these techniques properly can dramatically increase the reuseability and hence the value of almost any program.

PART III

Coding Techniques

CHAPTER 9

Servlets and the Servlet API

Servlets are the gateway to server-side Java programming. In a sense, they are like CGI programs, only more powerful and flexible. In this chapter we explain how servlets relate to the Java Web Server, their life cycle, and their architecture. We also discuss the way servlets implement the HTTP protocol and remove a lot of the tedious details from programmers. Finally, we take a look at a few ways that servlets can communicate with each other, and we take a peek at what lies ahead for the Servlet API.

We finish the chapter by starting to build the Game application we introduced in Chapter 2. Although there are many classes that make up this application, it is a servlet that makes it useful.

In a sense, servlets play the same role in the Java Web Server (JWS) that CGI programs play in other Web servers. In a CGI-based system, the Web server is configured to treat all URLs within a directory such as /cgi-bin, or with a certain extension such as .cgi, as programs. When the Web server sees such a URL it looks up the associated file just as it would with a regular html document, but instead of sending it to the user, it asks the operating system to execute it. It also makes the socket connection back to the user look like normal input and output streams to the program, so that anything the program prints is sent back to the user.

In a sense, this activity can be thought of as extending the Web server's functionality. A Web server may not know how to play tic-tac-toe, but a programmer can write a program in Perl to do so, make it a CGI, and from then on, at least as far as users are concerned, the Web server is able to play with them.

Unfortunately this "extension" of the Web server is very inefficient. In order to handle a CGI request, the Web server must first make a copy of itself in memory, and then have that copy load the Perl interpreter into memory, and then run the program. The operations of copying the Web server process (called *forking*) and starting the Perl interpreter (called *exec-ing*) are very time consuming.

In addition, the CGI model greatly limits the way Web server functionality can be extended. Once the Perl interpreter starts up, it is almost completely removed from the rest of the Web server. All it can do is read data from the user and write data back to the user, although the Web server may be able to capture the output and manipulate it on the way back.

Servlets are like CGI applications in a couple of ways. Servlets are small individual pieces of code that may be added to the Web server at any time. As with CGI applications, the Java Web Server has a mapping between a servlet and a URL or set of URLs and routes particular requests to particular servlets. Servlets may perform any kind of function, and that function may be thought of as extending the Java Web Server's own functionality. However, that is where the comparison ends.

When a servlet is called, no fork or exec is performed. Instead, the first time a servlet is needed, the Java Web Server loads it, and from then on whenever the servlet is needed, the JWS has direct access to it. Instead of starting a separate process for each request and talking to it through the standard intput and output mechanisms, the JWS calls a special method in the servlet and gives it objects representing the request from the user and the response it should send back.

Servlets extend the JWS in a way that CGIs simply do not, and hence they overcome both major limitations of CGIs. Because the servlet is local to the Web server, execution is fast. Also, any servlet may at any time get more information or resources from the Web server.

In addition, note that CGI applications are very transient creatures. The Web server starts them up, they do their job, and then they exit. This means that a CGI can recreate every resource it needs every time it is called—it cannot hold onto any data or resources between calls. Since servlets are loaded once and then forever remain a part of the JWS, they can retain of all sorts of things, which can provide a significant boost to performance.

It is worth noting that in the Java Web Server everything that gets sent to the user is generated by a servlet. Most Web servers handle requests for regular files directly. In the JWS a servlet called the FileServlet reads the file from disk and sends it out. This allows for great flexibility: if a programmer wanted all URLs to come from a database instead of from the local disk, it would just be necessary to replace FileServlet.

A Closer Look at Servlet Classes

The obvious question after "What do servlets do?" is "What are they made of?" To answer this, we present all the interfaces and classes in version 2.1 of the Servlet API in the following sections. For clarity, the methods are in the left column and their purposes are described in the right column.

NOTE: The application programming interface (API) is split between two packages. The first, `javax.servlet`, contains interfaces and classes that define the most basic notion of servlets. The second, `javax.servlet.http`, contains classes that extend the awareness of `javax.servlet` interfaces and classes to the specifics of the HTTP protocol.

`javax.servlet` *Interfaces and Classes*

Interface `javax.servlet.Servlet`

This interface is the heart of the API. It is therefore somewhat surprising that it is quite minimal. It states that servlets are initialized, service requests, and later may be destroyed. It also allows the servlet (or other parts of the system) to get the `ServletConfig` that was used to initialize the servlet and may provide a string describing itself.

`void init(ServletConfig)`	Initializes the servlet. `ServletConfig` provides information the servlet may need to start up.
`void service(ServletRequest, ServletResponse)`	Handles a request.
`void destroy()`	Destroys the servlet.
`ServletConfig getServletConfig()`	Returns a `ServletConfig`, almost always the one passed to `init()`.
`String getServletInfo()`	Returns a description of the servlet.

Interface `javax.servlet.ServletConfig`

This interface provides information that servlets may need to initialize themselves. In the JWS, this is the glue between the servlet parameter screen in the administration tool and the servlets.

`String getInitParameter(String)`	Returns a parameter. In the JWS, these are set in the administration tool.

`Enumeration getInitParameterNames()`	Returns all provided parameter names.
`ServletContext getServletContext()`	Returns current servlet context.

Interface `javax.servlet.ServletContext`

This interface provides a great deal of information about the environment a servlet is running in, and it provides access to other parts of the system.

`Object getAttribute(String)`	Returns the named attribute.
`Enumeration getAttributeNames()`	Returns all provided attribute names.
`ServletContext getServlet-` `  Context(String)`	Returns the servlet context for the given URI.
`int getMajorVersion()`	Returns the major number of the program the servlet is running in.
`int getMinorVersion()`	Returns the minor number of the program the servlet is running in.
`String getMimeType(String)`	Returns the MIME type of the named file.
`String getRealPath(String)`	Given a URL path, returns the operating system directory path.
`URL getResource(String)`	Returns a URL to a resource on the same server.
`InputStream getResource` `  AsStream(String)`	Returns a `Stream` that can be used to load a resource.
`RequestDispatcher getRequest-` `  Dispatcher(String)`	Returns a `RequestDispatcher` for the named URI.
`String getServerInfo()`	Returns information about the server.
`void log(String)`	Logs a message.
`void log(String, Throwable)`	Logs a message and accompanying `Exception` or other `Throwable`.
`void setAttribute(String,Object)`	Sets a named attribute.
`void removeAttribute(String)`	Removes the named attribute.

Interface `javax.servlet.ServletRequest`

This interface encapsulates information about a specific request to a servlet.

`Object getAttribute(String)`	Returns an attribute from the underlying context.
`Enumeration getAttributeNames()`	Returns names of all available attributes.
`String getCharacterEncoding()`	Returns the current character encoding.

`int getContentLength()`	Returns the length of any data provided with this request.
`String getContentType()`	Returns the MIME type of any data provided with this request.
`ServletInputStream getInputStream()`	Returns an input stream that can be used to obtain any data provided with this request.
`String getParameter(String)`	Returns a parameter provided with this request, such as a form variable.
`Enumeration getParameterNames()`	Returns the names of all available parameters.
`String[] getParameterValues(String)`	Returns an array of all values provided for a given parameter.
`String getProtocol()`	Returns the protocol used to make this request, for example HTTP/1.0.
`BufferedReader getReader()`	Returns a `Reader` that can be used to obtain any data provided with this request.
`String getRemoteAddr()`	Returns the address at which this request originated.
`String getRemoteHost()`	Returns the name of the machine on which this request originated.
`String getScheme()`	Returns the scheme portion of the URL, for example HTTP or FTP.
`String getServerName()`	Returns the name of the server the servlet is running on.
`int getServerPort()`	Returns the port the server is running on.
`void setAttribute(String,Object)`	Sets an attribute in the underlying context.

Interface `javax.servlet.ServletResponse`

This interface defines an object that servlets use to send data back to the user, along with information about that data.

| `String getCharacterEncoding()` | Returns the character set encoding for the MIME body. |
| `ServletOutputStream getOutputStream()` | Returns an `OutputStream`, meant for sending binary responses. |

`PrintWriter getWriter()`	Returns a `PrintWriter` for sending formatted text responses.
`void setContentLength(int length)`	Specifies the length of data to be sent back to the user.
`void setContentType(String type)`	Specifies MIME type of the content to be sent back to the user.

Interface `javax.servlet.SingleThreadModel`

This interface has no methods. It serves only to indicate that the servlet should handle only a single request at a time.

Abstract Class `javax.servlet.GenericServlet`

This class implements most of the `Servlet` and `ServletContext` interfaces. It is not particularly useful on its own but rather is provided as a class that protocol-aware servlets can extend.

Class `javax.servlet.ServletInputStream`

This class provides a means for servlets to get data from the source of the request. For example, in the JWS, it would be used to get `POST` data. It extends `java.io.InputStream` and adds only one method of its own: `int readLine(byte[],int,int)`, which reads bytes into the given array between the positions specified by the `int` arguments.

Class `javax.servlet.ServletOutputStream`

This class provides a means for servlets to send data back. For example, in the JWS this is used to actually write out the HTML. It overloads `OutputStream` and provides methods such as `print(int)`, `print(long)`, `println(int)`, `println(long)`, and so on for all the fundamental Java types.

Class `javax.servlet.ServletException`

This exception may be thrown by a servlet in the event that it encounters a problem it cannot deal with. The Java Web Server will do different things depending on which method throws this exception. Usually programmers prefer to use `UnavailableException`.

Class `javax.servlet.UnavailableException`

This is a particular type of `ServletException` that indicates that one of the life cycle methods could not do what it needed to do. There are two kinds of unavailable exceptions. The first is constructed with `UnavailableException (Servlet,String)`, which specifies the servlet that threw the exception and a reason why it was thrown. This version indicates a permanent problem. If `init()` throws it, the servlet will never be available to handle requests. The second type is constructed with `UnavailableException(int,Servlet,String)`. The first parameter is a time in seconds. If `init()` or `service()` throws it, the JWS will try again after that many seconds.

Interface `javax.servlet.RequestDispatcher`

This interface can be used by one servlet to pass control to another servlet, JSP, or even a flat HTML page. See the subsection "`RequestDispatcher`" toward the end of this chapter for more about how this interface is used.

`void forward(ServletRequest, ServletResponse)`	Transfers the current request to another servlet.

`javax.servlet.http` *Interfaces and Classes*

Interface `javax.servlet.http.HttpServletRequest`

This interface extends `javax.servlet.ServletRequest` and provides a great deal of additional information meaningful to the HTTP protocol.

`String getAuthType()`	Returns the authentication scheme, currently only `Basic` or `Digest`.
`Cookie[] getCookies()`	Returns the array of cookies that was sent with this request.
`long getDateHeader(String)`	Returns the value of the requested header as seconds since midnight, 1/1/1970.
`String getHeader(String)`	Returns the value of the named header or `null` if the header was not provided.
`Enumeration getHeaderNames()`	Returns the names of all provided headers.
`int getIntHeader(String)`	Gets the value of a header field as an integer.
`String getMethod()`	Gets the request method `GET`, `POST`, etc.
`String getPathInfo()`	Returns the part of the URL after the servlet and before the query string.
`String getPathTranslated()`	Returns the `PathInfo`, translated to a real path.
`String getQueryString()`	Returns the `QueryString`, or `null` if not provided.

`String getRemoteUser()`	If the user has logged in, returns the user's name.
`String getRequestedSessionId()`	Gets the requested session ID.
`String getRequestURI()`	Returns all the URLs but QueryString.
`String getServletPath()`	Returns the portion of the URL that names the servlet.
`HttpSession getSession()`	Returns the current user's session object.
`HttpSession getSession (boolean create)`	Returns the current user's session object. Creates a new one if the user does not yet have one.
`boolean isRequestedSessionId Valid()`	Returns true if the session is valid.
`boolean isRequestedSessionId FromCookie()`	Returns true if the session ID was specified in a cookie from the user.
`boolean isRequestedSessionId FromURL()`	Returns true if the session ID was specified in the URL.

Interface `javax.servlet.http.HttpServletResponse`

This interface extends `javax.servlet.ServletResponse` and allows the servlet to return more information relevant to the HTTP protocol. In addition to the methods shown here, this class also has a static final `int` value for each possible HTTP status return code.

`void addCookie(Cookie)`	Sends the cookie to the user.
`boolean containsHeader(String)`	Returns true if the named header has already been specified.
`String encodeURL(String)`	Returns the given URL, modified to include the session ID if necessary.
`void sendError(int)`	Sends specified error code to the user.
`void sendError(int,String)`	Sends the specified error code to the user and includes the given `String` as the page body.
`void sendRedirect(String)`	Sends a redirect to the given URL. The URL must be absolute.
`void setDateHeader(String, long)`	Sets the value of the named header to be the date and time specified, as the number of seconds since midnight 1/1/1970.
`void setHeader(String,String)`	Sets the value of the named header.
`void setIntHeader(String,int)`	Sets the value of the named header to be the given `int`.
`void setStatus(int)`	Sets the status code of the response.

Interface `javax.servlet.http.SingleThreadModel`

This interface has no methods. It serves only to indicate to the JWS that this servlet should be asked to handle only a single request at a time.

Session Interfaces

The following interfaces define a system for keeping arbitrary data between HTTP requests:

- `javax.servlet.http.HttpSession`
- `javax.servlet.http.HttpSessionBindingListener`
- `javax.servlet.http.HttpSessionContext`
  `javax.servlet.http.HttpSessionBindingEvent`

For example, a session could hold a list of all merchandise that a user had placed in a virtual shopping cart. (Sessions are covered in Chapter 7.)

Class `javax.servlet.http.Cookie`

This class represents an *HTTP cookie,* a small piece of data that a user carries between requests.

`Cookie(String,String)`	Creates a new cookie, with the given name and value.
`String getDomain()`	Returns the domain for which this cookie is valid.
`int getMaxAge()`	Returns the number of seconds this cookie has to live.
`String getName()`	Returns the name of this cookie.
`String getPath()`	Returns the path for which this cookie is valid.
`boolean getSecure()`	Returns `true` if this cookie will only be sent with `https` requests.
`String getValue()`	Returns the value of this cookie.
`int getVersion()`	Returns the version number of this cookie.
`void setComment(String)`	Sets a comment.
`void setDomain(String)`	Sets the domain for which this cookie is valid. By default, cookies are sent back only to the machine that issued them.
`void setMaxAge(int)`	Sets the number of seconds this cookie should live. Negative values mean that the cookie should only last as long as the current browser session.

void setPath(String)	Sets the path for which this cookie is valid. By default cookies are sent with requests only to URLs in the same "directory" or sub-directories of the URL that issued them.
void setSecure(boolean)	Sets to true if this cookie should be sent only with https requests.
void setValue(String)	Sets the value of this cookie.
void setVersion(int)	Sets the version number of this cookie.

Class javax.servlet.http.HttpServlet

This is the class almost all servlets in the JWS will start with. It defines methods for each kind of HTTP request. Creating a new servlet is as simple as overriding the methods for the request types that the programmer wishes to support.

void doDelete(HttpServletRequest, HttpServletResponse)	Handles a delete request. Called by service().
void doGet(HttpServletRequest, HttpServletResponse)	Handles a get request. Called by service().
doHead(HttpServletRequest, HttpServletResponse)	Handles a head request. Called by service().
doOptions(HttpServletRequest, HttpServletResponse)	Handles an options request. Called by service().
doPost(HttpServletRequest, HttpServletResponse)	Handles a post request. Called by service().
doPut(HttpServletRequest, HttpServletResponse)	Handles a put request. Called by service().
doTrace(HttpServletRequest, HttpServletResponse)	Handles a trace request. Called by service().
long getLastModified(HttpServlet Request)	Returns the time the output of this servlet would have last changed. Called by service().
service()	Handles an arbitrary request, dis patching it to the appropriate method. Programmers typically do not override it.

Class javax.servlet.http.HttpUtils

This class contains a few useful utility methods and is mainly used internally by the JWS; there are easier ways for programmers to get its functionality.

However, if a programmer wishes to call these methods explicitly, it is certainly possible. These methods are static, so this class never needs to be instantiated.

`static StringBuffer getRequest URL(request)`	Returns the original URL, as the user entered it.
`static Hashtable parsePostData(int,Servlet-InputStream)`	Constructs a `Hashtable` mapping form names to values from POST data.
`static Hashtable parseQuery String(String)`	Construsts a `Hashtable` mapping form names to values from a `QueryString`.

This is a fairly large number of classes, but in practice the programmer will not need to be aware of all of them all the time. For the most part writing a servlet consists of creating a class that extends `HttpServlet` and provides implementations of one or more of the request methods and possibly `init()` and `destroy()`. Init() uses values from the `ServletConfig` to initialize itself, and the request method gets information about the request from the `HttpServletRequest` and sends the results back to the user through the `HttpServletResponse`.

Servlet Life Cycle

The life cycle of a CGI application is quite simple. The Web server gets a request, forks itself, and execs the program or an interpreter for the program. The program then reads parameters and other data, writes the HTML or other data, and exits. End of story.

Servlets could be almost this simple. Of necessity, they have to be loaded into the Web server, but after that they could do nothing more than handle requests as they come in. However, this would be inefficient. As we have noted, servlets are persistent within the Java Web Server, so if a servlet is likely to need some resource, such as a connection to a database, every time it services a request, there is no reason why it should not create that resource just once.

There is a place in the servlet's life cycle where it may allocate such resources, and there is another point where the servlet can be sure it will no longer need them and then do any needed cleanup. The following sections discuss, in detail, every step in the servlet life cycle, which is shown in Figure 9.1.

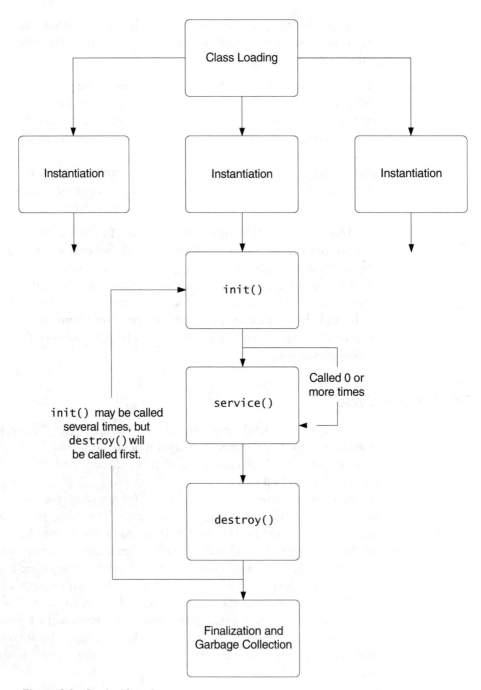

Figure 9.1   Servlet life cycle

Class Loading

A Java class file is very much like a blueprint; it tells the Java virtual machine (JVM) how much raw material, in this case memory, is needed to build an object, where the parts go, what kind of class it is, and so on. Before any class, including a servlet, can be built, the Java virtual machine must find and load its blueprint.

The class can be loaded by one of two mechanisms. If the servlet is somewhere in the Java Web Server's class path, it is loaded just like any other class. However, if the servlet is in the special <server_root>/servlets directory, it is loaded by a special class loader unique to the Java Web Server.

This class loader checks the time stamp of the .class file and, if it has changed since the last time the class was loaded, all servlets of that type are destroyed and the class reloaded. Although this is a very convenient mechanism for quickly testing and changing simple servlets consisting of only a single class, as we noted in Chapter 3 there are numerous problems with it, and it is best avoided.

Regardless of which class loader is used, if the class has a static block this block is executed when the class is loaded. Servlets almost never need a static block, though. Static blocks are usually used to load dynamic libraries for native methods, and although servlets can use native methods, doing so is dangerous. One missing delete or free and all of Java's sophisticated memory management goes out the window; one mistake with a pointer, and all the exception-handling code in the world can not stop the entire Web server from crashing.

Note that it is possible for a servlet class to be loaded more than once, even if it uses the default class loader. This is because the JVM can garbage collect classes as well as objects. If there are no active instances of a class and space is tight, the class may be dumped from memory and reloaded if and when it is next needed. This could be a concern if the class had a static block that was doing something that should only be done once, another good reason to skip static blocks entirely.

Construction

A blueprint does not actually do anything, apart from maybe rustle gently in the breeze. A servlet, like a machine, must be constructed before it can really be used. Constructing a java object entails the JVM allocating enough memory to hold all the object's instance members and possibly setting a number of fields to some known state.

Usually programmers provide a constructor that does some special work in order to set up the objects. However, this is not necessary for servlets, because they do not need to do anything when they are first built. A servlet may need to do some work before it starts handling requests, but that is exactly what the `init()` method, which we discuss next, is for.

Besides being unnecessary, providing a constructor for a servlet may be dangerous. The Java Web Server looks for a constructor with no arguments to build the servlet. If for some reason only a constructor with a different signature is present, an error will occur for the class, and the servlet will not be able to be built. This error will not show up in any log file and may be extremely difficult to track down. It could be avoided by providing a no-argument constructor as well, but it is better to not provide an explicit constructor at all.

After construction, there is now a servlet, but it still is not doing very much. After a coffee machine has been built, it does not do anything by itself. Both the coffee machine and the servlet need to start handling requests, but they also both have to set themselves up first. In servlets, this is handled by the `init()` method.

`init()` *Method*

A servlet may need to do any of several things before it starts handling requests. They include accessing configuration parameters, setting up a log file, opening a pool of connections to a database or daemon, constructing some utility objects, and so on. Before the `init()` method starts doing this, though, it should call `super.init()` to ensure that the underlying parts of the `HttpServlet` are set up properly.

`init()` is guaranteed to be called before the servlet has to handle any requests. It is also guaranteed that only one thread will ever be in the `init()` of any given instance of a servlet at a time, so no special care is needed regarding thread safety in this method. Enjoy this simple, carefree time, because it will not last long!

`init()` may be called several times, although it is called only once for each instance of the servlet in the server, and if a servlet is shut down and restarted, it is called again when the new instance is created. In this case the `destroy()` method is called before `init()` is called again.

If a servlet runs into problems while trying to do its initialization, it can notify the Java Web Server by throwing an `UnavailableException`. This exception can report the reason why the initialization failed and can specify whether the Java Web Server should try calling `init()` again later and if so, how long it should wait first.

UnavailableException extends javax.servlet.ServletException. Programmers will probably not want to use ServletException directly, as it does not allow for retrying.

If any resources are successfully allocated before the point where the init() method cannot continue, they should be cleaned up before the Unavailable-Exception is thrown. Otherwise they may be allocated again when the JWS tries calling init() again.

service() *Method*

After initialization the servlet is all ready to start handling requests. The Java Web Server tells a servlet to handle a request by invoking the servlet's service() method.

There is no way to know how fast or in what order requests may come in from users, and this means that one request may cause the service() method to be called while another request is already in the middle of service(). This could be a problem if service() is using some global resource. For example, if service() is talking to a database, and another request starts running through service() at the same time, the communication could be garbled.

This problem can be avoided by having the servlet implement the SingleThreadModel interface. This interface contains no methods; it serves only to tell the Java Web Server that only one thread should ever be in the service() method at a time. The JWS honors this by making each request wait until the previous ones have finished. This is a safe and easy way to program, but it is not very efficient.

It is much better to make your code *thread safe,* which is the process of allowing multiple threads to access service() simultaneously. This may be more difficult than it seems. As in our database example, servlets may need to be careful about how multiple requests are interleaved. This complex issue is dealt with in Chapter 10.

The service() method is called with an HttpServletRequest and an HttpServletResponse object. The servlet can use the HttpServletRequest to get all the kinds of information normally available to CGI programs, such as the URL that was called, the IP address of the requester, any cookies the user may have, and so on. If the user is performing a POST operation, the HttpServlet-Request also has an InputStream through which the data is sent.

Likewise, the servlet can use the response object to set various headers, such as MIME type, content length, and so on. It also contains an OutputStream that the servlet can use to send back the actual data.

The service() method can also throw an UnavailableException, either the permanent or the temporary variety. However, it is important to realize that once this exception is thrown, the servlet is essentially declaring itself dead. So service() should not simply throw this exception if it gets some sort of bad input from the user. In a case like this, it should simply send out a page describing the problem, possibly setting the return code to some error condition. UnavailableException should be thrown only if some necessary resource, such as a database connection, has somehow become unavailable.

Methods for Handling Specific HTTP Requests

The HttpServlet class provides a default service() method that determines what kind of operation is requested and passes the request to whichever of these methods is appropriate. Servlets that extend HttpServlet can override the service() method, but it is generally better to allow service() to do the dispatching and override the method or methods that handle the specific request type. These methods are doGet(), doPost(), doDelete(), doOptions(), doPut(), and doTrace().

This dispatching is an important component of how HttpServlets abstract the HTTP protocol. By default these methods all set the return code to the HTTP BAD_REQUEST code, which shows up to a user as an error page. Any of these protocol-specific methods may also throw a ServletException, but the same warnings that apply to the service() method apply here.

destroy() Method

The Java Web Server may at some point determine that a servlet is no longer needed. This could happen if another servlet is replacing an older version or if the JWS is about to shut down. When this happens, the servlet should clean up any resources it allocated when its init() method was called, so that other servlets or even completely seperate processes can use them. Servlets implement this cleanup phase by the destroy() method, although this name is somewhat misleading because the servlet instance is not actually destroyed or removed from memory.

As with init(), the destroy() method is single threaded, so it does not have to worry about another thread trying to clean up objects it is in the process of cleaning up.

If there are threads that are in the service() method when a servlet is unloaded, the JWS waits some time before calling destroy() to give those threads a chance to finish. No new requests are accepted during that interval. If the time expires and there are still threads in service, destroy() is called anyway. This means that it is possible, though unlikely, that some resource will become unavailable in the middle of the service() call. Programmers should be aware of this possibility and plan accordingly.

Garbage Collection and finalize() Method

After a servlet has been retired with destroy(), at some unpredictable time in the future the grim reaper of garbage collection may claim it. But don't feel bad. If this was a good, honest, hardworking servlet that managed lots of requests and was never greedy with system resources, Boddhisatva Duke will send it to servlet nirvana.

Before it goes completely, the JVM will execute the servlet's finalize() method, the "Last Will and Testament," if it has specified one. Because there is no way to guarantee when this will happen, programmers should not use finalize(). Any servlet cleanup should be handled in the destroy() method.

Simple Servlet

Enough talk, time for some code! Anyone who has ever read a book about computers can probably guess what is coming next. That's right, it is the ever-popular "Hello World," servlet edition. This one returns "Hello, world!" as flat text in response to any GET request.

Listing 9.1   Simple servlet.

```
import java.io.*;
import javax.servlet.*;
import javax.servlet.http.*;

public class HelloServlet extends HttpServlet {
   public void doGet(HttpServletRequest request,
                     HttpServletResponse response)
       throws UnavailableException, IOException
  {
    response.setStatus(response.SC_OK);
    response.setContentType("text/plain");
    // The string "Hello, world!" is probably copyright
    // Kernighan and Ritchie, but they seem to have placed it
    // into the public domain.
    response.getOutputStream().println("Hello, world!");
  }
}
```

NOTE: This servlet does not have an init() or destroy() method, which means it will inherit HttpServlet's version of the methods. Default init() sets up a number of things under the covers; default destroy() does nothing.

Let's now take a closer look at the request and response objects that have been passed to this servlet.

HttpServletRequest

This is the class that encapsulates a user's request to the servlet. It contains an input stream containing POST data and a list of the headers the browser has sent. A full list of headers in the HTTP protocol is available at

http://www.w3.org/Protocols/Specs.html

The HttpServletRequest class provides a general method to get any header, as well as a way to get a list of the headers that were sent. As a convenience, methods that get a specific header are also provided. This level of functionality is roughly equivalent to getting elements of %ENV in a Perl/CGI program. It is illustrated in Listing 9.2. This will get all available data from a GET request except cookies, which are covered in the next section.

Listing 9.2   Servlet that prints HTTP headers.

```
import java.io.*;
import javax.servlet.*;
import javax.servlet.http.*;
import java.util.*;

public class PrintHeaders extends HttpServlet {
  public void doGet(HttpServletRequest request,
                    HttpServletResponse response)
      throws IOException
{
  ServletOutputStream out = response.getOutputStream();
  response.setStatus(response.SC_OK);
  response.setContentType("text/plain");

  out.println("Here are the headers you sent: ");
  for(Enumeration e=request.getHeaderNames();
      e.hasMoreElements();)
  {
    String name = (String) e.nextElement();
    out.println(name + " = " + request.getHeader(name));
  }

  out.println();
  out.println("You are coming from IP address: " +
              request.getRemoteAddr());
  out.println("Your query string was " +
              request.getQueryString());
  if(request.getRemoteUser() == null) {
    out.println("You have not logged into this server");
  } else {
    out.println("You have logged into this server as " +
                request.getRemoteUser());
  }
```

```
        out.flush();
        out.close();
    }
}
```

POST data is not sent in the headers but rather through an input stream. To modify Listing 9.2 to include POST data, the doGet method would be changed to doPost, and the following code should be added after the getQueryString() line:

```
int postLength = request.getContentLength();
int count      = 0;
int totalCount = 0;

if(postLength == 0) {
  out.println("No post data");
} else {
  byte postData[]  = new byte[postLength];
  InputStream in   = request.getInputStream();
  while((count = in.read(postData,totalCount,
                         postLength-totalCount)) != -1)
    totalCount += count;

  // If we got too little data, flag an error, otherwise display
  // the data
  if(totalCount < postLength) {
    out.println("Bad POST data:  expected " + postLength +
                " bytes, and got " + totalCount);
  } else {
    out.println("Post Data: " + new String(postData,0,postLength));
  }
}
```

Note that this code should be added after the call to getQueryString(); it should not replace it. This is because it is quite possible for a request to have both a QueryString and POST data, although in practice it is rare. A form would provide both by including data after the question mark in the <ACTION> tag, as in

```
<FORM ACTION="a/b/c?some_data" METHOD="POST">
```

The Web browser knows that this is a POST request because of the method argument, but it still passes the information after the question mark in the query string.

Cookies

The one browser attribute that is not directly available though the getHeader() method is the user cookies. This is because there may be many cookie lines in the request header, unlike all the other headers, where there is only one per line.

`HttpServletRequest` provides a means to get cookies called, not surprisingly, `getCookies()`. It returns an array of cookie objects that contain information about the cookie's value, its time to live, the region for which it is valid, and so on.

Here is some sample cookie code that can be added to the `printHeaders` servlet, before the `out.flush()` line.

```
out.println("");
Cookie cookies[] = request.getCookies();
if(cookies.length == 0) {
  out.println("You have no cookies for this domain and this path.");
} else {
  out.println("<TABLE BORDER=1>");
  out.println("<TR><TH>Name</TH><TH>Value</TH><TH>Domain</TH>");
  out.println("<TH>Path</TH><TH>Max Age</TH><TH>Comment</TH></TR>");
  for(int i = 0;i<cookies.length;i++) {
    out.println("<TR><TD>" + cookies[i].getName() + "</TD>" +
                "<TD>" + cookies[i].getValue()   + "</TD>" +
                "<TD>" + cookies[i].getDomain()  + "</TD>" +
                "<TD>" + cookies[i].getPath()    + "</TD>" +
                "<TD>" + cookies[i].getMaxAge()  + "</TD>" +
                "<TD>" + cookies[i].getComment() + "</TD></TR>");
  }
  out.println("</TABLE>");
}
```

The Comment field will almost always be empty, because this field is not widely used by sites that issue cookies.

HttpUtils

Although servlets can obtain the query string via `HttpServletRequest.getQueryString()`, the string is not returned in a particularly useful form. All the values are URL encoded, and they are all combined into a single string. Getting POST data adds another level of annoyance to this process. For Perl programmers used to the convenience of CGI.pm, a Perl module containing a variety of methods for getting form variables and headers, this simply will not do.

The Java Web Server's equivalent of CGI.pm is a class called `HttpUtils`, which provides methods for breaking query strings and POST data into component form values. Its use is illustrated in the following code fragment, which can be added at the bottom of the `doPost` method in Listing 9.2.

```
Hashtable formValues =
  HttpUtils.parseQueryString(request.getQueryString());
for(Enumeration e = formValues.keys();e.hasMoreElements();) {
  String name   = (String) e.nextElement();
  String values[] = (String[]) formValues.get(name);
  if(values == null || values.length == 0) {
```

```
      out.println(name + ": (no value)");
  } else if (values.length == 1) {
      out.println(name + ": " + values[0]);
  } else {
      out.println(name + ": ");
      for(int i = 0;i<values.length;i++) {
        out.println("      " + values[i]);
      }
  }
}
```

Notice that it is not necessary to create an instance of HttpUtils, as all the methods are static. Also notice that we have to check the size of the returned array. This is because some HTML form elements, such as buttons, can have multiple values.

Getting POST data is almost as easy. Just do something like

```
try {
  formValues = HttpUtils.parsePostData(request.getContentLength(),
                            request.getInputStream());
} catch (IllegalArgumentException e) {
    out.println("Unable to continue - bad post data");
    return;
}
```

which returns a Hashtable that can be processed the same way. The IllegalArgumentException will be thrown if there is something wrong with the POST data—for example if the number of bytes promised by getContent-Length() is not delivered.

As convenient as the HttpUtils class is, there is an even easier way to get form data, using HttpServletRequest's getParamterNames() and get-ParameterValues(). The greatest advantage to this approach is that it hides the distinction between GET and POST from the programmer. Using these methods, the example would be rewritten as

```
for(Enumeration e = request.getParameterNames();
                    e.hasMoreElements();) {
  String name      = (String) e.nextElement();
  String values[] = request.getParameterValues(name);
  if(values == null || values.length == 0) {
    out.println(name + ": (no value)");
  } else if (values.length == 1) {
    out.println(name + ": " + values[0]);
  } else {
    out.println(name + ": ");
    for(int i = 0;i<values.length;i++) {
      out.println("      " + values[i]);
    }
  }
}
```

HttpServletResponse

The HttpServletResponse is how the servlet responds to the Java Web Server after it receives a request. It encapsulates everything a servlet needs to complete the HTTP round trip. It provides methods to set return codes, the MIME type of the returned data, the length, and numerous other headers. It also allows the servlet to set cookies and, most important, provides an output stream to send back the information itself.

Setting Headers

The examples in this chapter have set the two most important headers, the status and the type of the content. At a minimum, every servlet should set these two; if they do not, the browser may not know how to treat the received data.

There is a final static integer variable for every valid status code, as defined by the WWW consortium. See the javadoc entry for HttpServletRequest for a full list, which is available at

> *http://jserv.javasoft.com/products/java-server/documentation/webserver1.1/apidoc/*
> *javax.servlet.http.HttpServletResponse.html*

The most commonly used value is HttpServletResponse.SC_OK, which indicates that the request succeeded normally. At least we hope this is the most common response!

Sending Redirects and Errors

Servlets often need to redirect to other pages, and HttpServletRequest provides SC_MOVED_PERMANENTLY and SC_MOVED_TEMPORARILY variables for doing this. Even better, it provides a utility method called sendRedirect(), which handles appropriate setting of headers and sending a message body with the appropriate URL. All URLs sent through the sendRedirect() method should be run through the encodeRedirectUrl() method first. In addition to ensuring that all characters such as spaces are properly encoded, it is necessary for session tracking (see Chapter 7).

HttpServletResponse also provides a utility method for handling errors, so servlets do not need to handle setting error codes. They can simply call the sendError() method, which takes an integer status code and a string. This method sets the status header to the provided code and sends the string as the page body. sendError() even surrounds the specified body with <body></body> tags. For example, if a servlet supports only GET requests, it may define doPost() as

```
public void doPost(HttpServletRequest request,
                   HttpServletResponse result)
   throws IOException
{
    result.sendError(HttpServletResponse.SC_METHOD_NOT_ALLOWED,
                     "This servlet does not handle POST requests");
}
```

This shows up to the user as a page with the text in quotes. Some browsers indicate the status code somewhere, others do not.

Setting Cookies

Setting cookies is as easy as getting them. Just construct a new javax. servlet.http.Cookie object and send it to the user with HttpServlet-Response.addCookie, as shown in Listing 9.3. There are many other properties that can be set in a cookie, but browsers are somewhat inconsistent about how they treat them, so servlets should not rely too heavily on them.

Listing 9.3 Setting cookies.

```
public void doPost(HttpServletRequest request,
                   HttpServletResponse response)
     throws IOException
{
  // Create a new cookie with the user's IP address and the
  // current system time
  Cookie newCookie = new Cookie("myCookie",
                                 request.getRemoteAddr() + "|" +
                                 System.currentTimeMillis());

  // Indicate that this cookie should only be sent to URLs under
  // /servlets. If this is not set, it will be sent to all URLs
  // within this domain.
  newCookie.setPath("/servlets");

  // Indicate that this cookie should live for one day. If this is
  // not specified, the cookie will last only for the duration
  // of the browser session
  newCookie.setMaxAge(60 * 60 * 24);

  // Send it to the user
  response.addCookie(newCookie);
. . .
}
```

At the time of this writing, the cookie specification was still being finalized. The full draft of the working specification is available at

http://www.internic.net/rfc/rfc2109.txt

The addCookie() method cooperates with the sendError() and sendRedirect() methods as expected; if addCookie() is called before sendRedirect(), a servlet can both set a cookie and send the user to a new location.

Sending Data

As the examples have shown, sending data is simply a matter of getting the output stream from the HttpServletRequest via getOutputStream and writing to it. The output stream returned is actually a ServletOutputStream, which, despite the name, actually has more in common with the Writer classes than the OutputStream classes. If it were truly an OutputStream, the only way to write strings of data would be to use the write(byte[]) method, and programmers would have to convert everything to byte arrays before printing. The Servlet-OutputStream supports all the print() and println() methods that avoid this manual conversion (although, as we will see in Chapter 12, there may be times where it is more efficient to do this conversion by hand).

For all practical purposes, data sent through the output stream goes directly to the user. Although it may be buffered for a time in the JWS or some operating system buffer, once it has been written, the servlet loses control over it. Not only does this mean that it cannot be changed, but because the HTTP protocol specifies that all headers must precede data, once the first byte of data has been written, no headers can be set or changed. Among other things, this means that servlets cannot determine the content length of data as they are writing it.

While failing to set the content length is usually not fatal to the browser, communication between the browser and the server can be a lot more efficient if they agree on how much data is being sent. In the worst case, the browser may not know when all the data has been received and so will keep the connection open, leaving the user to sit and watch a spinning E, meteor shower, or surfing Duke for longer than anyone would really want to. The following code, which tries to set the content length, is wrong.

```
int length    = 0;
String data = getSomeData();
length        += data.getLength();
out.print(data);
data           = getSomeMoreData();
length        += data.length;
out.print(data);
result.setContentLength(length);    // Nope, too late!
```

By the time setContentLength() is called, the data may have already gone out, so the call will be ignored. The only way around this is to write the data to a buffer, then set the content length, then send the data.

```
String data = getSomeData();
data        += getSomeMoreData();
int length  = data.length;
result.setContentLength(length);
out.print(data);
```

As we will see in Chapter 12, this transformation can have some implications for performance and must be done with some care. Even in this simple example, suddenly another `String` is being created and used extensively. Neither the string construction nor the appending happens instantaneously, so this version of the code, although correct, will run slower.

In version 1.1 and later of the Java Web Server, servlets can get an output stream via `getWriter` as well as `getOutputStream`. This returns a `Writer` object that automatically internationalizes any data sent through it. This is a very quick and easy way to ensure that the servlet will behave appropriately for all locales, but it may have a serious impact on performance. All that conversion from one country's representation of data to another's takes time, and it even takes some effort to determine what the appropriate conversion is.

ServletConfig *and* ServletContext

When the `init()` method is called, it is given a `ServletConfig` object, which the servlet can use to get the initialization parameters that were set using the administration tool or specified in an `.initArgs` file in the `<server_root>/servlets` directory. Getting these values is very straightforward.

```
public void init(ServletConfig config)
     throws ServletException
{
  super.init(config);
  String param = config.getInitParameter("myParameter");
  if(param == null)
    throw new UnavailableException(this,"myParameter not specified");
}
```

Note that here it is appropriate to throw an `UnavailableException`, as the servlet cannot continue without this information.

There is also a method, `getInitParameterNames()`, that returns an enumeration of all the names that have been provided. This is useful if the servlet has default values for its parameters and wishes to allow the administrator to override some subset of them (see Listing 9.4).

Listing 9.4 Getting initialization parameters.

```
private String param1 = "default1";
private String param2 = "default2";
  ...
```

```
public void init(ServletConfig config)
  throws UnavailableException,IOException
{
  super.init(config);
  for(Enumeration e=config.getInitParameterNames();
      e.hasMoreElements;;)
  {
    String name = (String) e.nextElement();
    String value = config.getInitParameter(name);
    if(name.equals("param1"))
      param1 = value;
    else if(name.equals("param2"))
      param2 = value;
    else ...
  }
}
```

Servlets can also use the `ServletConfig` object to get the server's `Servlet-Context`. This object allows the servlet to get various objects related to the environment, most notably the system log. For example, the servlet could log that it had started successfully by doing something like this:

```
ServletContext sc = config.getServletContext();
if(sc != null) sc.log("The servlet has awoken...");
```

The servlet context should never be null; if it is, something is very wrong with the system. However, it is good programming practice to use intermediate values and check them before using them. In addition to the log, the `Servlet-Context` can be used to obtain or use many other objects in the Java Web Server, most notably other servlets. The possibilities this offers are discussed in the Interservlet Communication through `ServletContext` section later in this chapter.

Servlet Coding Techniques

Servlets are clearly an exciting and powerful technology, but like nuclear power and genetic engineering, they can turn on those who use them carelessly. The most important rule to keep in mind is *do not get drunk on servlets!* Servlets make excellent glue between the Web server and applications or databases or other systems, but they should not be the only class for a huge, complex application. This rule is really nothing more than an implication of good object-oriented programming style. A subclass should not add everything and the kitchen sink to its parent. If that much new functionality is needed, it should be in a separate class that the servlet will have an instance of, perhaps constructing it in the `init()` phase.

Performance and the Servlet Classes

As useful as the HttpUtils class is, it internally uses the String class, which in Java Development Kit (JDK) version 1.1 has some serious performance issues. It also has no way of knowing in advance which form variables have multiple values and which are single valued, so it has to be conservative and create an array for each. Worst of all, the URL decoding operation is very costly. When it is necessary to determine only whether or not a value has been provided or when a single simple value is needed from a query string, it may be much faster to do so with some custom code such as what's shown in Listing 9.5.

Listing 9.5 Finding an integer value in a queryString.

```
// Go through a query string represented as a byte array, and find an
// integer value
public int getSimpleIntValue(byte queryString[], byte fieldName[])
     throws IllegalArgumentException
{
  int i,j,pos=0;
  int ret          = 0;
  boolean ok       = true;
  byte fieldName2[] = new byte[fieldName.length + 1];
  // Create a new field name that is the original name
  // plus a trailing =.  This will prevent the problem
  // of having two parameters that start with the same
  // characters, such as coffee and coffeeFlavor
  System.arraycopy(fieldName,0,fieldName2,0,fieldName.length);
  fieldName2[fieldName.length] = '=';
  for(i=0;i<queryString.length-fieldName2.length;i++) {
    // Assume we're looking at the start of the field
    ok = true;
    for(j=0;j<fieldName2.length && ok;j++) {
      ok = (queryString[i+j] == fieldName2[j]);
    }
    // If we made it through and we're still OK,
    // then we really do have the field we want
    if(ok) {
      pos = i + fieldName2.length;
      break;
    }
  }

  // If we're OK, we have the field.  Otherwise, the field
  // isn't in the query string
  if(!ok) {
    throw new IllegalArgumentException(
            "Name not found: " + new String(fieldName));
  }

  // Read digits until the string runs out or we hit a
  // character that is not a digit
```

```
for(i=pos;
    (i < queryString.length &&
     queryString[i] >= '0'  &&
     queryString[i] <= '9');
    i++)
  {
    ret = (ret * 10 + (queryString[i]-'0'));
  }
  return ret;
}
```

It would not be too difficult to invent a general method that finds a particular name in a query string. However, at a certain point, using the routine over and over again becomes more expensive than using HttpUtils, since the cost of looking over the entire query string each time will start to mount up.

Threads and Servlets

Programmers, especially those used to UNIX's fork/exec model of handling CGI requests, may think that the first thing a servlet needs to do is kick off a new thread to handle each request so that the Web server can get back to the business of listening for new connections. Not so! The JWS maintains a pool of threads, and when it gets a new request, the first thing it does, before it even invokes the servlet, is to assign it to one of the threads in its pool. If there are no currently free threads, the server creates new ones, up to the limit specified in the administration tool. The service() method can take as long as it needs to satisfy the request, safe in the knowledge that it is already in a thread of its own, and only the user who made the particular request is kept waiting.

Even if, in some unusual case, it seems as if service() should create a new thread, it will not work. The most common way to start a new thread is to define a class that implements the Runnable interface and hence has a no-argument run method. In a servlet situation, presumably an object of this class would be created and perhaps given the request and response objects, or at least the OutputStream so that it can send back data. A new thread would then be created and passed this object, and then the thread's start method would be called. This in turn would call the run() method in a new thread. Although the run() method takes as long as it needs to do its job, both the thread constructor and the start call return immediately. So if this is all the service() method does, it also exits immediately, and the Java Web Server closes the output stream. The user gets no data, and when the auxiliary thread finishes its job and tries to send the data back—bang!—IOException.

In fact, a servlet does not often need to start a new thread. The one major exception is when there is some value or resource that changes often enough that it cannot be created only once in init(), but that is too time consuming to get on every `service()` request. An example might be a file that contains some data that will be included in the response. The servlet might handle this by having `init()` start a thread that periodically checks the time stamp and reloads the file when it has changed. Listing 9.6 shows a shell of a servlet that does just that.

Listing 9.6   Servlet that uses an auxiliary thread.

```
import java.io.*;
import javax.servlet.*;
import javax.servlet.http.*;
import java.util.Enumeration;
public class UpdatingFile extends HttpServlet
      implements Runnable
{
  private String fileName          = null;
  volatile private byte fileData[] = null;
  private long updateTime          = 0;
  private Thread fileChecker       = null;
  private boolean stillLiving      = true;

  public void init(ServletConfig s)
        throws ServletException
  {
    super.init(s);
    if((fileName = s.getInitParameter("fileName")) == null) {
      // If the parameter doesn't exist, we cannot
      // continue
      throw new UnavailableException(
                          this,
                          "Filename was not specified");
    }
    // Check whether the file exists.  If not, we
    // can wait a bit and try again
    if(!(new File(fileName)).exists()) {
      throw new UnavailableException(
                          300,
                            this,
                            "File does not exist");
    }
    updateFile();

    fileChecker = new Thread(this);
    fileChecker.start();
  }

  public void doGet(HttpServletRequest request,
                    HttpServletResponse result)
        throws UnavailableException,IOException
  {
    OutputStream out = result.getOutputStream();
    // We create a local reference to the file data in case
```

```
      // the other thread tries to change it between the check
      // for null and the use
      byte myFileData[] = fileData;
      if(myFileData == null) {
        out.write("The file is not available".getBytes());
      } else {
        out.write(myFileData);
      }

        out.flush();
        out.close();
  }

  public void destroy() {
      // When the servlet shuts down, it should clean up
      // the auxiliary thread too
      stillLiving = false;
  }

  public void run() {
      while(stillLiving) {
        try {Thread.sleep(60 * 1000 * 5);} catch (Exception e) {}
        updateFile();
      }
  }

  public void updateFile() {
      long timeStamp;

      try {
        File file = new File(fileName);
        if(!file.exists()) return;
        if((timeStamp = file.lastModified()) > updateTime) {
          updateTime = timeStamp;
          FileInputStream in = new FileInputStream(file);
          byte newFileData[] = new byte[(int) file.length()];
          in.read(newFileData,0,(int) file.length());
          in.close();
          fileData = newFileData;
        }
      } catch (IOException e) {
        // Log the error message...
      }
  }
}
```

There are several interesting things about the example in Listing 9.6. First, this is the first time we have used an UnavailableException with a time parameter. This is because the file may show up sometime in the next few minutes.

Even more interesting, this example does not have any synchronized methods. It might look as if it should, because updateFile() updates fileData and doGet() uses fileData. What would happen if updateFile() were changing it at the same time doGet() was using it? As it turns out, this is not a problem. The use of fileData is restricted to two assignments. updateFile() reads into a different array, then makes fileData refer to it. Likewise, doGet() first creates a reference to fileData and then uses only this local reference. As we discuss in greater depth in Chapter 12, these assignments are *atomic*, so there is no danger of one happening in the middle of the other.

In some implementations of the Java virtual machine there is some possibility that each thread will have its own copy of the fileData field, so the service() threads may never see the updated one. If a servlet exhibits strange behavior along these lines, it may be necessary to protect a variable with synchronized, or delcare it to be transient.

init() *Method and Static Members*

If a servlet has any static members that need to be allocated before they are used, some care must be taken when doing the allocating and destroying. This is because static members are shared across multiple instances of a servlet that may be active at any time and also across multiple instances of the same servlet as it is restarted. init() cannot just go ahead and allocate them, because another init() may already have done so. Correspondingly, destroy() cannot just deallocate or close these resources, because another instance of the servlet may still need them. The solution is to keep a static count of how many instances of the servlet are really active, as shown in Listing 9.7.

Listing 9.7   Multiple servlets using a common resource.

```
init(ServletConfig s) {
   super(s);
   incMaybeCreate();
}
destroy() {
   decMaybeDestroy();
}
private synchronized void incMaybeCreate {
   if(count == 0) ...; // allocate the resource
   count++;
}

private synchronized void decMaybeDestroy() {
   count--;
   if(count == 0) ...; // free the resource
}
```

A better approach is to take the static members out of the servlet class entirely and put them in a separate class. This class would have a public static method that would return an instance of the class and a private constructor that would ensure that only one instance is created.

Interservlet Communication

One huge strength of the Java Web Server is that servlets can talk to each other. This opens up a wide vista of possibilities: multiple servlets can track a set of users and adapt themselves to the users' interests, or a master servlet can watch a collection of other servlets and generate reports for administrators. It is even possible for one servlet to get the output of another one and manipulate it in all sorts of fancy ways.

Calling Another Servlet through HTTP

If one servlet needs data from another, it can get the data exactly the same way a user would—by going through the network and asking the Web server for it. This may seem like a rather roundabout way of doing things, but for many applications it is the simplest and most straightforward way for two servlets to communicate. For example, Listing 9.8 shows a servlet that gets the output of another servlet, and puts it on a green page.

Listing 9.8   Servlet that turns other servlets green.

```
import java.io.*;
import java.net.*;
import java.util.*;
import javax.servlet.*;
import javax.servlet.http.*;
public class MakeGreen extends HttpServlet {
  public void doGet(HttpServletRequest req,
                    HttpServletResponse res)
      throws IOException
  {
    ServletOutputStream out = res.getOutputStream();
    res.setContentType("text/html");

    out.println("<HTML>");
    out.println("<HEAD>");
    out.println("<TITLE>");
    out.println("A servlet included in another servlet");
    out.println("</TITLE>");
    out.println("</HEAD>");
    out.println("");
    out.println("<BODY BGCOLOR=#00FF00>");
    out.println("");

    // Open a connection back to ourselves
    String ourAddress = req.getHeader("Host");
    if(ourAddress == null) {
      out.println("Odd, we did not come from anywhere!");
      out.println("</BODY>");
      out.println("</HTML>");
```

```
      return;
    }
    // Now we construct a full URL. The path info for this
    // servlet will be the servlet we wish to invoke, and the
    // query string to this servlet will be passed down to the
    // other servlet
    String fullUrl = "http://" + ourAddress + "/" +
      req.getPathInfo() + "?" + req.getQueryString();

    // Now open the URL, and send out all the data
    try {
      URL url = new URL(fullUrl);
      InputStream in = url.openStream();
      byte buffer[] = new byte[1024];
      int count;

      while((count = in.read(buffer)) > 0) {
        out.write(buffer,0,count);
      }
      in.close();
    } catch (Exception e) {
      out.println("Unable to get other servlet: " + e);
    }
    out.println("</BODY>");
    out.println("</HTML>");
  }
}
```

To use this servlet, use the administration tool to assign it to /MakeGreen. Then you can turn the output of a servlet, such as the HelloServlet shown in Listing 9.1, green by going to

http://<your_machine>:<your_port>/MakeGreen/HelloServlet

NOTE: MakeGreen will contain everything from the other servlet, including the headers. It is certainly possible to check the output and remove these headers, but in version 2.1 of the Servlet API there is an easier way for doing this using the servlet context.

Interservlet Communication through ServletContext

As we mentioned earlier, servlets can get an object called ServletContext through a call to the getServletContext() method. ServletContext has access to all the servlets in the system and so can enable one to access another. Three methods are provided for doing this: using the getResource() method to get a

URL to a servlet or page, using the `getServlet()` method to get another servlet object, and using the `getRequestDispatcher()` method to pass control to another servlet or include another servlet's output.

getResource() Method

The `getResource()` method for connecting servlets through the `ServletContext` is new to version 2.1 of the Servlet API. It is very similar to the HTTP technique we looked at earlier, except instead of constructing a URL that will make a new connection back to the Web server, `ServletContext`'s `getResource()` method is used to obtain the URL. This URL works the same way as in Listing 9.8, but instead of going the long way around and getting data through a new connection, all the information is passed internally through the JWS from one servlet to the next, as shown in Listing 9.9.

Listing 9.9   Another way for one servlet to include another.

```java
import java.io.*;
import java.net.*;
import java.util.*;
import javax.servlet.*;
import javax.servlet.http.*;

public class MakeGreen2 extends HttpServlet {
  public void doGet(HttpServletRequest req,
                    HttpServletResponse res)
      throws IOException
  {
    ServletOutputStream out = res.getOutputStream();
    ServletContext theServletContext = getServletContext();
    res.setContentType("text/html");

    out.println("<HTML>");
    out.println("<HEAD>");
    out.println("<TITLE>");
    out.println("A servlet included in another servlet");
    out.println("</TITLE>");
    out.println("</HEAD>");
    out.println("");
    out.println("<BODY BGCOLOR=#00FF00>");
    out.println("");

    // Now we construct the new URL.  The path info for this
    // servlet will be the servlet we wish to invoke.
    // Unfortunately this method does not allow us to pass a
    // query string.

    String fullUrl = reg.getPathInfo();
```

```
    // Now have the ServletContext access the URL
    try {
      URL url = theServletContext.getResouce(fullUrl);
      InputStream in = url.openStream();
      byte buffer[] = new byte[1024];
      int count;

      while((count = in.read(buffer)) > 0) {
        out.write(buffer,0,count);
      }
      in.close();
    } catch (Exception e) {
      out.println("Unable to get other servlet: " + e);
    }
    out.println("</BODY>");
    out.println("</HTML>");
  }
}
```

Note that once the URL is obtained, we get an `InputStream` and use it as we did before. Also note that using `getResource()`, the headers are stripped out of the returned data, which will make the output of `MakeGreen2` cleaner than that of `MakeGreen`.

getServlet() Method

The second way `ServletContext` enables interservlet communication is by allowing one servlet to actually get another one. The `ServletContext`'s `getServlet()` method can be used to get any other servlet known to the Web server or to get an enumeration of all servlets.

Once a servlet has obtained another servlet, what can it do? Almost anything! As powerful as this may seem, it is potentially very dangerous. No servlet should ever call `init()`, `service()`, or `destroy()` directly, because the Java Web Server expects that it will be the only one doing so, and things may get seriously out of sync if anyone else does. For example, if one servlet tries to call another's `service()` method, the first has no way to be sure that the other's `service()` method has been initialized. If one servlet tries to initialize another, it has no way of knowing if the JWS is currently trying to destroy it. In addition there are some potential security issues here. If one servlet is open to the public and it has code that calls some protected servlet's methods, a malicious user may be able to use the first servlet to gain access to the second.

For these reasons, in version 2.1 of the servlet API the methods that allow servlets to get other servlets have been deprecated. We recommend against using them even in earlier versions of the API. However, for the sake of completeness, we will look at how this might work. For example, consider a servlet

that maintains a count of how many times it has been called. The `HelloServlet`
class could be given this functionality by adding the following methods.

```
private int count = 0;
private synchronized void incCount() {
   count++;
}

public synchronized int getCount() {
   return count;
}
```

Assuming the `HelloServlet` was installed with the name "hello", the servlet in
Listing 9.10 could then be used to access `Count` information.

Listing 9.10   Servlet that accesses another servlet's data.

```
import java.io.*;
import javax.servlet.*;
import javax.servlet.http.*;
public class ViewInfo extends HttpServlet {
   public void doGet(HttpServletRequest request,
                     HttpServletResponse response)
       throws ServletException,IOException
   {
      ServletContext sc = getServletContext();
      ServletOutputStream out = response.getOutputStream();

      response.setContentType("text/plain");

      if(sc == null) {
        throw new UnavailableException(
                          this,
                          "This servlet has no context!");
      }

      Servlet theServlet = sc.getServlet("hello");
      if(theServlet == null) {
        throw new UnavailableException(
                          this,
                          "The hello servlet is not installed");
      }
      HelloServlet theHelloServlet;
      try {
         theHelloServlet = (HelloServlet) theServlet;
      } catch (ClassCastException e) {
         throw new UnavailableException(
                  this,
                  "The servlet named hello is not a hello servlet!");
      }
```

```
        out.println("The hello servlet has been called " +
                theHelloServlet.getCount() + " times");
    }
}
```

This example may not be all that useful as it stands, but considered as the start of a master servlet that monitors custom information about all the others, it is the start of something many Web programmers and administrators might find useful. In particular, the only way to get this kind of usage information in most other Web servers is to painstakingly sift through the log files.

Fortunately, it is possible to pass this kind of information between servlets even without using the deprecated `getServlet()` method. A better approach is to use an auxiliary class with static members or methods and have all servlets use that class. For example, here is a class that can be used to pass `Count` information.

```
public class Counter {
  private static int helloCount = 0;

  public static void incHelloCount() {
    helloCount++;
  }
  public static int getHelloCount() {
    return helloCount;
  }
}
```

`HelloServlet` now can call `Counter.incHelloCount()`, and `ViewServlet` can call `Counter.getHelloCount()`. If an administrator was interested in how many times multiple servlets had been called, new count fields could be added to the `Counter` class.

RequestDispatcher Interface

Version 2.1 of the Servlet API defined a new interface, called `Request-Dispatcher`. This interface specifies a class that handles passing a request to a resource such as a servlet, HTML page, JSP, and so on. While this functionality was always available in the Java Web Server, this class makes it possible for servlets to explicitly pass control to another servlet. This can happen in two ways. Either a servlet can tell another servlet to handle a request by calling the `forward()` method, or a servlet can have another servlet generate some output that it will then include, by calling the `include()` method.

Both these methods have limitations. If a servlet is going to forward a request to another servlet, the first servlet is not allowed to write any output. This is because, as we have previously noted, a servlet must send out all headers before any data is sent. If the second servlet wanted to set or change some headers, such as the content length, and the first servlet had already written data, the output could become corrupted. To ensure that this does not happen, the forward() method throws an IllegalStateException if the calling servlet has already called getWriter() or getOutputStream().

For exactly the same reason, a servlet invoked by include() cannot set any headers, because data may have already been sent by the calling servlet. In this case, no exception is thrown, but the call may have no effect.

Listing 9.11 shows a servlet that does both forwarding and including; it could be used on a "Joke of the Day" site. This is a service that users would sign up for, and after signing up would be given a cookie called SignedUp. The servlet first checks to see if the user has this cookie. If not, the request is forwarded to a servlet where the user can register. If the user has the cookie, a page that includes the joke is generated.

Listing 9.11   Servlet that uses cookies.

```
import java.io.*;
import javax.servlet.*;
import javax.servlet.http.*;

public class WelcomeServlet extends HttpServlet {
   public void doGet(HttpServletRequest request,
                     HttpServletResponse response)
      throws UnavailableException, IOException
  {
    boolean signedUp        = false;
    ServletContext context = getServletContext();
    RequestDispatcher theDispatcher;
    // See if this user has the SignedUp cookie
    Cookie cookies[] = request.getCookies();
    if(cookies != null) {
      for(int i=0;i<cookies.length;i++) {
      if(cookies[i].getName().equals("SignedUp")) {
        signedUp = true;
        break;
      }
     }
    }
    // If the user has not signed up, send the user
    // to the register screen
    if(!signedUp) {
      theDispatcher = context.getRequestDispatcher("/signup");
      theDispatcher.forward(request,response);
      return;
    }
    // The user has signed up, so give the user the page.
    // We can now get the output writer safely, since
```

```
    // we know we will not be forwarding
    Writer out = response.getWriter();
    // We can now also set headers safely
    response.setStatus(response.SC_OK);
    response.setContentType("text/plain");
    out.println("<HTML>");
    out.println("<HEAD>");
    out.println("<TITLE>");
    out.println("Welcome");
    out.println("</TITLE>");
    out.println("</HEAD>");
    out.println("<BODY>");
    out.println("Welcome to the joke of the day!");
    out.println("Here is today's joke:");
    theDispatcher = context.getRequestDispatcher("/joke.html");
    theDispatcher.include(request,response);

    out.println("<P>Hope you laughed!");
    out.println("</BODY>");
    out.println("<HTML>");
  }
}
```

Note that the caution about setting headers does not apply to getting headers, as we show here by getting the cookies at the top of doGet(). The other thing to notice in this example is how the RequestDispatcher is actually used. First the object is obtained by calling getRequestDispatcher() with the URL of the desired page, and then either forward() or include() is called and passed the current HttpServletRequest and HttpServletResponse. Finally, the target of a forward() or include() does not need to be a servlet; it can be a simple HTML page or anything else. Here we include a file called joke.html. Using an include() here makes it very easy to include the same joke on multiple pages. Tomorrow, when a new joke is published, it will just be necessary to change joke.html.

We do not include the code for the sign-up page here, because it does not do anything we have not already seen. It would only need to prompt a user for any information that the administrator wanted to track and then issue the cookie. Again, making this a separate servlet, instead of a part of Welcome, makes a great deal of sense, since it allows multiple servlets to use the same sign-up mechanism.

Servlet Chaining

Perhaps the most exciting possibility for interservlet communication is to plug the output of one servlet directly into the input of another. This technique is called *servlet chaining* or *filtering,* and it is the most flexible of all the techniques we have looked at so far.

The servlet chaining technique works somewhat like the HTTP technique. In the HTTP method a servlet, which we will call the consumer, makes a request back to the Web server, which in turn invokes another servlet, which we will call the producer. The producer's output is sent to the consumer via a URL, and the consumer can then modify it. By comparison, in the servlet chaining approach the Web server calls the producer first, and the producer sends some data to its output stream. Then the consumer is called, and it gets a ServletInputStream from the HttpServletRequest, which it uses to directly read the data that was sent through the ServletOutputStream. The consumer then sends modified data to its output stream. This data could go to the user or could be sent to yet another servlet, and so on.

Listing 9.12 shows a servlet that can act as a consumer. It looks for the special sequence of characters <!--#date--> in the data and replaces it with the current date. One thing to notice about this code is that it uses the get-ContentLength() method from the HttpServletRequest. This will not work if the producer servlet does not use setContentLength(), which is another good reason why all servlets should set their content length before sending out data.

Listing 9.12   Server-side include example.

```
import java.io.*;
import java.util.*;
import java.text.*;
import javax.servlet.*;
import javax.servlet.http.*;
public class DateFilter extends HttpServlet {
   public void service(HttpServletRequest req,
                       HttpServletResponse res)
       throws IOException
  {
    ServletInputStream in   = req.getInputStream();
    ServletOutputStream out = res.getOutputStream();
    int count               = req.getContentLength();
    byte buffer[]           = new byte[count];
    int pos;

    res.setContentType("text/plain");

    in.read(buffer);

    String tmp          = new String(buffer);
    StringBuffer result = new StringBuffer(tmp.length()+30);

    if((pos = tmp.indexOf("<!--#date-->")) != -1) {
      // Send out the first part of the string
```

```
        result.append(tmp.substring(0,pos));

        // Send out the date
        Date theDate  = new Date();
        DateFormat df = DateFormat.getDateInstance(
                                        DateFormat.LONG);
        result.append(df.format(theDate));

        // Send out the rest of the page. Note we skip past the
        // <!--#date--> piece
        result.append(tmp.substring(pos+12));
        tmp = result.toString();
        res.setContentLength(tmp.length());
        out.print(tmp);
      } else {
        // If the producer did not send out a page with the
        // <!--#date-->, then just send it out unchanged
        res.setContentLength(tmp.length());
        out.print(tmp);
      }
    }
}
```

Once this servlet has been compiled, installed, and given a name through the administration tool, it can be used in one of two ways. The first associates it with a specific producer. To see this in action, modify `HelloServlet` so that it sends out `"Hello, world, today is <!--#date-->"`. Then go into the administration tool and create a new servlet alias, where the alias is `/hellotoday` and the `ServletInvoked` is specified as `helloServlet,dateServlet`. Make sure that servlet chaining is enabled in the administration tool. Then go to `http:<your_machine>/hellotoday` and gaze in wonder at the magic of servlet chaining.

But wait, it gets even more amazing! Besides creating chains by explicitly listing them, it is also possible to tell the Java Web Server that all output of a particular type should be sent through another servlet. There is not yet a way to do this through the administration tool, but it is still quite easy. Just edit `<server_root>/properties/process/javaserver/webpageservice/` and add a line containing `"text/plain=dateFilter"`, then restart the server. This line states that if any servlet calls `setContentType("text/plain")`, then its output should be sent through `dateFilter`.

Once this has been done, go to `http://<your_machine>/servlet/ helloServlet`, or any name that has been associated with `HelloServlet`. The date will be filled in! Even better, note that in Chapter 4 we said that the `FileServlet` uses the MIME-type mappings from the administration tool. This means that the `FileServlet` will set the content type to `text/plain` when it sends out a file with the `.txt` extension. Create a `.txt` file under

<server_root>/public_html, and put <!--#date-->. Then use a browser to view this page. Yup, the date has been dropped into the page!

This is a simple example of something available in many Web servers called server-side include. Server-side includes are HTML comments, like <!--#date-->, that the server replaces with appropriate information. The JWS provides a general version of a server-side include through a servlet called SSInclude. SSInclude grabs any page whose MIME type is java-internal/ parsed-html and looks for the special <servlet> tag. If it finds one, it will replace the tag with the result of invoking the specified servlet. More information on this is provided with the Java Web Server and is available at

http://<your_machine>/system/doc/servlets/core_servlets.html

Future Directions: Servlet Beans

Conceptually, a bean is a reusable software component. In programming terms, a bean is a class that supports certain naming conventions and interfaces. A servlet can be a bean.

This should not come as any great surprise, since there is no reason why a servlet class cannot support the bean naming conventions or implement the Serializable interface. The cool thing is that the Java Web Server can use servlet beans *as* beans, with all the benefits of component reuse, shipping, and automatic detection of properties the bean specification was designed for.

Servlet beans come in two flavors and no, they are not regular and decaffeinated. Well, on second thought, maybe they are. The decaffeinated variety is simply a class file that follows the get and set naming conventions or a serialized instance of that class stored as a .ser file. These are as tasty as any other servlet, and the Java Web Server can load them and init() them and ask them to handle service() requests and so on. But they do not really provide any extra kick.

The caffeinated variety is a class file, possibly with a serialized instance, stored in a .jar file. These beans offer the rich flavor of any other servlet plus the jolt of enhanced configuration through the administration tool. Sun refers to .class or .ser beans as *not installed,* or *dropped-in,* and the kind that live in .jar files as *installed.*

Any servlet can get parameters through the ServletConfig object passed to init(), but if the administrator is not the same person as the programmer or if good documentation has not been provided (or read!), there may be no way to know what the possible options for the parameter line are. Perhaps a servlet outputs a page with green text on a red background, and the administrator would like to change it to a nice, readable white-on-black. If the administrator knows that "fgcolor=white;bgcolor=black" can be specified in the administration tool, fine; if not, users are just going to have to live with eyestrain.

But if the administrator is using the installed version of the servlet, the administration tool will be able to use Introspection to determine the parameters the servlet accepts and automatically present an input box for each, as shown in Listing 9.13.

Listing 9.13 Servlet bean.

```java
import java.io.*;
import javax.servlet.*;
import javax.servlet.http.*;

public class ColorBean extends HttpServlet
    implements Serializable
{
  private String fgColor = "#00FF00";   // Green text...
  private String bgColor = "#FF0000";   // on a red background.

  public void setBgColor(String c) {bgColor = c;}
  public String getBgColor() {return bgColor;}

  public void setFgColor(String c) {fgColor = c;}
  public String getFgColor() {return fgColor;}

  // Note that even though this uses parameters, it does not need
  // an init() method or any of that primitive getInitParameter
  // stuff!

  public void doGet(HttpServletRequest request,
                    HttpServletResponse result)
      throws UnavailableException,IOException
  {
    ServletOutputStream out = result.getOutputStream();
    StringBuffer text = new StringBuffer();

    text.append("<HTML>\n");
    text.append("<BODY BGCOLOR=");
    text.append(getBgColor());
    text.append(" TEXT=");
    text.append(getFgColor());
    text.append(">\n");
    text.append("Hello again world!\n");
    text.append("</BODY>\n");
    text.append("</HTML>\n");

    result.setStatus(HttpServletResponse.SC_OK);
    result.setContentType("text/html");
    result.setContentLength(text.length());

    out.print(text.toString());
    out.flush();
```

```
      out.close();
   }

   public static void main(String argv[]) throws Exception {
      ColorBean theBean = new ColorBean();
      FileOutputStream f =
          new FileOutputStream("theColorBean.ser");
      ObjectOutputStream out = new ObjectOutputStream(f);
      out.writeObject(theBean);
      out.flush();
      out.close();
   }
}
```

There is nothing really special about this servlet except that it implements the serializable interface and has accessor methods for the two variables. The main method does not really have anything to do with the servlet; it's provided as a convenient way to create a .ser file. It could be in a different class, or a bean editor such as JavaSoft's BeanBox could be used for the same purpose.

To see it in action, compile the example, and then run

```
java colorBean
```

to create the theColorBean.ser file. Then create a .jar file with this command:

```
jar -cv0f colorBean.jar theColorBean.ser colorBean.class
```

Move colorBean.jar into the servletBeans directory under the JWS distribution. Then go into the administration tool, click on the Servlets button, then click Add in the servlet tree. This servlet is added as is any other, but specify that it is a bean that lives in the colorBean.jar file. After clicking Save there will be a new Properties screen, with fgColor and bgColor as options, already filled in with the ugly defaults. This is shown in Figure 9.2.

Try loading this page in a browser. Ugh! Then change the color properties and click Modify, then have the browser reload the page. Much better. By the way, we did not really need to create the theColorBean.ser file. If the .jar file had just contained the class file, the Java Web Server would have allowed the administrator to create a new instance and then set the color parameters the same way.

Servlet beans open up a wide vista of other possibilities. Of particular interest is the servlet infobus, which allows data such as an HTTP request or user-provided data to be shared between many beans. Full details of the infobus are outside the scope of this book, but more information is available at

http://developer.javasoft.com/developer/technicalArticles/infobus/infobus.html

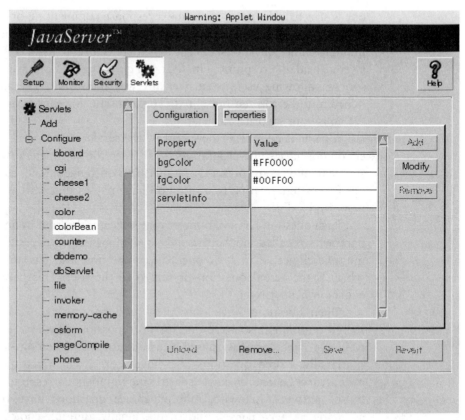

Figure 9.2 Administration tool with Bean values

Only registered members of the Java Developers Connection can get this page, but registering is free.

A Sample Application: The Game Engine

In this section we introduce the first sample application—a rudimentary, yet hopefully useful, game engine. The servlet component of this application is simple, even simpler than some of the other examples we have looked at in this chapter. However, it uses the `init()` method and the `ServletConfig` class to build the game and the `service()` method and the `HttpServletRequest` and `HttpServletResponse` classes to allow the user to play it.

To start with, let's review the specification we presented in Chapter 2. A game consists of one or more questions, and each question may be one of three types. Multiple-choice questions give players a list of possible answers; when one is selected, the game can issue a response commenting on the choice. One answer may also be designated as the right one. Scored questions are like multiple-choice questions, except that there is a score associated with each answer instead of a response. Finally, open questions do not have a fixed set of responses, allowing users to answer any way they want. The answers are then tallied and the top ten presented. This is useful for survey questions, such as "Who is your favorite musician?"

A game is completely specified by the servlet parameters, so game designers do not have to be programmers. To keep the parameters straight, we use a simple naming convention. Questions are named `question0`, `question1`, and so on. Parameters relating to a question have names that start with the question name and a dot.

Each question has a parameter that indicates the kind of question it is. This parameter is called, not surprisingly, `question_name.type`, and it may be either multiple choice, scored, or open. Each question also has an associated text, which is the actual question presented to the user. This parameter is called `question_name.text`.

Open questions have only these two parameters. Multiple-choice and scored questions also have one or more possible answers. These are named `question_name.answer0`, `question_name.answer1`, and so on.

Finally, scored questions also have scores, which are named `question_name.score0`, `question_name.score1`; the numbers correspond to the numbers in the answers. Likewise, multiple-choice questions have responses called `question_name.response0` and so on. Finally, multiple-choice questions may also have a parameter called `question_name.rightAnswer`, whose value should be a number corresponding to an answer number.

Here are the parameters that define a simple game about servlets.

```
name=Servlet Game
question0.type=open
question0.text=What do you like best about servlets?
question1.type=multiple
question1.text=What is the signature for HttpServlet.service()?
question1.answer0=service(Cheese,Squid)
question1.response0=Uh, you must live in an interesting world...
question1.answer1=service(ServletRequest,ServletResponse)
question1.response1=Close, but you can be more specific
question1.answer2=service(HttpServletRequest,HttpServletResponse)
question1.response2=Right!
question1.rightAnswer=2
question2.type=scored
question2.text=What are some of the benefits of servlets?
question2.answer0=Softens hands while you do dishes
question2.score0=0
```

```
question2.answer1=speed of execution and speed of development
question2.score1=10
question2.answer2=cross-platform
question2.score2=8
```

We discuss how to design applications more formally in Chapter 16, but fortunately, it is pretty easy to come up with an object model for this application. Since the specification talks about things like games and questions, these are our classes. Specifically, we have a Game class that contains a number of Question objects. There is a base Question class, which will have name and text questions, since these are common to all questions. There are also classes called MultipleQuestion, ScoredQuestion, and OpenQuestion, which extend Question and implement each question's special behavior.

We also need some way of accumulating things like total score and number of right answers. It does not make sense to try to put this functionality into the questions, since they should not need to know anything about the other questions in the system. The accumulation could happen in the game, but it is slightly better design to have an auxiliary class do this. This class we call GameTallies.

Have we forgotten any classes? Oh, yes, the servlet itself. Of course the entry into the application is a servlet, but we follow our own advice and do not go overboard with code in the servlet class. In fact, the servlet is the dullest one in this chapter and does not do much more than set up an instance of Game and call its methods.

The other side is that the servlet does not pass any objects from the Servlet API to any of the game classes. The Game and related classes are conceptually completely independent of servlets, which is how it should be. Of course these classes generate HTML, which in practice ties them to the Web. However, if it is ever desired to deploy the games in some other form, say as an applet, it will be possible to do so without having to go back and remove all the servlet-specific code. It will be necessary just to replace code that prints HTML with code that uses various AWT classes. The servlet code is shown in Listing 9.14.

Listing 9.14 Game servlet.

```
import javax.servlet.*;
import javax.servlet.http.*;
import java.io.*;
import java.util.*;
/**
 * The servlet class. It is pretty miminal—all it does is
 * construct a Game in init() and use it to play or render
 * in service().
 */
public class GameServlet extends HttpServlet
                         implements SingleThreadModel
{
```

```
/**
 * The Game object, which does all the real work
 */
private Game theGame;
/**
 * Constructs the game
 */
public void init(ServletConfig conf)
     throws ServletException
{
   // Build a Properties object from the ServletConfig,
   // because Game objects shouldn't need to know anything
   // about Servlet API classes
   Properties  p = new Properties();
   Enumeration e = conf.getInitParameterNames();
   String name;
   while(e.hasMoreElements()) {
     name = (String) e.nextElement();
     p.put(name,conf.getInitParameter(name));
   }
   theGame = new Game(p);
}
/**
 * If service() is being called with a query string, play the
 * game and have it display the results. Otherwise, have
 * the game display the question screen.
 */
public void service(HttpServletRequest req,
                    HttpServletResponse res)
     throws IOException
{
   PrintWriter out = res.getWriter();
   // Set up the output
   res.setStatus(res.SC_OK);
   res.setContentType("text/html");
   // If we've been given a query string, someone is
   // playing the game. Otherwise, just render the game
   // for them
   if(req.getQueryString() != null) {
     // Get the values from the request, and pack them
     // into a Properties, because Games shouldn't need
     // to know anything about the servlet classes
     Properties p  = new Properties();
     Enumeration e = req.getParameterNames();
     String name;
     String values[];
     while(e.hasMoreElements()) {
       name   = (String) e.nextElement();
       values = req.getParameterValues(name);
       if(values != null && values.length > 0) {
         p.put(name,values[0]);
       }
```

```
        }
      theGame.play(p,out);
    } else {
      theGame.render(req.getRequestURI(),out);
    }
    out.close();
  }
}
```

As we said, cut and dried. Note that we implement the `SingleThreadModel` interface. This will ensure that we don't have to worry about running into any problems with many people playing the game at once, although it will present a performance problem. At the end of Chapter 12 we show how to make this game safe for multiple simultaneous players in a much more efficient way. Next, let's have a look at the Game class (see Listing 9.15).

Listing 9.15   Game class.

```java
import java.io.*;
import java.util.*;
/**
 * The game class, which handles all interactions and
 * renderings of a game
 */
class Game {
  /**
   * The questions in the game
   */
  private Vector questions;
  /**
   * The name of the game
   */
  private String gameName;
  /**
   * The constructor sets up some instance variables and
   * uses the Properties to generate questions
   */
  public Game(Properties props) {
    questions = new Vector(10);
    int i;
    Question q;

    // Get the game name
    gameName = props.getProperty("name");
    if(gameName == null) gameName = "Untitled Game";
    // Build questions until we get an indicator that there
    // are no more
    for(i=0;
        (q = Question.buildQuestion(props,i)) != null;
        i++)
    {
      questions.addElement(q);
```

```java
    }
  }
  /**
   * A game is rendered by sending the beginning of a page,
   * rendering each of the questions, and then sending the
   * end of the page
   */
  public void render(String uri,PrintWriter out)
        throws IOException
  {
    int i;
    // Send out the beginning of the page, including the
    // start of the form
    out.println("<HTML>");
    out.println("<HEAD>");
    out.println("<TITLE>" + gameName + "</TITLE>");
    out.println("</HEAD>");
    out.println("<BODY>");
    out.println("<FORM ACTION=" +
                uri +
                " METHOD=GET>");
    // Render each of the questions. Each will have a
    // form field that the user will respond to when playing
    // the game
    for(i=0;i<questions.size();i++) {
      ((Question) questions.elementAt(i)).render(out);
    }
    // Close the form and the page
    out.println("<INPUT TYPE=SUBMIT VALUE=Play!>");
    out.println("</FORM>");
    out.println("</BODY>");
    out.println("</HTML>");
  }
  /**
   * To play a game, the beginning of the result page is sent
   * out, then each of the questions is played, and finally
   * the page is closed
   */
  public void play(Properties props, PrintWriter out)
        throws IOException
  {
    int i;
    // Start the page
    out.println("<HTML>");
    out.println("<HEAD>");
    out.println("<TITLE>" + gameName + ": Results </TITLE>");
    out.println("</HEAD>");
    out.println("<BODY>");
    // Create an object to hold running tallies
    GameTallies t = new GameTallies();
    // Play each question
    for(i=0;i<questions.size();i++) {
      ((Question) questions.elementAt(i)).play(props,out,t);
```

```
        }
        // Print the summary info
        if(t.getMaxScore() != 0) {
          out.println("<P>You scored " +
                      t.getScore() +
                      " out of a possible " +
                      t.getMaxScore() +
                      " points</P>");
        }
        if(t.getNumMultiple() != 0) {
          out.println("<P>You got " +
                      t.getNumRight() +
                      " out of " +
                      t.getNumMultiple() +
                      " right</P>");
        }
        // Close the page
        out.println("</BODY>");
        out.println("</HTML>");
    }
}
```

The game generates only questions, then renders them onto a page or plays them. In keeping with our design, a Game should not know anything more about questions than it needs to. In particular, it does not need to know about our conventions for parameter names. So the code that gets parameters is left for the buildQuestion() method in Question, rather than having it in Game. Moving to the next of our application classes, Listing 9.16 is the code for the base Question class.

Listing 9.16 Question class.

```
import java.io.*;
import java.util.*;
/**
 * The base question class provides some basic
 * functionality, but most of the interesting stuff happens
 * in the subclasses. The one exception is the
 * buildQuestion method, which constructs a
 * question of the appropriate type
 */
public abstract class Question {
  /**
   * The prefix is a string of the form question0,
   * question1, etc. It indicates the prefix of values
   * in the servlet parameters that are relevant to
   * this question, and it is also used to indentify the
   * question itself
   */
  private String prefix;
  /**
   * The text of the question, in other words,
```

```
 * what the user should be asked
 */
private String text;
/**
 * The constructor sets the prefix and text,
 * since all questions have
 * these properties
 */
public Question(String qname,Properties props) {
  prefix = qname;
  text    = props.getProperty(qname + ".text");
}
/**
 * Method to get the prefix
 */
public String getPrefix() {return prefix;}
/**
 * Method to get the question text
 */
public String getText() {return text;}
/**
 * This method looks for the type specifier in the properties
 * and dispatches to the appropriate constructor
 */
public static Question buildQuestion(Properties props,
                                     int index)
{
  String type;
  String qname = "question" + index;
  if((type = props.getProperty(qname + ".type")) == null)
    return null;
  if(type.equals("open")) {
    return new OpenQuestion(qname,props);
  } else if(type.equals("multiple")) {
    return new MultipleQuestion(qname,props);
  } else if(type.equals("scored")) {
    return new ScoredQuestion(qname,props);
  }
  // If it's nothing we recognize, we can't return a
  // meaningful question
  return null;
}
/**
 * The default render method is abstract, since it should
 * never be called
 */
public abstract void render(PrintWriter out)
     throws IOException;
/**
 * The default play method is abstract, since it should
 * never be called
 */
```

```
public abstract void play(Properties props, PrintWriter out,
                 GameTallies tallies) throws IOException;
}
```

The major point of interest here is the buildQuestion() method. Note that this is an *abstract* class, which cannot be instantiated, because it makes sense not to play a generic question but to play a specific subclass, which will define how the question should be rendered and played. These classes are presented in Listings 9.17, 9.18, and 9.19. Finally, Listing 9.20 is the GameTallies class, which, as promised, collects only tally information.

Listing 9.17 MultipleQuestion class.

```java
import java.io.*;
import java.util.*;
/**
 * A MultipleQuestion has a fixed list of possible answers.
 * Each has an associated response, and one may be designated
 * as the right answer
 */
class MultipleQuestion extends Question {
  /**
   * The possible answers
   */
  private Vector answers;
  /**
   * The responses associated with each answer
   */
  private Vector responses;
  /**
   * Which answer is right?
   */
  private int    rightAnswer;

  /**
   * The constructor sets up the answer and response vectors
   */
  public MultipleQuestion(String prefix,Properties props) {
    super(prefix,props);

    String tmp =
      props.getProperty(getPrefix() + ".rightAnswer");
    if(tmp != null) rightAnswer = Integer.parseInt(tmp);
    else rightAnswer = -1;
    answers   = new Vector();
    responses = new Vector();
    String answer;
    String response;
    String tmp1 = getPrefix() + ".answer";
    String tmp2 = getPrefix() + ".response";
    // If our question is named question<n>,
    // we look for properites called question<n>.answer0,
```

```
        // question<n>.answer1, and so on
        // until we fail to find one
        for(int j=0;
            (answer = props.getProperty(tmp1 + j)) != null;
            j++)
        {
          answers.addElement(answer);
          responses.addElement(props.getProperty(tmp2 + j));
        }
    }
    /**
     * MultipleQuestions render as a dropdown box of possible
     * answers
     */
    public void render(PrintWriter out) throws IOException {
      int i;
      out.println("<P>" + getText() + "</P>");
      out.println("<P><SELECT NAME=" + getPrefix() + ">");
      for(i=0;i<answers.size();i++) {
        out.println("<OPTION VALUE=" +
                    i +
                    ">" + answers.elementAt(i));
      }
      out.println("</SELECT>");
      out.println("</P>");
    }
    /**
     * When a MultipleQuestion is played, it prints the user's
     * answer and the correct response. If the answer
     * was the right one, it increments the tally
     */
    public synchronized void play(Properties props,
                                  PrintWriter out,
                                  GameTallies tallies)
          throws IOException
    {
      String answer = props.getProperty(getPrefix());
      int i;
      int whichEntry = 0;
      tallies.incNumMultiple();
      if(answer != null) {
        whichEntry = Integer.parseInt(answer);
      }
      if(whichEntry == rightAnswer) tallies.incNumRight();
      out.println("<P>");
      out.println(getText());
      out.println("You said: " +
                  answers.elementAt(whichEntry) + "<BR>");
      out.println(responses.elementAt(whichEntry).toString());
      out.println("</P>");
    }
}
```

Listing 9.18 OpenQuestion class.

```java
import java.io.*;
import java.util.*;
/**
 * An open question is a question without a fixed set
 * of predefined answers. Users can respond with anything,
 * and the question keeps a list of responses with
 * an associated count of how many times each response
 * has been given. When played, this question prints
 * the top ten answers
 */
public class OpenQuestion extends Question {
  /**
   * All the answers we've seen, mapped to counts of how
   * many times we've seen them
   */
  private Hashtable answers;
  /**
   * The keys from the answers Hashtable, sorted by number
   * of times each has been given
   */
  private String sortedAnswers[];
  /**
   * Sets up the answers Hashtable
   */
  public OpenQuestion(String prefix,Properties props) {
    super(prefix,props);
    answers = new Hashtable();
  }

  /**
   * OpenQuestions render as a simple text input box
   */
  public void render(PrintWriter out) throws IOException
  {
    out.println("<P>" + getText() + "</P>");
    out.println("<P><INPUT TYPE=TEXT NAME=" +
                getPrefix() + "></P>");
  }
  /**
   * When an OpenQuestion is played, the entry for the
   * answer given is incremented or set to 1 if this is
   * the first time it has been seen. The sorted array
   * is then resorted, and the top answers are printed
   */
  public void play(Properties props,
                   PrintWriter out,
                   GameTallies tallies)
        throws IOException
  {
    String answer = props.getProperty(getPrefix());
    int i;
    if(answer != null) {
```

```
        Integer entryCount = (Integer) answers.get(answer);
        if(entryCount == null) {
          entryCount = new Integer(1);
        } else {
          entryCount = new Integer(entryCount.intValue() + 1);
        }
        answers.put(answer,entryCount);
      }
      sortAnswers();
      // We can't print the top ten if we've seen fewer than
      // ten different answers
      int howMany = (sortedAnswers.length < 10) ?
        sortedAnswers.length : 10;
      out.println("<P>" + getText() + "</P>");
      out.println("Top " + howMany + " answers:");
      out.println("<UL>");
      for(i=0;i<howMany;i++) {
        out.println("<LI>" + sortedAnswers[i] + " (" +
                    answers.get(sortedAnswers[i]) + ")");
      }
      out.println("</UL>");
      out.println("You said: " + answer);
    }
    /**
     * Resorts the sortedAnswers table, using a simple bubble sort
     */
    private void sortAnswers() {
      int i,j;
      int count1;
      int count2;
      String tmp;
      int numAnswers    = answers.size();
      sortedAnswers     = new String[numAnswers];
      Enumeration keys = answers.keys();
      i=0;
      while(keys.hasMoreElements()) {
        sortedAnswers[i++] = (String) keys.nextElement();
      }
      for(i=0;i<numAnswers;i++) {
        for(j=0;j<numAnswers;j++) {
          count1 = ((Integer)
                    answers.get(sortedAnswers[i])).intValue();
          count2 = ((Integer)
                    answers.get(sortedAnswers[j])).intValue();
          if(count2 < count1) {
            tmp               = sortedAnswers[i];
            sortedAnswers[i] = sortedAnswers[j];
            sortedAnswers[j] = tmp;
          }
        }
      }
    }
  }
}
```

Listing 9.19   ScoredQuestion class.

```java
import java.io.*;
import java.util.*;
/**
 * A ScoredQuestion has a fixed set of responses,
 * each of which has an associated score. When played,
 * it adds the appropriate score to the tally
 */
public class ScoredQuestion extends Question {
  /**
   * All possible answers
   */
  Vector answers;
  /**
   * The scores associated with each answer
   */
  Vector scores;
  /**
   * The maximum score for this question, which is needed
   * for the final 'you scored n out of m possible points'
   * message
   */
  int maxScore;
  /**
   * The constructor sets up the answers and scores vectors
   */
  public ScoredQuestion(String prefix,Properties props) {
    super(prefix,props);

    answers  = new Vector();
    scores   = new Vector();
    maxScore = 0;
    String res;
    String score;
    int    iscore;
    String tmp1 = getPrefix() + ".answer";
    String tmp2 = getPrefix() + ".score";
    // If our question is named question<n>, we look for
    // properites called question<n>.answer0,
    // question<n>.answer1, and so on
    // until we fail to find one.
    for(int j=0;
        (res = props.getProperty(tmp1 + j)) != null;
        j++)
    {
      answers.addElement(res);
      score = props.getProperty(tmp2 + j);
      if(score != null) {
        iscore = Integer.parseInt(score);
        if(iscore > maxScore) maxScore = iscore;
      } else {
        iscore = 0;
```

```
        }
        scores.addElement(new Integer(iscore));
    }
}
/**
 * ScoredQuestions render as a drop-down menu of
 * possible answers
 */
public void render(PrintWriter out) throws IOException {
    int i;
    out.println("<P>" + getText() + "</P>");
    out.println("<P><SELECT NAME=" + getPrefix() + ">");
    for(i=0;i<answers.size();i++) {
        out.println("<OPTION VALUE=" + i + ">" +
                    answers.elementAt(i));
    }
    out.println("</SELECT>");
    out.println("</P>");
}
/**
 * When playing a ScoredQuestion, the appropriate score and
 * the maximum possible score are added to the
 * running tallies
 */
public synchronized void play(Properties props,
                              PrintWriter out,
                              GameTallies tallies)
        throws IOException
{
    String answer = props.getProperty(getPrefix());
    int i;
    int whichEntry = 0;
    tallies.incMaxScore(maxScore);

    if(answer != null) {
        whichEntry = Integer.parseInt(answer);
    }
    tallies.incScore(
        ((Integer) scores.elementAt(whichEntry)).intValue());
    out.println("<P>");
    out.println(getText());
    out.println("You said: " +
                answers.elementAt(whichEntry));
    out.println(" which is worth " +
                scores.elementAt(whichEntry) +
                " points");
    out.println("</P>");
    }
}
```

Listing 9.20   GameTallies class.

```java
import java.io.*;
import java.util.*;
/**
 * A utility class to keep track of various tallies,
 * such as number of
 * right answers and cumulative score.
 */
class GameTallies {
  private int maxScore;
  private int score;
  private int numMultiple;
  private int numRight;
  public GameTallies() {
    maxScore    = 0;
    score       = 0;
    numMultiple = 0;
    numRight    = 0;
  }
  public void incNumMultiple()      {numMultiple++;}
  public void incNumRight()         {numRight++;}
  public int getNumMultiple()       {return numMultiple;}
  public int getNumRight()          {return numRight;}
  public void incScore(int add)     {score += add;}
  public void incMaxScore(int add)  {maxScore += add;}
  public int getScore()             {return score;}
  public int getMaxScore()          {return maxScore;}
}
```

That completes our introduction to the Game application. Compile the classes, place them somewhere in the class path, start up the administration tool, and set up some parameters. Have fun!

Conclusion

That should be all the information necessary for entering the exciting world of servlets: the classes that make up the servlet package and how they relate to each other, the servlet life cycle and methods, and a handful of programming tips.

One of the hardest parts of writing servlets is making them thread safe, that is, ensuring that many threads can be in the service() method at once. This is critical for good performance and well-behaved code, but it is a topic that is complex enough to warrant a whole separate chapter to really do it justice. Fortunately, that very chapter is coming up next.

CHAPTER 10

Writing Thread-Safe Code

Without a doubt, threads are the hardest part of servlet programming. If you have heard that Java makes threads easy, don't feel bad if you still have trouble with them. Threads are just plain hard to understand. But once you do understand them, Java makes them easier to work with than most other languages do.

A lot of people skip over thread chapters in Java books because they think they can write good programs without understanding threads. But if we are going to write servlets, we have to bite the bullet. The Java Web Server makes extensive use of threads, so we won't be accomplished servlet programmers until we thoroughly understand them. That doesn't mean we have to stop writing servlets until we become expert. While we are learning, we can do two things to make sure servlets work with threads.

First, we make our servlet class implement the `javax.servlet.Single-ThreadModel` interface.[1] There aren't any methods in that interface: It is just a way to tell the Java Web Server (JWS) not to send more than one thread at a time through an instance of the servlet. Second, if there are any class (static) fields, they should either be changed to object fields or made final. These two steps will make a servlet safe for threads. Of course, there is a cost. The `SingleThreadModel` interface makes servlets slower and less efficient. We don't really recommend using it; we're only telling you that the option is there.

Before we get into the nitty-gritty of threads, let's look at a little history. In the early days of computing, operating systems were like playgrounds after school, and programs were like kids. Nice kids are supposed to play together

---

[1] If you don't know about Java interfaces, now would be a good time to read Chapter 4 of the Ken Arnold and James Gosling book (see Appendix for publication details).

politely and not bother anyone else; if a bully interferes with the nice kids' game, there is no teacher around to stop him.

Way back when, operating systems didn't control access to shared resources like memory or printers. A program could be chugging away when all of a sudden another program could write to its memory and corrupt it. A program could be in the middle of sending a file to the printer when another program tried to print; their output would both end up on the same piece of paper, completely garbled. It was rare for someone to deliberately write a bully program, but not rare at all for someone to write a program that went haywire and accidentally harmed other programs. Programmers had to work together to make sure their programs cooperated with each other to share everything, and that was a lot of overhead.

To take this burden off the shoulders of regular programmers, newer operating systems began to control access to shared resources and to build walls between programs to keep them from interfering with each other. Today, modern operating systems build such strong walls that it is difficult for programs to interact with each other at all, and even Windows NT rarely lets a badly written application crash the whole machine. Programmers don't have to worry much about sharing the computer's resources; the OS takes care of that for them.

Unfortunately, there were some unintended consequences of this good idea. For instance, the operating system spends so much time and memory keeping track of each individual program that it takes a while to start a new one. Actually, starting a single new program isn't too bad, but starting 50 programs is terrible. Also, sometimes we want programs to work closely with each other, and we'd like them to be able to exchange data just by changing each other's variables.

To address these issues, operating system designers came up with a way for one program to do several things at once without creating several new copies of itself. Now a program can start a new thread of control. One program can have many threads that share memory and other resources. Also, it is relatively inexpensive to start a new thread. The downside? We are right back where programmers were 40 years ago. If we use threads, we have to write code like our grandfathers did—very carefully—to make sure that one thread doesn't change any memory while another thread is using it.

Thread Basics

So what is a thread? Have you ever read a program listing to figure out what the program does? You start from the beginning, putting your finger on the first line of code, reading it, and then moving to the next line. You skip some lines when you come to if-then-elses and repeat some lines in while loops. You might keep track of what's in the variables on a piece of scratch paper. You can think of your finger as a thread. A thread executes a single stream of instructions. Simple, isn't it? Most programs are single threaded—in other words, you need only one finger to read them, and you never have to worry about somebody else writing on your scratch paper (memory) at the same time you are.

Most of the time, a single-threaded program is good enough. Unfortunately, it does not scale well. As an example, imagine that you want to write a simple Web server (see Listing 10.1). You write code that opens a socket on port 80 and then starts a loop, where it waits for a browser to connect to the socket, read the URL to see what file the browser asks for, read the file, and finally write the file out to the socket. At the end of the loop, it starts over again, listening at the socket.

Listing 10.1 BadServer and ConnHandler.

```
public class BadServer  {

    public static void main(String argv[])  {
        ServerSocket incoming = new ServerSocket(80);

        while (true)  {
            Socket       s = incoming.accept();    // fast
            ConnHandler c = new ConnHandler(s);    // fast
            c.processRequest();                    // slow
        }
    }
}


class ConnHandler  {

    ConnHandler(Socket s)  {
        ...
    }

    void processRequest()  {
        ...
    }
}
```

That's all you need—as long as only one person at a time wants to browse your Web site. If two requests come in one after the other, the second has to wait for the first request to finish. That isn't too bad, but what if 25 requests come in close together? The last browser in line will have to wait a long time. In other words, this Web server design doesn't scale well past two simultaneous users.

The reason multithreaded programs tend to scale better than single-threaded ones is because they use the CPU much more efficiently. In the single-

threaded Web server, the CPU spends most of its time waiting around. It waits
to read the URL from the socket (which, depending on the network connection,
could take a long time), it waits to read the HTML file from disk, and it waits
while writing the file out over the network to the browser. What a waste! The
CPU could be doing something in that dead time. It could be executing another
thread.

A multithreaded web server would work pretty much the same way as a
single-threaded one (see Listing 10.2). First, one thread would open a socket on
port 80 and start listening for requests. However, when a request came in, this
master thread would not enter a loop; it would just start a new thread to handle the request and go right back to listening at the socket. The new thread
would handle the request with code that used to be in a loop and then die when
it was finished. That way, if the first request is only halfway through when the
second one comes in, the master thread just starts a new thread to handle it. If
25 requests come in, it starts 25 threads.

Listing 10.2   BetterServer and ConnHandler.

```
public class BetterServer  {

    public static void main(String argv[])  {
        ServerSocket incoming = new ServerSocket(80);

        while (true)  {
            Socket      s = incoming.accept();    // fast
            ConnHandler c = new ConnHandler(s);   // fast
            Thread      t = new Thread(c);        // fast
            t.start();         // starts the new thread, returns
                               // immediately--fast.
        }
    }
}


class ConnHandler implements Runnable  {

    ConnHandler(Socket s)  {
        ...
    }

    void run()  {
        processRequest();  // This method is still slow, but now
                           // it won't slow down the main loop
    }

    void processRequest()  {
        ...
    }
}
```

To trace the execution of this program, it isn't enough to move your finger line by line. You need several fingers. Finger one starts in `BetterServer.main()` with the line that opens a socket on port 80, then enters a loop that accepts a new request, creates a connection handler to answer the request, creates a new thread to run the connection handler code, and then starts that thread. At this point, finger one goes back to the beginning of the loop, but you need another finger to start following the code in `ConnHandler.run()`. Finger two traces through the code in `ConnHandler.processRequest()` while finger one keeps spawning new threads in `BetterServer.main()`. Each new thread requires yet another finger. Multithreaded (or concurrent) programming might use the computer's resources more efficiently, but it is definitely harder to follow.

If the computer has two CPUs, one thread can run on one CPU and the other thread can run on the other. But if it has only one CPU, the threads take turns. (To put it less gently, threads preempt each other.) When one thread starts reading a file, it can go to sleep for a few milliseconds while it waits for the slow disk. During that time, other threads can use the CPU, and when the first thread's turn comes again, the first few blocks of the file are right there in memory. The thread won't even know it was asleep during the read. You might have some older relatives who do the same thing while reading the morning paper.

The point is that disk and network I/O cause so many delays that there is enough time for hundreds of threads to run at once without straining the CPU. (Multithreading also uses modern disk controllers more efficiently, since they can schedule many concurrent disk reads to take just a little bit longer than a single read.) Multithreaded programs are so much more efficient than single-threaded ones that sometimes they can do ten times as much with only 10 percent more work from the computer.

Multithreading Problems: Resource Contention and Race Conditions

Writing a multithreaded program is hard—that's the catch to threads. Even writing code that won't malfunction in a multithreaded environment (thread-safe code) is hard. It is so hard that no one ever gets it right on the first try, and most people give up in frustration before they ever learn to master threads.

Why is it so difficult? Because threads can interfere with each other. Doesn't sound too bad, does it? All we have to do is avoid writing threads that bother other threads, right? Wrong! Programmers don't write threads, they write code that threads execute. That is a subtle distinction, but it is a very important one. In the Web server example, `ConnHandler.processRequest()` is just plain Java code. It doesn't have to adhere to any kind of thread API in order to be used in a multithreaded context. In fact, the programmer who wrote it might not have even known how it would be used.

We cannot run just any code within a multithreaded environment (like a servlet). Code that works fine in a single-threaded environment may fail miserably in a multithreaded environment. Single-threaded code is like an only child; it takes what it wants when it wants it. If it wants a one-of-a-kind resource, fine, since it is the only one around to use it. On the other hand, many threads that want to use a single resource are just as bad as a room full of toddlers with only one Furby. This situation is called *resource contention.*

For instance, say we have a database connection object that takes queries, sends them to a database server over a permanent connection, and returns the results. We know it works because we have used it in lots of applications. We should not be surprised if it returns garbled results when we use it in a servlet. One thread might be using the object to send its query when another thread comes along and uses the same method of the same object to send *its* query over the exact same connection. The database gets two queries together, so it returns either garbage or an error code.

This situation is a *race condition.* Whenever there is code that only one thread at a time can safely use, the thread has to *race* through the code as fast as it can before another thread shows up. A section of code where a race condition could occur is a *critical section.* To prevent race conditions, we have to ensure that only one thread at a time can run a critical section of code.

We could try adding a boolean flag, *available,* to the database connection object. Threads could set this field to tell each other when it was busy. (Since we are good OO programmers, we don't make it a public field; instead, we control access to it with public methods.) For instance,

```
if (dbConn.isAvailable()) {
    dbConn.setAvailable(false);
    response = dbConn.query(request);
    dbConn.setAvailable(true);
}
```

One thread would be able to tell when another thread was sending a query and wouldn't interfere. But what if two threads get to the first line at the same time and see that the connection is available? If they both get inside the if block, another race condition occurs.

Let's think this through. Imagine that two threads are taking turns executing the code, one line at a time, and that no other threads are using the dbConn. First, thread A checks to see if isAvailable() returns true (Table 10.1). It is, so A proceeds to the next line of code. Second, thread B checks to see if isAvailable() returns true. It still does, so B goes to the next line. Third, A sets available to false (too late). Fourth, B sets available to false, even though it

Table 10.1   A *Race Condition* Timeline

Thread A . . .	Then Thread B . . .	`IsAvailable()` returns . . .
Checks `isAvailable()`	Checks `isAvailable()`	True
Calls `setAvailable(false)`	Calls `setAvailable(false)`	False
Calls `query(requestA)`	Calls `query(requestB)` at the same time	False

already is. Fifth, A starts sending its request. Sixth, B does the same thing, causing the query to fail for both of them. This is a race condition!

Clearly, flags are no good for protecting critical sections, since a thread can be pre-empted between checking and setting the flag. What we need is a way to make absolutely sure that two threads can't execute the same critical section of code at the same time. Java uses monitors to do this.

Java's Solution Is Monitors

Every Java object has a monitor. A *monitor* is something that allows only one thread at a time inside it. That makes it perfect for protecting critical sections of code. A section of code that should be run by only one thread at a time can be protected with a monitor. Don't worry; there is no `Monitor` class you have to learn about. You need to know only one word: *synchronized*. For instance, instead of

```
if (dbConn.isAvailable()) {
    dbConn.setAvailable(false);
    response = dbConn.query(request);
    dbConn.setAvailable(true);
}
```

we can say

```
synchronized (dbConn)     {
    response = dbConn.query(request);
}
```

This contrived example tells the Java compiler to generate bytecodes to enter the monitor of the `dbConn` object, run its `query()` method, and then exit the monitor. If you compile the example code and disassemble the bytecodes with `javap`, you will see the `monitorenter` and `monitorexit` instructions around the method call (this is not the case with synchronized methods, discussed later in this chapter).

When a thread A executes a `monitorenter` command on an object, the Java virtual machine checks to see if there is some other thread B already inside that object's monitor. If there is, then A's call to `monitorenter` blocks. Once thread B exits the monitor, thread A enters and `monitorenter` completes.

But isn't `monitorenter` basically the same as our flag idea earlier? You check a condition and then do something about it, so why isn't it a race condition here? Because Java guarantees that `monitorenter` is atomic. In other words, a thread can't be preempted right in the middle of a `monitorenter` instruction, between the check and the execution.

Why did the creators of Java decide to hide monitors from us? Don't they trust us? No, they don't. We're the ones who can't manage our own memory, remember? They know we would put `monitorenter` statements in our code, forget to put in corresponding `monitorexits`, and so end up with threads that never left certain monitors. Also, they know we would get confused with multiply nested `monitorenters` and `monitorexits`. And we would, too. Thank goodness they chose the synchronized keyword. It makes it very easy to see where a thread enters a monitor and where it exits. It also makes it impossible to have a `monitorenter` without a matching `monitorexit`, and vice versa. To do so would mean leaving out a curly brace, and the Java compiler won't let us do that.

A metaphor for monitors might be a public toilet stall: many can enter, but only one at a time, and nothing can interrupt what is going on in there. However, there is a little more to monitors than that. First, a thread can be in more than one monitor at a time. It might do that if it wanted to use two objects and didn't want any other thread to interfere with either one of them. Second, a thread can enter the same monitor more than once. That is to say, monitors are reentrant. That seems even less useful, but there is a good reason for it.

To return to our example, say that the `query()` method contains a block of code synchronized on the `dbConn` object. Since the method call is already in a synchronized block, the thread is already in the monitor when it executes the method. What happens when it gets to the nested `monitorenter` call? The thread just enters the monitor again. However, if monitors weren't reentrant, the thread would wait forever; it couldn't release the monitor until it finished the `query()` method, and it couldn't finish the `query()` method until it released the monitor. That kind of situation is called *deadlock,* and it is bad news. Fortunately, monitors are reentrant, so we have to worry about deadlock only when two or more threads each have a monitor another one wants.

Here's something that may be surprising. When one thread enters an object's monitor, other threads can still use the object. One of the biggest misconceptions about monitors is that they somehow guarantee exclusive access to their objects. They don't. Java promises that only one thread can execute a block of code that is synchronized on an object, but if that object has any code that isn't synchronized, as many threads as want to can run that code. For instance, if the `dbConn` object has two methods with signatures `public boolean isConnected()` and `public synchronized void connect()`, only one thread at a time can run `connect()`. However, many threads can run `isConnected()`, even if another thread is running `connect()` at the same time.

Threads have to enter the object's monitor to execute `connect()`, but there is no monitor required to run `isConnected()`. Also, synchronization protects only code, not data. There is no way to synchronize a field, so if there is a non-final public field in a class, there is no way to keep many threads from changing it at the same time. That's one of the reasons good object-oriented programmers use `getX()` and `setX()` methods instead of making some field `X` public. The lesson here is that if an object has any unsynchronized blocks of code or unprotected fields, then any thread can use them, even if another thread is in that object's monitor.

Don't feel bad if you are struggling with the concept of monitors. There probably is no real-world analogy that could capture all the different aspects of monitors (clearly the toilet stall is sadly inadequate). Most Java books do not even talk about monitors; they say that every Java object has a lock and that the synchronize keyword "obtains the lock" or "locks the object." A lock probably is not a good analogy. For instance, if someone says that a thread has locked an object, we naturally think that no other thread can use the object, but that is not true. If a thread has locked an object, no other thread can lock it, but any thread can read or write the object's public fields and run the object's unsynchronized code.

The only way to completely lock an object is to synchronize every one of its methods and protect all its fields so that no other object can use them. This is one of the most widespread misconceptions about Java synchronization, and it stems from the misleading term, *lock*. Unfortunately, the term has become standard usage, and no one, not even Bill Gates, can change it now. Well, maybe someone could, but we certainly cannot. So we say "lock" in this book even though we do not really mean *lock*.

Deadlock Is the Problem with Monitors

Deadlocks are bad news. The technical definition of a *deadlock* goes something like this: Deadlock is the state that occurs when a set of two or more threads of execution are blocked indefinitely, each waiting for another thread in the set to give up exclusive access to a shared resource. In other words, deadlock

happens when some threads that are already in monitors try to get into each
other's monitors, too. Here's an example.

Say the program that uses the dbConn object also has a dbLog object to control access to its log. The synchronized dbConn.query() method calls the synchronized dbLog.write() method to record every query. Now say dbLog has
another synchronized method, recordErrors(), that calls the synchronized
method dbConn.checkForErrors(). A deadlock can occur if a thread calls
dbConn.query() at about the same time another thread calls dbLog.record-
Errors(). Table 10.2 shows why. Since each thread is waiting for the other, neither does anything; they just sit there waiting forever. That is deadlock.

It often happens that there are several threads involved in a cycle like this,
so it can be very difficult to figure out what causes a deadlock. Even worse,
sometimes it's not evident that a deadlock has occurred. An application can be
running along just fine, when suddenly all or part of it freezes up. There is
no error message or any other external indication. If a problem like this occurs
and we suspect deadlock, the JDK's program can provide a thread dump: hit
Ctrl-\ on Solaris and Ctrl-<Break> on Windows.

A thread dump is a lot of output, but we are interested only in the Monitor
Cache section, which looks something like this.

```
Monitor Cache Dump:
    dbConn@1080376832/1080782608: owner "Thread A"(0x413b5f04,
        1 entry)
      Waiting to enter:
        "Thread B" (0x413d6f04)
    dbLog@1080376816/1080782720: owner "Thread B" (0x413d6f04,
        1 entry)
      Waiting to enter:
        "Thread A" (0x413b5f04)
```

If there are several threads in monitors, it is helpful to draw a diagram of which
threads hold which monitors and which threads are waiting to get into which

Table 10.2   Deadlock Timeline

Thread action	Monitor result
Thread A runs dbConn.query()	Thread A enters the dbConn monitor
Thread B runs dbLog.recordErrors()	Thread B enters the dbLog monitor
Thread A tries dbLog.write()	Thread A tries to enter dbLog monitor, waits for B to leave.
Thread B tries dbConn.checkForErrors()	Thread B tries to enter dbConn monitor, waits for A to leave.

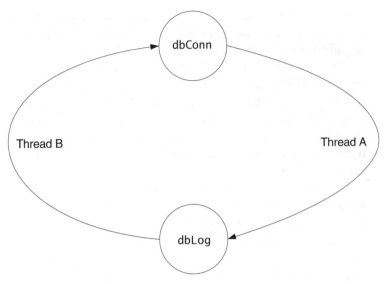

Figure 10.1   Deadlock

monitors. In the example, the diagram would look like Figure 10.1. Just by looking at it, we can see a deadlock.

Some databases can automatically detect deadlocks and fix them, but it is harder to do than it seems and requires a lot of overhead, so Java does not even attempt it. If a program causes a deadlock, it is up to us to figure it out and fix it. That takes all the luck we can get. Now that we have gone over the background, let's go on with some concrete details.

Java Language Specifics: Thread Class and Runnable Interface

If you are interested only in writing servlets, you can skip this section and go on to the next one. Here, we deal with starting new threads, which is not required reading for servlet developers. In fact, it is a pretty bad idea to start new threads from within servlets unless we really *really* know what we are doing. Since the servlet code is already running in a thread created by the Java Web Server, we probably won't derive any benefit from starting a new thread anyway.

To actually start creating threads, we have to know about two things: the `java.lang.Thread` class and the `java.lang.Runnable` interface. The Thread class has a constructor that takes a Runnable argument and a method called `start()`. The Runnable interface is pretty simple—it has only one method, called `run()`, that takes no arguments and returns nothing. `run()` is basically a thread's main() method. To write a Runnable class, we need to know that the first line of code in run() is the first thing a thread will do and that the last line of code in run() is the last thing the thread will do.

When we have written a Runnable class, we are ready to start a new thread. This is done in Java by constructing an object of the class and then constructing a new Thread instance with the object as a constructor argument. Once we have the Thread object, we call its start() method. start() calls your object's run() method, which then executes in its own thread. When run() returns (or something within run() throws an exception that run() doesn't catch), the thread dies.

For the sake of completeness, there is another way to start threads, even though we do not recommend it. Some people subclass java.lang.Thread and override Thread's run() method, which does nothing. Then they construct an instance of the subclass without a Runnable object so that when they start() the instance, it uses its own run() method. One good thing about this way of starting threads is that only one object is needed, not two. The bad thing is that once we start subclassing Thread, we are tempted to override more than just run(). For instance, some people override the constructor and call start() from it. It makes sense to them that a Thread should start running as soon as it is created. However, that doesn't make sense to other people, who are surprised when that happens. Once we start interfering with the basic functionality of Thread, we ensure that other programmers won't be able to reuse the code easily.

While we are on the subject of what not to do, *DON'T USE* stop() *OR* suspend()! JDK 1.2 calls those Thread methods "deprecated," but we really shouldn't use them with any version of Java. If we call stop() on a Thread, it immediately gives up its monitors and dies. If it is right in the middle of something and doesn't try to catch the ThreadDeath error to clean things up, then it may leave one or more objects in an inconsistent state. Even if the code does catch ThreadDeath, it probably isn't clear exactly where the thread died, making cleanup difficult.

As bad as stop() is, suspend() is even worse: A suspended Thread doesn't give up its monitors. If the Thread is getting memory out of the heap when it is suspend()ed, the heap locks permanently, and no other Thread can allocate any more memory.

If an application requires stopping and/or suspending threads, we should add methods to the Runnable class that set boolean flags so that the main code (in run() or called from run()) can check to see if a stop or suspension has been requested. The code should then tidy things up before stopping or suspending itself. It should not stop or suspend while it has a monitor. That is a lot of extra work, but it is better than using Thread's stop() or suspend().

Servlet Thread Model

Now might be a good time to review the Servlet Life Cycle section in Chapter 9. First, the servlet is instantiated. Under most conditions, only one instance of the servlet exists at any one time. Once it has been created, a single thread runs the `init()` method. As soon as `init()` completes successfully, and not before, one or more threads run the `service()` method. Remember that the default `service()` is what runs `doGet()` and `doPost()` and all the other `doX()` methods, as well as `getLastModified()`. When the Java Web Server decides that it is time to run `destroy()`, it makes sure that there are no threads still running `service()`, and then one thread runs `destroy()`. It may then start the cycle over again, but the JWS guarantees that only one thread will run `init()` and `destroy()`, whereas many threads will run `service()` and the other methods.

Now, if the servlet implements `javax.servlet.SingleThreadModel`, we never have to worry about more than one thread calling the same object's `service()` method at the same time. If a request comes in before the last one is finished, the Java Web Server creates a new instance of the object. We end up with as many instances of the class as there are simultaneous requests for it. This means that we do not need to protect object fields from race conditions: they are not shared by multiple threads. However, even though we now have several objects to work with, we still don't have a separate class for every thread, so class (static) fields are still shared.

`SingleThreadModel` does not guarantee that there will never be a race condition; it just promises that there will never be one with an object field. Class fields still need to be protected, unless they are final. There are other problems with `SingleThreadModel`. Creating a new instance and running its `init()` method takes time, so there can be a delay before incoming HTTP requests are fulfilled. It also increases the Java Web Server's memory consumption and overhead, since it has to keep track of all the copies of the `SingleThreadModel` servlets. Most people don't use `SingleThreadModel`.

Making Code Thread Safe

Thread-safe code is code that can be safely run in many threads at the same time, meaning that two threads running that code won't interfere with each other. Thread-safe code forces threads to take turns using shared resources such as sockets, buffers, or even simple integer fields. Every class and instance field is a shared resource. (Since every thread stores method parameters and local variables in its own private memory, we do not have to worry about them; see Chapter 11 for more information.)

Every method that reads or modifies a field is a potential critical section of code. Listing 10.3 is an example.

Listing 10.3   UnSafe.java.

```
public class UnSafe {
    long field;

    public void unSafeSetField(long newField) {
        field = newField;    // modifies field: critical section
    }

    public long unSafeGetField() {
        return field;        // reads field: critical section
    }

    public long safe(long a, long b) {
        long c;

        c = a + b;           // parameters and local variables
        return c;            // only, no fields: not critical
    }
}
```

NOTE: When one fully understands this section, he or she will be a competent Java threads programmer. To become even more competent, read the definitive reference *Concurrent Programming in Java: Design Principles and Patterns* by Lea. The rest of this section covers only a small part of the material presented in that mighty tome.

Immutable Objects Are Safe

If an object such as a string can't be changed after it has been created, then we don't have to worry about other threads changing it. A class whose instances don't change can be made immutable with a few simple modifications. First we make sure that all its nonfinal fields are hidden, and we give access to the fields through set() and get() methods. Public fields can be accessed by any code at all, thread safe or not.

Next we make sure that the class's constructors initialize every field. Once we've done that, we can take away the set() methods.

Finally, we make sure that no method changes any field. If we realize that there must be methods to change objects' (or classes') fields, then the class can't be made immutable. Listing 10.4 is an example of a class that can easily be made immutable. After going through the steps in Listing 10.4, we get Listing 10.5.

Listing 10.4 UnSafePoint.java.

```java
public class UnSafePoint {
    public double x, y;

    public void setX(double newX) {
        x = newX;
    }

    public void setY(double newY) {
        y = newY;
    }

    public double getX() {
        return x;
    }

    public double getY() {
        return y;
    }
}
```

Listing 10.5 ImmutablePoint.java.

```java
public class ImmutablePoint {
    private double x, y;

    public Point(double x, double y) {
        this.x = x;
        this.y = y;
    }
    public double getX() {
        return x;
    }

    public double getY() {
        return y;
    }
}
```

Fully Synchronized Objects Are Safe

Objects that never change are all well and good, but in practice most classes cannot be made immutable without losing too much functionality. What do we do with those? The brute-force method is to make every field private and then synchronize every single method. What does "synchronize every single method" mean? If we do not have any class (static) methods, it means "put the synchronized keyword in front of all method declarations." A thread must lock the object before it can execute an object's synchronized method. Putting the synchronized keyword in a method declaration is equivalent to putting the whole method body inside a `synchronized(this)` block. (But not exactly the same: synchronized methods don't use `monitorenter` or `monitorexit` byte-codes—the Java virtual machine (JVM) takes care of monitor management in this case.)

For class methods, synchronized methods lock the whole class. If a class has a mixture of instance and class methods, putting the synchronized keyword in front of both won't work because they are getting two different locks, the class's lock and the object's lock. To get around that, we synchronize the class methods and change the instance methods so that the whole body of each method is in a `synchronized(getClass())` block (see Listing 10.6). That way, both class and instance methods are synchronizing on the same thing: the class. As long as no fields are exposed, the only way to change an object's state is through methods, and if every one of them is synchronized, we are perfectly safe.

Listing 10.6   `FullySynchronizedPoint.java`.

```
public class FullySynchronizedPoint {
    private double x, y;

    public synchronized void setX(double newX) {
        x = newX;
    }

    public synchronized void setY(double newY) {
        y = newY;
    }

    public synchronized double getX() {
        return x;
    }

    public synchronized double getY() {
        return y;
    }
}
```

Full synchronization is the easiest way to ensure thread safety, but it is not recommended for many cases. First of all, lots of synchronization slows down the code. Second, the looser we are with synchronization, the greater the like-lihood of deadlock. Finally, it's just not very elegant.

Objects Contained by Safe Objects Are Safe

A contained object is one that is kept in a nonpublic field of another object and that cannot be directly accessed by any object except its containing object: a reference to it can't be returned by a get() method, for example. If only one thread can manipulate it at a time, it becomes thread safe automatically. If it turns out that only one class ever needs to use this unsafe object, we can make that class thread safe and completely contain the unsafe object within it. Listing 10.7 is an example.

Listing 10.7 LineSegment.java.

```java
public class LineSegment {
    private UnSafePoint begin, end;

    public LineSegment() {
        begin = new UnSafePoint();
        end = new UnSafePoint();
    }

    public synchronized void setBeginPoint(double i, double j) {
        begin.setX(i);
        begin.setY(j);
    }

    public synchronized void setEndPoint(double k, double l) {
        end.setX(k);
        end.setY(l);
    }

    public synchronized void getBeginX() {
        return begin.getX(i);
    }

    public synchronized void getBeginY() {
        return begin.getX(i);
    }

    public synchronized void getEndX() {
        return end.getX(i);
    }

    public synchronized void getEndY() {
        return end.getX(i);
    }
}
```

LineSegment is fully synchronized, and because the UnSafePoint()s are completely contained, there is no way for two different threads to concurrently manipulate an UnSafePoint(). Containment is an especially good strategy for classes that are not thread safe but that cannot be changed (for instance, third-party classes whose methods are all final).

Making Code Thread Hot

It should be clear by now that multithreaded programming is the way to go for high-performance applications. All those threads competing for the CPU and other resources ensure that very few resources are wasted. Making the application thread safe takes work, but the advantages of threads are worth the effort. (Of course, if we are writing servlets, we do not have much choice.) Once code is safe for threads, it can be made optimal for threads. Such optimized code is called *thread hot.*

Why isn't thread safe good enough? Why don't programmers just synchronize everything? For one thing, if every piece of code is synchronized, then we are back to single-threaded code. Actually, we are worse off, because in the reference implementation of the Java virtual machine, too much synchronization makes code extremely slow. Java doesn't create a monitor every time it creates an object. Since few objects ever use their monitors, that would be a waste. Therefore, Java creates a monitor only when it is needed. It keeps track of which monitor belongs to which object in a monitor cache. To add a new monitor to the cache or even to look inside the cache, Java must lock and unlock it (since the cache is a shared resource). While this scheme conserves memory, locking and unlocking make for significant overhead. If 20 threads are all trying to enter monitors at the same time, *even if they are different monitors,* then the monitor cache has to be locked and unlocked 19 times before the last thread gets a chance. Sun's current Java implementations (those since JDK version 1.1.5) give each thread a local cache, which they can use for monitor lookups without having to lock or unlock anything.

With a superoptimized Java implementation, such as Sun's HotSpot, synchronization is not nearly so slow. However, it is true for all implementations that if threads are doing a lot of synchronization with different objects, deadlock becomes more likely. So the key to making code thread hot is to first make it thread safe, then take away as much synchronization as possible without making it unsafe.

Obviously, "removing unnecessary synchronization" is not as easy as it seems. If the class is completely synchronized, then chances are good that some of the synchronization can be deleted while maintaining thread safety. But which synchronization must be decided on a case-by-case basis. For instance,

```
private int employeeSalary;

public synchronized void setEmployeeSalary(int salary) {
```

```
        this.employeeSalary = salary;
    }

    public synchronized int getEmployeeSalary() {
        return this.employeeSalary;
    }
```

We might think that the set method should be synchronized because two threads might try to write to the same variable at once, and that variable would have garbage as the result. On the contrary. The Java virtual machine guarantees that `int` assignments are atomic; if you assign any value of type `byte`, `char`, `short`, `int`, `float`, or `reference`, that assignment cannot be interrupted or interfered with in any way. (`boolean` is implementation-dependent.) If the line

```
        this.employeeSalary = salary;
```

were executed by two threads at exactly the same time, Java would make sure that one whole value and then another would be assigned to `employeeSalary`. It would not allow `employeeSalary` to end up with the two high bytes of one thread's salary and two low bytes of another thread's salary. Java guarantees that multiple threads cannot write anything smaller than a `double` or `long` to the same memory location at the same time.

So we do not have to worry about two `set()`s hurting each other. Moreover, we do not need synchronization to keep the `get` from happening right in the middle of the `set`. For the same reason that two `writes` cannot be done at once, a `read` cannot be done halfway through a `write`. All this means is that we can mix `sets` and `gets` without getting weird numbers. And that means that we can take the synchronization away from these two methods.

Before leaving this example, however, we should discuss the volatile keyword. Most people just ignore it because it does not do anything in Sun's current JVM implementation. However, it might become important in future versions of Java. On multiprocessor systems, different threads can sometimes run on different CPUs. One day, frequently accessed fields may be copied from main memory into a CPU's cache so that they can be used more efficiently. If that happens, Java will need a way to specify when fields can be copied into or out of a CPU cache.

No one knows exactly how that will work, but right now it looks as if regular fields will be copied into the cache when a thread enters a monitor and copied back to main memory when the thread leaves a monitor. Volatile fields will be copied every time they are used. Therefore, it is a good idea to declare a field volatile if it is used in a multithreaded context in unsynchronized code. It won't make a difference now, but it might keep code running smoothly in future versions of Java.

This is our thread-hot version of `setEmployeeSalary()` and `getEmployee-Salary()`.

```
private volatile int employeeSalary;

public void setEmployeeSalary(int salary) {
    this.employeeSalary = salary;
}

public int getEmployeeSalary() {
    return this.employeeSalary;
}
```

What about these methods?

```
private long managerSalary;

public synchronized void setManagerSalary(long salary) {
    this.managerSalary = salary;
}

public synchronized long getManagerSalary() {
    return this.managerSalary;
}
```

We cannot take the synchronization away from these methods because Java does not guarantee the atomicity of `long`s or `double`s. The assignments might be atomic on some platforms, but they aren't necessarily so on every platform; therefore the methods still need to be synchronized. If two `setManager-Salary()`s were done at once, the first thread might write the high 32 bits and then the low, and the second thread might write the low-order bits first, so a *race* condition could occur when `managerSalary` ends up with the high-order bits of one salary and the low-order bits of another.

In other words, if `setManagerSalary()` is called with two different values, we might end up with a third, completely different salary. Also, if a `set` and a `get` occur at the same time, the `set` might write 32 bits, then the `get` could get all 64 bits before the `set` wrote the last 32 bits. That means that the `get` could return a value that was a mixture of old and new salaries, not a valid salary at all.

An example is shown in Table 10.3. The call to `getSalary()` returns with `0x0000000100000004`, a combination of the old and new salaries. This is called a *transient value* because it is an invalid value that exists for only a little while. (Don't confuse this with Java's transient keyword.) Since we never want objects to return false values, synchronization cannot be removed from these methods. What about this?

```
public synchronized void setPoint(Point p) {
    this.point = p;
}
```

Table 10.3 Transient Value Caused by Race Condition

Thread A . . .	Thread B . . .	managerSalary has value . . .
Calls setSalary() with 0x0000000100000002	Calls getSalary()	0x0000000300000004
Thread writes high 4 bytes **0x00000001**	<pre-empted>	0x**0000000l**00000004
<pre-empted>	Thread reads all 8 bytes	0x0000000100000004
Thread writes low 4 bytes **0x00000002**		0x0000000l**00000002**

```
public synchronized Point getPoint() {
    return this.point;
}
```

This code can be safely unsynchronized because the Java virtual machine guarantees that object reference assignments are atomic. (Remember to declare object field point as volatile.) We could try to strip the synchronization using this:

```
public synchronized void setPoint(int x, int y) {
    this.x = x;
    this.y = y;
}
```

because we are dealing only with ints, but unfortunately we are dealing with *two* ints. If Thread A runs setPoint(1, 2) and Thread B runs setPoint(3, 4) at the same time, a race condition occurs. Table 10.4 shows one possible outcome. Even though Thread A calls setPoint() with (1, 2) and Thread B calls setPoint() with (3, 4), the point ends up with mismatched x and y values (1, 4). Whenever an object's fields conflict with each other, the object is said to be in an inconsistent state. Because that is something we want to avoid, we should not remove synchronization from this method.

Table 10.4 Inconsistent State Caused by Race Condition

Action	x is . . .	y is . . .
Thread B writes its x value	Set to 3	
Thread A writes its x value	Changed to 1	
Thread A writes its y value	unchanged(1)	Set to 2
Thread B writes its y value	unchanged(1)	Changed to 4

Thread Implementations

Although many programmers are still unfamiliar with threads, operating system designers have known about them for quite some time. Unfortunately, every OS that claims to support threads manages to do so in a slightly different way. Some operating systems, like DOS, do not even pretend to have threads. That makes it tough for the folks at Sun Microsystems to consistently port Java to different platforms. That's why green threads were created.

Green Threads

Some people think of the green threads package as a thread emulator. A program that runs in one OS-level thread can use the green threads package to create and manage its own program-level threads. The green threads package helps keep Java consistent across all platforms, even platforms that do not support multithreading. Because Java has full control over green threads, it can perform certain optimizations that are impossible with native threads, which are controlled by the underlying OS. Best of all (for developers), a green thread is much more lightweight than a native thread, which means that it requires less memory and is faster to create.

The green threads package does have its drawbacks. It cannot take advantage of more than one processor. Also, it requires the programmer to take a lot of responsibility for thread scheduling, which can be difficult for novice thread programmers. Many native thread implementations use *time slicing*, where each thread is given some small amount of time to run, then is put to sleep while another thread takes its turn. High-priority threads get more time than low-priority threads, but every thread typically gets some time. This is called *fair scheduling*. Time slicing and fair scheduling make it easy for beginners to write working programs. However, these policies can be frustrating to advanced programmers who want full control over scheduling, so many people prefer green threads scheduling to native threads scheduling.

Here is how green threads scheduling works. A high-priority thread preempts (interrupts) lower-priority threads. However, threads of equal priority do not usually preempt each other, so unless a running thread calls Thread.yield(), or performs some action that causes it to go to sleep for a while (like calling Thread.sleep()), it can inadvertently prevent all other equal- or lower-priority threads from ever running again. This is called *starvation*. Of course, lower-priority threads cannot preempt higher-priority threads, but even if the higher-priority threads call Thread.yield(), the green threads scheduler still will not allow lower-priority threads to run. To prevent low-priority threads from starving, high-priority threads need to sleep(), wait(), or perform some kind of I/O operation that keeps it waiting for a while.

Native Threads

Native threads are threads supported by the underlying operating system. Sun produces a native threads Java runtime for Solaris, as well as Windows 95, 98, and NT. Because these operating systems have fair, time-slicing thread schedulers, starvation is not normally a problem with native threads. Also, the threads of one process can usually run on different CPUs.

Solaris (SunOS 5)

The green threads Java runtime for Solaris that ships with the Java Web Server has been reported to exhibit strange behavior after running continuously for several days. The JWS startup scripts invoke Java with -noasyncgc, and some people say this has a salutary effect. To see for yourself, visit

http://developer.java.sun.com/developer/bugParade/bugs/4108795.html

Another problem is inconsistent behavior with blocking I/O. Luckily, network I/O works just fine. If a thread blocks while reading from a socket, other threads are unaffected. Unluckily, the same is not true for keyboard or named pipe I/O. If one thread tries to read from System.in or a FileInputReader opened on a named pipe, then *every single thread comes to a halt;* every single green thread stops running until the read call returns. According to Sun, the System.in problem is a problem with UNIX and therefore cannot be fixed. The named pipe problem, however, has been a bug in the JDK since 1.1, and it still existed at the time of this writing (1.1.6 and 1.2 beta 2). To see if your version of the JDK suffers from it, check the status of bug number 4040621 at the Java Developer's Connection,

http://developer.java.sun.com/developer/bugParade/bugs/4040621.html

If it does, make sure your servlets do not try to communicate with back-end processes through named pipes, or they could block the whole Java Web Server from running.

Threading and the Game Application

In Chapter 9, the GameServlet class, the entry point to the application, implemented the SingleThreadModel interface. This was a quick and easy way to ensure thread safety, but as this chapter has pointed out, we can definitely do better.

Let us consider what would happen if we just removed this interface. Looking over the code, we see that there are not many places where we would be in trouble. This is because most of the methods in most of the classes do not update any shared or global resources. The Question objects are created once, at init() time, and then never changed. There is a separate GameTallies object created for each request, which in turn means one per thread, so this is not a concern. The render() methods in the Question classes do not change any values, so they are safe. Likewise, most of the play() methods do not touch any shared data. It looks as if we are almost completely thread safe without having to do any extra work.

Unfortunately, the one notable exception is OpenQuestion's play() method. Consider this code, which updates the count for a given answer.

```
Integer entryCount = (Integer) answers.get(answer);
if(entryCount == null) {
    entryCount = new Integer(1);
} else {
    entryCount = new Integer(entryCount.intValue() + 1);
}
answers.put(answer,entryCount);
```

If two threads, A and B, come into this chunk of code at the same time with the same answer, the chain of events might look something like this:

Thread A gets the current value out of answers. Call this number N.
Thread B gets the current value out of answers.
Thread A creates a new Integer with value N+1
Thread B creates a new Integer with value N+1
Thread A updates the entry in the answers table to N+1
Thread B updates the entry in the answers table to N+1

The net result is that we have lost one vote for this answer. Note that the fact that the hash table's get() and put() methods are synchronized does not help us here, because the problem comes from the code between the get and put.

The sortAnswers() method presents another problem. If one thread is re-sorting the array while another is printing the results, they may print out in some random order. Even worse, if the printing thread happens to run just as the other thread gets to the sortedAnswers = new String[numAnswers] line, the printing thread may suddenly try to print a null string.

Now that we have isolated the potential thread problems in the application, we can think about how to fix them. One easy solution would be to synchronize OpenQuestion's play() method. Since sortAnswers() is called only from play(), this will fix all the thread problems at once. The downside is that any games that have an OpenQuestion will still essentially be single threaded, as each player may have to "wait in line" to play the OpenQuestion. On the other hand, if it is expected that few if any games will have such questions, this is not a bad solution.

However, users seem to like open questions. Nothing seems to draw users to a site faster than the ability to vote for something, like a favorite TV show, so it is worth figuring out a better solution.

We could try synchronizing just the parts of the code that present potential conflicts, such as the `sortAnswers()` method and the incrementing code presented. This will help—the less code that is wrapped in synchronized blocks, the smaller the chance that two or more threads will try to enter it at the same time and have to wait in line. However, there are large sections of the play code that would need to be protected, and most of the time will be spent in the `sortAnswers()` method anyway, so this approach does not get us far.

Unfortunately, as long as we are changing global data, we cannot do much better. However, there is an interesting trade-off we can make that will enable us to improve the situation. When a user plays an open question, it may not be important that the results seen are up-to-the-second accurate, as long as they are consistent. In other words, if 15 votes come in at the same time, it probably doesn't matter whether all 15 people see the version of the Top Ten list with all 15 votes counted. If each person sees only his or her vote, that's probably good enough.

This simple cheat makes a big difference. It means that we can now use a *local* version of the answers hash table and `sortAnswers()` array, which means that almost all the synchronization issues go away. In practice, this involves four steps.

1. Before doing anything else, the `play()` method makes a local copy of the answers hash table. This step is synchronized, to ensure that the two agree. The vote is added to this local copy.

2. A local sorted array is built, just like the global one was, and the results are printed.

3. The vote is then placed on a global "pending votes" list. This action is synchronized, since it changes global data.

4. An auxiliary thread periodically adds all the pending votes to the global answers and `sortedAnswers()`. It does this by also creating a local hash table, adding all the data from the pending list to this local table, sorting it, and then swapping the local ones for the global ones. Listing 10.8 is the new version of `OpenQuestion`.

Listing 10.8 `OpenQuestion.java`.

```
import java.io.*;
import java.util.*;
/**
```

```
 * An open question is a question without a fixed set of
 * predefined answers. Users can respond with anything,
 * and the question will keep a list of of responses, with
 * an associated count of how many times each response has
 * been given. When played, this question will print the
 * top ten answers
 */
public class OpenQuestion extends Question implements Runnable {
  /**
   * All the answers we've seen, mapped to counts of how
   * many times we've seen them
   */
  private transient Hashtable answers;
  /**
   * The keys from the answers hashtable, sorted by number
   * of times each has been given
   */
  private transient String sortedAnswers[];
  /**
   * Answers that are waiting to be processed
   */
  private Vector pending;
  /**
   * An auxiliary thread that will periodically take all
   * the pending answers and add them into the answers table
   */
  private Thread runner;
  /**
   * Sets up the answers Hashtable and the pending vector and
   * kicks off the new thread
   */
  public OpenQuestion(String prefix,Properties props) {
    super(prefix,props);
    answers = new Hashtable();
    pending = new Vector();
    runner  = new Thread(this);
    runner.start();
  }

  /**
   * OpenQuestions render as a simple text input box
   */
  public void render(PrintWriter out) throws IOException
  {
    out.println("<P>" + getText() + "</P>");
    out.println("<P><INPUT TYPE=TEXT NAME=" +
                getPrefix() +
                "></P>");
  }
  /**
   * When an OpenQuestion is played, the entry for the answer
   * given is incremented or set to 1 if this is the first
   * time it has been seen. The sorted array is then resorted
```

```
 * and the top answers are printed
 */
public void play(Properties props,
                 PrintWriter out,
                 GameTallies tallies)
     throws IOException
{
  String answer = props.getProperty(getPrefix());
  int i;
  // The local copies
  Hashtable myAnswers;
  String    mySortedAnswers[];
  // Copy the global data into our local variables
  synchronized(this) {
    myAnswers = (Hashtable) answers.clone();
  }
  if(answer != null) {
    Integer entryCount = (Integer) myAnswers.get(answer);
    if(entryCount == null) {
      entryCount = new Integer(1);
    } else {
      entryCount = new Integer(entryCount.intValue() + 1);
    }
    myAnswers.put(answer,entryCount);
  }
  mySortedAnswers = sortAnswers(myAnswers);
  // We can't print the top ten if we've seen fewer than
  // ten different answers
  int howMany = (mySortedAnswers.length < 10) ?
    mySortedAnswers.length : 10;
  out.println("<P>" + getText() + "</P>");
  out.println("Top " + howMany + " answers:");
  out.println("<UL>");
  for(i=0;i<howMany;i++) {
    out.println("<LI>" + mySortedAnswers[i] + " (" +
                myAnswers.get(mySortedAnswers[i]) + ")");
  }
  out.println("</UL>");
  out.println("You said: " + answer);
  // Finally, store the answer in the pending vector.  The
  // runner thread will eventually add it to the master list.
  // Note that this does not need to be explicitly synchronized,
  // because  addElement already is
  pending.addElement(answer);
}
/**
 * Once a minute, the run method takes all the pending
 * answers and adds them into the answer table, then
 * resorts everything
 */
public void run() {
  Vector    myPending;
  Hashtable myAnswers  = null;
```

```
String     mySortedAnswers[];
Integer    entryCount = null;
String     answer;
int        i;
while(runner != null) {
  try {Thread.sleep(60 * 1000);} catch (Exception e) {}
  //If there are no pending results, let's not waste
  // CPU cycles
  if(pending.size() == 0) continue;
  // Make a local copy of the pending list and answer
  // tables, and clear the global pending list. This
  // must be synchronized to ensure that no vote comes
  // in between making the local copy and creating
  // the new global one
  synchronized(this) {
    myPending = pending;
    pending   = new Vector();
    myAnswers = (Hashtable) answers.clone();
  }
  // Go through myPending, and add the elements to myAnswers
  for(i=0;i<myPending.size();i++) {
    answer     = (String)  myPending.elementAt(i);
    entryCount = (Integer) myAnswers.get(answer);
    if(entryCount == null) {
      myAnswers.put(answer,new Integer(1));
    } else {
      myAnswers.put(answer,
                    new Integer(entryCount.intValue() + 1));
    }
  }
  // Now sort the table
  mySortedAnswers  = sortAnswers(myAnswers);
  // Now replace the global answers and sortedAnswers
  // with our local copy. Again, this needs to be
  // synchronized to ensure that we don't mess up play()
  synchronized(this) {
    answers       = myAnswers;
    sortedAnswers = mySortedAnswers;
  }
 }
}
/**
 * Sorts the given Hashtable in order of the values
 */
private String[] sortAnswers(Hashtable myAnswers) {
  int i,j;
  int count1;
  int count2;
  String tmp;
  String mySortedAnswers[];
  int numAnswers      = myAnswers.size();
  mySortedAnswers     = new String[numAnswers];
  Enumeration keys = myAnswers.keys();
```

```
      i=0;
      while(keys.hasMoreElements()) {
        mySortedAnswers[i++] = (String) keys.nextElement();
      }
      for(i=0;i<numAnswers;i++) {
        for(j=0;j<numAnswers;j++) {
          count1 = ((Integer) myAnswers.get(mySortedAnswers[i])).
              intValue();
          count2 = ((Integer) myAnswers.get(mySortedAnswers[j])).
              intValue();
          if(count2 < count1) {
            tmp                  = mySortedAnswers[i];
            mySortedAnswers[i] = mySortedAnswers[j];
            mySortedAnswers[j] = tmp;
          }
        }
      }
      return mySortedAnswers;
  }
}
```

Listing 10.8 is a straightforward implementation of the algorithm described just before the listing. However, it is worth pointing out the clone() calls in play() and run(). If we had used simple assignment, we would still not be thread safe. Remember that in Java, variables hold references to objects, which means that after a simple assignment such as myAnswers = answers, two variables would be referring to the same Hashtable. This would mean that any changes to answers would affect myAnswers, which in turn would mean that we really had not solved the global data problem. Calling clone() creates a new object that is identical to the original one, which will be truly local. On the other hand, the assignment of answers = myAnswers at the bottom does not need to be a call to clone() because we really do want to throw out the reference to the old version of answers and replace it with the new one that has just been built.

So we have succeeded in making the application thread safe, while minimizing the time that users must wait at synchronized blocks. But at what cost? clone() is a very expensive operation. Not only does a new Hashtable need to be constructed, the old one needs to be laboriously traversed and copied. When the answers table gets big, it will begin to hurt performance more than just synchronizing the play() method would have.

In Chapter 12, we discuss how to get the best performance out of the Java class libraries. This will enable us, at the end of the next chapter, to remove the burden of calls to clone(). We will also find that there are many other inefficiencies in this code, and we will be able to eliminate them.

Conclusion

Multithreaded programming is the way to go for server-side programming. Understanding all the subtleties of threads is not easy, but it is worth the effort. If you want to make a serious study of threads, a good starting point is Lesson 16 (Doing Two or More Tasks at Once: Threads) in the book by Mary Campione and Kathy Walrath, *The Java Tutorial: Object-Oriented Programming for the Internet*. A more thorough treatment can be found in Chapter 9 (Threads) in the Ken Arnold and James Gosling book, *The Java Programming Language*. Once you are comfortable with the mechanics of threading and are ready for deep thoughts about design, read Doug Lea's book, *Concurrent Programming in Java: Design Principles and Patterns* (see Appendix for complete cites).

CHAPTER 11

Optimizing Code for the Java Runtime Environment

This chapter is about ways to optimize code for an implementation of the Java virtual machine. In other words, it violates the spirit of "write once, run anywhere." If you adopt the techniques presented here, your code may run faster on a particular version of Sun's Java implementation but slower on others. Your code will probably be harder to read and maintain. Finally, putting the chapter's ideas into practice can take a lot of work.

Treat this chapter like a book of black magic—the information it contains comes with a price and should only be used as a last resort. Chapter 17, Servlet Debugging Techniques, tells you how to track performance problems to their source; only after you know for certain what part of your code is the bottleneck should you consider applying these tips. And remember: better algorithms always trump souped-up code. A highly optimized bubble sort cannot compete with a naïvely implemented quicksort.

An Overview of the JVM

The Java™ Virtual Machine Specification, Second Edition, by Tim Lindholm and Frank Yellin (see Appendix for complete cite) is the standard that allows a compiled Java program to run on any platform. You might hear people talk about "Sun's JVM" or "Microsoft's JVM," but there is only one Java *virtual machine* (JVM). What people mean to say is "Sun's Java runtime" or "Microsoft's JVM implementation." Before we get into what the JVM is not, though, let's define what it is.

The Metaphor

Have you ever used a flight simulator? There are some pretty complicated ones out there. These virtual airplanes have fuel tanks, wings, flaps, altimeters, and landing gear, just as real airplanes do. When you start the engine, the virtual airplane starts lowering its fuel level and increasing its speed. When you raise the flaps, the virtual airplane changes its pitch, which changes its altitude and air speed. Writing a flight simulator cannot be easy. There must be a million things to keep track of, such as air speed, direction (in three dimensions), fuel level, roll, pitch, and yaw.

A computer simulator would be much simpler to write. The virtual computer would have a lot fewer properties to keep track of: main memory, registers, program counters, and a few other things. If we wanted to simulate an operating system as well, it would be harder, especially for complicated operating systems (which is why DOS emulators work better than Windows emulators do). But if you didn't care about the software and wanted to write virtual hardware, it wouldn't be too bad, especially if the hardware you were modeling were simple and had a well-defined instruction set.

Why would anyone want to write virtual machine (VM) software? It wouldn't be as much fun as creating a virtual airplane. And implementing the same virtual machine on ten different platforms would be ten times as boring. There would be one interesting thing about it, though. Once you had an implementation on ten platforms, you could run a program written for that virtual machine on all ten platforms without rewriting (or even recompiling) the program.

The Real Thing

The creators of the Java programming language wanted to write a language that would enable compiled programs to run on any platform. They decided to do that by writing a language for a specific architecture—the JVM architecture—and then writing a software model of that architecture (a JVM implementation or Java runtime) for every major platform. That way, once a program in that language is complied, the compiled code (or bytecode) runs on any implementation. The Java language is only half the story. The other half is the JVM.

The JVM is pretty straightforward. Conceptually, it has multiple CPUs, one for each thread. Therefore each thread needs at least one register, the program counter (or pc) register. Each thread also has its own stack. A stack is where a thread stores things like local variables. The JVM stores all of the code it is executing in an area of memory called the method area, which is shared among all threads. The JVM stores constants and literals (e.g., `final String foo = "bar"`) in constant pools, contained within the method area. It has a heap, in other words, a store of memory from which programs can allocate whatever they want, as in `byte buf[] = new byte[1024]`. While the JVM can have many stacks, it has only one heap and method area (Figure 11.1).

Different groups have come up with their own JVM implementations, and each one is unique. The one from Sun's Java software division, included with its Java Development Kit (JDK) and Java Runtime Environment (JRE), is the reference implementation. We discuss that one initially and later on compare it with Sun's highly optimized HotSpot.

Stack

Before a JVM can execute a method, it must set aside memory for the method's parameters, local variables, and operand stack. The parameters are the variables that hold the arguments with which the method is called. They are treated just like local variables. *Local variables* are "local" to a method because they are declared inside it and cannot be used outside the method. An *operand stack* is a little more exotic. It's like a scratch pad, a place in memory where a method can keep track of what it is doing. For instance,

```
public int add(int op1, int op2) {
    return op1 + op2;
}
```

adds its two parameters and uses its operand stack to store the results. What are the steps the method takes? First, it pushes the value of op1 onto the operand stack. Second, it pushes the value of op2. Then it executes the `iadd` in-

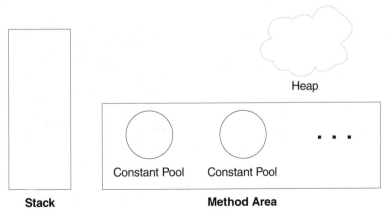

Figure 11.1   The JVM memory layout

struction, which pops the two values from the operand stack, adds them, and
then pushes their sum back onto the operand stack. Finally, the method returns
the value on the operand stack to whatever called it (Figure 11.2).

The chunk of memory that holds local variables (including parameters) and
the operand stack is called a *frame*. A frame is allocated every time a new
method is called, and it is freed whenever the method terminates, either because
it finished or because of an exception. The size of a frame depends on the
method. A method with one local variable, an `int`, probably won't need as big
a frame as a method with ten `long`s.

We can always tell how big the frame needs to be just by looking at the
method. In the example, there are three local variables (the two explicit parameters op1 and op2, as well as the implicit parameter "this," even though it isn't
used) and an operand stack that only needs to hold two `int`s. Of course, different JVM implementations might assign different amounts of memory to `int`s
and references, but the point is that any implementation can tell how much
memory a method needs by inspection.

What about arrays? If a method has a statement like the following

```
byte[] buf = new byte[size];
```

how can the JVM know how much space `buf` will take up without knowing the
value of `size`? That's a trick question, because technically `buf` is a reference to
an array, and a reference always takes the same amount of size, no matter how
big its referent object is. The "referent object," in this case a byte array, is allocated from the heap, not from a frame, so it does not affect the frame size.
(That's the trick.) Java objects (and an array is an object) always live in the
heap, not the stack. That way, the JVM always knows how much memory each
frame takes up, and frames never grow or shrink.

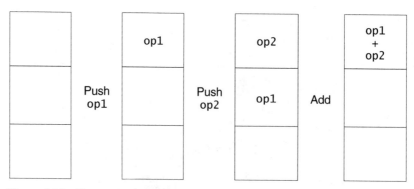

Figure 11.2   The operand stack for op1 + op2

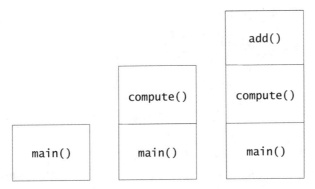

Figure 11.3   A method call stack

The fact that frames never change size allows the JVM to stack them, one on top of the other. That is why we say that all of a thread's frames form the thread's stack. This is just conceptual, of course. There is no reason for frames to be stored contiguously in memory. We talk about a stack as if it had its own area in memory only in order to make it easier to understand, as in the diagram shown in Figure 11.3.

The traditional way to think about stacks is that they begin at the bottom of a computer's memory and grow toward the top, one frame at a time. In Figure 11.3, the first stack frame is for method main(). main() calls compute(), so compute()'s frame follows main()'s. compute() in turn calls add(), so add()'s frame follows compute()'s. As one method calls another, the stack grows and grows. Only when a method exits (normally or abnormally, with an exception) can the JVM reclaim its frame. As methods exit, the stack shrinks, until it is back where it started, with main().

Heap

The *heap* is the area of memory where all objects live. It is just a big pile of memory. While the stack is rigidly segmented into frames, one after another, the heap does not have much structure. Two objects allocated in a row are not necessarily laid out contiguously in the heap.

Since there is only one heap, shared among all threads, a JVM implementation has to lock the heap while a thread is getting its memory, then unlock it. If the heap couldn't be locked, then two threads could take memory from it at the same time, which would mean that they could get overlapping pieces of memory (Figure 11.4).

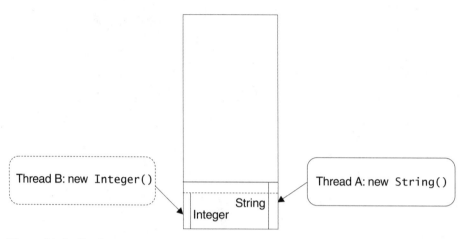

Figure 11.4   Simultaneous memory requests, without locking

Method Area (and Constant Pools)

Where does the JVM keep constant and literal values? Where does it keep the code it is executing? Those things do not directly affect programmers, but they are useful to know about for understanding how the JVM works. When the JVM loads a Java class, it puts it into the method area. Each class gets its own spot in the method area, and within each spot is a constant pool, one per class. The constant pool is where most constants and literals are stored (although integer-type constants are stored within the code that uses them).

Monitor Cache

The Lindholm and Yellin book mentions monitors (see Section 11.1.2) but does not discuss their implementation. Sun chose to use something called a global monitor cache, which is shared among all threads. Rather than take up memory and CPU cycles to create a monitor for every object, the reference JVM implementation creates monitors only when they become necessary. It keeps track of them by putting them in a cache.

Shared Resources Are the JVM's Slow Spots

Using shared resources is slower than using private ones. Sharing means taking turns, and taking turns means waiting for a turn. In the dark ages before computers, people lived in huts, ate tubers and roots, and had to get their water from the village well. If a lot of people wanted water at the same time, there was a long wait in line at the well. A pump brings the water out faster, but no matter how fast it comes, there is always a wait for it if there is a line. In other words, sharing does not scale well.

Memory

Computer programs cannot do without memory any more than humans can do without water. Unfortunately, there is only one place for a thread to go for more memory: the heap. If two threads want memory at the same time, one must wait while the other goes first. If they both allocated from the heap at the same time, they would get overlapping segments of memory, and each time one thread wrote to that memory (by assigning a value to an array index or object field, for example), it would affect the other thread's memory. So the threads have to take turns, sharing the heap, so that each gets its own discrete chunk of memory.

In other words, the heap must be locked and unlocked for every memory allocation. Locking and unlocking don't take too much time, but if 20 threads want memory at the same time, the last thread will be waiting awhile. The worst-case scenario is when lots of threads constantly ask for many little chunks of memory. Then the whole JVM is reduced to running only as fast as it can lock and unlock the heap.

The Java memory management has another source of overhead: automatic garbage collection, or GC. Garbage collection means reclaiming the memory that a program allocated for objects that it does not use any more. Languages like C or C++ don't have automatic GC, so the unlucky souls who write programs in those languages have to do it themselves. Ask one, and he or she will say that it can be quite difficult and prone to serious error. The reference GC uses an algorithm called *mark-and-sweep*. Whenever the JVM runs out of memory, it tries to reclaim unused objects. Since it has a list of all objects, all it has to do is figure out which ones are still being used and reclaim the rest.

In the first phase (mark), the GC starts with objects referred to by class variables, local variables in each thread's stack, and similar places. These objects are called root objects, and the collector marks each of them as used. Of course, each root object might have fields that refer to other objects, and those objects might have fields that refer to yet more objects, so the collector has to follow the chain of references to mark all of these objects. When the collector has followed all the references of all the roots and marked each one as read (see Figure 11.5), it begins the second phase (sweep). It sweeps every object that was not marked in the first phase into the finalization queue, where its `finalize()` method can be run by another thread. Once an object has been finalized, its memory can be reclaimed. That's a lot of work to do, and the bigger the heap, the more time it takes.

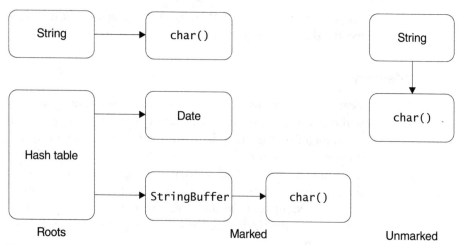

Figure 11.5   Garbage collection: Results of mark phase

Memory in the Reference Implementation

What do we do about slow memory allocations? That's simple. Use them as rarely as possible. Here are two helpful suggestions. First, if you know that your application is eventually going to use 1,000 objects of a certain type, allocate them all at once (at the beginning of the program or in the init() method of the servlet) instead of one at a time as they are needed. Second, if you know your program will use 1,000 objects but only one at a time, just allocate it once and then reuse it 999 times. For example,

```
public copy(InputStream in, OutputStream out) throws IOError {
    int n = 0;

    while (n != -1) {
        byte buffer[] = new byte[1];
        n = in.read(buffer);
        if (n > 0) out.write(buffer, 0, n);
    }
}
```

This code allocates one byte of memory at a time. That's pretty dumb, so let's try "preallocation." Instead of allocating one byte at a time, we get our bytes in 1K chunks, like the following.

```
public copy(InputStream in, OutputStream out) throws IOError {
    int n = 0;

    while (n != -1) {
        byte buffer[] = new byte[1024];
        n = in.read(buffer);
```

```
        if (n > 0) out.write(buffer, 0, n);
    }
}
```

This method might make less than one tenth of 1 percent as many memory allocations as it did before.

Can it do even better? We can try "recycling." We allocate the byte buffer once, outside the loop, and then reuse it. For example,

```
public copy(InputStream in, OutputStream out) throws IOError {
    int n = 0;
    byte buffer[] = new byte[1024];

    while (n != -1) {
        n = in.read(buffer);
        if (n > 0) out.write(buffer, 0, n);
    }
}
```

This version uses the heap much more efficiently.

The memory situation improved with JDK 1.1.5. As of this version of Sun's Java runtime, every thread has its own thread-local buffer. That means that threads do not have to go to the heap for every memory allocation. Small requests (a few kilobytes or so) can be fulfilled by the local buffer, which does not have to be locked and unlocked because it serves only one thread. When the local buffer is empty, it allocates another small chunk from the heap. Thread-local buffering does not make a big difference to small applications, but it allows Java programs to scale up to use many threads without sacrificing performance.

Another painful thing about the reference implementation is that its GC is not incremental. The whole Java runtime comes to a halt for as long as the garbage collector runs, which can be as long as a few seconds at a time. In Sun's green threads implementation, there is a low-priority thread that attempts a garbage collection when no other thread is running, but if it gets only halfway done before another thread becomes runnable, then it bails out immediately and has to start from scratch.

Memory in HotSpot

HotSpot is significantly more sophisticated about memory than the reference implementation. It has what is called a generational garbage collector. In addition to the regular heap, HotSpot has an area of memory called the *nursery*. All requests for small memory blocks are satisfied by the nursery. The nursery reclaims space very quickly, much faster than the regular collector. Remember, the worst-case scenario for the reference memory system—lots of small, short-lived objects—is the best case for HotSpot. With no more than about 500K of objects at a time and old ones discarded before new ones are created, the oh-so-slow heap is not needed. If an object sticks around for a while, though, it is tenured out of the nursery and into the heap whenever the nursery fills up and needs more room.

That brings us to the worst case for HotSpot: allocating a few large objects and keeping them around for a long time. The bad news is that this is the best case for the reference implementation, and forms the basis for the recommendations in the preceding memory reference implementation subsection. If you follow the recommendations, then your program will not be much faster under HotSpot than it was under the reference implementation. The good news is that your program won't be any slower. If you went through the trouble to preallocate objects and then keep them around so you can reuse them, all to make your program really fast under another JVM, it will still be really fast under HotSpot. It just won't take advantage of generational garbage collecting.

Another advantage of HotSpot is incremental garbage collection. Instead of freezing the whole Java runtime for as long as it takes to do GC for the entire heap, HotSpot just does it bit by bit, 5 to 10 milliseconds at a time. This makes programs run more smoothly.

Monitor Cache

The JVM specification says that the Java synchronization primitive is the monitor (see Chapter 10), but it is silent on the issue of monitor implementation. For instance, every object must be able to use its own monitor. This does not mean that a monitor must be created every time an object is created. Sun decided not to allocate a monitor for every object because most objects never use their monitors. Instead, the reference implementation creates a monitor on demand and keeps track of which monitors belong to which objects in a global data structure called the monitor cache. The *monitor cache* is a shared resource, just as the heap is. Chapter 10 discusses this in more detail.

Monitor Cache in the Reference Implementation

Prior to JDK 1.1.5, the reference implementation relied exclusively on a global monitor cache. Like the single global heap, the single global monitor cache did not allow Java programs to scale well. Starting with JDK 1.1.5, each thread also has its own local monitor cache, which it can use to see if an object already has a monitor. Since threads are less reliant on the global monitor cache, Java applications are better able to scale up to use more threads.

Monitor Cache in HotSpot

HotSpot also has a global monitor cache, but it does not use it in most cases. Because of this and other improvements, synchronization takes much less time under HotSpot than under the reference implementation.

Another Slowdown: Dynamic Method Dispatch

One of the most unusual object-oriented terms is *polymorphism* (from the Greek meaning *having many forms*). If you read a book that describes Java as "polymorphic," it isn't trying to claim that Java turns into a werewolf during a full moon. It is referring to the fact that a class's implementation of a method might be overridden later on by a subclass. For instance, say we are writing a method that takes an argument of type Shape, which has a nonfinal instance method getArea(). Of course, the actual object that is passed in might be an instance of a subclass of Shape such as Circle or Square. When you invoke the argument's getArea() method, you don't not know whether it will be the getArea() implemented by Shape or the getArea() overridden by a subclass. The compiler does not know either, so it cannot store an absolute reference to any code. Therefore, Java uses something called late binding. *Late binding* means that the Java runtime has to wait until a program is actually running to figure out which version of getArea() to run. The process it uses to execute the right method definition is called *dynamic method dispatch.*

Dynamic method dispatch is not blindingly fast. In the reference implementation, the only way to avoid the overhead of dynamic method dispatch is to declare methods static and/or final. Neither static nor final methods can be overridden, so the compiler can store an absolute reference to the right code. This means not having to wait around at runtime for the JPE to track down a method and also that the compiler and/or the runtime can better optimize the program. Sometimes the compiler can even copy the method definition straight into its caller's definition. That is called *inlining,* and it is the fastest way of all to execute a method—no lookups or even jumps. Unfortunately, declaring methods static or final means that no one can derive other classes from yours, so reusability goes out the window.

What can we do? Use HotSpot. When it loads a class, it checks to see how many versions of the same methods it and its superclasses share. If it turns out that a method is defined only once, then HotSpot treats it as if it were static and final and optimizes it accordingly. HotSpot's optimizer is adaptive, so if it decides to inline a method that later turns out to be overridden in a new class, it can throw out the inlined code and start over.

Unbuffered I/O Is a Universal Problem

Unbuffered I/O is less efficient than buffered I/O in every language and on every platform. The Java programming language is no exception. Reading from a network connection or from a tape file is slow, so we want to do it as few times as possible. For example, if we want to read ten bytes from a file, we could read one byte at a time, which would result in ten read operations, or we could read all ten bytes at once, with just a single read operation. If a program looks at the input one byte at a time, we should read all ten bytes into a buffer at once and then look at the buffer one byte at a time. This will reduce the time the program spends in I/O by a factor of 10. Using kilobyte buffers can speed up a program by as much as three orders of magnitude.

Managing buffers can be a pain, so Java makes it easy. Whether we are reading or writing with byte streams or character streams, java.io has a class. If we have an unbuffered InputStream, for example, we can make a buffered one from it:

```
InputStream in;
. . .
BufferedInputStream bin = new BufferedInputStream(in);
```

We just use bin instead of in from that point on. When we call bin's close() method, it will automatically close in as well. And for Writers:

```
Writer out;
. . .
BufferedWriter bout = new BufferedWriter(out);
```

Closing bout will flush the buffer and then close out.

Conclusion

Virtual machine technology is much better developed than most people realize. Smalltalk and LISP environments have employed VMs for many years. Researchers have been studying algorithms for things like garbage collection and dynamic method dispatch for quite some time. Java is still in its infancy, and JVM implementations are only now beginning to take advantage of the accumulated experience of Smalltalk and LISP. One day, Sun hopes to produce JVM implementations so advanced that currently expensive operations, such as thread synchronization and memory allocation, will take almost no time at all. Until then, programmers who need every last iota of performance out of their code will want to be aware of the code's execution environment.

That is not easy. There are not very many JVM books available as of this writing. The standard reference is Lindholm and Yellin, *The Java™ Virtual Machine Specification, Second Edition*. Bill Venners, of *JavaWorld* fame, wrote *Inside the Java™ Virtual Machine*, which has some great applets that demonstrate VM concepts such as garbage collection. Jon Meyer (one of this book's reviewers) and Troy Downing of NYU wrote *Java™ Virtual Machine*, which goes into the kind of detail needed to implement the JVM or write a compiler to translate a favorite language into Java bytecodes.[1]

CHAPTER 12

Optimizing Use of the Java Class Libraries

As we showed in Chapter 11, memory allocation and thread synchronization can have dramatic impacts on performance. Programmers who want their servlets to run at top speed must be aware that these factors affect not only their classes but everything in the Java Class Libraries as well. This should not be surprising, as the bulk of these classes are themselves written in Java. In addition, some of the methods in the Java Class Libraries do unexpectedly complicated things, which may affect servlet performance, and programmers need to watch for this problem, as well.

In the following sections we look at each of the major packages in the Java Class Libraries and point out some of the classes and methods that may present performance problems. Most notably, these problems manifest themselves in classes that depend on locale information, such as `String` and `Calendar`, and in classes that use a lot of synchronized code, such as many of the I/O classes and `Hashtable`. We also discuss how to track down these kinds of problems and code around them.

`java.lang` Package

Most of the classes in this package are well optimized and can be used without concern. Unfortunately the `String` class, one of the most used and useful of the Java classes, is also one of the most problematic. This is especially troubling in servlets, which tend to do a great deal of text processing and manipulation.

Inside `java.lang.String`

Strings are problematic for a couple of reasons. One is that, appearances to the contrary, Strings are *immutable*. In a sense Strings are like statues carved out of marble. They are quite beautiful, but it takes a lot of time to make one, and once built, they cannot just be erased or modified. Most string operations, such as appending another string or replacing a character, actually construct new strings. This is a fairly expensive proposition, since not only does memory need to be allocated for the new string, but the data from the old one need to be copied.

Consider the following code fragment:

```
String hello1 = new String("Hi ");
String hello2 = new String("there!");
hello1 += hello2;
```

This clearly constructs two strings, but what is not as obvious is that it also constructs a third string and an auxiliary object called a `StringBuffer` as well.

We certainly do not expect anyone to believe us when we talk about invisible strings and string buffers; after all, we did not believe the drunk who stumbled over to us the other night complaining about invisible elves. To bring these hidden objects into plain sight, create a simple class containing the given three lines, and compile it as normal. Then `javap` with the `-c` option can be used to show exactly what virtual machine (VM) codes this turned into. The relevant part should look something like Listing 12.1.

Listing 12.1   Compiled form of a `String` operation.

```
 0 new #4 <Class java.lang.String>
 3 dup
 4 ldc #1 <String "Hi ">
 6 invokespecial #8 <Method java.lang.String(java.lang.String)>
 9 astore_1
10 new #4 <Class java.lang.String>
13 dup
14 ldc #2 <String "there!">
16 invokespecial #8 <Method java.lang.String(java.lang.String)>
19 astore_2
20 new #5 <Class java.lang.StringBuffer>
23 dup
24 aload_1
25 invokestatic #12 <Method java.lang.String
                      valueOf(java.lang.Object)>
28 invokespecial #9 <Method java.lang.StringBuffer(
                      java.lang.String)>
31 aload_2
```

```
32 invokevirtual #10 <Method java.lang.StringBuffer
                            append(java.lang.String)>
35 invokevirtual #11 <Method java.lang.String toString()>
38 astore_1
```

The details of what most of those mysterious words, such as astore_1 and dup, mean are unimportant, although they are completely described in *The Java™ Virtual Machine Specification, Second Edition,* by Tim Lindholm and Frank Yellin, for anyone who is interested in knowing more. Of interest right now are the two ldc calls on lines 4 and 14, which retrieve character data from the constant pool. This operation is fast, since no memory is allocated and no data are copied.

Now look at all the calls to new. The ones on lines 0 and 10 allocate memory for the hello1 and hello2 strings. The constructors on lines 6 and 16 allocate space for their data and copy the characters from the constant pool into the strings. In other words, each of the constructors in the original code turns into an allocation for the string, an allocation for data, and a copy, all of which are slow.

The call to new on line 20 constructs the invisible StringBuffer. If a String is a block of marble, a String Buffer is a lump of clay. It is much more mutable, and in particular, it is possible to append to a StringBuffer, just as it is possible to add another lump of clay if the first turns out to be too small. The append method is called on line 32.

The third, invisible string is constructed on line 35. Even under the microscope of javap it is not directly visible, as it is hiding in the call to StringBuffer.toString. However, it is documented in the javadoc page from Sun on the StringBuffer class, which states "A new String object is created and initialized to contain the character sequence represented by this StringBuffer."

The immutability of Strings and the corresponding need to construct extra objects is one problem with Strings. Another problem arises when a servlet wants to actually send a string to a user. Before a String can be sent over a network or saved to a file, it needs to be converted to bytes. This is because the underlying hardware and networks do not understand Java strings directly. This conversion may seem like a simple operation, but remember that Java was designed for international use. Consequently it uses Unicode characters, each of which is 2 bytes, and the way in which these 2-byte entities are converted to a stream of single bytes varies widely depending on the locale. For example, the character *I* is represented as the single byte 0x49 in the United States and the 2 bytes—0x01 0x31—in Turkey. Not surprisingly, the logic to determine the appropriate translation, as well as to actually do it, is very complex.

Optimizing by Removing Unnecessary Calls to new

The complexities of the String class make it an excellent case study for how to optimize programs for speed, although because strings are so ubiquitous, most of the techniques that suggest themselves have already been implemented by the compiler or the virtual machine.

One easy improvement that can and should be done immediately is to *not* do what our three-line example did, construct new Strings from constants. Where we had

```
String hello1 = new String("Hi ");
```

it would have been much better instead to write

```
String hello1 = "Hi ";
String hello2 = "there!";
```

If this code is compiled and then run through javap -c, it will be obvious that now two fewer strings are constructed. This is because constant strings, that is, strings that appear literally in a program, are stored in a special place in the class file called the constant pool. The VM is able to just grab them, without having to construct new instances.

We can also write the program as seems most logical, run it under a simulated heavy load, and see if it is fast enough. There is a great deal of wisdom in "If it ain't broke, don't fix it." But for very complex programs or programs that need to be extremely scalable, there comes a time when the simple, obvious code just does not keep up. The first step to optimizing is to spend some time looking at and perhaps profiling the code to figure out everything it is doing and where the problems may lie. Consider the servlet in Listing 12.2 that prints the number of times it has been accessed.

Listing 12.2   Servlet that counts the number of times it has been used.

```
import java.io.*;
import javax.servlet.*;
import javax.servlet.http.*;

public class Counter extends HttpServlet {
  private int count = 0;

  public void service(HttpServletRequest req,
                  HttpServletResponse res)
      throws IOException
  {
    ServletOutputStream out = res.getOutputStream();
    out.println("This page has been accessed " + incCount() +
             " times.");
  }
```

```
private synchronized int incCount() {
  int oldcount = count;
  count++;
  return oldcount;
  }
}
```

This certainly looks innocuous, but consider all the activity that is going on behind the scenes, in particular the things that are happening on the single line where println() is called.

1. The characters containing "This page has been accessed " are retrieved from the class's constant pool, and a new string is created to hold them.

2. The result of incCount() is converted to a string, causing another memory allocation.

3. A StringBuffer is created to handle appending the second String to the first.

4. The characters " times." are retrieved from the constant pool and a new String is created to hold them.

5. This String is appended to the StringBuffer.

6. The result of appending all these strings together is pulled out of the StringBuffer, resulting in the construction of a new String.

7. The resulting String is then converted to a byte array, which must also be constructed.

In other words, the one line results in a whopping six memory allocations and four hidden method calls.

If this simple, straightforward use of strings is too slow, there is a continuum of optimizations that can be applied to the code. As science fiction author Larry Niven is fond of pointing out, though, "There ain't no such thing as a free lunch." At each step, the cost of making the code a bit faster is that it gets a bit more complex. Finding the right balance between code that screams but also makes maintainers scream with pain, and slower code that humans can live with depends entirely on the application and may be hard to determine.

The simplest change would be to print each component out individually, instead of appending them together first. That is, replace

```
out.println("This page has been accessed " + incCount()
            + "times.");
```

with

```
out.print("This page has been accessed ");
out.print(incCount());
out.println(" times.");
```

This saves the overhead of creating the intermediate `StringBuffer`, as well as the string to hold the representation of the value returned from `incCount()` and the `String` that holds all the other strings appended together. Not to mention the two extra calls to print, which, as might be expected, are pretty expensive themselves. We discuss just how expensive the I/O classes are in the java.io Package section later in this chapter.

Because the `"This page has been accessed "` and `" times."` strings never change, they can be made into class variables, as shown in Listing 12.3. The translation means that those `ldc`s will be called only once, when the class is first loaded, instead of each time the `service()` method is invoked.

Listing 12.3 Counter servlet using class variables.

```
import java.io.*;
import javax.servlet.*;
import javax.servlet.http.*;

public class Counter2 extends HttpServlet {
  private int count = 0;
  static final String text1 = "This page has been accessed ";
  static final String text2 = " times.";

  public void service(HttpServletRequest req,
                       HttpServletResponse res)
      throws IOException
  {
    ServletOutputStream out = res.getOutputStream();
    out.print(text1);
    out.print(incCount());
    out.println(text2);
  }

  private synchronized int incCount() {
    int oldcount = count;
    count++;
    return oldcount;
  }
}
```

But we have definitely paid for our lunch with this technique. The text has been taken out of the context in which it is used, and if in the future some of the wording needs to be changed or new material needs to be added, it will not be as easy to locate the text in question.

Optimizing by Using StringBuffers

If `StringBuffer`s are good enough for the compiler, they should be good enough for mere programmers. Indeed, `StringBuffer`s can be used directly in an attempt to eliminate some of the intermediate steps of the + operator.

At the 1998 JavaOne Conference, Tony Squire, a software engineer at Sun, showed that using `String Buffers` instead of strings could be as much as 175% faster! He also suggested creating `StringBuffers` with a sufficiently large start size. By default, a `StringBuffer` has enough room for 16 characters. Once it has 16 it must get another "lump of clay," which takes some time. If a programmer thinks a string will never be more than 200 characters, the `StringBuffer` could be created with new `StringBuffer(200)`. Using `StringBuffers` with an appropriately large start size can improve speed as much as 245% over plain `Strings`! Yes, that is no typo: 245%! The slides from the talk at which this information was presented are available at

http://java.sun.com/javaone/javaone98/sessions/T200/index.html

In particular, the slide showing these amazing results is at

http://java.sun.com/javaone/javaone98/sessions/T200/misc_slide_4.html

Using `StringBuffers`, the `service()` method would now become

```
public void service(HttpServletRequest req, HttpServletResponse res)
  throws IOException
 {
   ServletOutputStream out = res.getOutputStream();
   StringBuffer tmp       = new StringBuffer(text1);
   tmp.append(incCount());
   tmp.append(text2);
   out.println(tmp.toString());
}
```

In this case, this change actually hurts performance, because a new string now needs to be constructed in order to print the result. Most of the `append()` methods in the `StringBuffer` are synchronized, so there are now issues of locking the monitor cache that did not come up in the previous version. However, if there were many strings that needed to be concatenated instead of just three, as would probably be the case in a real-life page, the benefits of using a `String-Buffer` would soon overtake its disadvantages.

If removing the extra memory allocations and moving to `StringBuffers` does not sufficiently improve performance, it will be necessary to actually delve into what all the library classes are really doing.

Optimizing by Studying the Library Classes

Most of the time it is appropriate to treat the Java library classes as magic black boxes. It usually does not matter to programmers what sort of wondrous gears and wires are spinning and humming inside the `String` class, as long as characters go in and come out the right way. However, when it comes to optimization, it is sometimes necessary to open the black boxes up and see if perhaps some of the gears are not spinning quite as fast as they need to.

The first step of this process is to determine what methods are being called, and as we have seen, javap -c can help here. The second step is to figure out what the method calls are doing. Fortunately, JavaSoft provides the source code for all the core classes for exactly this purpose. It is available from

http://www.javasoft.com/products/index.html

Under the appropriate version of the JDK is a documentation pack that comes with a file called src.zip, which file contains a .java file for each library class.

In our counter example, javap shows a call to getBytes(), and the source code reveals that getBytes() is a very complicated method, dealing with all sorts of international issues. In JDK 1.1 this overhead was huge, as each conversion had to find, load, and invoke the right conversion class. It makes much less of an impact in JDK 1.2, which introduces caching and reuse of the conversion classes.

In some cases it may be possible to use different methods or a different set of methods to eliminate the overhead of a particularly complex and time-consuming method. However, in this case the only way to eliminate the overhead is, sadly, to abandon Strings. The strings text1 and text2 would become byte arrays. Experienced C programmers might be inclined to write this as

```
static final byte text1[] = {'T','h','i','s',' ','p','a','g',
                             'e',' ','h','a','s',' ','b','e',
                             'e','n',' ','a','c','c','e','s',
                             's','e','d',' '};
static final byte text2[] = {' ','t','i','m','e','s','.'};
```

The Java programming language allows for a much cleaner representation:

```
static final byte text1[] = "This page has been accessed ".getBytes();
static final byte text2[] = " times.".getBytes();
```

This may seem strange—if the whole point is to get rid of the conversion from strings to bytes, why would we use two strings and call getBytes()? The method to our apparent madness is that now the getBytes() calls will only happen once, when the class is first loaded, which is a much better situation than having to do it every time the service method is called. The other advantage to writing the code this way is that it will still use internationalization, and the strings will be translated appropriately for the locale where the code is run. Note, however, that this will not necessarily be the locale where the Web browser is actually located, which is where the localization really matters. We discuss internationalization and related issues more fully in Chapter 8.

The service() method would use byte arrays exactly as it used strings:

```
ServletOutputStream out = res.getOutputStream();
out.write(text1);
out.write(incCount());
out.write(text2);
```

This is a slightly more expensive lunch, and the code has become slightly more complex. Programmers now need to remember to add .getBytes() at the end of all their static strings. On the positive side, though, this is as about as fast as this code can possibly get.

Unfortunately there is another complication. As we pointed out in Chapter 9, not every string in a servlet is used only once, as it is printed, and discarded immediately afterwards. One reason to hold onto the string would be to get the content length. Servlets should set the content-length header, but in most cases this will not be known until the full message has been assembled. This length cannot be counted as each piece of the message is sent out, because once any data has been sent it is too late to set the headers. In the simple counter example, the length could be computed based on the size of the two constant parts and the size of the integer, but in a more realistic situation it is not that easy.

The perfect class in this instance would be something that stores data in a byte array so that the conversion cost can be avoided but to which programmers could append data like a string buffer. Of course the servlet programmer could write one, but why recreate work that JavaSoft has already done? One of the best things a Java programmer can do is become as familiar with the core packages as possible. There are lots and lots of wonderfully useful classes hiding in them, and it will frequently happen that a program needs some seemingly strange piece of functionality that is already available. In this case, looking through the library APIs will soon uncover java.io.ByteArrayOutputStream, which is exactly what this situation calls for. The service() method would use it in almost exactly the same way it used the string buffer:

```
public void service(HttpServletRequest req, HttpServletResponse res)
   throws IOException
  {
  ServletOutputStream out    = res.getOutputStream();
  ByteArrayOutputStream tmp = new ByteArrayOutputStream();
  tmp.write(text1);
  tmp.write(count):
  tmp.write(text2);
  res.setContentLength(tmp.size());
  out.write(tmp.toByteArray());
}
```

At this point, the extraneous memory allocations have been eliminated, and only fast method calls are being used. If performance is still a problem, it is time to start looking even deeper into the Java environment.

Optimizing by Removing Synchronized Method Calls

From the beginning, Java was designed as a multithreaded language, and consequently all the classes in the libraries need to be prepared to be used by many threads simultaneously. One place this comes up is the write() methods of all the output streams, ByteArrayOutputStream included. This is a really good thing. It means that programmers can write() servlets in a straightforward logical way, without needing to worry about the text for two different pages becoming interwoven, which could result in such horrors as one user's credit card number showing up in another user's page. However, the downside of this convenience is the cost of going through synchronization, as we discussed in Chapter 11. This cost is paid even if only one thread is actually using a class. For example, a local variable, that is, one that is declared in a method and used only within that method, is always thread safe. But even if Java could prove that a variable was used only locally, it could not unsynchronize the method calls.

Unsynchronization cannot be done because synchronization is a property of the method, not the way the method is called. However, there is an even easier way to tell if a program is using synchronized calls: check the javadocs for the classes that are being used. This is another good reason to become intimate with all the class library documentation. Although all synchronization issues will not be revealed, since methods can and do contain synchronized blocks, it will reveal the ones that programmers are most likely to need to worry about.

It is worth mentioning that the HotSpot compiler does a number of very clever things to reduce the impact of synchronized method calls. However, even if HotSpot makes synchronization a really cheap lunch, anything put in a really tight loop starts to mount up. If the synchronized calls do present a performance problem, the code will need to be rewritten to avoid classes with synchronized methods. For ByteArrayOutputStream, the simplest way to do this is to write everything directly to a byte array, as in Listing 12.4.

Listing 12.4 Using a byte array to avoid synchronization.

```
public void service(HttpServletRequest req,
                    HttpServletResponse res)
   throws IOException
{
    ServletOutputStream out = res.getOutputStream();
    byte tmp[]              = new byte[50];
    int bytecount           = 0;

    // Note the use of System.arraycopy, which is almost certainly
    // faster than copying the array by hand
    System.arraycopy(text1,0,tmp,bytecount,text1.length);
    bytecount += text1.length;
    bytecount += intwrite(tmp,bytecount,incCount());
    System.arraycopy(text2,0,tmp,bytecount,text2.length);
```

```
        bytecount += text2.length;
        res.setContentLength(bytecount);
        out.write(tmp,0,bytecount);
    }
```

There is no quick and easy way to convert an integer to a byte array, at least not without going through an intermediate string, as `Integer.parseInt()` does. So the servlet needs to handle this itself (see Listing 12.5). Finally! A version of the `Counter` servlet that has no extra memory allocations, uses only fast method calls, has no extra synchronizations, and yet still holds on to constructed data so that it can get the length.

Listing 12.5   Fast method to convert integers to byte arrays.

```
public int intwrite(byte b[],int offset,int value) {
    int digit = 1000000000;    // The largest power of ten that can
                               // be stored in an int
    boolean firstNonZero = false;
    int indx              = offset;

    while(digit > 0) {
        if(value >= digit) {
            b[indx++] = (byte) ((value/digit) + '0');
            firstNonZero = true;
        } else if(firstNonZero) {
            b[indx++] = (byte) '0';
        }
        value = value % digit;
        digit = digit/10;
    }
    return (indx-offset);
}
```

Who could ask for anything more? Any Java programmer who has ever gotten an `ArrayIndexOutOfBoundsException`! In this example, 50 bytes will always be enough space to hold the message, since the representation of an integer can be at most 13 bytes and the rest of the message is only 35 bytes. In real situations, it may be impossible to put such a firm upper limit on the size of the message. In this case, the array will have to grow dynamically, as needed, to become something with the functionality of a `ByteArrayOutputStream` but none of the synchronized overhead. A utility class that does this is not hard to write, and it is used in the final version of the `Counter` servlet shown in Listing 12.6.

Listing 12.6   Counter servlet using a growable array of bytes.

```
import java.io.*;
import javax.servlet.*;
import javax.servlet.http.*;

public class Counter3 extends HttpServlet {
    private int count = 0;
```

```java
        static final byte text1[]
            = "This page has been accessed ".getBytes();
        static final byte text2[]
            = "times.".getBytes();

        public void service(HttpServletRequest req,
                            HttpServletResponse res)
            throws IOException
        {
          ServletOutputStream out = res.getOutputStream();
          GrowableByteArray tmp    = new GrowableByteArray(100,100);
          tmp.write(text1);
          tmp.write(incCount());
          tmp.write(text2);

          res.setContentLength(tmp.getSize());
          out.write(tmp.getBytes(),0,tmp.getSize());
        }

        private synchronized int incCount() {
          int oldcount = count;
          count++;
          return oldcount;
        }
}
/**
 * Note that this class is NOT thread safe!  Be sure to use it only
 * as a local variable
 */
class GrowableByteArray {
  private byte theArray[];
  private int  size;
  private int  sizeIncr;

  public GrowableByteArray(int initSize,int sizeIncrP) {
    theArray = new byte[initSize];
    size     = 0;
    sizeIncr = sizeIncrP;
  }

  private void expandArray(int dataSize) {
    int incr = (dataSize > sizeIncr) ? dataSize : sizeIncr;

    byte newArray[] = new byte[theArray.length + incr];
    System.arraycopy(theArray,0,newArray,0,size);
    theArray = newArray;
  }

  public int getSize()     {return size;}
  public byte[] getBytes() {return theArray;}

  public void write(byte b[]) {
    try {
```

```
      System.arraycopy(b,0,theArray,size,b.length);
    } catch (ArrayIndexOutOfBoundsException e) {
      expandArray(b.length);
      System.arraycopy(b,0,theArray,size,b.length);
    }
    size += b.length;
  }

  public void write(int value) {
    int digit = 100000000000;
    boolean firstNonZero = false;

    if(theArray.length > size + 13) expandArray(13);
    while(digit > 0) {
      if(value > digit) {
        theArray[size++] = (byte) ((value/digit) + '0');
        firstNonZero = true;
      } else if(firstNonZero) {
        theArray[size++] = (byte) '0';
      }

      value = value % digit;
      digit = digit/10;
    }
  }
}
```

There is an interesting technique used in the write(byte[]) method. It might seem that the logical thing to do is to check whether the current size plus the length of the array was greater than the length of the array and call expandArray() if it is. However, note that System.arraycopy() is already doing this check, so doing it in our code would be duplicating effort and hence be less efficient. Simply catching the Exception, although it may look stranger, is in fact faster. Java does a great deal of bounds checking on arrays, so in general, it is not worth doing it in user code.

We have gone from one line in the service() method to four, plus a couple of hard-to-manage byte arrays, plus a whole extra class. However, on the *Money Magazine* site, which was running under JDK 1.1.3 with the Solaris JIT, we found that making these kinds of changes could improve performance by a factor of as much as 20.

That concludes our walkthrough of String optimizations. Most of the techniques we discuss should be applicable to any servlet or other program. Optimizing is as much an art as it is a science, so it is impossible to give hard-and-fast rules about how to go about it. However, in general here are the things to look for.

- Extraneous object allocations, both in programmer code and in code the compiler generates, which can be seen with javap

- Unexpectedly complex method calls, which can be found by examining the library source code
- Extra synchronizations where they are not needed, such as on local variables. Find them by looking through the class documentation, and eliminate them by writing equivalent classes without synchronized methods.

In the remainder of this chapter, we look at some of the major packages and point out things that may require special attention when optimizing.

java.io Package

It is a basic fact of life that I/O is slow. First the program must make a request to the operating system through what are called *system calls,* which on many platforms can take a fairly long time. Then the operating system has to manipulate all sorts of internal data. And worst of all, a big, slow, physical disk head needs to be moved around, or sluggish electrons need to be sent through an Ethernet card to contact a remote address, or something equally complex needs to happen. A good Java program could probably compute π (or κ) to a hundred places in this time!

Because this all happens at a snail's pace compared to the speed of the Java virtual machine, there is not much Java per se can do to significantly improve I/O performance. However, a few rules of thumb help minimize the impact.

Imagine the output of a servlet as several gallons of water and transmitting the data as moving the water from one large basin to another. No one would want to do this a drop at a time. It would all get to the destination, but it would take forever. It would go much faster to take a full bucket on each trip. Likewise, no one would want to transmit a Web page by sending only one byte at a time. Each tiny transmission would require a big, slow system call. Since they are so slow, programs want to make as few of them as possible and send as much data as possible each time.

The Java I/O libraries help do this by providing buffered classes. Buffered classes provide an invisible bucket in memory. When data is given to the write() methods of a class, it is not sent out immediately but get stored in memory until the object decides it has enough, or is explicitly forced to send it out, or is closed or finalized. This means that data can be written out in whichever way makes the most sense for the application, and still only a few system calls are made. Like buffered output classes, buffered input classes read as much data as can fit in their internal buffers, store it in memory, and then pass it on to programs in whatever chunks are asked for.

Although buffered classes can save a great deal of operating system overhead, they have some disadvantages. All the read() and write() methods of the buffered I/O classes are synchronized, so once again monitor locking rears its ugly head. Sending data to the end user using buffered classes means that no data reach the user until it has all been generated or until the internal buffer fills up. If the generating process is slow, it may be better to send out whatever is available as soon as possible.

If byte arrays, as discussed in the string sections, are being used, then they also act as buckets, buckets the programmer instead of the Java library has control over. This does not help when sending data to the user, since the ServletOutputStream buffers output automatically. However, when talking to other processes, servlets can bypass the buffering classes and use only the write(byte[]) method of whatever output stream is being used.

When writing to a file or communicating with a back-end daemon, there is no hard-and-fast rule as to whether buffering data manually versus using the buffered I/O classes will be better. We recommend letting Java do the buffering initially, and if there are performance problems in the IO section of the code, try buffering to a byte array and sending it out in one large chunk.

java.net **Package**

There are no hidden gotchas in the java.net package. However, building a network connection has as much or more overhead than local I/O, regardless of the language. Here are a few programming tips that help minimize the impact.

First and foremost, opening a connection or a pool of connections and reusing it instead of opening a new connection for each request will help tremendously. Managing this sort of pool can be difficult, but there are many classes that do this already available.

If it is necessary to open a connection to the same machine repeatedly, do not use the machine name to construct the socket. The easiest way to construct a socket is to do something like

```
theSocket = new Socket(machineName, port);
```

The operating system does not use the machine name directly to build the connection; instead, it must first look up the machine's IP address. This process can be extremely slow, as the operating system may need to make several network connections to domain name servers.

Once an address is looked up, the operating system may cache it, but even then subsequent connections must go through the operating system's tables. This process can be bypassed by getting an InetAddress object, either in the servlet's init() method or the first time there is a need to build the socket, and then storing it somewhere. For example,

```
public void init() throws ServletException, IOException {
  try {
     machineAddress = InetAddress.getByName(machineName);
  } catch (UnknownHostException) {
     // Log the error
     throw new servletNotInitialized(
            "Couldn't find IP address for"
            + machineName);
  }
}
public void service(HttpServletRequest req,
                    HttpServletResponse res)
   throws ServletException, IOException
{
     theSocket = new Socket(machineAddress, port);
     ...
}
```

Setting various socket parameters, such as SO_LINGER and SO_TIMEOUT, may also affect overall performance, but tuning at this level is beyond the scope of this book.

java.text Package

The classes in this package were designed to separate various kinds of information from their representations to allow them to be represented differently in different locations. As with the translation from characters to bytes, this internationalized code can get very complex and hence very slow. Most of these methods end up producing strings, and there is a good deal of string manipulation going on behind the scenes as well, which further affects the performance of these classes.

Whenever possible, cache the representation built with the text classes to avoid recomputing them. This is another good rule of thumb when optimizing: never compute several times what can be computed once and stored.

If code will only be run in one locale, it may be possible to bypass this package entirely. The one exception is the DateFormat class, which so greatly simplifies the task of printing dates and times that programmers almost always want to use it. However, if requests do not require the date and time accurate to the second the representation generated by the DateFormat could be cached to avoid the cost of using it. The representation could be stored in a class variable that caches the representation of the current time, and the init() method could kick off a thread that would update this variable once every minute or so. This procedure also avoids the cost of getting the current time at each request, which is itself an expense due to the overhead of making a system call.

If only the current day is needed, the cache only needs to be refreshed, not surprisingly, once a day. init() would compute the time until the day changes, and the refresh thread would sleep until then. After refreshing the first time, each subsequent refresh would happen after sleeping a full 24 hours. One of the great things about the Java Web Server is that it is so stable that programmers need to worry about how their code will cross day, week, and even month boundaries! For an example, see Listing 12.7.

Listing 12.7 Using a thread to avoid recomputations.

```java
import java.io.*;
import java.text.*;
import java.util.*;
import javax.servlet.*;
import javax.servlet.http.*;
public class ShowDay extends HttpServlet implements Runnable {
  /**
   * This will store the text containing today's date.
   * We will keep it in a byte array instead of a string
   * so that we do not have to convert to bytes every time we
   * print it
   */
  private byte[] today;
  private Thread runner;
  private Calendar myCalendar;
  private int timeToMidnight;
  // Midnight in milliseconds
  private final static int midnightMillis = 24 * 60 * 60 * 1000;
  public void init(ServletConfig config)
       throws ServletException
  {
    super.init(config);
    setToday();
    runner = new Thread(this);
    runner.start();
  }

  public synchronized void setToday() {
    Date theDate  = new Date();
    long now      = theDate.getTime();
    timeToMidnight = midnightMillis -
      (int) (now % midnightMillis);
    DateFormat df;
    // The string version of today's date
    StringBuffer todayS = new StringBuffer("Today is ");
    // Get the day of the week
    StringBuffer dow = new StringBuffer();
    FieldPosition fp =
      new FieldPosition(DateFormat.DAY_OF_WEEK_FIELD);
    dow = DateFormat.getDateInstance(DateFormat.FULL).
       format(theDate,dow,fp);
```

```
      todayS.append((new String(dow)).substring(
                          fp.getBeginIndex(),
                          fp.getEndIndex()-fp.getBeginIndex()));
      todayS.append(", ");
      // Get the day of the month and the month
      df = DateFormat.getDateInstance(DateFormat.LONG);
      todayS.append(df.format(theDate));
      // Convert the string to a byte array for
      // efficiency when we print
      today = (new String(todayS)).getBytes();
    }

    public void run() {
      while(true) {
        try {Thread.sleep(timeToMidnight);} catch (Exception e) {}
        setToday();
      }
    }

    public void service(HttpServletRequest req,
                        HttpServletResponse res)
          throws ServletException,IOException
    {
      ServletOutputStream out = res.getOutputStream();
      out.write(today);
    }
  }
```

java.util Package

The classes in this package were designed to provide high-level utilities to make life easier for programmers. Unfortunately, some of the classes do this by making more work for the JVM, which in turn makes for slow programs. Physicists call this the "conservation of energy"; programmers call it "another &@*(% night with the Java profiler."

java.util.Date

Prior to JDK 1.1, the Date class was used to get a variety of date and time information. Most of this functionality has been moved into the Calendar class, and Date is now little more than a wrapper around the current system time in milliseconds. If all that is needed is quick access to the time, it is slightly faster to use System.currentTimeMillis() than to construct a new Date object and use Date.getTime(), simply because it avoids the overhead of constructing the Date.

NOTE: The system time may not exactly equal the calendar time. The science of keeping and coordinating global calendar date and time is very complex. See JavaSoft's documentation for the java.util.Date class and *http://tycho.usno. navy.mil/* for more information. For most applications, this distinction between system time and Coordinated Universal Time does not matter.

java.util.Calendar

As with the String class, the Calendar class was designed support full internationalization, and hence it may be expensive to use, at least in JDK 1.1. In JDK 1.2, the classes that do the conversion are reused, making them much more efficient.

If simple formatting will suffice and internationalization is not a concern, it may be easier and faster to use this class instead of java.text.DateFormat. Listing 12.8 shows how the setToday() method of showDay would be rewritten to avoid the overhead of the text classes. Note that this code does not follow JavaSoft's recommended use of the Calendar class. The official way to get date and time representations is through the java.text.DateFormat class.

Listing 12.8 Printing dates without the Calendar class.

```
public synchronized void setToday() {
  // The string version of today's date.
  String todayS;

  Calendar myCalendar = Calendar.getInstance();
  timeToMidnight = 24*60-(myCalendar.get(Calendar.HOUR)*60+
                   myCalendar.get(Calendar.MINUTE));
  todayS = "Today is ";
  switch(myCalender.get(Calendar.DAY_OF_WEEK)) {
    case Calendar.MONDAY:    todayS += "Monday";    break;
    case Calendar.TUESDAY:   todayS += "Tuesday";   break;
    case Calendar.WEDNESDAY: todayS += "Wednesday"; break;
    case Calendar.THURSDAY:  todayS += "Thursday";  break;
    case Calendar.FRIDAY:    todayS += "Friday";    break;
    case Calendar.SATURDAY:  todayS += "Saturday";  break;
    case Calendar.SUNDAY:    todayS += "Sunday";    break;
  }
  todayS += ", ";
  switch(myCalendar.get(Calendar.MONTH)) {
    case Calendar.JANUARY:   todayS += "January ";  break;
    case Calendar.FEBRUARY:  todayS += "February "; break;
    case Calendar.MARCH:     todayS += "March ";    break;
    case Calendar.APRIL:     todayS += "April ";    break;
    case Calendar.MAY:       todayS += "May ";      break;
    case Calendar.JUNE:      todayS += "June ";     break;
```

```
        case Calendar.JULY:      todayS += "July ";        break;
        case Calendar.AUGUST:    todayS += "August ";      break;
        case Calendar.SEPTEMBER: todayS += "September "; break;
        case Calendar.OCTOBER:   todayS += "October ";   break;
        case Calendar.NOVEMBER:  todayS += "November ";  break;
        case Calendar.DECEMBER:  todayS += "December ";  break;
    }

    todayS += + myCalendar.get(Calendar.DAY_OF_MONTH);
    // Convert the string to a byte array for efficiency when we print
    today = todayS.getBytes();
}
```

java.util.Hashtable

Unfortunately most methods for both insertion and retrieval are synchronized. If a program needs the functionality of a hash table and must run at absolutely top speed there are two ways to avoid synchronization overhead.

If only *very* small sets of data are being maintained, it may be possible to use a pair of arrays, one for keys and one for values. Finding a value would then be a matter of walking through the array of keys and then looking at the corresponding position in the array of values. However, the cost of iterating through the key array soon overtakes the cost of synchronization.

A better solution is to use the HashMap class, which was introduced in Java 1.2 as part of the new collection hierarchy. The details of this hierarchy are beyond the scope of this book, but we will note that in version 1.2 both Hashtable and HashMap implement an interface called Map. This interface specifies all the methods that programmers are used to in the Hashtable class. The difference is that Hashtable implements these methods with synchronization and HashMap implements them unsynchronized.

A hash map can be used exactly like a hash table:

```
HashMap record = new HashMap();
record.put("name","Tinderbox");
record.put("artist","Siouxsie and the Banshees");
record.put("year",new Integer(1986));
System.out.println(record.get("name") + " was released in " +
                    record.get("year"));
```

If a hash map is to be used locally in a method, or if it can be proven that only one thread will ever be using it at a time, no other thought needs to be given to it. However, if there is a chance that multiple threads will be accessing or modifying a hash map simultaneously, care must be taken to ensure that the program is well behaved.

There are two different ways a hash map can be modified. First, some existing key can be assigned to a new value. If this is the only kind of change a program or servlet is making, every thread will see a consistent version of the hash map. That is, if one thread is doing a `get()` at the same time another is doing a `put()`, the first thread will unpredictably see either the old value or the new one, but in either case no error will occur.

The second kind of change is the insertion or deletion of keys. This kind of change is called *structural,* and it is more potentially dangerous. If one thread is doing a `get()` while another thread is inserting a new value, it is possible that the `get()` will happen while the innards of the hash map are being rearranged, which could result in some random value being returned by the `get()`. In the preceding record example, for example, the title might be returned for `get("year")`, which could be disastrous if the program then tries to cast the result to an `Integer` and do arithmetic on it.

There are a few ways to avoid problems with structural changes. The first is to tell the collection system to synchronize all structural changes. This can be done when the hash map is constructed, as in

```
Map record = Collections.synchronizedMap(new HashMap());
```

It is also possible for the program to do its own synchronization around any `gets` and `puts` that might happen simultaneously. Since the programmer is in explicit control of the synchronization, it may be possible to leave some access unsynchronized, leading to slightly better performance.

There are two other performance issues to be aware of. First, constructing both hash tables and hash maps can be expensive, so if possible, reuse them between requests. Also, for every new key used, another object of type `Hash-tableEntry` is created. This may have an impact on both memory usage and performance.

Despite the potential performance problems with hash tables, they are unquestionably useful. Judicious use of them may improve overall servlet performance significantly. For the *Money* site, we keep a cache of stock data, one of the most critical parts of the site, indexed by hash tables. Retrieval may lock the monitor table, but this is still much better than having to go over the network for each quote request or iterating over a huge set of symbols looking for the one we want.

If hash tables or hash maps are going to be used, note Sun's guidelines about the initial creation parameters. Try to get a sense of how large the hash table will grow, and preallocate that much space when it is created. This is especially important, as dynamically resizing a hash table is very expensive.

If there is no way to know in advance how large the tables are likely to be, consider adding some code to occasionally write the size of the hash table to the log. Once the application has been running for a while, this data will help fine-tune the initial parameters.

It is most common to use strings as the keys in a Hashtable, and in recent versions of the JDK, String's hashCode() method has been tuned to support this, although it is worth noting that the hash value is not cached but must be recomputed every time a string is used to store or retrieve a value from a Hashtable.

If a custom class is being used as keys, it may be worth considering writing a custom hashCode() method. If no class-specific method is provided, all classes use the object's hashCode(). What this method does is implementation dependent: the reference implementation uses the underlying machine pointer to the object. This method is fast, but under some circumstances it may not provide the best distribution of objects in the hash buckets. If retrieving data from a hash table seems slow, a data-based hash algorithm may be better. The one in the String class can serve as a good model for writing such a method.

Vector

As with hash tables, most methods for both insertion and retrieval are synchronized. It is possible to avoid this overhead by using the ArrayList class, which is part of the Java 1.2 collection hierarchy. ArrayList corresponds to Vectors in exactly the same way that HashMap corresponds to Hashtable. That is, ArrayList may be thought of as an unsynchronized version of Vectors. As with HashMaps, care must be taken with structural changes (see the previous section for details).

If a firm upper limit can be set on the number of elements and if all elements are of the same type, it is significantly more efficient to use an array instead of a vector. Using an array avoids the synchronization overhead and the overhead of calling the elementAt() and insert() methods, and the repeated casting from Object can be avoided.

If Vector or ArrayList is going to be used, note Sun's guidelines about the initial creation parameters, because resizing a vector on the fly may be expensive. Also note that it is slightly more efficient to walk a vector with

```
for(int i=0;i<theVector.size();i++)
```

than with an enumeration, as it avoids the overhead of constructing the enumeration object.

StringTokenizer

This class does not introduce a great deal of new overhead, beyond that of using strings at all. However, if the string is being split on only one character, it is slightly more efficient to use indexOf, as this avoids constructing the String-Tokenizer object. It might look something like this:

```
int pos = -1;
String remainder = theString;
 while((pos = remainder.indexOf(theChar)) != -1) {
    token    = theString.substring(0,pos);
    // Do something with token
    remainder = theString.substring(pos+1);
}
```

This would work, but if it is viewed through a pair of optimization-colored glasses, the two substrings calls will stand out like big ugly warts. Remember that the substring() methods construct new strings, which cost both time and space. An even better way to write this is

```
int pos     = -1;
int lastPos = 0;
 while((pos = theString.indexOf(theChar,lastPos)) != -1) {
    token = theString.substring(lastPos,pos);
    // Do something with the token
    lastPos = pos;
}
```

which constructs only one string per iteration.

Replacing the Java Core Classes

As we have seen, there are many instances where a Java core class is almost exactly what is needed but the overhead is high due to internationalization or synchronization that may be unnecessary because the object is used in only a single locale or a single method. Since the source for the Java core classes is available from Sun, at some point it may be tempting to obtain it; simply remove the word "synchronized" everywhere it appears, recompile, and use this new class instead.

It is not quite so simple. For one thing, the new class would need to sit outside the Java packages. Although it is in principle possible to replace the classes in the Java core, it is *extremely* dangerous to do so. These classes are used by the Java Web Server, the Java compiler, and other classes within the core library. Making what seems like even a small change may produce bugs that are almost impossible to locate and fix.

In addition to putting the derived classes into a new package, the package should be given a different name so that it is impossible to mistake the new class for the Java original. If the modified version has had all the synchronized qualifiers removed, prepending threadUnsafe to the class name clearly labels it as what it is.

Even given these two conditions, we recommend against tampering with the Java core classes. No aspect of these classes was introduced by accident, and making what seems like a minor change may introduce weird behavior that is difficult to track down. Using a new package and a new name will at least limit this behavior to code within the servlets that use it, but even so it is best to leave these classes as God, Duke, and JavaSoft intended them.

Optimizing Library Use in the Game Application

In this section we once again revisit the Game application introduced at the end of Chapter 9. At the end of Chapter 10, we made it thread safe without overly harming performance by introducing local copies of some global variables, which could then be used freely without worrying about some other thread affecting or needing global data. The cost was the need to clone a hash table, which could become quite large. As we noted, such operations can be very time consuming. In addition to the single expensive clone operation, the Game application makes heavy use of Vectors and Hashtables. All the classes that make up the game also make heavy use of Strings and Print-Writers, which have their own performance issues. We are now in a position to fix all these problems and create one of the fastest game engines on the Web.

We start by fixing the easy things first. In particular, we can replace almost all the strings in this application with byte arrays. Unfortunately, this means we also lose the convenience of PrintWriters and have to fall back on Output-Streams, since PrintWriter does not have a write(byte[]) method.

This will require a few simple changes. First, GameServlet should call not getWriter() but getOutputStream() instead. Also, all the render() and play() methods in Game, Question, and the subclasses of Question should be changed to accept an OutputStream instead of a PrintWriter. We can now change Game to get rid of Strings, as shown in Listing 12.9.

Listing 12.9   Version of the Game class that uses Writers.

```java
import java.io.*;
import java.util.*;
/**
 * The game class, which handles all interactions and
 * renderings of a game
 */
class Game {
  /**
   * The questions in the game
   */
```

```
private Question questions[];
/**
 * The name of this game
 */
private String gameName;
/**
 * The name of the game in byte form for quick printing
 */
private byte gameNameBytes[];
// Some byte arrays for printing
byte openHTML[]    = "<HTML>".getBytes();
byte openHEAD[]    = "<HEAD>".getBytes();
byte openTITLE[]   = "<TITLE>".getBytes();
byte closeHTML[]   = "</HTML>".getBytes();
byte closeHEAD[]   = "</HEAD>".getBytes();
byte closeTITLE[]  = "</TITLE>".getBytes();
byte openFORM1[]   = "<FORM ACTION=".getBytes();
byte openFORM2[]   =  " METHOD=GET>".getBytes();
byte openBODY[]    = "<BODY>".getBytes();
byte closeBODY[]   = "</BODY>".getBytes();
byte submit[]      = "<INPUT TYPE=SUBMIT VALUE=Play!>".getBytes();
byte closeFORM[]   = "</FORM>".getBytes();
byte scoreMessage1[] = "<P>You scored ".getBytes();
byte scoreMessage2[] = " out of a possible ".getBytes();
byte scoreMessage3[] = " points</P>".getBytes();
byte rightMessage1[] = "<P>You got ".getBytes();
byte rightMessage2[] = " out of ".getBytes();
byte rightMessage3[] = " right</P>".getBytes();
/**
 * The constructor sets up some instance variables and then
 * uses the Properties to generate questions
 */
public Game(Properties props) {
  Vector tmpQuestions = new Vector(10);
  int i;
  Question q;

  // Get the game name
  gameName = props.getProperty("name");
  if(gameName == null) gameName = "Untitled Game";

  gameNameBytes = gameName.getBytes();
  // Build questions until we get an indicator that there
  // are no more
  for(i=0;
      (q = Question.buildQuestion(props,i)) != null;
      i++)
  {
    tmpQuestions.addElement(q);
  }
  // Now move the questions into the array to make using them
  // faster
```

```java
      questions = new Question[tmpQuestions.size()];
      for(i=0;i<tmpQuestions.size();i++) {
        questions[i] = (Question) tmpQuestions.elementAt(i);
      }
    }
    /**
     * A game is rendered by sending the begining of a page,
     * rendering each of the questions, and then sending the
     * end of the page
     */
    public void render(String uri,OutputStream out)
          throws IOException
    {
      int i;
      // Send out the beginning of the page, including the
      // start of the form
      out.write(openHTML);
      out.write(openHEAD);
      out.write(openTITLE);
      out.write(gameNameBytes);
      out.write(closeTITLE);
      out.write(closeHEAD);
      out.write(openBODY);
      out.write(openFORM1);
      out.write(uri.getBytes());
      out.write(openFORM2);
      // Render each of the questions.  Each will have some
      // form field that the user will respond to when playing
      // the game
      for(i=0;i<questions.length;i++) {
        questions[i].render(out);
      }
      // Close the form and the page
      out.write(submit);
      out.write(closeFORM);
      out.write(closeBODY);
      out.write(closeHTML);
    }
    /**
     * To play a game, the beginning of the result page is sent
     * out, then each question is played, and finally
     * the page is closed.
     */
    public void play(Properties props, OutputStream out)
          throws IOException
    {
      int i;
      out.write(openHTML);
      out.write(openHEAD);
      out.write(openTITLE);
      out.write(gameNameBytes);
      out.write(closeTITLE);
      out.write(closeHEAD);
```

```
    out.write(openBODY);
    // Create an object to hold running tallies
    GameTallies t = new GameTallies();
    // Play each question
    for(i=0;i<questions.length;i++) {
      questions[i].play(props,out,t);
    }
    if(t.getMaxScore() != 0) {
      out.write(scoreMessage1);
      out.write((""+t.getScore()).getBytes());
      out.write(scoreMessage2);
      out.write((""+t.getMaxScore()).getBytes());
      out.write(scoreMessage3);
    }
    if(t.getNumMultiple() != 0) {
      out.write(rightMessage1);
      out.write((""+t.getNumRight()).getBytes());
      out.write(rightMessage2);
      out.write((""+t.getNumMultiple()).getBytes());
      out.write(rightMessage3);
    }
    // close the page
    out.write(closeBODY);
    out.write(closeHTML);
  }
}
```

Admittedly it is ugly, but it is not really that complicated. We have just introduced a byte array for every string we had in the old version. Note that because we are still calling getBytes() explicitly, this code is still able to be internationalized. It just means that the translation from characters to the local representation in bytes will happen once, when the class is loaded, instead of each time the strings are printed.

We have also taken the opportunity to replace the vector of questions with an array. Every call to Vector.elementAt() is synchronized, and there is the overhead of the method call itself, so an array is much better. An array may not be thread safe in instances where a vector would be, but that is not an issue in this case because the elements are never changed outside the constructor.

We could do exactly the same thing for the Question classes: replace strings with byte arrays and vectors with arrays. We will, in fact, do this, but we will better it. Note that the render() methods all produce the same thing each time they are called. This means that rather than calling write() several times inside render(), a single byte array containing the text could be built in the constructor and then simply written in render().

Likewise, there are only a few possible outputs of play() in the Scored-Question and MulipleQuestion classes. There will be a different output for each possible answer, but that set is likely to be pretty small. This means that we can

construct an array of byte arrays containing every possible response and then
play() can just write out the proper one. Listing 12.10 shows how this would
be done in ScoredQuestion.

Listing 12.10   Optimized version of ScoredQuestion.

```
import java.io.*;
import java.util.*;
/**
 * A ScoredQuestion has a fixed set of responses, each of
 * which has an associated score.  When played, it adds the
 * appropriate score to
 * the tally
 */
public class ScoredQuestion extends Question {
  /**
   * The scores assocated with each answer
   */
  int scores[];
  /**
   * The maximum score for this question, which is needed
   * for the final 'you scored n out of m possible points'
   * message
   */
  int maxScore;
  /**
   * The bytes containing the rendered version of this question
   */
  private byte renderBytes[];
  /**
   * The bytes containing each possible output of play()
   */
  private byte playBytes[][];
  /**
   * The constructor sets up the answers and scores Vectors
   */
  public ScoredQuestion(String prefix,Properties props) {
    super(prefix,props);
    int i,j;
    Vector answers   = new Vector();
    Vector tmpScores = new Vector();
    maxScore = 0;
    String res;
    String score;
    int    iscore;
    String tmp1 = getPrefix() + ".answer";
    String tmp2 = getPrefix() + ".score";
    // If our question is named question<n>, we look for
    // properties called question<n>.answer0,
    // question<n>.answer1, and so on
    // until we fail to find one
    for(j=0;(res = props.getProperty(tmp1 + j)) != null;j++) {
      answers.addElement(res);
```

```
      score = props.getProperty(tmp2 + j);
      if(score != null) {
        iscore = Integer.parseInt(score);
        if(iscore > maxScore) maxScore = iscore;
      } else {
        iscore = 0;
      }
      tmpScores.addElement(new Integer(iscore));
    }
    // Copy the scores into an array, which will allow
    // play() to be faster
    scores = new int[tmpScores.size()];
    for(i=0;i<tmpScores.size();i++) {
      scores[i] = ((Integer) tmpScores.elementAt(i)).intValue();
    }
    // Set up the render array
    ByteArrayOutputStream bout = new ByteArrayOutputStream();
    PrintWriter pout = new PrintWriter(bout);
    pout.println("<P>" + getText() + "</P>");
    pout.println("<P><SELECT NAME=" + getPrefix() + ">");
    for(i=0;i<answers.size();i++) {
      pout.println("<OPTION VALUE=" +
                       i + ">" + answers.elementAt(i));
    }
    pout.println("</SELECT>");
    pout.println("</P>");
    pout.close();
    renderBytes = bout.toByteArray();
    // Similiarly, there are only as many possible outputs of
    // play() as there are possible answers.  So if we
    // generate the full text of each now, the play()
    // method can just send out the appropriate one
    playBytes = new byte[answers.size()][];
    for(i=0;i<answers.size();i++) {
      bout = new ByteArrayOutputStream();
      pout = new PrintWriter(bout);
      pout.println("<P>");
      pout.println(getText());
      pout.println("You said: " + answers.elementAt(i));
      pout.println(" which is worth " +
                       tmpScores.elementAt(i) +
                       " points");
      pout.println("</P>");
      pout.close();
      playBytes[i] = bout.toByteArray();
    }
  }
  /**
   * ScoredQuestions render as a dropdown menu of
   * possible answers
   */
  public void render(OutputStream out) throws IOException {
    out.write(renderBytes);
  }
```

```
/**
 * When playing a ScoredQuestion, the appropriate score and
 * the maximum possible score are added to the running
 * tallies
 */
public synchronized void play(Properties props,
                              OutputStream out,
                              GameTallies tallies)
      throws IOException
{
  String answer = props.getProperty(getPrefix());
  int i;
  int whichEntry = 0;
  tallies.incMaxScore(maxScore);

  if(answer != null) {
    whichEntry = Integer.parseInt(answer);
  }
  tallies.incScore(scores[whichEntry]);
  out.write(playBytes[whichEntry]);
 }
}
```

One of the nice things about this technique is that we can once again use
PrintWriters, since they are used only in the constructors and will not slow
anything down when the pages are generated. Note that it is very important to
close PrintWriters before getting the bytes out of the ByteArrayOutputStreams.
This is because PrintWriter buffers output internally and does not write it out
to the underlying stream until it fills up, is flushed, or is closed. This means that
if we did not close the PrintWriters, toByteArray() might well return empty
arrays.

Note that we have also replaced the vector of scores with an array, again
using a vector only as an intermediate. This removes the overhead of getting the
score in play() and also saves the cost of converting from an Object to an
Integer and then getting the intValue(). We can do the same thing with
MultipleQuestion, but since there is nothing new or interesting there, we will
not present it here. It is available on the CD-ROM that accompanies this book.

That brings us to optimizing OpenQuestion. Once again, we can start by
prebuilding the output of render(). play(), however, is much more difficult,
because there is no fixed set of responses. The major problem with play() is
the use of the hash table.

As we noted earlier in this chapter, every call to get() and put() is synchronized—which can slow things down. And as we noted in Chapter 11, in a
sense it is not synchronized enough. We had to create a local copy to ensure
that answers and sortedAnswers would stay in sync, without having to make
all of play() synchronized.

It is starting to look as if the answers hash table is more trouble than it is worth. All it is really doing in play() at this point is providing a quick way to look up the user's answer. The value of this activity should not be underestimated—for large sets of data it is always faster to use a hash table than to look at every element in an array to find the one that is wanted. However, in this case we do not have to look at every element.

Consider what happens when a user submits an answer to play(). The thread we introduced in Chapter 10 takes care of adding it to the master list, so in play() the only real concern is how it affects what is in the top list that is printed. There are really only a few ways this can happen.

- The answer is a new one, and less than ten items are on the top list.
- The answer is already on the top list.
- The answer would move into the top list based on this addition vote.

In most cases all these can be checked without having to look at every answer. Typically, no more than the top entries will need to be looked at, which is a small enough number that doing so will be faster than using the hash table. Another benefit of this approach is that we can avoid resorting the whole array each time. If the user's answer is in the top list, at most one swap will have to be done.

To do this, we introduce an array of sortedCounts, which parallel sortedAnswers. play() still makes a local copy of these arrays, but this is just a local reference, without all the pain of clone(). After the local copies are made, we look through the top answers for the one the user has given. If we get beyond the current top count, we can stop. Listing 12.11 shows the code.

Listing 12.11 Optimized version of OpenQuestion.

```java
import java.io.*;
import java.util.*;
/**
 * An open question is a question without a fixed set of
 * predefined answers. Users can respond with anything, and
 * the question will keep a list of responses, with an
 * associated count of how many times each response
 * has been given.  When played, this question will print
 * the top ten answers
 */
public class OpenQuestion extends Question implements Runnable
{
  /**
   * All the answers we've seen, mapped to counts of how
   * many times we've seen them
   */
  private transient Hashtable answers;
  /**
```

```
 * The keys from the answers hashtable, sorted by number
 * of times each has been given
 */
private transient String sortedAnswers[];
/**
 * The counts associated with each answer
 */
private transient int sortedCounts[];
/**
 * Answers that are waiting to be processed
 */
private Vector pending;
/**
 * The bytes containing the rendered version of this question
 */
private byte renderBytes[];
/**
 * An auxiliary thread that will periodically take all
 * the pending answers and add them into the answers table
 */
private Thread runner;
/**
 * Sets up the answers hashtable and the pending vector, and
 * kicks off the new thread
 */
public OpenQuestion(String prefix,Properties props) {
  super(prefix,props);
  answers = new Hashtable();
  pending = new Vector();
  sortedAnswers = new String[0];
  sortedCounts  = new int[0];
  ByteArrayOutputStream bout = new ByteArrayOutputStream();
  PrintWriter pout           = new PrintWriter(bout);
  pout.println("<P>" + getText() + "</P>");
  pout.println("<P><INPUT TYPE=TEXT NAME=" +
               getPrefix() +
               "></P>");
  pout.close();
  renderBytes = bout.toByteArray();
  runner = new Thread(this);
  runner.start();
}

/**
 * OpenQuestions render as a simple text input box
 */
public void render(OutputStream out) throws IOException
{
  out.write(renderBytes);
}
/**
 * When an OpenQuestion is played, the entry for the
 * answer given is incremented or set to 1 if this is
 * the first time it has been seen.  The sorted array is
```

```
 * then resorted, and the top answers are printed
 */
public void play(Properties props,
                 OutputStream out,
                 GameTallies tallies)
    throws IOException
{
  String answer = props.getProperty(getPrefix());
  int i;
  // The local copies
  String mySortedAnswers[];
  int    mySortedCounts[];
  // Copy the global data into our local variables
  synchronized(this) {
    mySortedAnswers = sortedAnswers;
    mySortedCounts  = sortedCounts;
  }
  if(answer == null) {
    answer = "";
  }
  // How many results will we show?
  int howMany = (mySortedAnswers.length < 10) ?
    mySortedAnswers.length : 10;
  // Find the answer in the list of answers
  boolean answerMatters = true;
  int ranking            = -1;
  for(i=0;i<sortedAnswers.length;i++) {
    // If we have passed the top list, and this entry is less
    // than the last one that is in the top list, then this
    // answer won't matter to the display
    if(i > howMany &&
       sortedCounts[i] < sortedCounts[howMany])
    {
      answerMatters = false;
      break;
    }
    if(answer.equals(sortedAnswers[i])) {
      ranking = i;
      break;
    }
  }
  // If we didn't find the answers it is new!  But that
  // only matters if there are fewer than ten entries;
  // otherwise this entry won't make the top list
  if(ranking == -1) {
    if (howMany < 10) {
      int oldcount = mySortedAnswers.length;
      String myNewAnswers[] = new String[oldcount+1];
      int myNewCounts[]     = new int[oldcount+1];
      System.arraycopy(mySortedAnswers,
                       0,
                       myNewAnswers,
                       0,
                       oldcount);
```

```
            System.arraycopy(mySortedCounts,
                             0,
                             myNewCounts,
                             0,
                             oldcount);

        myNewAnswers[oldcount] = answer;
        myNewCounts[oldcount]  = 1;
        howMany++;
        mySortedCounts  = myNewCounts;
        mySortedAnswers = myNewAnswers;
      }
    } else {
      // This isn't a new entry.  If it matters, add it
      if(answerMatters) {
        mySortedCounts[ranking]++;
      }
      // Do we need to sort the array again?
      if(ranking != 0) {
        if(mySortedCounts[ranking] >
          mySortedCounts[ranking-1])
        {
          // Fortunately, if we do it is much simpler, since only
          // one swap will be needed
          String temps                = mySortedAnswers[ranking];
          mySortedAnswers[ranking]    = mySortedAnswers[ranking-1];
          mySortedAnswers[ranking-1]  = temps;
          int tempi                   = mySortedCounts[ranking];
          mySortedCounts[ranking]     = mySortedCounts[ranking-1];
          mySortedCounts[ranking-1]   = mySortedCounts[ranking];
        }
      }
    }
    // At this point the rankings are all set.
    // Display the results
    StringBuffer bout = new StringBuffer(512);
    bout.append("<P>");
    bout.append(getText());
    bout.append("</P>");
    bout.append("Top ");
    bout.append(howMany);
    bout.append(" answers:");
    bout.append("<UL>");
    for(i=0;i<howMany;i++) {
      bout.append("<LI>");
      bout.append(mySortedAnswers[i]);
      bout.append(" (");
      bout.append(mySortedCounts[i]);
      bout.append(")");
    }
    bout.append("</UL>");
    bout.append("You said: ");
    bout.append(answer);
```

```
      out.write(bout.toString().getBytes());
      // Finally, store the answer in the pending vector.
      // The runner thread will eventually add it to the
      // master list. Note that this does not need to be explicitly
      // synchronized, because  addElement already is
      pending.addElement(answer);
}
/**
 * Once a minute, the run method takes all the pending
 * answers and adds them into the answer table, then
 * resorts everything
 */
public void run() {
   Vector     myPending;
   String     mySortedAnswers[];
   int        mySortedCounts[];
   Integer    entryCount = null;
   String     answer;
   int        i;
   while(runner != null) {
      try {Thread.sleep(5000);} catch (Exception e) {}
      // If there are no pending results, let's not waste
      // CPU cycles
      if(pending.size() == 0) continue;
      // Make a local copy of the pending list and answer
      // tables, and clear the global pending list.  This
      // must be synchronized to ensure that no vote comes
      // in between making the local copy and creating
      // the new global one
      synchronized(this) {
        myPending = pending;
        pending   = new Vector();
      }
      // Go through myPending, and add the elements to answers
      for(i=0;i<myPending.size();i++) {
        answer     = (String) myPending.elementAt(i);
        entryCount = (Integer) answers.get(answer);
        if(entryCount == null) {
           answers.put(answer,new Integer(1));
        } else {
           answers.put(answer,
                      new Integer(entryCount.intValue() + 1));
        }
      }
      // Now sort the table
      mySortedAnswers = sortAnswers(answers);
      // and rebuild the sorted counts
      mySortedCounts   = new int[mySortedAnswers.length];
      for(i=0;i<mySortedAnswers.length;i++) {
        mySortedCounts[i] =
          ((Integer)
           answers.get(mySortedAnswers[i])).intValue();
      }
```

```
    // Now replace the global answers and sortedAnswers
    // with our local copy. Again, this needs to be
    // synchronized to ensure that we don't mess up play()
    synchronized(this) {
       sortedAnswers = mySortedAnswers;
       sortedCounts  = mySortedCounts;
    }
  }
}
/**
 * Sorts the given hashtable in order of the values
 */
private String[] sortAnswers(Hashtable myAnswers) {
  int i,j;
  int count1;
  int count2;
  String tmp;
  String mySortedAnswers[];
  int numAnswers     = myAnswers.size();
  mySortedAnswers    = new String[numAnswers];
  Enumeration keys = myAnswers.keys();
  i=0;
  while(keys.hasMoreElements()) {
     mySortedAnswers[i++] = (String) keys.nextElement();
  }
  for(i=0;i<numAnswers;i++) {
     for(j=0;j<numAnswers;j++) {
       count1 = ((Integer)
                   myAnswers.get(mySortedAnswers[i])).intValue();
       count2 = ((Integer)
                   myAnswers.get(mySortedAnswers[j])).intValue();
       if(count2 < count1) {
          tmp                 = mySortedAnswers[i];
          mySortedAnswers[i] = mySortedAnswers[j];
          mySortedAnswers[j] = tmp;
       }
     }
  }
  return mySortedAnswers;
}
}
```

Note that the auxiliary thread still uses the hash table. This is as it should be, since when adding the data the whole array would need to be searched, so a hash table will quickly be more efficient. However, we can avoid copying the hash table in run(). The answers hash table is now no longer shared by run() and play(), only the sorted arrays are, so run() can use and modify it without worrying that some other thread will be trying to access it at the same time. While the elimination of clone() in run() is not directly important for performance, since it will not affect the time for run() to complete, it is still worth doing as little work as possible. This will free up CPU cycles and also prevent allocating huge copies of the hash table that would just need to be garbage collected anyway.

Believe it or not, this concludes the optimization of the game servlet! We do not claim that this is "provably the optimal implementation"; there probably are one or two things we could do to tweak performance just a bit more. Anyone who can think of one is invited to share it with other readers by logging on to the Addison Wesley Longman Web site at the address shown on this book's copyright page. However, assuming that the application is run on reasonably fast hardware, this implementation will be fast enough for all real-world instances.

Conclusion

The rich class libraries of the Java programming language are unquestionably a large part of the language's huge success. Most of the time, servlet programmers will have no reason to abandon this richness and convenience in favor of performance, for the most part, because the classes in the core library are very well tuned. When it is necessary to squeeze the last few drops of speed out of an application, the suggestions given in this chapter should help.

Although we have now finished looking at optimization techniques, there is still much to say about sample applications. In Chapter 14 we discuss a wide variety of methods for connecting servlets with external applications. One of the most common kinds of external applications are databases, and at the end of Chapter 14, we show how to store the answers to OpenQuestions in a database so that they can be preserved even if the Java Web Server is shut down.

CHAPTER 13

Communicating with External Applications: Sockets and Mail

By now we should have conveyed that there is pretty much nothing a servlet cannot do. However, that does not mean that in a given application the servlet *should* do everything. More often than not, some of the functionality of an application resides outside the servlet and indeed outside the Java Web Server (JWS) altogether. There are many reasons why this may be necessary. Perhaps the servlet is acting as a middle-layer interface to some legacy system or a gateway to some other application. Or there may be some central facility, such as a database, that many applications besides the Java Web Server need access to. For example, there may be some functionality that is exported to the Web through a servlet but for which there is a better application available to local users.

In this chapter we look at *sockets,* the simplest and most general mechanism two applications use for talking to each other. Sockets can connect two or more processes on the same machine or across a network. When a Web browser talks to the JWS, the data is sent over a socket. The data the Java Web Server gets from a database goes over a socket, as well. Therefore, even if a developer is never going to use sockets directly, understanding how they work makes it easier to understand all the other methods of talking to remote applications. We conclude the chapter by looking at how servlets can send mail, which we consider as a simple socket-based protocol.

What Are Sockets?

A socket is a simple two-way communication channel between two processes, which may or may not be on the same machine. Typically, either process may read or write to the socket and be sure that the data it receives or transmits is valid. From the beginning, Java was designed to be network aware. Consequently, it is much easier to construct sockets in Java than it is in other languages. It also means that most Java programmers do not need to worry about the details of what sockets really are, beyond noting that socket communication happens in three distinct steps.

1. One application, called the *server* or *daemon*, runs on a particular machine and listens to a particular "port," which is identified by a number, for incoming connections.

2. The other application, the *client*, requests a connection on the server's machine and the port it is listening to. The two applications can then communicate back and forth.

3. When either application decides that the conversation is over, it closes its end of the connection. The other application detects this and cleans itself up.

For those who are interested in the details of transmission control protocol (TCP) and related protocols, we recommend *Java Network Programming* by Elliotte Rusty Harold.[1] For those interested in how to program sockets at the lowest levels, we recommend W. Richard Stevens's *UNIX Network Programming*, a book that is likely to be found on any system programmer's bookshelf.[2]

Listing 13.1 is a very simple servlet that uses sockets. It simply acts as a client to some server running on the same machine at port 4567. It does not send any data to the server, and it simply forwards any data it receives to the user.

Listing 13.1   Servlet that makes a socket connection.

```
import javax.servlet.*;
import javax.servlet.http.*;
import java.net.*;
import java.io.*;
public class SocketServlet extends HttpServlet {
  public void doGet(HttpServletRequest req,
                    HttpServletResponse res)
```

---

[1]See Appendix for complete publication information.
[2]Copyright © 1990. Available from Prentice Hall PTR, Upper Saddle River, NJ, or Amazon.com Books.

```
        throws IOException
{
   res.setContentType("text/plain");
   getData(res.getOutputStream());
}
public void doPost(HttpServletRequest req,
                   HttpServletResponse res)
       throws IOException
{
   res.setContentType("text/plain");
   getData(res.getOutputStream());
}
public void getData(ServletOutputStream out)
       throws IOException
{
   try {
      // Make the connection to the server
      Socket s = new Socket("localhost",4567);
      // Get an input stream from the socket
      InputStream in = s.getInputStream();
      byte buffer[]  = new byte[1024];
      int count;
      // Read all the data the server feeds us,
      // and send it to the user
      while((count = in.read(buffer)) > 0)  {
         out.write(buffer);
      }
      in.close();
   } catch(Exception e) {
      out.println("Unable to read data for daemon");
   }
   out.close();
 }
}
```

At this point it is important to consider the differences between Java data types and the bytes that represent them. As we noted in the discussion on strings in Chapter 12, the translation from strings to bytes can vary greatly depending on the location. If this servlet is running in Greece and the daemon is running in Egypt, the bytes sent by the daemon might not look at all like strings.

Potentially, exchanging data can be more complex if the daemon is not written in the Java programming language. Frequently a client may want to get numeric data from a daemon, and it is tempting to use calls like `DataInput-Stream`'s `readInt()` or `readFloat()`. However, C or Pascal's representation of an integer may be very different from Java's. The C representation is also likely to differ between Intel-based systems and Motorola or Sparc-based systems.

What this means in practical terms is that if the daemon is not written in Java, the data passed back and forth should be as simple and low-level as possible. Instead of trying to send integers, send four bytes with well-defined rules about how to combine them. Instead of sending strings, send bytes with an agreement between client and server about how to combine them back into strings. In short, remember that on the wire it is all just ones and zeros, and any more sophisticated structure to data must come from the programs.

By the way, it may seem confusing that the servlet is a client and yet is part of the JWS. The resolution of this apparent paradox is that a *server* is something that listens for connections, and a *client* is something that initiates a connection. It is perfectly possible for the same program to be both a server and a client, as this is.

Writing the Server-Side of the Socket Connection

In principle, it is possible to extract any piece of functionality in a servlet and pull it out into a separate process. Normally, it does not make any sense to do so, but there are some situations where it may.

The first and most obvious is if there is some service or functionality available on a machine other than the one that is running the Web server. For example, a laboratory might have a special computer dedicated to controlling an electron microscope. It would not make sense to put the Web server on this machine, and yet it may be useful to allow the microscope to be controlled or images to be obtained through the Web server. In this case a small server could be written for the controller machine, with which a servlet would then communicate. This would also allow multiple Web servers to use the same equipment.

The other major reason to write a server is to isolate code from the Web server. In particular, there may be some system resource that is available only by writing native methods. Native methods in general are dangerous to the Web server, since they may not cooperate properly with other threads, and a buggy native method can potentially crash the entire Web server. If native methods are needed, a small server can be written with which a servlet will communicate, and if worse comes to worst and there is a problem with the native code, at least the Web server will stay up and running. Of course, this slows down the servlet's performance to some extent. This performance impact needs to be weighed against how "trustworthy" the native code is.

It is as easy to write servers in Java as it is to write clients. Listing 13.2 is the code for a simple server that the socket servlet can connect to. Sadly, it does not do anything as exciting as control an electron microscope, but it does send "Hello, World" to all clients that connect to it.

Listing 13.2 Simple server.

```
import java.net.*;
import java.io.*;
public class SocketServer1 {
  public final static byte[] message="Hello, world!".getBytes();
  public static void main(String argv[]) throws Exception {
    ServerSocket theServerSocket = new ServerSocket(4567);
    Socket connection;
    OutputStream out;
    while(true) {
      // Wait for an incoming connection.  This line
      // will hang until a connection comes in
      connection = theServerSocket.accept();
      // When we get here, we have a connection. Get an
      // output stream, and send some data
      out        = connection.getOutputStream();
      out.write(message);
      out.close();
      connection.close();
    }
  }
}
```

Compile and run this code. Then telnet to <your_machine> 4567. Telnet will print out "Hello, world!" and exit. The servlet can now be compiled and installed, and it will, as expected, return "Hello, world."

Although this server is functional, it has one major problem, besides the fact that it does not do anything useful. If a request comes in while the server is already handling a request, the second client has to wait until the server is finished talking to the first one and goes back up to the accept line. It does not take very long to send a few bytes of text, but if the server was doing something much more complicated, the delay could be a problem. A better solution would be to start a new thread for each connection so that the main loop can immediately go back and listen for new ones. This version would look like Listing 13.3.

Listing 13.3 Threaded version of the server.

```
import java.net.*;
import java.io.*;
public class SocketServer2 implements Runnable {
  public final static byte[] message="Hello, world!".getBytes();
  private Socket theSocket;
  private Thread runner;
  public SocketServer2(Socket s) {
    theSocket = s;
    runner    = new Thread(this);
    runner.start();
  }
```

```
public void run() {
  try {
    OutputStream out = theSocket.getOutputStream();
    out.write(message);
    out.close();
    theSocket.close();
  } catch(Exception e) {
    System.err.println("Unable to send data: " + e);
    e.printStackTrace(System.err);
  }
}
public static void main(String argv[]) throws Exception {
  ServerSocket theServerSocket = new ServerSocket(4567);
  Socket connection;
  while(true) {
    connection = theServerSocket.accept();
    new SocketServer2(connection);
  }
}
}
```

UDP Sockets

The sockets we discussed in the previous section are all *TCP* sockets. TCP stands for transmission control protocol, and it is a very reliable method of transmitting data from one point to another. TCP breaks large amounts of data into smaller chunks called *datagrams* and it ensures that the datagrams are received and processed in the correct order and that if any pieces are lost in transmission they are resent. This high reliability is the reason TCP is used almost exclusively in Web-based programs.

However, the reliability comes with some cost. TCP takes some processing power to knit all the datagrams back together, which has a small but real effect on the performance of programs that use it. There is also a lot of auxiliary information that needs to be transmitted when using TCP, such as where in the final message a given datagram belongs. This means that when transmitting 10K of data, possibly 11K or more will be sent. This also has some effect on final program speed.

More significantly, however, it is very hard to write code that understands TCP from the ground up. This is not an issue for most Java programmers, since most of the hard work is done by the operating system and the rest is done by the Java.net package. However, it may be a very serious problem for people trying to interface the Java Web Server with legacy systems running on mainframes without TCP implementations.

For these people, there is a much simpler network protocol called *UDP*, for user datagram protocol. As might be expected from the name, in this protocol the programmer is responsible for managing the datagrams. Using UDP, there is no built-in assurance that data has been received as it was sent or even that it has been received at all. If TCP is like a number of people having civilized conversations on a bunch of separate phone lines, UDP is more like a room full of people just shouting their messages out loud. When someone shouts something, the shouter cannot be sure that the person intended to hear the message did unless that person shouts a response. This kind of potential data loss is not likely to be a real problem on well-behaved local networks, and it is possible to build checks on top of UDP.

Listing 13.4 shows a sample servlet that uses UDP. It connects to a mythical UDP server running on a machine called "legacy," and asks for data by sending the server a datagram consisting of the message send data and a sequence number. It then waits for a response datagram that contains the same sequence number and sends the data in that datagram on to the user. The sequence number is used to ensure that the response matches the request. This is precisely the sort of thing that TCP takes care of invisibly.

Listing 13.4   Servlet that uses a UDP socket.

```
import javax.servlet.*;
import javax.servlet.http.*;
import java.net.*;
import java.io.*;
public class UDPServlet extends HttpServlet {
  private int sequenceNumber = 0;
  public void doGet(HttpServletRequest req,
                    HttpServletResponse res)
      throws IOException,UnavailableException
  {
    res.setContentType("text/plain");
    getData(res.getOutputStream());
  }
  public void doPost(HttpServletRequest req,
                     HttpServletResponse res)
      throws IOException,UnavailableException
  {
    res.setContentType("text/plain");
    getData(res.getOutputStream());
  }
  public void getData(ServletOutputStream out)
      throws IOException,UnavailableException
  {
    DatagramSocket theSocket;
    DatagramPacket thePacket;
    byte data[] = new byte[1024];
    try {
      theSocket = new DatagramSocket();
    } catch (SocketException e) {
      throw new UnavailableException(10,this,
                              "Unable to build socket");
```

```
        }
        int mySeqNumber = getSequenceNumber();
        String message   = "Send data:" + mySeqNumber;

        thePacket = new DatagramPacket(
                        message.getBytes(),
                        message.length(),
                        InetAddress.getByName("legacy"),
                        3000);
        try {
          theSocket.send(thePacket);
        } catch (IOException se1) {
        }
        thePacket = new DatagramPacket(data,1024);
        // Look for data until we see the thing we want
        boolean foundPacket = false;
        String received     = "";
        int pos             = 0;
        int receievedSeqNum;

        while(!foundPacket) {
          theSocket.receive(thePacket);
          received = new String(thePacket.getData());
          pos = received.indexOf(":");
          if(pos != -1) {
            try {
              receivedSeqNum =
                Integer.parseInt(received.substring(0,pos));
              foundPacket = (receivedSeqNum == mySeqNumber);
            } catch (NumberFormatException ne) {
            }
          }
        }
        out.println(received.substring(pos+1));
        out.close();
    }
    private synchronized int getSequenceNumber() {
      sequenceNumber++;
      return sequenceNumber;
    }
}
```

A number of issues would have to be resolved if this servlet were ever to be put into production. Most serious, if the response is somehow lost, the servlet loops forever waiting for it. This could be addressed by exiting if received-SeqNumber is ever much larger than mySeqNumber, assuming that all responses take roughly the same amount of time and are handled more or less in the order they are sent.

The warning about distinguishing between Java data types and bytes being transmitted is especially true here. Many legacy systems do not even use ASCII, so the sequence of bytes that represent send data:1 may mean nothing to the remote system. It would have been better in this example to use an even more abstract protocol, such as a single byte giving the command and another specifying the count.

Mail

Before the arrival of HTTP and the Web, most sockets across the Internet were transmitting mail from one place to another. The details of how Internet mail works are beyond the scope of this book, but in concept, at least, it is not much more complex than the other socket-based examples we have looked at. An application on the sender's machine connects to a server and sends the message. Later, the recipient may use another application, which uses a socket to retrieve the message.

A programmer might have many reasons to want a servlet to send mail. If some serious error occurs, rather than just logging it and throwing an exception, the servlet could immediately send a mail alert to the administrator. It could even send mail to some mail-to-pager gateway, enabling a servlet to wake up the administrator at any time of night. This is a good thing, even though the administrator might not think so at the time.

In addition to sending out alerts, there may be situations where part of the task must be done by a human, possibly a human who does not have access to the Web logs or local databases. Mail may be the best way to alert the person to what must be done.

There are lots of different kinds of mail systems out there, with acronyms like SMTP and POP. If Java programmers do not have to concern themselves with the system-specific details of sockets, why should they have to know about how particular systems send mail? JavaSoft does not think they should, so they have introduced a set of classes that encapsulate mail behavior and hide all the low-level specifics. It is considered essential enough to have been made a standard extension to the Java language; it lives in the `javax.mail` and `javax.mail.internet` packages.

There may be many commercial implementations of these packages built for specific mail systems, much like there are many JDBC drivers. However, JavaSoft provides a standard implementation that is free for download and should work on most common UNIX or NT systems. As of this writing, the latest version was 1.1 and was available at

http://www.javasoft.com/products/javamail/

It also requires the JavaBeans Activation framework, available from

http://www.javasoft.com/beans/glasgow/jaf.html

Once the necessary packages have been downloaded and installed, using
them to send mail requires only a few steps. First a Session object (not to be
confused with the JWS session tracking) is created and told about the local mail
environment. Then a Message object is created that contains the mail text, as
well as information such as the subject and recipients. Then the Transport class
is used to actually send the message. Listing 13.5 is a sample servlet that takes
orders for a mythical candy company and sends the request to an operator who
fulfills it.

Listing 13.5   Servlet that sends orders via mail.

```
import javax.servlet.*;
import javax.servlet.http.*;
import javax.mail.*;
import javax.mail.internet.*;
import java.util.*;
import java.io.*;
public class OrderServlet extends HttpServlet {
  private String mailFrom              = "orderservlet";
  private String mailTo                = "";
  private Session theSession           = null;
  private InternetAddress theAddress[] = null;
  public void init(ServletConfig conf) throws ServletException {
    String mailHost;
    // Get the various information we need to set up the session
    if ((mailHost = conf.getInitParameter("mailHost")) == null)
      throw new ServletException("mailHost not provided");
    // Set up the session
    Properties mailProps = new Properties();
    mailProps.put("mail.smtp.host",mailHost);
    theSession = Session.getDefaultInstance(mailProps,null);
    if ((mailTo = conf.getInitParameter("mailTo")) == null)
      throw new UnavailableException(
                    this,
                    "mailTo not provided");
    // Set up the address
    theAddress     = new InternetAddress[1];
    try {
      theAddress[0] = new InternetAddress(mailTo);
    } catch (AddressException e) {
      throw new UnavailableException(
                    this,
                    "Specified recipient address is invalid");
    }
  }
  public void doGet(HttpServletRequest req,
                    HttpServletResponse res)
      throws UnavailableException,IOException
  {
    ServletOutputStream out = res.getOutputStream();
    String queryString      = req.getQueryString();
```

```java
res.setContentType("text/html");
out.println("<HTML>");
out.println("<HEAD>");
out.println("<TITLE>Yummy Candy Co. order form</TITLE>");
out.println("</HEAD>");
out.println("<BODY BGCOLOR=#FFFFFF>");
// If we don't have an order yet, print the order form
if(queryString == null) {
  out.println(
      "Specify how many of each item you would like:<P>");
  out.println("<FORM ACTION=/servlet/OrderServlet " +
              "METHOD=GET>");
  out.println("Raspberry Swirl: ");
  out.println("<INPUT TYPE=TEXT NAME=item1 VALUE=0><BR>");
  out.println("Fascination Sweet: ");
  out.println(
  "<INPUT TYPE=TEXT NAME=item2 VALUE=0><BR>");
  out.println("Crunchy Frog: ");
  out.println("<INPUT TYPE=TEXT NAME=item3 VALUE=0><BR>");
  out.println("<P>");
  out.println("Please provide your shipping address :");
  out.println("<TEXTAREA NAME=address></TEXTAREA>");
  out.println("<P>");
  out.println("<INPUT TYPE=SUBMIT NAME=Send VALUE=Send>");
  out.println("</FORM>");
} else {
StringBuffer buffer = new StringBuffer(1024);
String values[];
// We have the info we need, so construct the message
// and send it
buffer.append("Order for the following:");
buffer.append(Character.LINE_SEPARATOR);

buffer.append("Raspberry Swirl: ");
values = req.getParameterValues("item1");
buffer.append(values[0]);
buffer.append(Character.LINE_SEPARATOR);
buffer.append("Fascination Sweet: ");
values = req.getParameterValues("item2");
buffer.append(values[0]);
buffer.append(Character.LINE_SEPARATOR);
buffer.append("Crunchy Frog: ");
values = req.getParameterValues("item3");
buffer.append(values[0]);
buffer.append(Character.LINE_SEPARATOR);

// Build the message object
Message msg = new MimeMessage(theSession);
try {
  // Specify the subject
```

```
            msg.setSubject("Candy order");

            // Set the message content
            msg.setContent(buffer.toString(),"text/plain");

            // Specify the recipient
            msg.setRecipients(Message.RecipientType.TO,theAddress);
            // Send it
            Transport.send(msg);
        } catch (MessagingException e) {
            e.printStackTrace(System.err);
            out.println("We were unable to process your order.");
            out.println("Please try again later");
            out.println("</BODY>");
            out.println("</HTML>");
            return;
        }
        out.println("Your order is being processed.");
        out.println("Please expect one to two weeks delivery ");
        out.println("time");
    }
    out.println("</BODY>");
    out.println("</HTML>");
  }
}
```

There are a couple of things to notice in the code in Listing 13.5. The first is the way the Session is constructed. The properties that are passed to the getDefaultInstance() method can specify a number of things about the local mail environment. Here, we tell it that we will be using SMTP and what machine serves as our SMTP host. If we had been using some other type of mail system, it might have been necessary to specify other properties, such as a username and password, with which to connect to the mail server.

Another thing to notice is that we specify a content type for the mail, text/plain. The JavaMail API allows for the transmission of data of any MIME type, as well as multipart messages with "attachments" of many different types. So it would be possible, for example, to write a servlet that allowed users to draw on a virtual canvas and then submit their art in a contest. The judge could receive the submissions as mail messages with GIF attachments.

Adding E-mail to the Project Management Application

The last time we changed the project management application, in Chapter 6, we made it easier to maintain by separating out the HTML presentation into a JSP page. However, that didn't make the project plans any easier to maintain. Project managers still have to keep track of all the relevant e-mail flying back and forth and remember to keep the project archive up to date. Wouldn't it be great if the archive could keep itself up to date by reading the e-mail itself? Using the JavaMail API, it can (see Listing 13.6).

Listing 13.6 Version of `ManageServlet` that sends mail.

```java
package com.awl.cseng.jws.project;
import javax.servlet.*;
import javax.servlet.http.*;
import java.util.*;
import java.io.*;
/**
 * Allows users to manage project plans via HTML forms.
 *
 * @see Project
 */
public class ManageServlet extends HttpServlet
implements ArchiveConstants {
  // Constants
  public static final String PAGE_URL      = "PageUrl";
  public static final String ARCHIVE_STORE = "Store";
  public static final String ARCHIVE_PATH
                                           = "SerializedArchivePath";
  public static final String SERIALIZED    = "Serialized";
  public static final String EMAIL         = "Email";
  public static final String PROVIDER      = "JavaMailProvider";
  public static final String HOST          = "Host";
  public static final String FOLDER        = "Folder";
  public static final String USER          = "MailUser";
  public static final String PASSWD        = "MailPassword";
  // Instance data members
  Archive archive;
  String  pageUrl;
  String  archivePath;
  String  provider;
  String  folder;
  String  user;
  String  passwd;
  String  host;
  // Servlet API methods
  /**
   * Requires initialization parameters whose names are defined
   * by PAGE_URL and ARCHIVE_STORE.  PAGE_URL is the (relative)
   * URL of the Java Server Page that displays the output of this
   * servlet.  If ARCHIVE_STORE is SERIALIZED, then ARCHIVE_PATH
   * must be defined as the location of a serialized Archive
   * object.  If one does not exist, it will be created when the
   * servlet is shut down.  If ARCHIVE_STORE is EMAIL, then
   * PROVIDER, HOST, FOLDER, USER, and PASSWD must be defined for
   * the servlet to access the appropriate email folder via
   * JavaMail.
   *
   * @see Archive
   * @see #PAGE_URL
```

```
 * @see #ARCHIVE_STORE
 * @see #SERIALIZED
 * @see #ARCHIVE_PATH
 * @see #EMAIL
 * @see #PROVIDER
 * @see #HOST
 * @see #FOLDER
 * @see #USER
 * @see #PASSWD
 */
public void init(ServletConfig conf) throws ServletException {
  super.init(conf);
  pageUrl = conf.getInitParameter(PAGE_URL);
  if ( pageUrl == null ) {
    throw new UnavailableException(this,
                                   "Init parameter "
                                   + PAGE_URL
                                   + " must be set.");
  }
  try {
    String archiveStore = conf.getInitParameter(ARCHIVE_STORE);
    if ( archiveStore.equalsIgnoreCase(SERIALIZED) ) {
      archivePath = conf.getInitParameter(ARCHIVE_PATH);
      if ( archivePath == null ) {
        archive = new Archive();
      } else {
        FileInputStream    fileIn
                              = new FileInputStream(archivePath);
        ObjectInputStream objIn
                              = new ObjectInputStream(fileIn);
        archive = (Archive)objIn.readObject();
        objIn.close();
      }
    } else if ( archiveStore.equalsIgnoreCase(EMAIL) ) {
      provider = conf.getInitParameter(PROVIDER);
      folder   = conf.getInitParameter(FOLDER);
      user     = conf.getInitParameter(USER);
      passwd   = conf.getInitParameter(PASSWD);
      host     = conf.getInitParameter(HOST);
      archive  = new EmailArchive();
      ((EmailArchive)archive).updateFromFolder(provider,
                                                 host,
                                                 folder,
                                                 user,
                                                 passwd);
    }
  } catch (Exception e) {
    log("init(): " + e.getLocalizedMessage());
    throw new UnavailableException(this, "init() caught " + e);
  } finally {
    if ( archive == null ) archive = new Archive();
  }
```

```
  }
  /**
   * Writes the updated, serialized archive object to the file
   * defined by the ARCHIVE_PATH parameter
   */
  public void destroy() {
    try {
      FileOutputStream   fileOut
                                 = new FileOutputStream(archivePath);
      ObjectOutputStream objOut
                                 = new ObjectOutputStream(fileOut);
      objOut.writeObject(archive);
      objOut.close();
    } catch (IOException e) {
      log("destroy(): " + e.getLocalizedMessage());
    } finally {
      archive = null;
    }
  }
  /**
   * Updates the archive and then prints the same output as
   * doGet()
   *
   * @see #doGet
   */
  public void doPost(HttpServletRequest req,
                     HttpServletResponse resp)
  throws ServletException {
    try {
      int len = req.getContentLength();
      if (len > 0) {
        Hashtable ht = HttpUtils.parsePostData(len,
                          req.getInputStream());
        archive.update(ht);
      }
    } catch (IOException e) {
      log("ProjMgmtServlet.doPost() caught " + e);
    }
    doGet(req, resp);
  }
  /**
   * Prints HTML using the Java Server Page defined in the
   * PAGE_URL parameter
   */
  public void doGet(HttpServletRequest req,
                    HttpServletResponse resp)
  throws ServletException {
    ((com.sun.server.http.HttpServiceRequest)
                        req).setAttribute("archive", archive);
    try {
      ((com.sun.server.http.HttpServiceResponse)
                        resp).callPage(pageUrl, req);
```

```
    } catch (FileNotFoundException f) {
      throw new UnavailableException(this,
                              "Servlet initialized with bad "
                              + PAGE_URL
                              + " parameter: "
                              + pageUrl);
    } catch (IOException e) {
      throw new UnavailableException(this,
                              "Servlet encountered "
                              + e.getLocalizedMessage());
    }
  }
}
```

The servlet does not need to change much. It just has to have some more
configuration information so that it can know how and where to look for
project-related e-mail. This version of the servlet only checks at startup, but it
would not be difficult for `init()` to spawn a thread that keeps checking the
mail folder for new messages. The major changes need to happen to the `Archive`
class. For ease of presentation, we create a subclass of `Archive` called `Email-
Archive` with a method for updating an archive via e-mail (see Listing 13.7).
Another benefit of extending `Archive` is that we can keep the original class free
of dependencies on the `javax.mail.*` packages.

Listing 13.7   Project management class that handles e-mail.

```
package com.awl.cseng.jws.project;

import java.util.*;
import java.text.*;
import javax.mail.*;
/**
 * A subclass of Archive that can be modified by data stored in
 * an e-mail folder, using the JavaMail API.
 */
public class EmailArchive extends Archive
implements java.io.Serializable {
  // instance methods
  /**
   * Reads the subject: lines from e-mail messages from folder on
   * host via provider.  Looks for the following fields in
   * those lines: PROJECT_NAME, ACTION, TYPE, NAME, DESCRIPTION,
   * and DUE_DATE.
   *
   * @see ArchiveConstants
   * @see javax.mail.URLName
   *
   * @exception MessagingException if something goes wrong while
   * reading from the folder
   * @exception NoSuchProviderException if the specified provider
   * cannot be found (if you are using third-party providers, you
   * will need to create a javamail.providers registry)
```

```java
    */
    public int updateFromFolder(String provider,
                                String host,
                                String folder,
                                String user,
                                String passwd)
    throws NoSuchProviderException, MessagingException {
      URLName url = new URLName(provider,
                               host,
                               -1,
                               folder,
                               user,
                               passwd);
      Properties props = System.getProperties();
      props.put("mail.smtp.host", host);
      Session session = Session.getDefaultInstance(props, null);
      session.setDebug(false);
      Store store = session.getStore(url);
      int numMessagesProcessed = 0;
      store.connect();
      Folder f = store.getDefaultFolder();
      if (f == null) return 0;
      f = f.getFolder(folder);
      if (f == null) return 0;
      f.open(Folder.READ_ONLY);
      try {
        int count = f.getMessageCount();
        for (int i = 1; i = count; i++) {
          Message msg = f.getMessage(i);
          String subject = msg.getSubject();
          Hashtable subj = parseSubject(subject);
          if (subj != null) {
            update(subj);
          }
          ++numMessagesProcessed;
          msg = f.getMessage(++i);
        }
      } catch (IndexOutOfBoundsException e) {
        // we have read all the messages--let's quit
      }
      return numMessagesProcessed;
    }
    /**
     * Takes single-word arguments from PROJECT_NAME, ACTION, TYPE,
     * NAME, DESCRIPTION, and DUE_DATE fields.
     *
     * @return a Hashtable of field values indexed by field names.
     */
    protected Hashtable parseSubject(String subject) {
      Hashtable ht = new Hashtable();
      // use space and tab characters for delimiter
      StringTokenizer scanner = new StringTokenizer(subject,
                                                    " ");
```

```
    while (scanner.hasMoreTokens()) {
      String tok = scanner.nextToken();
      if (tok.equalsIgnoreCase(PROJECT_NAME + ':'))          {
        ht.put(PROJECT_NAME, scanner.nextToken());
      } else if (tok.equalsIgnoreCase(ACTION + ':'))          {
        ht.put(ACTION, scanner.nextToken());
      } else if (tok.equalsIgnoreCase(TYPE + ':'))          {
        ht.put(TYPE, scanner.nextToken());
      } else if (tok.equalsIgnoreCase(NAME + ':'))          {
        ht.put(NAME, scanner.nextToken());
      } else if (tok.equalsIgnoreCase(DESCRIPTION + ':')) {
        ht.put(DESCRIPTION, scanner.nextToken());
      } else if (tok.equalsIgnoreCase(DUE_DATE + ':'))          {
        ht.put(DUE_DATE, scanner.nextToken());
      }
    }
    return ht;
  }
}
```

This class can parse the Subject headers from all the e-mail messages in a folder and use the information to build (or update) an archive. Everyone on a project can copy all their mail to a special address that EmailArchive can use to retrieve it later. As long as they use the right strings in their subjects, EmailArchive can keep track of the changes to the project as they are announced. For instance, if the deadline for fixing a bug has been changed, the project manager can send a message with the subject project_name: moneymag type: bug name: StickyButton action:update due_date: 10/10/98. As soon as a developer fixes it, he or she can send e-mail with the subject project_name: moneymagtype: bug name: StickyButton action: close.

Conclusion

Mail is a socket-based system where an application writes some data to a server, in this case a piece of mail, which another application may later retrieve. This notion of sending and retrieving data is fundamental to all the external applications a servlet may wish to use. The next chapter looks at databases, which specialize in storing vast quantities of data and allowing lots of applications to retrieve it.

CHAPTER 14

Communicating with External Applications: Databases and the JDBC

Perhaps the most common kind of external application that servlets need to communicate with are databases. In part this is because many Web applications are essentially HTML interfaces to existing databases. A major component of the `Money.com` site, for example, consists of a database of various stock information. It would, in principle, be possible to take this data and put it in flat files or something else the program could access directly, but we would then lose the benefits of fast, indexed retrieval and concurrency control that any modern database provides.

In addition to putting existing databases on the Web, servlets often need to store their own data. A servlet can keep track of small quantities of data in a file or keep track of per-user data using the session tracking mechanism, but for anything beyond the simplest kinds of data, it pays to let a real database worry about managing the updates and speed of retrieval.

In this chapter we explore how servlets use databases to both retrieve and store data. We start with an overview of how databases work, then discuss the Java Database Connectivity (JDBC) classes, which are the standard way for Java applications to talk to relational databases. We conclude by looking at some other database technologies.

How Do Databases Work?

Before jumping into JDBC, it will be useful to review how a database works and introduce some terminology. To start with, databases follow the socket-based client-server model we discussed in Chapter 13. A process called the *database server,* or sometimes just the *database,* contains all the data, indexes, security information, and so on. This process is the one responsible for the real work. It has a socket that listens for connections over the network, which consists of requests for data, or instructions to add or change data. In a sense, databases are much like the Java Web Server (JWS) itself.

Typically only one or two kinds of applications ever connect to the Java Web Server to make requests. However, many different kinds of applications may connect to a database. Most databases ship with a command line utility that lets users interactively make requests. From the user's perspective, a conversation with the database using this command line program might look something like Listing 14.1.

Listing 14.1   Sample dialog with a database.

```
1. User starts the program and provides a username and password
2. The program responds: OK
3. The user types: create table test1(int a, char b(4));
4. The program responds: OK
5. The user types:  insert into table test1 values(1,"hi");
6. The program responds: OK
7. The user types:  insert into table test1 values(2,"hello");
8. The program responds: OK
9. The user types:  select * from test1;
10. The program responds:
a    b
---------
1    hi
2    hello
```

Behind the scenes, however, the conversation looks very different. The transmission of the username and password may be encrypted, and the commands to create, insert, and retrieve data may be compiled into some internal representation. The returned data probably is not sent all at once, but instead a count of rows is returned, and the program then asks for the data in each row. The exact bytes that are sent back and forth to communicate these requests and responses vary widely among databases.

In the old days, when a programmer wanted to write a new client program that used a database, the programmer had to be somewhat familiar with the details of this protocol and intimately familiar with the *client library*—a set of routines usually written in C that could be called to send a query, get the number of rows, get a particular row, and so on. Programmers spent months learning the details of a particular library; if a company purchased a new database the next month, they had to start from scratch.

This was a pretty sad state of affairs for programmers, companies, and ultimately database vendors, as well. Two important developments improved things somewhat. The first was the development of open database connectivity (ODBC). People noticed that, although specific details about what a database could do and how it did it varied widely, many supported essentially the same functionality. This enabled the creation of client libraries that consisted of a set of functions common to all databases. These functions still talked to a database in a particular protocol, but at least programmers did not have to relearn a new library for every new database.

The other important development was the notion of writing layers on top of the C functions to provide database access for non-C programmers. This meant that Perl or Python programmers could write applications in their favorite language without having to learn C. Sometimes the layers simply gave access to the underlying client library routines, and in other cases much more sophisticated functionality was provided, which could translate into dozens of low-level C routines. In either case, using the libraries meant installing the C libraries on every machine where the programs would run.

JDBC and JDBC Drivers

JDBC combines both ODBC and the layering concept. Like ODBC, it provides for a database-independent set of methods for interacting with any database, and like the various language wrappers, it hides details of the specific API behind a set of Java classes.

There is enough information on how to use JDBC to fill several books, and in fact several have been written. We recommend *JDBC: Database Access with Java* by Graham Hamilton, R.G.G. Cattell, and Maydene Fisher.[1] However, there are only a few steps required to do simple kinds of database access. The first step is to select a driver. A JDBC *driver* is a set of classes that wrap the particular details of a particular database's client-server interface and provide the JDBC functionality. There are four kinds of drivers.

The simplest kind of driver to write takes the existing client library and uses the functions in it as native methods, adding additional Java methods to provide the JDBC functionality. As we have previously indicated, native methods in the JWS are potentially a problem. Commercial JDBC drivers are unlikely to introduce any memory leaks or corruption, but they still may not cooperate with the Java threading system as well as pure Java would, and thus can introduce some hard-to-find performance problems or even deadlocks. Native drivers may also interact strangely with the just-in-time (JIT) compilers, the presence of native methods means that applets cannot use the driver and that a

---

[1]See Appendix for publication details.

different version of the libraries must be purchased for each kind of system on which the servlet is to run.

Similar to the native driver, there are drivers that act as bridge between JDBC and ODBC. They sit on top of an existing ODBC installation in the same way the first kind of driver sits on top of the raw client libraries. The drivers require that the ODBC code be available as native methods, and they frequently require the database-specific native libraries as well.

For situations where native methods are a problem, it is possible to write a middle-level daemon. This daemon can contain the native methods and talk directly to the database, and then a pure Java JDBC driver can be written to talk to the daemon. This removes the native code from the servlet at the cost of introducing an intermediate step in getting and sending data, which may affect ultimate performance.

Finally, it is possible to reimplement the low-level client libraries in pure Java, giving a pure JDBC driver. Writing this kind of driver requires intimate knowledge of the database-client protocol, which is typically available only to the database vendor.

There are well over 30 vendors selling JDBC drivers. An up-to-date list is maintained at

http://www.javasoft.com/products/jdk/1.2/docs/guide/jdbc/index.html

Database URLs

Because JDBC is database independent, it needs a way to specify which database is to be used, where on the network it is, what kind of driver to use, and possibly the username and password with which to make the connection. Fortunately there is already a universal way to locate resources: *URLs*. The URLs that specify databases under JDBC look a little different from those used to specify Web pages, but the concept is the same.

The most general form of a JDBC URL is

```
<general driver type>:<specific driver type>://<machine>:<port>/<database>
```

The general driver type is usually JDBC, but sometimes ODBC. The specific driver type usually indicates either the kind of database to connect to or the vendor of the driver. This field may have a value such as `sybase`, `oracle`, `weblogic`, or `msaccess`. The machine and port that specify where the database is running, in some cases, may be omitted. They may be specified in some auxiliary configuration file; some databases may provide default values. Finally, the database field specifies which database to use. Most database servers allow for many different databases to be active simultaneously.

Using JDBC

It may appear that using JDBC is a formidable undertaking, but once the basics are understood, JDBC is much easier to use than it is to talk about. The first step is to decide on a database to use and choose a driver. For the remainder of this section, our examples will use a database called *PostgreSQL,* an open-source, commercial-quality database that is available for most versions of UNIX including Linux, with an NT port currently underway. PostgreSQL comes with a pure Java–DBC driver, so any system with an available Java implementation can use it, as long as there is a UNIX system on which to run the server. For PostgreSQL URLs, the general type is JDBC, the specific type is `postgresql`.

Depending on the exact task, the next step may be to use some other tool to set up a database. The next example uses a table called `testdb`, which contains an integer value called `foo` and a string of 16 characters called `bar`. This table can be built using `psql`, the PostgreSQL command-line utility. We also put in some data at the same time.

```
create table testdb (foo int,bar char(16));
insert into testdb values(1,'Hello, world');
insert into testdb values(17,'JDBC rules!');
```

It is next necessary to add the JDBC classes to the Java Web Server's CLASS-PATH so that the server will have access to the classes. The details of how to do this are different for pure Java drivers than for drivers with native methods. For PostgreSQL, the easiest way is to put a copy of the `postgresql.jar` file in the `<server_root>/lib` directory. All `.jar` files in this directory are automatically added to the class path. If this driver had a native component, under UNIX it would have to be added to the LD_LIBRARY_PATH of the Java virtual machine running the JWS. Under NT, the Installation Wizard would place the libraries where they belong.

When a servlet that uses JDBC starts up, the driver class must be loaded. When a JDBC driver is loaded, it registers itself and specifies what kinds of URLs it can handle so that when JDBC encounters a URL that begins with something like `jdbc:postgresql:...`, it will know what class should handle the connection.

There are two ways to load this class. First, each servlet can explicitly do the loading, using the default class loader somewhere in the `init()` method. For PostgreSQL, it would be done with the following code:

```
Class.forName("postgresql.Driver");
```

The advantage of this method is that multiple drivers can be loaded by different servlets. The downside is that if there are many servlets using the same driver, time will be wasted for the second and subsequent calls to Class.forName(), because once a class is loaded it does not need to be reloaded. In this case, it is more efficient to just tell the JWS which driver to load. This can be done by starting the Java Web Server with a special parameter, as in

```
httpd -Djdbc.drivers=postgresql.Driver
```

Everything is now in place for servlets to use databases. This use happens in a couple of steps. First a connection to the database is established, by specifying a database URL and often a username and password. Then a Statement object is created. There are many kinds of statements, but we concern ourselves only with java.sql.Statement, which allows a single command to be sent to the database, and java.sql.PreparedStatement, which can be more efficient when many similar commands are sent. After the statement has been issued a command, if data is being returned, a ResultSet object is obtained. The ResultSet is used to get each row of data and each value within each row.

Listing 14.2 shows a simple servlet that retrieves data from the test database we constructed above. As usual, compile it and put it in the /servlets directory or somewhere in the JWS class path. It assumes that certain site-specific information will be provided in the Properties screen of the administration tool: the database URL, the user's name, and the password.

Listing 14.2   Servlet that uses JDBC to get data.

```
import java.io.*;
import java.sql.*;
import java.text.*;
import javax.servlet.*;
import javax.servlet.http.*;
public class SQLServlet extends HttpServlet
{
  private static String dbUrl;
  private static String userName;
  private static String password;
  public void init(ServletConfig conf) throws ServletException {
    if ((dbUrl = conf.getInitParameter("dbUrl")) == null)
      throw new ServletException("dbUrl not provided");
    if ((userName = conf.getInitParameter("userName")) == null)
      throw new ServletException("userName not provided");
    if ((password = conf.getInitParameter("password")) == null)
      throw new ServletException("password not provided");
  }
  public void doGet(HttpServletRequest req,
                    HttpServletResponse res)
      throws IOException
  {
    ServletOutputStream out = res.getOutputStream();
```

```
      res.setContentType("text/html");
      out.println("<HTML>");
      out.println("<HEAD><TITLE>JDBC Servlet</TITLE></HEAD>");
      out.println("<BODY>");
      try {
        Connection db;     // The connection to the database
        Statement  st;     // Our statement to run queries with

        // Load the driver
        Class.forName("postgresql.Driver");

        // Connect to database
        db = DriverManager.getConnection(dbUrl,
                                         userName,
                                         password);
        // Create a statement to use to send queries
        st = db.createStatement();

        // Get all the data from our test database
        ResultSet rs =
          st.executeQuery("select foo, bar from test");

        if(rs != null) {
          out.println("<TABLE BORDER=1>");
          out.println("<TR>");
          out.println("<TH>Foo</TH><TH>Bar</TH>");
          out.println("</TR>");
          while(rs.next()) {
            int foo    = rs.getInt("foo");
            byte bar[] = rs.getBytes("bar");
            out.println("<TR>");
            out.println("<TD>" + foo + "</TD><TD>" +
                        new String(bar) + "</TD>");
            out.println("</TR>");
          }
          out.println("</TABLE>");
          // To ensure that resources are properly
          // cleaned up, ResultSets should be closed when
          // we're done with them
          rs.close();
        } else {
          out.println("This database is empty");
        }

        // Finally close the database
        st.close();
        db.close();
      } catch (Exception e) {
        out.println("Unable to get data: " + e);
      }
      out.println("</BODY>");
      out.println("</HTML>");
  }
}
```

The code in Listing 14.2 exactly follows the programming pattern we described before. A connection to the database is obtained, a `Statement` is constructed and used to issue a query, and a `ResultSet` is then iterated over to get the data. However, notice that in this example all the work is done in the `doGet()` method. This may seem redundant—why open a new connection to the database each time? For that matter, why construct a new statement each time? The answer has to do with thread safety and performance.

JDBC drivers are required to be *thread safe,* meaning that it is possible to send several requests simultaneously and be sure that the results will not interfere with each other. However, the driver may fulfill this requirement by being single threaded internally. This means that if one thread issues a query, all other threads may have to wait until the first one completes. Creating a separate connection ensures that each will run in its own thread, and no one will have to wait for anyone else. In the next section we present some solutions to the problem of creating multiple threads and the overhead (cost) of creating a new connection each time.

Efficiency Issues and JDBC

Now that we know how to make servlets talk to databases, the issue becomes how to do so as efficiently as possible. It can be especially difficult in the multithreaded servlet environment, where simple performance enhancements, like precreating single instances of all the required objects once in `init()`, do not work.

Stated another way, the problem is using an essentially single-threaded resource in a multithreaded situation. There are two possible solutions to this dilemma: designate a single thread to deal with the resource, or create enough instances of the resource so that every thread can have one of its own. The first solution leads to *caching,* the second to *pooling.*

Caching

In a caching scheme, we keep as much data as possible in some local shared data structure, and we create an auxiliary thread that is responsible for synchronizing the local version of the data with the persistent version that lives in the database. In addition to providing a solution to the problem of JDBC and threading, this process can be much more efficient because the data is local. Database access may be the fastest way to deal with large data stores, but it is still slow compared to the speed of executing Java code. The disadvantage of caching is that the data presented to any given user may be somewhat inaccurate, as the data could have changed since the last time the cache was updated. Caching also becomes a much more difficult problem when the quantity of data becomes too large to hold in memory all at once.

Listing 14.3 is a modified version of the servlet presented in the last section. This version keeps track of IP addresses and comments and allows users to add new comments. Data is stored locally in two vectors, and an auxiliary thread periodically inserts new data into the database.

The other new feature in this example is the use of a `PreparedStatement`. Some JDBC drivers translate SQL statements into an internal representation before sending it to the database. For drivers that do this, `PreparedStatements` can be more efficient than `Statements`, because they do this translation only once. Other drivers send the raw SQL directly to the database, and for these `PreparedStatements` are no better than `Statements` but are not worse. The logical conclusion is that if a statement is to be used multiple times, it should be a `PreparedStatement`.

Listing 14.3   Servlet that uses a `PreparedStatement` for efficiency.

```
import java.io.*;
import java.sql.*;
import java.text.*;
import javax.servlet.*;
import javax.servlet.http.*;
import java.util.Vector;
import java.util.Hashtable;
public class SQLServlet2 extends HttpServlet implements Runnable
{
  private Connection        theConnection;
  private PreparedStatement theStatement;
  private Vector ips;
  private Vector entries;

  private Vector newIps;
  private Vector newEntries;
  private Thread runner;
  public void init(ServletConfig conf) throws ServletException {
    String dbUrl;
    String userName;
    String password;
    if ((dbUrl = conf.getInitParameter("dbUrl")) == null)
      throw new ServletException("dbUrl not provided");
    if ((userName = conf.getInitParameter("userName")) == null)
      throw new ServletException("userName not provided");
    if ((password = conf.getInitParameter("password")) == null)
      throw new ServletException("password not provided");
    try {
      // Set up the connection to the database
      Class.forName("postgresql.Driver");
```

```java
    } catch (ClassNotFoundException ce) {
      throw new UnavailableException(
                     this,
                     "Could not load JDBC driver");
  }

  try {
    // Connect to database
    theConnection =
      DriverManager.getConnection(dbUrl, userName, password);

    // Create a PreparedStatement to insert new data
    theStatement = theConnection.prepareStatement(
                     "insert into test value(?,?)");

    // Initializes the local data store
    ips     = new Vector();
    entries = new Vector();

    newIps     = new Vector();
    newEntries = new Vector();

    Statement st = theConnection.createStatement();
    ResultSet rs =
      st.executeQuery("select foo, bar from test");

    if(rs != null) {
      while(rs.next()) {
        ips.addElement(new String(rs.getBytes("ip")));
        entries.addElement(new String(rs.getBytes("entry")));
      }
      rs.close();
    }
    st.close();
  } catch (SQLException se) {
    throw new UnavailableException(
                     this,
                     "Unable to set up database");
  }
  // Start a new thread to periodically move information
  // into the database
  runner = new Thread(this);
  runner.start();
}
public void doGet(HttpServletRequest req,
                  HttpServletResponse res)
  throws IOException
{
  ServletOutputStream out = res.getOutputStream();
  String queryString;
  int i;
  // If the user has provided a value, insert it
```

```java
    if((queryString = req.getQueryString()) != null) {
      String values[] = req.getParameterValues("entry");

      if(values != null &&
         values[0] != null &&
         !values[0].equals(""))
      {
        synchronized(this) {
           ips.addElement(req.getRemoteAddr());
           entries.addElement(values[0]);
        }
        synchronized(this) {
          newIps.addElement(req.getRemoteAddr());
          newEntries.addElement(values[0]);
        }
      }
    }

    res.setContentType("text/html");
    out.println("<HTML>");
    out.println("<HEAD><TITLE>JDBC Servlet</TITLE></HEAD>");
    out.println("<BODY>");
    out.println("<TABLE BORDER=1>");
    out.println("<TR>");
    out.println("<TH>Foo</TH><TH>Bar</TH>");
    out.println("</TR>");

    for(i=0;i<ips.size();i++) {
      out.println("<TR>");
      out.println("<TD>" + ips.elementAt(i) + "</TD>");
      out.println("<TD>" + entries.elementAt(i) + "</TD>");
      out.println("</TR>");
    }

    out.println("</TABLE>");
    out.println("</BODY>");
    out.println("</HTML>");
  }
  public void run() {
    Vector saveIps;
    Vector saveEntries;
    int i;
    while(runner != null) {
      try {Thread.sleep(1000 * 5 * 60);} catch (Exception e) {}
      synchronized(this) {
        saveIps     = newIps;
        saveEntries = newEntries;
        newIps      = new Vector();
        newEntries  = new Vector();
      }
      for(i=0;i<saveIps.size();i++) {
        try {
```

```
      theStatement.setBytes(1,
        ((String) saveIps.elementAt(i)).getBytes());
      theStatement.setBytes(2,
        ((String) saveEntries.elementAt(i)).getBytes());
      theStatement.execute();
    } catch (Exception e) {
    }
   }
  }
 }
 public void destroy() {
   runner = null;
   try {
     theStatement.close();
     theConnection.close();
   } catch (SQLException e) {}
  }
}
```

The caching used in the example in Listing 14.3 is somewhat different from the caching in most examples, where incoming data is stored for reuse; here it is the outgoing data that is stored. This means that when the JWS shuts down, some data can be lost. This problem could be reduced by having the destroy() method flush any remaining data to the database, but if the machine on which the JWS is running suddenly goes down, there is still the possibility of lost data. Also, note that after the initial load this servlet never tries to get data from the database. If something other than this servlet is adding data to the table, it never shows up to the user.

Pooling

A caching solution may not be appropriate for many reasons, most often because there is either too much data or the data needs to be absolutely up to date when it is sent to the user. In this case, a pooling solution may be more appropriate. In this model, a number of database connections and statement objects are prepared in advance and placed in a pool. When a thread needs a connection or object, it gets one from the pool, uses it, and then places it back in the pool. If the pool is sufficiently large, every request should be able to get a connection.

The following example (Listings 14.4–14.7) does the same thing as Listing 14.3, but using a connection pool. Free of charge, this example also introduces a completely general Pool class that can manage a pool of any kind of item that implements the Poolable interface.

First, Listing 14.4 introduces the Poolable interface, which represents an object that can be placed in a pool.

Listing 14.4 General class to store pools of objects.

```
public interface Poolable {
  public boolean isAvailable();
  public void setAvailable(boolean b);
  public void destroy();
}
```

Essentially a poolable item is one that can be marked as in use. The `Pool` class has an array of such items. When it is asked for one, it looks through the array for one that is not currently being used, marks that it is in use, and returns it. When the program is done with an item, it returns it to the pool, which marks it as no longer in use (Listing 14.5). Note that `getItem()` is synchronized, since otherwise two threads could see that the same item was available and return it.

Listing 14.5 Class representing an object that can be stored in a pool.

```
import java.util.*;
/**
 * A Pool of Poolable objects
 */
public class Pool {
  private int numItems    = 0;
  private int capacity    = 0;
  private int increment   = 0;
  private Poolable items[];

  /**
   * Constructor.  Specifies how many items to allocate
   * initially and how many more to add when none is
   * available
   */
  public Pool(int capacity,int increment) {
    items          = new Poolable[capacity];
    this.capacity  = capacity;
    this.increment = increment;
  }

  /**
   * Add an item to the pool
   */
  public synchronized void addItem(Poolable p) {
    if (numItems == capacity) {
      Poolable newItems[] =
        new Poolable[capacity + increment];

      System.arraycopy(newItems,0,items,0,capacity);
      capacity += increment;
      items = newItems;
    }
```

```java
    items[numItems++] = p;
  }

  /**
   * Get an item from the pool
   */
  public synchronized Poolable getItem() {
    for(int i=0;i<numItems;i++) {
      if(items[i].isAvailable()) {
        items[i].setAvailable(false);
        return items[i];
      }
    }
    return null;
  }

  /**
   * Put an item back into the pool
   */
  public synchronized void releaseItem(Poolable p) {
    // Find the item
    for(int i=0;i<numItems;i++) {
      if(items[i].equals(p)) {
        // Mark it as available
        p.setAvailable(true);
        return;
      }
    }
  }

  /**
   * When we're done with the items, clean them up
   */
  public synchronized void destroyItems() {
    for(int i=0;i<numItems;i++) {
      items[i].destroy();
    }
    numItems = 0;
  }
}
```

We can now write a class that wraps a database connection (Listing 14.6) and implements the `Poolable` interface.

Listing 14.6 `Poolable` database connection.

```java
import java.sql.*;
import java.util.*;
public class DBConnection implements Poolable {
  private boolean available = true;
  private Connection theConnection;
  private Statement  theStatement;
  private Hashtable  preparedStatements;
```

```java
    public DBConnection(String dbUrl,String user,String pwd)
        throws SQLException
    {
      preparedStatements = new Hashtable();
      // Connect to database
      theConnection =
        DriverManager.getConnection(dbUrl, user, pwd);

      // Create a statement to use to send queries
      theStatement = theConnection.createStatement();
    }
    public void addPreparedStatement(String name,String sql)
        throws SQLException
    {
      preparedStatements.put(name,
                          theConnection.prepareStatement(sql));
    }
    public Statement getStatement() {return theStatement;}
    public PreparedStatement getPreparedStatement(String name) {
      return (PreparedStatement) preparedStatements.get(name);
    }

    public boolean isAvailable()          {return available;}
    public void setAvailable(boolean b) {available = b;}
    public void destroy() {
      try {
        theStatement.close();
        theConnection.close();
      } catch (SQLException e) {}
    }
}
```

Finally, Listing 14.7 shows the servlet that will use the `Pool`. The `init()` method creates the `Pool` and loads it with `DBConnection` items. `doGet()` then requests a connection from the `Pool` when it starts, and returns it to the pool when it is done.

Listing 14.7 Servlet that uses a pool of database connections.

```java
import java.io.*;
import java.sql.*;
import java.text.*;
import javax.servlet.*;
import javax.servlet.http.*;
import java.util.*;
public class SQLServlet3 extends HttpServlet
{
  private Pool dbConnections;
  private int ipIndex;
  private int entryIndex;
  public void init(ServletConfig conf)
      throws ServletException
  {
```

```java
String dbUrl;
String userName;
String password;
if ((dbUrl = conf.getInitParameter("dbUrl")) == null)
  throw new ServletException("dbUrl not provided");
if ((userName = conf.getInitParameter("userName")) == null)
  throw new ServletException("userName not provided");
if ((password = conf.getInitParameter("password")) == null)
  throw new ServletException("password not provided");
try {
  // Load the driver
  Class.forName("postgresql.Driver");

  // Build the pool of connections
  dbConnections = new Pool(5,5);
  for(int i=0;i<5;i++) {
    DBConnection d =
      new DBConnection(dbUrl,userName,password);
    // The first time through, take the opportunity to
    // look up the column indexes
    if(i == 0) {
      Statement   s = d.getStatement();
      ResultSet rs =
        s.executeQuery("select * from example2");
      ResultSetMetaData md = rs.getMetaData();
      for(int j=0;j<md.getColumnCount();j++) {
          String name = md.getColumnName(j);
          if(name == null) continue;
          if(name.equals("ipIndex")) ipIndex = j;
          else if(name.equals("entryIndex")) entryIndex = j;
      }
      rs.close();
    }
    d.addPreparedStatement(
            "addEntry",
            "insert into example2 values(?,?)");
    dbConnections.addItem(d);
  }
} catch (Exception e) {
  e.printStackTrace();
  throw new UnavailableException(
                    this,
                    "Could not load db driver");
}
}
public void doGet(HttpServletRequest req,
                  HttpServletResponse res)
  throws IOException
{
  ServletOutputStream out = res.getOutputStream();
  String queryString;
  res.setContentType("text/html");
  out.println("<HTML>");
```

```
out.println("<HEAD><TITLE>JDBC Servlet</TITLE></HEAD>");
out.println("<BODY>");
try {
  DBConnection d = (DBConnection) dbConnections.getItem();
  if(d == null) {
    throw new UnavailableException(
                         5,
                         this,
                         "No DB Connection available");
  }
  // If the user has provided a value, insert it
  if((queryString = req.getQueryString()) != null) {
    String values[] = req.getParameterValues("entry");

    if(values != null &&
       values[0] != null &&
       !values[0].equals(""))
    {
      PreparedStatement ps =
        d.getPreparedStatement("addEntry");
      ps.setBytes(1,req.getRemoteAddr().getBytes());
      ps.setBytes(2,values[0].getBytes());
      ps.execute();
    }
  }
  // Select everything currently in the database
  Statement st = d.getStatement();

  // Get all the data from our test database
  ResultSet rs =
    st.executeQuery("select ip, entry from example2");

  out.println("Previous entries:");
  if(rs != null) {
    out.println("<TABLE BORDER=1>");
    out.println("<TR>");
    out.println("<TH>IP</TH><TH>Entry</TH>");
    out.println("</TR>");
    while(rs.next()) {
      byte ip[]    = rs.getBytes(ipIndex);
      byte entry[] = rs.getBytes(entryIndex);
      out.println("<TR>");
      out.println("<TD>" + new String(ip) + "</TD>");
      out.println("<TD>" + new String(entry) + "</TD>");
      out.println("</TR>");
    }
    out.println("</TABLE>");
    // In order to ensure that resources are properly
    // cleaned up, ResultSets should be closed when
    // we're done with them
    rs.close();
  } else {
    out.println("This database is empty");
```

```
      }
    } catch (Exception e) {
      out.println("Unable to get data: " + e);
      e.printStackTrace();
    }
    out.println("Now you say something:");
    out.print("<FORM ACTION=");
    out.print(HttpUtils.getRequestURL(req).toString());
    out.println(" METHOD=GET>");
    out.println("<INPUT TYPE=TEXT NAME=entry>");
    out.println("<INPUT TYPE=SUBMIT>");
    out.println("</FORM>");
    out.println("</BODY>");
    out.println("</HTML>");
  }
}
```

We slipped in one additional optimization. In the `init()` method, we take the opportunity to look up the column indexes for the columns `IP` and `Entry`. Internally, the database knows columns by number, so the various `ResultSet` `get()` methods, when given a name, first have to look up the column number. Rather than do this lookup for each request, as we have done until now, we do it once at the beginning.

Object Databases

So far, all the communication methods we have discussed have used primitive data types, mostly sequences of bytes. Even JDBC gives us only slightly more sophisticated kinds of data, mostly various numeric types. Java is an object-oriented language; wouldn't it be great if a database could actually store Java objects directly, including all the rich hierarchies and objects within objects? As it turns out, there are two ways it can.

The first is an *object database*. As the name suggests, this is a database that stores objects. We could build a very simple object database right now, using serialization. To construct a database of objects of some class `Foo`, we could simply have `Foo` implement `Serializable`, construct a `Vector` or array of `Foo`s, and serialize it back and forth to disk as needed. We could even build indexes on this "database" using serializable binary trees or hash tables.

This solution would work, but it would not scale well at all. The problem with serialization is there is no way to just pull a few objects of interest out of a stream. In the example, perhaps we would want to get a hold of only 2 out of 500 `Foo`s in a `Vector`. We would still have to unserialize all 500, which would take a very long time, before we could start looking for the ones we want. This could become even more wasteful if `Foo` has some members that we are not always interested in. If Foo has a member of type `Bar` and another of type `Baz`, and we only want the `Bar` in a particular program, we would still have to pay the penalty of unserializing all the `Bazes`. What we really want is something like serialization but that only "pulls in" the parts of an object tree we really want.

This may sound impossible, but a company called Object Design has done it, in a product called the ObjectStore Personal Storage Edition (PSE). What is even better is that they have done it in pure Java, so everyone can use it. More information and a 20-day trial version are available from

http://www.odi.com

The PSE works by running a *postprocessor* over one or more class files. The postprocessor rewrites a lot of the code in the class file. For example, it may replace simple references to members with code that determines whether the member has been loaded into memory yet and pulls it in from disk if it has not. Likewise, any constructors are modified so that after the object is created it is saved to disk. The result is that the object has become *persistent*—that is, its lifespan extends beyond that of the process that created it.

The postprocessor is very careful about the code it generates, so if it is given a pure Java class as input, the resulting modified class is still pure Java. The resulting class also still has all the defined methods with all the same signatures. This means that programmers can write classes, run the postprocessor, and then use the persistent objects exactly as if they were unmodified, making it very easy to make any class persistent.

In the following example (Listings 14-8–14.10), we use ObjectStore to implement a simple bulletin board system. We have two persistent classes. A message contains a name, a subject, and text, as well as an array of response messages. There are also top-level `Board` objects, which contain the root message and an array of all messages in the system. This array is used to quickly find a particular message without traversing the whole message tree.

First we define the message object. Note that there is nothing special about the code in Listing 14.8; it is not even serializable.

Listing 14.8 Message class.

```
import java.util.Vector;
public class Message {
    private String name;
    private String subject;
    private String text;
    private int index;
    private Message[] followups;
    private int size;
    private int capacity;
```

```
public Message(String name, String subject, String text) {
  this.name    = name;
  this.subject = subject;
  this.text    = text;
  followups    = new Message[20];
  size         = 0;
  capacity     = 20;
}
public String getName()          {return name;}
public String getSubject()       {return subject;}
public String getText()          {return text;}
public int getIndex()            {return index;}
public void setIndex(int index) {this.index = index;}
public Vector getFollowups() {
  Vector v = new Vector(size);
  for(int i=0;i<size;i++) v.addElement(followups[i]);
  return v;
}
public void addMessage(Message newMessage) {
  if(size == capacity) {
    Message newArray[] = new Message[capacity + 20];
    for(int i=0;i<capacity;i++) newArray[i] = followups[i];
    capacity += 20;
    followups = newArray;
  }
  followups[size] = newMessage;
  newMessage.setIndex(size);
}
}
```

Now we define the Board object. Most of this class is also ignorant of persistence, except for main(). The main() method here creates a database and then constructs a Board object and puts it in the database, associating the name theBoard with it. Later, programs will be able to access the Board object by asking for the object with this name.

Listing 14.9   Board class that contains messages.

```
import COM.odi.*;
import java.util.Properties;
public class Board {
  private Message[] messages;
  private int capacity;
  private int size;
  public Board(String name,String subject,String text) {
    messages = new Message[20];
    capacity = 20;
    size     = 1;
    // Create the first message
    messages[0] = new Message(name,subject,text);
  }
```

```
public Message getMessage(int i)
    throws IndexOutOfBoundsException
{
  if(i > size) throw new IndexOutOfBoundsException();
  return messages[i];
}
public synchronized void addMessage(Message parent,
                                    Message newMessage)
{
  parent.addMessage(newMessage);
  addMessage(newMessage);
}
private void addMessage(Message newMessage) {
  if(size == capacity) {
    Message newArray[] = new Message[capacity + 20];
    for(int i=0;i<capacity;i++) newArray[i] = messages[i];
    capacity += 20;
    messages = newArray;
  }
  messages[size] = newMessage;
  newMessage.setIndex(size);
}
public static void main(String argv[]) {
  String dbName = argv[0];

  Session theSession = Session.create(null,null);
  theSession.join();
  Database db = Database.create(dbName,
                  ObjectStoreConstants.ALL_READ |
                  ObjectStoreConstants.ALL_WRITE);
  // Start an update transaction
  Transaction tr =
    Transaction.begin(ObjectStoreConstants.UPDATE);
  // Create the board
  Board theBoard = new Board(argv[1],argv[2],argv[3]);
  // Create a database root and associate it with the board.
  // Programs using this datbase will get the board
  // through the name we give it here
  db.createRoot("theBoard", theBoard);
  // End the transaction. This stores the Board object
  // into the database
  tr.commit();
  theSession.terminate();
}
}
```

A servlet could use these classes as they are, but then all the messages would disappear if the servlet restarts. Also, it would mean that all messages would have to be in memory all the time, which may be wasteful. But with one command we can make them persistent. That command is itself a Java program.

Install the PSE, and make sure that tools.jar and pse.jar are in the class path. Then run

```
java COM.odi.filter.OSCFP -dest . -inplace Board.class Message.class
```

This code rewrites the class files and also generates two utility classes. The Board class can now be used to generate the database. Just run the following:

```
java Board boards.odb "<your name>" "<a subject>" "<a message>"
```

This code creates three files in the current directory: boards.odb, boards.odf, and boards.odt, which together make up the database.

We can now write the servlet that will use these persistent classes (see Listing 14.10). Its use of the classes themselves will be exactly as if they were not persistent, and there will need to be only a few lines in order to set up and use the ObjectStore system.

Listing 14.10   Servlet that allows users to read and post to boards.

```
import COM.odi.*;
import javax.servlet.*;
import javax.servlet.http.*;
import java.io.IOException;
import java.util.Vector;
import java.util.Hashtable;
public class BoardServlet extends HttpServlet {
  private Session theSession;
  private Database theDatabase;
  public void init(ServletConfig c) throws ServletException {
    super.init(c);
    String dbName = c.getInitParameter("dbName");
    if(dbName == null)
      throw new UnavailableException(
                      this,
                      "dbName parameter not given");

    try {
      // Try to set up ObjectStore
      Session theSession = Session.create(null,null);
      theSession.join();

      theDatabase =
        Database.open(dbName, ObjectStore.OPEN_UPDATE);
    } catch (Exception e) {
      throw new UnavailableException(
                      this,
                      "Could not set up ObjectStore");
    }
  }
}
```

```java
    public void doGet(HttpServletRequest req,
                      HttpServletResponse res)
        throws IOException
{
    String URI            = req.getRequestURI();
    int messageNumber     = 0;
    String queryString    = req.getQueryString();
    ServletOutputStream out = res.getOutputStream();
    Board theBoard;
    Message theMessage;
    res.setContentType("text/html");
    out.println("<HTML>");
    out.println("<HEAD><TITLE>ODI demo </TITLE></HEAD>");
    out.println("<BODY>");
    out.println("");

    if(queryString != null) {
      // Determine which message the user is reading
      String values[] = req.getParameterValues("messageNumber");
      if(values != null && values[0] != null) {
        messageNumber = Integer.parseInt(values[0]);
      }
      // If the user is posting a followup, add it
      values = req.getParameterValues("action");
      if(values != null &&
         values[0] != null &&
         values[0].equals("post"))
      {
        String name    = "Anonymous";
        String subject = "";
        String text    = "This person didn't say anything!";
        values = req.getParameterValues("name");
        if(values != null && values[0] != null)
          name = values[0];
        values = req.getParameterValues("subject");
        if(values != null && values[0] != null)
          subject = values[0];
        values = req.getParameterValues("text");
        if(values != null && values[0] != null)
          text = values[0];
        // Start an update transaction
        Transaction update =
          Transaction.begin(ObjectStoreConstants.UPDATE);

        // Create the new message
        Message newMessage = new Message(name,subject,text);
        // Add it to the board
        theBoard = (Board) theDatabase.getRoot("theBoard");
        theBoard.addMessage(theBoard.getMessage(messageNumber),
                            newMessage);
        // End the transaction
        update.commit();
      }
```

```
// Now print out the page.  First, start a read-only
// transaction to get the current message
Transaction read =
  Transaction.begin(ObjectStoreConstants.READONLY);
// Get the Board.  Note we have to do this even
// if we just got the update transaction, because
// persistent objects do not cross transaction boundaries
theBoard  = (Board) theDatabase.getRoot("theBoard");
theMessage = theBoard.getMessage(messageNumber);
out.println("<HTML>");
out.println("<HEAD>");
out.println("<TITLE>Bulletin Board Servlet</TITLE>");
out.println("</HEAD>");
out.println("<BODY BGCOLOR=#FFFFFF>");
out.println("");
out.println("<H2>From: " +
            theMessage.getName() +
            "</H2>");
out.println("<H2>Subject: " +
            theMessage.getSubject() +
            "</H2>");
out.println("");
out.println(theMessage.getText());
out.println("");
out.println("Replies:<BR>");
out.println("<UL>");
Vector v = theMessage.getFollowups();
for(int i=0;i<v.size();i++) {
  Message m = (Message) v.elementAt(i);
  out.println("<LI>" +
              m.getName() +
              " - " +
              m.getSubject());
}
out.println("</UL>");
out.println("");
out.println("Post a reply:<BR>");
out.println("<FORM ACTION=" +
            URI +
            " METHOD=GET>");
out.println("Your name: ");
out.println("<INPUT TYPE=TEXT NAME=name><br>");
out.println("Subject: ");
out.println("<INPUT TYPE=TEXT NAME=name VALUE="
            + theMessage.getSubject() + "><br>");
out.println("Your comments:<br>");
out.println("<TEXTAREA NAME=text>");
out.println("</TEXTAREA><P>");
out.println("<INPUT TYPE=SUBMIT " +
            " NAME=Post VALUE=POST>");
out.println("</FORM>");
out.println("");
```

```
        out.println("</BODY>");
        out.println("</HTML>");
    }
  }
}
```

The only ObjectStore-specific code is at the beginning and end of doGet(). The first thing doGet() does is create a session, which manages the interaction with the database. The join() call associates the current thread with the session.

After the session is created and joined, a connection to the database is opened. Then a transaction is started. Transactions help protect data. If there are several things that need to happen for an object to stay in a consistent state, and only some of them happen before an error occurs, the transaction can be canceled, meaning that the first set of changes is dropped. In this example, for the database to be consistent a new message must be added to both the parent message and the complete array in the board. If one of those additions did not happen for some reason, the one that did would be canceled. The message would be lost, but the integrity of the data would remain intact.

After the transaction is opened, the root object is obtained. From then on, the objects are used as normal.

ObjectStore and the Future

JavaSoft liked ObjectStore so much that they have elected to use it in the reference implementation of a system called *JavaSpaces*, which is modeled after a system called Linda developed by David Gelernter at Yale University.[2] This system is somewhat like a public notice board. Objects can post themselves to the board, and other objects can scan the board looking for particular types of objects, or objects with certain characteristics. Once they find an object of interest, they can either remove it from the board or take a copy.

This opens up whole new models of distributed computing. For example, a servlet at a record company could take orders and then drop them into a JavaSpace. A validator could continually scan the space for orders, ensure that the credit card numbers are valid, mark the objects as having been validated, and put them back in the space. The poster department could likewise look for validated poster orders and handle them, while the CD department looks for validated CD orders.

An evaluation version of the JavaSpaces Technology Kit (JSTK) is available to registered Java developers. For future developments, check

> *http://java.sun.com:80/products/javaspaces/index.html*

---

[2]For more information, see Yale's Web site at *http://www.cs.yale.edu/HTML/YALE/CS/Linda/linda.html* or contact Scientific Computing Associates (203/777-7442).

In addition to the view of JavaSpaces we have discussed, JavaSpaces may be thought of as a service provided by a distributed system called Jini. *Jini* is a system whereby any object or device with a JVM on a network will be able to discover the existence of the network and join it by announcing its presence and capabilities. Applications will also be able to ask a lookup service for objects that have registered. JavaSpaces fits naturally into this scheme, as such a space could act as the repository for the lookups.

Jini is available to registered developers, but the details are beyond the scope of this book, so we will do little more than hint at the exciting possibilities of having a servlet dynamically discover services or devices on the network and transparently make them available over the Web. Or having a servlet register itself as a resource, and providing both Web-based and Jini-based services. For more details, stay tuned to

http://java.sun.com/products/jini

Java™ Blend™

In addition to ObjectStore, there is another mechanism for putting objects into databases. Consider the following two classes:

```
public class Foo {
   public int    anInt;
   public float aFloat;
   public Baz    aBaz;
}
class Baz {
   public double aDouble;
   public byte[] someBytes = new byte[20];
}
```

Although they cannot be stored directly in a relational database, they can be simulated by the following two tables:

```
create table Foo (
    int    objectId,
    int    anInt,
    float  aFloat,
    int    aBaz
);

create table Baz (
    int    objectId,
    double aDouble,
    byte   someBytes(20)
);
```

In this scheme, primitive types in Java map to the corresponding primitive SQL type, and object references become indexes to the table representing those objects. Once the two tables are constructed, the program can be rewritten so that every member reference is a SQL select, every member assignment a SQL update, and every call to new an insert.

This is the idea behind Java Blend, a commercial product available from the Java Software Division of Sun, that was developed jointly with The Baan Company. Like ObjectStore, it contains a postprocessor that modifies class files. Where ObjectStore changes member references into calls that retrieve data from the file-based database, Java Blend converts references into JDBC calls. Java Blend can also set up the database tables and make sure that the class hierarchy is preserved. The nice thing about this system is that it sits entirely on top of JDBC, meaning that it can be used with any database that has a JDBC driver.

More information about Java Blend is available from the following URL; this page includes a link to the on-line store where the product can be purchased:

http://www.javasoft.com/products/java-blend/index.html

Connecting the Project Management Application to a Database

The last version of the project management application (Listings 14.11 and 14.12) can read project information from a database. Because the `Database-Archive` is used only in a single-thread context, we do not have to worry about thread safety. If we wanted the servlet to write updates back to the database, however, we would need to be careful to synchronize across to the `Connection` and `PreparedStatement` objects.

Listing 14.11 Version of `ManageServlet` that uses a database.

```
package com.awl.cseng.jws.project;

import javax.servlet.*;
import javax.servlet.http.*;
import java.util.*;
import java.io.*;
/**
 * Allows users to manage project plans via HTML forms
 *
 * @see Project
 */
public class ManageServlet extends HttpServlet
implements ArchiveConstants {
  // constants
  public static final String PAGE_URL      = "PageUrl";
```

```java
public static final String ARCHIVE_STORE = "Store";
public static final String ARCHIVE_PATH
                                      = "SerializedArchivePath";
public static final String SERIALIZED   = "Serialized";
public static final String DATABASE     = "Database";
public static final String JDBC_URL     = "JdbcUrl";
public static final String TABLE        = "JdbcTable";
public static final String USER         = "JdbcUser";
public static final String PASSWD       = "JdbcPassword";
// instance data members
Archive archive;
String  pageUrl;
String  archivePath;
String  user;
String  passwd;
String  jdbcDriver;
String  jdbcUrl;
String  jdbcTable;
// Servlet API methods
/**
 * Requires initialization parameters whose names are defined
 * by PAGE_URL and ARCHIVE_STORE.  PAGE_URL is the (relative)
 * URL of the Java Server Page that displays the output of this
 * servlet.  If ARCHIVE_STORE is SERIALIZED, then ARCHIVE_PATH
 * must be defined as the location of a serialized Archive
 * object.  If one does not exist, it is created when the
 * servlet is shut down.  If ARCHIVE_STORE is DATABASE, then
 * JDBC_URL, TABLE, USER, and PASSWORD must be defined for the
 * servlet to access the appropriate table via JDBC
 *
 * @see Archive
 * @see #PAGE_URL
 * @see #ARCHIVE_STORE
 * @see #SERIALIZED
 * @see #ARCHIVE_PATH
 * @see #DATABASE
 * @see #JDBC_URL
 * @see #TABLE
 * @see #USER
 * @see #PASSWORD
 */
public void init(ServletConfig conf) throws ServletException {
  super.init(conf);
  pageUrl = conf.getInitParameter(PAGE_URL);
  if ( pageUrl == null ) {
    throw new UnavailableException(this, "Init parameter "
                                       + PAGE_URL
                                       + " must be set.");
  }
  try {
    String archiveStore = conf.getInitParameter(ARCHIVE_STORE);
    if ( archiveStore.equalsIgnoreCase(SERIALIZED) ) {
      archivePath = conf.getInitParameter(ARCHIVE_PATH);
```

```
          if ( archivePath == null ) {
            archive = new Archive();
          } else {
            FileInputStream    fileIn
                                   = new FileInputStream(archivePath);
            ObjectInputStream objIn
                                   = new ObjectInputStream(fileIn);
            archive = (Archive)objIn.readObject();
            objIn.close();
          }
        } else if ( archiveStore.equalsIgnoreCase(DATABASE) ) {
          jdbcUrl   = conf.getInitParameter(JDBC_URL);
          user      = conf.getInitParameter(USER);
          passwd    = conf.getInitParameter(PASSWD);
          jdbcTable = conf.getInitParameter(TABLE);
          archive   = new DatabaseArchive();
          ((DatabaseArchive)archive).updateFromDatabase(jdbcDriver,
                                                        jdbcUrl,
                                                        jdbcTable,
                                                        user,
                                                        passwd);
        }
      } catch (Exception e) {
        log("init(): " + e.getLocalizedMessage());
        throw new UnavailableException(this, "init() caught " + e);
      } finally {
        if ( archive == null ) archive = new Archive();
      }
    }
    /**
     * Writes the updated, serialized archive object to the file
     * defined by the ARCHIVE_PATH parameter (NOT to the database)
     */
    public void destroy() {
      try {
        FileOutputStream    fileOut
                                   = new FileOutputStream(archivePath);
        ObjectOutputStream objOut
                                   = new ObjectOutputStream(fileOut);
        objOut.writeObject(archive);
        objOut.close();
      } catch (IOException e) {
        log("destroy(): " + e.getLocalizedMessage());
      } finally {
        archive = null;
      }
    }
    /**
     * Updates the archive and then prints the same output as
     * doGet()
     *
```

```
 * @see #doGet
 */
public void doPost(HttpServletRequest req,
                   HttpServletResponse resp)
throws ServletException {
  try {
    int len = req.getContentLength();
    if (len > 0) {
      Hashtable ht = HttpUtils.parsePostData(len,
                       req.getInputStream());
      archive.update(ht);
    }
  } catch (IOException e) {
    log("ProjMgmtServlet.doPost() caught " + e);
  }
  doGet(req, resp);
}
/**
 * Prints HTML using the Java Server Page defined in the
 * PAGE_URL parameter
 */
public void doGet(HttpServletRequest req,
                  HttpServletResponse resp)
throws ServletException {
  ((com.sun.server.http.HttpServiceRequest)
                        req).setAttribute("archive", archive);
  try {
    ((com.sun.server.http.HttpServiceResponse)
                        resp).callPage(pageUrl, req);
  } catch (FileNotFoundException f) {
    throw new UnavailableException(this,
                              "Servlet initialized with bad "
                              + PAGE_URL
                              + " parameter: "
                              + pageUrl);
  } catch (IOException e) {
    throw new UnavailableException(this,
                              "Servlet encountered "
                              + e.getLocalizedMessage());
  }
 }
}
```

Listing 14.12 Project management class that handles database interactions.

```
package com.awl.cseng.jws.project;

import java.text.*;
import java.util.*;
import java.sql.*;
import java.util.Date;
// This tells javac not to use java.sql.Date
/**
```

```
 * A subclass of Archive that can be modified by data stored in
 * a database table, or to be saved in a table, using the JDBC
 * API
 */
public class DatabaseArchive extends Archive
implements java.io.Serializable {
  // instance methods
  /**
   * Reads rows from the specified table, which must have columns
   * with names defined by the constants PROJECT_NAME, TYPE,
   * NAME, DESCRIPTION, DUE_DATE, OPEN_DATE, and CLOSE_DATE
   *
   * @see ArchiveConstants
   *
   * @exception ClassNotFoundException if jdbcDriver cannot be
   * found
   * @exception SQLException if something goes wrong while
   * opening the connection to or reading from the database
   */
  public int updateFromDatabase(String jdbcDriver,
                                String jdbcUrl,
                                String table,
                                String user,
                                String passwd)
  throws ClassNotFoundException, SQLException {
    Connection conn;
    PreparedStatement stmt;
    Class driver = Class.forName(jdbcDriver);
    conn = DriverManager.getConnection(jdbcUrl, user, passwd);
    stmt = conn.prepareStatement("SELECT "
                                  + PROJECT_NAME + ", "
                                  + TYPE         + ", "
                                  + NAME         + ", "
                                  + DESCRIPTION  + ", "
                                  + DUE_DATE     + ","
                                  + OPEN_DATE    + ","
                                  + CLOSE_DATE
                                  + " FROM "
                                  + table);
    ResultSet rs = stmt.executeQuery();
    int numMessagesProcessed = 0;
    while (rs.next()) {
      Hashtable row = new Hashtable();
      row.put(ACTION,        UPDATE);
      row.put(PROJECT_NAME, rs.getString(1));
      row.put(TYPE,         rs.getString(2));
      row.put(NAME,         rs.getString(3));
      row.put(DESCRIPTION,  rs.getString(4));
      row.put(DUE_DATE,     rs.getString(5));
      row.put(OPEN_DATE,    rs.getString(6));
      row.put(CLOSE_DATE,   rs.getString(7));
      update(row);
      ++numMessagesProcessed;
    }
```

```
      stmt.close();
      conn.close();
      return numMessagesProcessed;
}
/**
 * Reads rows from the specified table, which must have columns
 * with names defined by the constants PROJECT_NAME, TYPE,
 * NAME, DESCRIPTION, DUE_DATE, OPEN_DATE, and CLOSE_DATE
 *
 * @see ArchiveConstants
 *
 * @param df - the DateFormat object whose format() method can
 * write Date strings in a format acceptable to the database
 *
 * @exception ClassNotFoundException if jdbcDriver cannot be
 * found
 * @exception SQLException if something goes wrong while
 * opening the connection or writing to the database
 */
public void saveToDatabase(String          jdbcDriver,
                           String          jdbcUrl,
                           String          table,
                           String          user,
                           String          passwd,
                           DateFormat df)
throws ClassNotFoundException, SQLException {
   Connection conn;
   PreparedStatement stmt;
   Class driver = Class.forName(jdbcDriver);
   conn = DriverManager.getConnection(jdbcUrl, user, passwd);
   stmt = conn.prepareStatement("INSERT INTO "
                         + table
                         + "("
                         + PROJECT_NAME + ","
                         + TYPE         + ","
                         + NAME         + ","
                         + DESCRIPTION  + ","
                         + DUE_DATE     + ","
                         + OPEN_DATE    + ","
                         + CLOSE_DATE
                         + ") VALUES (?,?,?,?,?,?,?)");
   Enumeration projects = getProjects();
   while(projects.hasMoreElements()) {           // write projects
      Project proj = (Project)projects.nextElement();
      stmt.setString(1, proj.getName());
      stmt.setString(2, PROJECT);
      stmt.setString(3, proj.getName());
      stmt.setString(4, proj.getDescription());
      Date dueDate = proj.getDue();
      String dueString = (dueDate == null)
                      ? ""
                      : df.format(dueDate);
      stmt.setString(5, dueString);
```

```
          Date openDate = proj.getOpened();
          String openString = (openDate == null)
                               ? ""
                               : df.format(openDate);
          stmt.setString(6, openString);
          Date closeDate = proj.getClosed();
          String closeString = (closeDate == null)
                               ? ""
                               : df.format(closeDate);
          stmt.setString(7, closeString);
          stmt.executeUpdate();
          Enumeration subtasks = proj.getSubTasks();
          while (subtasks.hasMoreElements()) {
            // Write project subtasks
            Task t = (Task)subtasks.nextElement();
            stmt.setString(1, t.getName());
            stmt.setString(2, t.getType());
            stmt.setString(3, t.getName());
            stmt.setString(4, t.getDescription());
            stmt.setString(5, df.format(proj.getDue()));
            stmt.setString(6, df.format(proj.getOpened()));
            stmt.setString(7, df.format(proj.getClosed()));
            stmt.executeUpdate();
          }
        }
        stmt.close();
        conn.close();
    }
}
```

Connecting the Game Application to a Database

Over the past few chapters, we have done a pretty good job of making the game as fast and efficient as possible. However, it still has one glaring problem. All the tallies for the OpenQuestions are stored in memory. While this is a good thing for performance, it does mean that if the Java Web Server is shut down, all that data is lost. To prevent that problem, we have the OpenQuestion store its data in a database.

Fortunately, we are in an excellent position to do this easily. Ever since Chapter 12, we have been using an auxiliary thread to update the in-memory version of the data. We can very easy extend the run() method to also write the data to the database. Note that the use of the database here is almost exactly the same as in the caching example in Listing 14.3.

There is one major difference between what we are trying to do here and what we did in the caching example. In that example, all the data the thread placed in the database was new. Here, some data is new, and other data is updated. We could solve this problem by deleting all the data in the table and then inserting all accumulated data, but it would be awfully wasteful. True, the waste would not affect end users, since it would all be happening in a background thread. However, all that extra network traffic and load on the database would not be a good thing.

To avoid the problem, we do a comparison in memory between the current contents of the database and what the contents should be after the update. To do this, we once again have to clone answers and work on a local copy. As we pointed out in Chapter 12, cloning is a very expensive operation. However, it is almost certain to be less expensive than making lots of unnecessary database calls. Listing 14.13 shows the code.

This assumes that the database name, as well as the database user's name and password, are provided as properties to the servlet. Unlike the previous database examples, this one also looks for a table name, which allows each open question to have its own table. If one of the parameters is missing the connection remains equal to null, meaning that the database simply is not used.

Listing 14.13 Version of OpenQuestion that stores tallies in a database.

```
import java.io.*;
import java.util.*;
import java.sql.*;
/**
 * An open question is a question without a fixed set of
 * predefined answers. Users can respond with anything, and
 * the question will keep a list of responses with an
 * associated count of how many times each response has been
 * given. When played, this question will print the top ten
 * answers
 */
public class OpenQuestion extends Question implements Runnable {
    /**
     * All the answers we've seen, mapped to counts of how
     * many times we've seen them
     */
    private transient Hashtable answers;
    /**
     * The keys from the answers hashtable, sorted by number
     * of times each has been given
     */
    private transient String sortedAnswers[];
    /**
     * The counts associated with each answer
     */
    private transient int sortedCounts[];
    /**
     * Answers that are waiting to be processed
     */
    private Vector pending;
    /**
```

```
 * The bytes containing the rendered version of the question
 */
private byte renderBytes[];
/**
 * An auxiliary thread that will periodically take all the
 * pending answers and add them into the answers table
 */
private Thread runner;
/**
 * The name of the table with our data.  Each
 * OpenQuestion can have its own table
 */
private String tableName;
/**
 * Connection to the database
 */
private Connection theConnection;
/**
 * Sets up the answers hashtable and the pending vector and
 * kicks off the new thread
 */
public OpenQuestion(String prefix,Properties props) {
  super(prefix,props);
  int i;
  answers = new Hashtable();
  pending = new Vector();
  sortedAnswers = new String[0];
  sortedCounts  = new int[0];
  ByteArrayOutputStream bout = new ByteArrayOutputStream();
  PrintWriter pout           = new PrintWriter(bout);
  pout.println("<P>" + getText() + "</P>");
  pout.println("<P><INPUT TYPE=TEXT NAME=" +
               getPrefix() + "></P>");
  pout.close();
  renderBytes = bout.toByteArray();
  // Set up the connection to the database
  String dbUrl     = props.getProperty("dbUrl");
  String username = props.getProperty("username");
  String password = props.getProperty("password");
  tableName       = props.getProperty(getPrefix() +
                                        ".tableName");
  if(dbUrl != null && username != null && password != null) {
    try {
      // Load the driver
      Class.forName("postgresql.Driver");

      // Connect to the database
      theConnection = DriverManager.getConnection(
                              dbUrl,
                              username,
                              password);

      // Load up any data into the Hashtable
```

```
        Statement st = theConnection.createStatement();
        ResultSet rs =
          st.executeQuery("select answer, count from " +
                          tableName);

      if(rs != null) {
        while(rs.next()) {
          byte answer[] = rs.getBytes("answer");
          int count     = rs.getInt("count");
          int pos       = answer.length;

          for(i=0;i<answer.length;i++) {
            if(answer[i] == 0) {
              pos = i;
              break;
            }
          }

          answers.put(new String(answer,0,pos),
                      new Integer(count));
        }
        rs.close();
      }
      st.close();
    } catch (Exception e) {
    }
  }
  // Start the updating thread
  runner = new Thread(this);
  runner.start();
}

/**
 * OpenQuestions render as a simple text input box
 */
public void render(OutputStream out) throws IOException
{
  out.write(renderBytes);
}
/**
 * When an OpenQuestion is played, the entry for the answer
 * given is incremented, or set to 1 if this is the first
 * time it has been seen.  The sorted array is then resorted,
 * and the top answers are printed.
 */
public void play(Properties props,
                 OutputStream out,
                 GameTallies tallies)
    throws IOException
{
  String answer = props.getProperty(getPrefix());
  int i;
```

```
// The local copies
String mySortedAnswers[];
int     mySortedCounts[];
// Copy the global data into our local variables
synchronized(this) {
  mySortedAnswers = sortedAnswers;
  mySortedCounts  = sortedCounts;
}
if(answer == null) {
  answer = "";
}
// How many results will we show?
int howMany = (mySortedAnswers.length < 10) ?
  mySortedAnswers.length : 10;
// Find the answer in the list of answers
boolean answerMatters = true;
int ranking           = -1;
for(i=0;i<sortedAnswers.length;i++) {
  // If we have passed the top list, and this entry is less
  // than the last one that is in the top list, then this
  // answer won't matter to the display
  if(i > howMany &&
     sortedCounts[i] < sortedCounts[howMany])
  {
    answerMatters = false;
    break;
  }
  if(answer.equals(sortedAnswers[i])) {
    ranking = i;
    break;
  }
}
// If we didn't find the answers it is new.  But that
// only matters if there are less than ten entries;
// otherwise this entry won't make the top list
if(ranking == -1) {
  if (howMany < 10) {
    int oldcount = mySortedAnswers.length;
    String myNewAnswers[] = new String[oldcount+1];
    int myNewCounts[]     = new int[oldcount+1];
    System.arraycopy(mySortedAnswers,
                     0,
                     myNewAnswers,
                     0,
                     oldcount);
    System.arraycopy(mySortedCounts,
                     0,
                     myNewCounts,
                     0,
                     oldcount);

    myNewAnswers[oldcount] = answer;
    myNewCounts[oldcount]  = 1;
```

```
            howMany++;
            mySortedCounts  = myNewCounts;
            mySortedAnswers = myNewAnswers;
        }
    } else {
        // This isn't a new entry.  If it matters, add it
        if(answerMatters) {
            mySortedCounts[ranking]++;
        }
        // Do we need to resort?
        if(ranking != 0) {
            if(mySortedCounts[ranking] >
                mySortedCounts[ranking-1])
            {
                // Fortunately, if we do, it is much simpler, since only
                // one swap will be needed.
                String temps                = mySortedAnswers[ranking];
                mySortedAnswers[ranking]    = mySortedAnswers[ranking-1];
                mySortedAnswers[ranking-1]  = temps;
                int tempi                   = mySortedCounts[ranking];
                mySortedCounts[ranking]     = mySortedCounts[ranking-1];
                mySortedCounts[ranking-1]   = mySortedCounts[ranking];
            }
        }
    }
    // At this point the rankings are all set.  Display the
    // results
    StringBuffer bout = new StringBuffer(512);
    bout.append("<P>");
    bout.append(getText());
    bout.append("</P>");
    bout.append("Top ");
    bout.append(howMany);
    bout.append(" answers:");
    bout.append("<UL>");
    for(i=0;i<howMany;i++) {
        bout.append("<LI>");
        bout.append(mySortedAnswers[i]);
        bout.append(" (");
        bout.append(mySortedCounts[i]);
        bout.append(")");
    }
    bout.append("</UL>");
    bout.append("You said: ");
    bout.append(answer);
    out.write(bout.toString().getBytes());
    // Finally, store the answer in the pending vector.
    // The runner thread will eventually add it to the master
    // list.  Note that this does not need to be explicitly
    // synchronized, because  addElement already is
    pending.addElement(answer);
}
```

```
/**
 * Once a minute, the run method takes all the pending
 * answers, adds them to the answer table, then resorts
 * everything
 */
public void run() {
  Hashtable myAnswers;
  Vector    myPending;
  String    mySortedAnswers[];
  int       mySortedCounts[];
  Integer   entryCount = null;
  String    answer;
  int       i;
  while(runner != null) {
    try {Thread.sleep(5000);} catch (Exception e) {}
    // If there are no pending results, let's not waste
    // CPU cycles
    if(pending.size() == 0) continue;
    // Make a local copy of the pending list and answer
    // tables, and clear the global pending list.  This must
    // be synchronized to ensure that no vote comes in
    // between making the local copy and creating
    // the new global one
    synchronized(this) {
      myAnswers = (Hashtable) answers.clone();
      myPending = pending;
      pending   = new Vector();
    }
    // Go through myPending, and add the elements to answers
    for(i=0;i<myPending.size();i++) {
      answer       = (String)  myPending.elementAt(i);
      entryCount = (Integer) myAnswers.get(answer);
      if(entryCount == null) {
        myAnswers.put(answer,new Integer(1));
      } else {
        myAnswers.put(answer,
                    new Integer(entryCount.intValue() + 1));
      }
    }
    // Now sort the table
    mySortedAnswers  = sortAnswers(myAnswers);
    // and rebuild the sorted counts
    mySortedCounts   = new int[mySortedAnswers.length];
    for(i=0;i<mySortedAnswers.length;i++) {
      mySortedCounts[i] =
        ((Integer)
          myAnswers.get(mySortedAnswers[i])).intValue();
    }
    // Update the database
    if(theConnection != null) {
      try {
        Statement st = theConnection.createStatement();
```

```
        Enumeration keys = myAnswers.keys();
        String key;

        while(keys.hasMoreElements()) {
          key = (String) keys.nextElement();

          // If this key doesn't exist in the answers table,
          // it is new
          if(answers.get(key) == null) {
            st.executeQuery("insert into " + tableName +
                            "('" + key + "'," +
                            myAnswers.get(key) + ")");
          } else if(!answers.get(key).equals(
                                   myAnswers.get(key)))
          {
            // If the values differ, it is an update
            st.executeQuery("update " + tableName +
                            "set count= " +
                            myAnswers.get(key) +
                            " where answer= '" +
                            key +
                            "'");
          }
          // If the values are equal, we don't have to do
          // anything
        }
      } catch (Exception e) {
      }
    }
    // Now replace the global answers and sortedAnswers
    // with the local copy. Again, this needs to be
    // synchronized to ensure that we don't mess up play()
    synchronized(this) {
      answers       = myAnswers;
      sortedAnswers = mySortedAnswers;
      sortedCounts  = mySortedCounts;
    }
  }
}
/**
 * Sorts the given hashtable in order of the values
 */
private String[] sortAnswers(Hashtable myAnswers) {
  int i,j;
  int count1;
  int count2;
  String tmp;
  String mySortedAnswers[];
  int numAnswers      = myAnswers.size();
  mySortedAnswers  = new String[numAnswers];
  Enumeration keys = myAnswers.keys();
  i=0;
```

```
        while(keys.hasMoreElements()) {
          mySortedAnswers[i++] = (String) keys.nextElement();
        }
        for(i=0;i<numAnswers;i++) {
          for(j=0;j<numAnswers;j++) {
            count1 = ((Integer)
                      myAnswers.get(mySortedAnswers[i])).intValue();
            count2 = ((Integer)
                      myAnswers.get(mySortedAnswers[j])).intValue();
            if(count2 < count1) {
              tmp                = mySortedAnswers[i];
              mySortedAnswers[i] = mySortedAnswers[j];
              mySortedAnswers[j] = tmp;
            }
          }
        }
        return mySortedAnswers;
      }
    }
```

Conclusion

One thing all these database systems have in common, whether they store raw data or objects, is that the data are "frozen" within the database. In other words, a program must retrieve an object from a database, manipulate it, and restore it in order for it to do anything. As useful as this is, it could be even more powerful if the objects in a database could be doing things, such as running computations, whether or not a program had loaded them. This leads to the idea of *distributed objects*—objects that live on a network and that can be found and used by other objects. We explore this exciting idea further in Chapter 15.

CHAPTER 15

Communicating with External Applications: Distributed Objects

So far, in all the communication methods we have discussed, there has been a pretty sharp distinction between programs and data. Even in ObjectStore, where we are storing Java objects, the objects are "frozen," in a sense. They stay unchanging in a database until a program pulls them out, performs operations on them, and then puts them back.

It is often useful to think of objects in a much more dynamic sense, as entities living out on the network. In this model, objects act as peers and can make requests to each other by calling each other's methods. This may seem to be a subtle change in perspective, but it can have some profound effects on the way programs are built and used.

In this chapter, we look at three ways a servlet can use remote, live, objects. As the previous paragraph suggests, each works by invoking methods on the remote object. We start with *Remote Method Invocation* (RMI), which allows servlets to use Java objects anywhere on the network as if they were local. This leads into a discussion of *Common Object Request Broker Architecture* (CORBA), which is much like RMI but allows servlets to use objects written in almost any language.

Finally, we present interfacing with Microsoft's *Distributed Component Object Model* (DCOM) objects, which enable servlets to interface with Excel and other Windows applications.

How Does RMI Work?

How can an object sitting a whole network away from another object call its methods? In the strictest sense, it cannot. Invoking a method in a Java object is a complex process whereby the Java virtual machine (JVM) implementation looks up information about the object and the method and the arguments and starts executing some code based on the information. If an object is not present in the JVM, there is no way it can directly call one of the object's methods. Indirectly is another matter.

Consider a client and server written in the Java programming language. The server has a number of objects stored in a hash table, each with an identifying name. Each object has a method, setValue(), which takes an integer, and another method called getValue(), which returns an integer. The client opens a socket to the server and sends the name of an object to get out of the hash table. The client then sends the name of the method to invoke. If it is setValue(), it then follows the name with an integer, written with a call to writeInteger(). This call is safe here because both programs are written in Java, so they agree on what an integer is. The server then calls the object's setValue() method and passes the integer to it. Likewise, if the client tells the server to invoke getValue(), the server sends the result to the client with writeInteger().

This may not seem so exotic as the name Remote Method Invocation would imply, but RMI is exactly what it is! After all, the client is causing a method on a remote object to be called, though admittedly this is an indirect process. Now imagine another layer. Instead of writing directly to the socket, the client has its own collection of objects. These objects also have getValue() and setValue() methods. When these methods are invoked, they talk to the server over the socket. We have now constructed a system where we simulate directly calling remote methods by calling local ones. Because these local objects do not do any of the real work, we will call them *stubs*.

We could expand our hypothetical system to also allow passing float values around by using writeFloat and readFloat. It could even be expanded to pass arbitrary objects back and forth by using writeObject and readObject, although remember that for an object to be sent using readObject or receieved using writeObject, it must implement the java.io.Serializable interface.

Finally, we could do one more thing to make this system more flexible. Instead of having one server that contains all the objects, we could have a sort of superserver. Other servers would create objects, tell the superserver about them, and provide names for them. When the superserver gets a request for an object with a particular name, it would find the server that really has the object, pass the request and the arguments on to it, and then take the server's response and send it back to the client.

This is the core of how RMI works. The "superserver" is a program called the *rmiregistry*, and just as in our imaginary system it maps names (actually URLs) to objects. The other servers are classes that extend the `java.rmi.server.RemoteServer` class. And the clients are just that, clients that use the remote objects. But RMI provides one very important thing that our imaginary remote method system did not. In our system, programmers would need to write two versions of every class they wanted to use remotely, one that did the actual work and the stubs that would pass requests over the network. No programmer wants to have to do twice as much work. RMI provides a program called *rmic* that automatically generates the stubs. It also generates another class called the *skeleton*, which serves as the glue between the rmiregistry program and the actual object.

RMI Example

In this section we use RMI to actually do what we could only talk about in the last section: remotely call an object's `getValue` and `setValue` methods from a servlet.

Defining the Remote Object Interface

Before we write the remote class, there is one more issue we must face. We observed that the real class and the stub have the same methods. This is good, because servlets should be able to use the stub as if they were really using the remote object. However, the implementations of the real class and the stub are completely different. As interfaces are definitions of what methods a class has without saying anything about how they are implemented, remote objects in RMI are defined initially as interfaces. Here is ours:

```
import java.rmi.*;
public interface RMIClass extends Remote {
  public int getIntValue() throws RemoteException;
  public void setIntValue(int value) throws RemoteException;
  public String getStringValue() throws RemoteException;
  public void setStringValue(String value) throws RemoteException;
}
```

This interface extends the `Remote` interface, which contains no methods. `Remote` serves only to indicate which objects are going to be used remotely. All the methods throw `RemoteException` as a catchall for things that may go wrong during a remote invocation. These could include the network becoming unavailable, the remote server going down, and so on.

Defining the Remote Object Implementation

Now that the interface has been defined, an implementation can be written, as shown in Listing 15.1. Most of this class is a straightforward implementation of the interface, but there are some interesting things to notice.

Listing 15.1   Implementation of an RMI-capable class.

```
import java.rmi.*;
import java.rmi.server.*;
public class RMIClassImpl extends UnicastRemoteObject
                          implements RMIClass
{
  private int intValue       = 0;
  private String stringValue = "";
  public RMIClassImpl() throws RemoteException {
    super();
  }
  public int getIntValue() throws RemoteException {
    return intValue;
  }
  public void setIntValue(int value) throws RemoteException {
    intValue = value;
  }
  public String getStringValue() throws RemoteException {
    return stringValue;
  }
  public void setStringValue(String value)
       throws RemoteException
  {
    stringValue = value;
  }
  public static void main(String argv[]) {
    System.setSecurityManager(new RMISecurityManager());

    try {
      RMIClassImpl obj = new RMIClassImpl();
      Naming.rebind("//localhost/thing1", obj);
      System.out.println("RMIClass object now available");
    } catch (Exception e) {
      System.out.println("HelloImpl err: " + e.getMessage());
      e.printStackTrace();
    }
  }
}
```

First, in addition to implementing the RMIClass interface, this class extends UnicastRemoteObject. A UnicastRemoteObject is a particular kind of remote object that exists in one place, lives only as long as the server process that contains it is active, and communicates over transmission control protocol (TCP). It is in principle possible to define remote objects with different behaviors by extending UnicastRemoteObject's parent class, RemoteServer, but as of this writing no others have been defined.

The next thing to notice is the first thing the main method does, installation of a security manager. A security manager defines which operations may be performed. For example, one method defined in SecurityManager is checkRead(), which takes the name of a file as an argument and returns true if the application should be allowed to read the file. It is important to keep in mind that when a remote object is created, potentially everyone in the world has the ability to run code on your system. Even if the object does not have any methods that are obviously dangerous, it may be possible to get the object to load another class and execute its methods, which could do all sorts of nasty things. The RMISecurityManager sets a security policy that makes sense for remote objects and ensures that systems that run remote object servers will not be compromised. Readers are encouraged to check the documentation for java.rmi.RMISecurityManager to ensure that it is in line with their site's security policies. If it is not, it is quite easy to extend RMISecurityManager to make it either more or less restrictive.

After the security manager is installed, an instance of RMIClassImpl is created. It is then added to the system with the call to Naming.rebind(). This call associates the name thing1 with the object so that callers who want access to it can look it up by name. Actually, thing1 is an abbreviation. The full name is the URL *rmi://localhost:1099/thing1*, but since we will use the default port and run everything on the local machine, the full name can be omitted.

Generating the Stubs

Now that the class has been defined, we use rmic to automatically generate the stub class that will transparently handle all the communication. To run rmic, just type the following at the command prompt:

```
rmic RMIClassImpl
```

NOTE TO J++ USERS: J++ does not include rmic, although it can use the generated stubs. rmic is available by downloading the Java Development Kit (JDK) from JavaSoft.

After the program runs, there will be two additional files in the directory, RMIClassImpl_Skel.class and RMIClassImpl_Stub.class. Normally, programmers do not have to worry about them, since their roles are entirely behind the scenes. However, it is interesting to take a look inside the stub to get an idea of what it is doing. The javap program shows a list of what methods a class defines; running javap on RMIClassImpl_Stub gives the code shown in Listing 15.2.

Listing 15.2   The contents of the generated stub class.

```
Compiled from RMIClassImpl_Stub.java
public final synchronized class RMIClassImpl_Stub
extends java.rmi.server.RemoteStub
implements RMIClass, java.rmi.Remote
    /* ACC_SUPER bit set */
{
    public RMIClassImpl_Stub();
    public RMIClassImpl_Stub(java.rmi.server.RemoteRef);
    public int getIntValue();
    public java.lang.String getStringValue();
    public void setIntValue(int);
    public void setStringValue(java.lang.String);
    static static {};
}
```

Notice that it implements the RMIClass interface, and contains all the RMIClass methods. This is exactly as we would expect, since programs will be using this stub exactly as if they had a RMIClassImpl. It is also possible to run javap on the skeleton class, but as the skeleton is only used by the RMI internals it is more cryptic and not as interesting.

Running the Remote Object Server

Everything is now ready to actually create an RMIClass that is able to be used across the network or across the room. The first step is to run rmiregistry. This program acts as the "superserver." It associates names with objects that can be called remotely and hands back stubs for those objects to other objects that request them. In a sense, it "brokers" requests for objects. Keep this term in mind; it is important in the discussion of CORBA.

Once rmiregistry has been started, we can add an RMIClass to it by running RMIClassImpl from the command prompt java RMIClassImpl. After RMIClassImpl is started, it will print out "RMIClass object now available," but notice that it does not exit after doing so. This is because when the object is created another thread is started to handle the remote requests, and a Java program does not exit until all its threads have exited. It has to be this way, because all the Naming.rebind call does is tell rmiregistry where to find the object. All the actual work still has to be done by the RMIClassImpl, and if the program exited, the RMIClassImpl would no longer exist. Listing 15.3 is a servlet that uses a remote object.

Listing 15.3 Servlet that uses RMI.

```java
import java.io.*;
import javax.servlet.*;
import javax.servlet.http.*;
import java.rmi.*;
import java.rmi.server.*;
import java.util.Hashtable;
public class RMIServlet extends HttpServlet
{
  private RMIClass theObject = null;
  public void init(ServletConfig conf) throws ServletException {
    // Try to get the object from the registry
    try {
      theObject = (RMIClass) Naming.lookup("thing1");
    } catch (Exception e) {
      System.err.println("Unable to get remote object");
      e.printStackTrace(System.err);
    }
  }
  public void doGet(HttpServletRequest req,
                    HttpServletResponse res)
    throws IOException
  {
    ServletOutputStream out = res.getOutputStream();
    int intValue;
    String values[];
    String stringValue;

    res.setContentType("text/html");
    out.println("<HTML>");
    out.println("<HEAD><TITLE>RMI Servlet</TITLE></HEAD>");
    out.println("<BODY>");
    // If the user provided new values, use them
    String queryString = req.getQueryString();

    if(queryString != null) {
      values = req.getParameterValues("intValue");
      if(values != null && values.length > 0) {
        try {
          theObject.setIntValue(Integer.parseInt(values[0]));
        } catch(RemoteException re) {
          out.println("Could not set new string value<BR>");
        } catch(NumberFormatException ne) {
          out.println("Non-numeric value provided: " +
                      values[0] + "<BR>");
        }
      }
    }
```

```
      values = req.getParameterValues("stringValue");
      if(values != null && values.length > 0) {
        try {
          theObject.setStringValue(values[0]);
        } catch(RemoteException re) {
          out.println("Could not set new string value<BR>");
        }
      }
    }
    // Now print the current values
    try {
      out.println("Current int value: " +
                  theObject.getIntValue() + "<BR>");
      out.println("Current string value: " +
                  theObject.getStringValue() + "<BR>");
    } catch(RemoteException e) {
      out.println("Unable to get remote values");
    }
    // Allow the user to set new values
    out.println(
    "<FORM ACTION=/servlet/RMIServlet METHOD=GET>");
    out.println(
    "New int value: " +
    "<INPUT TYPE=TEXT NAME=intValue><BR>");
    out.println(
    "New string value: "+
    "<INPUT TYPE=TEXT NAME=stringValue> <BR>");
    out.println(
    "<INPUT TYPE=SUBMIT NAME=Go VALUE=Go>");
    out.println("</BODY>");
    out.println("</HTML>");
  }
}
```

Because of the security manager, this class cannot just be placed in the `<server_root>/servlets` directory. It and `RMIClassImpl_Stub.class` must be placed in the JWS's `CLASSPATH` and must be explicitly added through the administration tool.

After all that preparation, this code is almost boring. All the servlet does, after it obtains the class by calling `Naming.lookup("thing1")`, is call several sets and gets. It is as if the object weren't remote at all—the code looks the same as if it were just a plain old `RMIClassImpl` created in `init()`. But that is exactly the point! Once the setup has been done, remote objects look just like local objects, and with very few exceptions programmers do not need to know that they are remote. However, because they are remote, several applications can use them at the same time, and if the Java Web Server goes down, when it comes back up the object will be in exactly the same state it was left in.

More Complex RMI Example

In this section we look at a more complex RMI example and consider passing objects as arguments to remote methods or values returned from them. The example models a corridor off which are 10 rooms. Each room has a lamp that can be turned on or off. The rooms are remote objects, and the servlet allows users to move from room to room, changing the state of the lamps.

First, here is the definition of the Lamp class:

```
import java.io.*;
public class Lamp implements Serializable {
  private boolean on = false;
  public boolean isOn() {return on;}
  public void setOn(boolean state) {on = state;}
}
```

The only thing to notice here is that the class implements the Serializable interface. If it did not, programs trying to use this class would get lots of errors that look like this:

```
java.rmi.UnmarshalException: Error unmarshaling return; nested
                          exception is:
     java.io.WriteAbortedException: Writing aborted by exception;
     java.io.NotSerializableException: Lamp
```

Here is the interface definition for the Room class. As expected, it does not do much more than give access to the Lamp class.

```
import java.rmi.*;
public interface Room extends Remote {
  public Lamp getLamp() throws RemoteException;
}
```

Listing 15.4 shows the code for the RoomImpl. Again, nothing new here, except that main now creates 10 objects and gives each a different name in the registry.

Listing 15.4   RMI-ready implementation of the Room class.

```
import java.rmi.*;
import java.rmi.server.*;
public class RoomImpl extends UnicastRemoteObject
                        implements Room
{
  private Lamp theLamp;

  public RoomImpl() throws RemoteException {
    super();
    theLamp = new LampImpl();
  }
```

```
public Lamp getLamp() throws RemoteException {
  return theLamp;
}
public static void main(String argv[]) {
  System.setSecurityManager(new RMISecurityManager());
  RoomImpl rooms[] = new RoomImpl[10];
  try {
    for(int i=0;i<10;i++) {
      rooms[i] = new RoomImpl();
      Naming.rebind("room" + i,rooms[i]);
      System.out.println("Room object " + i +
                             " now available");
    }
  } catch (Exception e) {
    System.out.println("HelloImpl err: " + e.getMessage());
    e.printStackTrace();
  }
}
}
```

As in Listing 15.1, compile Lamp, Room, and RoomImpl classes, then run rmic on RoomImpl to generate RoomImpl_Skel and RoomImpl_Stub. The remote objects can now be made available by running rmiregistry (if it is not already running) and then starting RoomImpl.

Listing 15.5 is the servlet that allows users to move through the rooms. Compile this code, and place the class file along with the others somewhere in the JWS's CLASSPATH. Then add the servlet with the administration tool and go to

http://<your_machine>/servlet/RoomServlet

Go to room 1 and turn the light on. Then go to room 2 and back to room 1. The light is off!

Listing 15.5   Servlet that uses RMI on rooms.

```
import java.io.*;
import java.util.*;
import javax.servlet.*;
import javax.servlet.http.*;
import java.rmi.*;
import java.rmi.server.*;
public class RoomServlet extends HttpServlet
{
  public void doGet(HttpServletRequest req,
                    HttpServletResponse res)
    throws IOException
  {
    ServletOutputStream out = res.getOutputStream();
    String queryString     = req.getQueryString();
    int roomNumber         = 0;
```

```java
String action            = "";
Room theRoom;
Lamp theLamp;
if(queryString != null) {
  String values[] = req.getParameterValues("roomNumber");
  if(values != null && values.length > 0)
    roomNumber = Integer.parseInt(values[0]);
  values = req.getParameterValues("action");
  if(values != null && values.length > 0)
    action = values[0];
}
res.setContentType("text/html");
out.println("<HTML>");
out.println("<HEAD><TITLE>Room Servlet</TITLE></HEAD>");
// Get the object representing this room
try {
  theRoom = (Room) Naming.lookup("room" + roomNumber);
  if(theRoom == null) {
    out.println("<BODY>");
    out.println("No such room");
    out.println("</BODY>");
    out.println("</HTML>");
    return;
  }
  theLamp = theRoom.getLamp();
} catch (NotBoundException nbe) {
    out.println("<BODY>");
    out.println("Error getting lamp object");
    out.println("</BODY>");
    out.println("</HTML>");
    return;
}
// If the user changed the state of the lamp, change it
if(action.equals("on")) {
  theLamp.setOn(true);
} else if(action.equals("off")) {
  theLamp.setOn(false);
}

// If the lamp is off, print white text on a black
// background. If it is on, print black text on a
// white background
if(theLamp.isOn()) {
  out.println(
        "<BODY BGCOLOR=#FFFFFF TEXT=#000000>");
} else {
  out.println(
        "<BODY BGCOLOR=#000000 TEXT=#FFFFFF>");
}
out.println("<H1>You are in room #" + roomNumber + "</H1>");
// Also print the state of the lamp. Remember, not
// everyone has a browser that supports background colors
out.print("The lamp is");
```

```
out.print(theLamp.isOn() ? " on " : " off ");
out.println("<P>");
// Now print links to let the user move back,
// move forward, or toggle the light
if(roomNumber < 10) {
  out.print("<A HREF=/servlet/RoomServlet?roomNumber=");
  out.print(roomNumber+1);
  out.println(">Next room</A><BR>");
}
if(roomNumber > 0) {
  out.print("<A HREF=/servlet/RoomServlet?roomNumber=");
  out.print(roomNumber-1);
  out.println(">Previous room</A><BR>");
}
if(theLamp.isOn()) {
  out.print("<A HREF=/servlet/RoomServlet" +
            "?action=off&roomNumber=");
  out.print(roomNumber);
  out.print(">");
  out.println("Turn lamp off</A>");
} else {
  out.print("<A HREF=/servlet/RoomServlet" +
            "?action=on&roomNumber=");
  out.print(roomNumber);
  out.print(">");
  out.println("Turn lamp on</A>");
}
  }
}
```

Some people prefer dark rooms, but for those who need light, we uncover the bug in this example. The problem lies in the way the Lamp class was defined. It was made serializable but not remote. When the servlet called getLamp(), what was returned was a *copy* of the Lamp object as it existed in the room. This lamp was then completely local to the servlet, so any changes made to it were not reflected in the room.

There are a couple of ways this could be fixed. We could do away with the Lamp class entirely and make the state of the light a property of the room. Methods could be added to Room to turn the light on and off. Similarly, the room could still have a lamp, and Room's turnLightOn() method would simply call the Lamp's method in turn. In either case, the servlet would then only be making true remote calls.

This would work, but it is bad object design. There is no reason why a room object should know anything about how lamps work. As the Lamp object became more complex, perhaps to support a time limit on how long bulbs last, the Room object would also have to become more complex.

The second option would be to change the lamp's state by sending the room a new lamp. This would add a third step to the process:

```
theLamp=room.getLamp();
theLamp.setOn(true);
room.setLamp(theLamp);
```

This too would work, as the room now receives a lamp in the on state, which it uses to replace the previous lamp. But once again it is poor design, this time because it does not model the system in a sensible way. No one turns on a lamp by unplugging the one that is turned off and replacing it with one that is turned on. (How many RMI calls does it take to screw in a light bulb, anyway?)

The right way to fix this problem is to make the lamp itself a remote object. Then when the servlet calls getLamp(), it will get a stub, which when used will change the real lamp. Making this change is quite straightforward. As before, we first define lamp as an interface:

```
import java.rmi.*;
public interface Lamp extends Remote {
  public boolean isOn() throws RemoteException;
  public void setOn(boolean state) throws RemoteException;
}
```

Then we write the implementation shown in Listing 15.6.

Listing 15.6   RMI-ready implementation of the Lamp class.

```
import java.rmi.*;
import java.rmi.server.*;
public class LampImpl extends UnicastRemoteObject
    implements Lamp
{
  private boolean on = false;
  public LampImpl() throws RemoteException {
    super();
  }
  public boolean isOn() throws RemoteException {
    return on;
  }
  public void setOn(boolean state) throws RemoteException
  {
    on = state;
  }
}
```

Only one line in RoomImpl needs to change. Since interfaces cannot be instantiated, where we had done

```
theLamp = new Lamp();
```

we now do

```
theLamp = new LampImpl();
```

None of the type definitions need to change because a `LampImpl` is a `Lamp`. Best of all, the servlet code does not need to change at all, although it does need to be recompiled.

As in previous example listings, compile everything and run rmic on `RoomImpl` and `LampImpl`, then put all the class files in the JWS class path and restart the server. Users can now turn lights on at will. If they like that sort of thing.

Notes on Programming with RMI

For most purposes, remote objects act exactly as local objects would. However, programmers should pay attention to a few things when using them.

Thread Safety

None of the classes we have made remote thus far have had any synchronized methods. They haven't needed any, because all their actions have been atomic. However, if there had been one or more synchronized methods and we had compiled and run it through rmic and then viewed the resulting classes through javap, we would have noticed that none of the methods in the resulting stub remained synchronized.

RMI may appear to be introducing new potential thread problems, but in fact it is not. Use of the stubs is always safe, because the underlying socket communication is thread safe, as is the rmiregistry. RMI will not introduce any new causes of deadlock or data corruption through bad thread handling.

However, this does not mean that all objects run through rmic automatically become thread safe. In fact, objects that are to be used remotely may need to be more aware of thread issues than others. This is because every remote method call looks to the object like a separate thread, even if each request is coming from a separate program that may itself be using the resource in a thread-safe way.

The good news is that nothing special needs to be done to make remote object use thread safe beyond ensuring the safety of the implementation class. In an extreme case, declaring all the methods in the implementation class synchronized will keep everything safe, although at the cost of performance. See Chapter 10 for better ways to achieve thread safety.

The only other thing to watch for is the use of synchronized blocks, that is, chunks of code that achieve thread safety by synchronizing on some object, as in

```
synchronized (anObject) {
  // Do stuff with anObject
}
```

If anObject is a stub to a remote object, synchronization will not work. It will ensure that only one thread in the program is using the stub, but it will not guarantee that some other program is not using anObject in other ways. To be safe, keep all the synchronization code in the implementation class; it's better object-oriented design anyway.

Efficiency

It should not be surprising that calling a remote method is much more expensive than invoking a local one. At the very least some bytes representing the call have to go across the network and a response has to come back. Add this to the normal cost of invoking the method in the stub and the cost of invoking the method on the implementation at the other end, and suddenly one line of code may be keeping users of a servlet twiddling their thumbs.

There is nothing that can be done directly about this overhead; it is built into RMI. What can be done, however, is to reduce to the bare minimum the number of remote calls made. This can be done by caching data going to or from remote objects, using the same sorts of techniques we discussed in connection with databases (Chapter 14).

The other thing to be aware of is the cost of serialization, which has to be paid if objects are used as the arguments to remote procedures or returned from them. In addition to the CPU time required to convert an object to a stream of bytes and then reconstruct it at the other end, serialized objects are sometimes surprisingly large. What looks like a simple hash table in a program could turn into several kilobytes of data that need to be transmitted.

Fortunately, when true remote objects are sent from one process to another, much less information needs to be sent than if the objects were just serialized. This means that, in addition to sometimes being the only way to make a program work correctly, making more of the objects true remote objects may help efficiency, as well. However, this is not always true. The advantage of serialized objects is that once they have been sent, no further data needs to go over the network.

For remote objects, every method invocation turns into some network activity. In other words, sending a serialized object has one big cost up front, whereas remote objects have lots of little costs that mount up over the life of the object. All other factors being equal, which is better depends on the specifics of the servlet using the objects.

What Is CORBA?

Remote method invocation is a great way for Java programs to get access to Java objects that may live anywhere on the network. But it is a fact of life that not every object that a servlet might wish to use is written in Java. The control library for the hypothetical electron microscope we discussed earlier could be written in C++ or raw C or even FORTRAN. There might be some complex and sophisticated Perl modules or Python objects, written for a CGI-based system, that would take a lot of time to translate to Java. Or maybe the weird programmer in the next cubicle just prefers working in Smalltalk.

Consider once again the hypothetical remote method system we developed in the section on RMI. Nowhere in that discussion did we require the servers to be written in Java, although it certainly would make things simpler—both client and server could agree on how data is represented. However, in principle there is no reason why the stubs could not be written in one language and the skeleton and implementation class in another. Enter CORBA.

CORBA, or Common Object Request Broker Architecture, is an industry standard system to allow programs written in any language use objects written in any other. Although it has many complexities not present in RMI, the basic ideas are very much the same. In RMI, stubs and skeletons are generated by rmic from a compiled class file. In CORBA, the stubs and skeleton are generated by a program from a description written in the *interface definition language,* or IDL. An IDL file is very much like a Java interface file. It specifies what methods an object will have but says nothing at all about how the methods will be implemented or in what language. IDL even looks a lot like an interface, although in fact IDL is a subset of C++ with some additions.

In RMI, there is one rmiregistry that passes requests and responses to particular objects and associates names with objects. In CORBA, this is done by an *Object Request Broker,* or ORB. The 1.0 version of the CORBA specification had a single ORB that held all objects. This resulted in a system that was very much like RMI. There was one limitation to this architecture. Because the ORB holds the skeleton objects and they are written in a particular language, the 1.0 ORB could hold only objects written in that language, although clients for the ORB could be written in any language.

To get around this limitation, CORBA 2.0 introduced the idea of multiple ORBs passing requests between them. Now instead of one monolithic ORB holding all the objects, many ORBs exist concurrently, each with one or more objects written in a particular language. ORBs transmit data and requests between each other using a protocol called *Internet Inter-ORB Protocol,* or IIOP.

In addition to handling the passing of requests and responses and looking up objects by name, an ORB provides a number of services to both client and server objects. These services include various life cycle facilities, concurrency control and locking, and an event model where any object can listen for specific kinds of events or alert all listeners that a certain kind of event has occurred. ORBs also provide a dynamic discovery mechanism, whereby one object can learn about the methods another object supports, even if the two objects were not built from the same IDL. These advanced features of ORBs are beyond the scope of this book, but they are well covered in most books on CORBA.

CORBA Example

Using CORBA is very much like using RMI. An interface is specified in IDL, then a program is used to generate stubs and skeletons. Next the implementation is written, including a program that creates an ORB and a server object and tells the ORB about the object. Finally, a client is written that uses another ORB to send requests.

Over the next few sections we develop a servlet that uses CORBA to get data from a remote object. In general, if both the client and server are going to be written in Java it is much easier to use RMI than CORBA, so this time our server will be written in C++. This language and technology is used to, once again, print out one of several messages, one of which will, of course, be "Hello, World."

Writing the IDL File

Like a Java interface, an IDL file specifies what an object will do without specifying how. The following is the language-neutral IDL file for our class, which has only one method. This method takes an integer that is used to look up a particular string, which is returned to the client and later sent to the user.

```
module HelloApp
{
  interface Hello
  {
    string getMessage(in unsigned short which);
  };
};
```

Anyone squinting really hard might almost mistake this for a Java interface. There are some important differences, though. First, IDL calls the highest level of object a *module* instead of a class. Next, note that string, the return type, is lowercase. This may seem minor, and in actual use the servlet obtains a real Java String. However, string with a lowercase s is not a Java type; it is a

CORBA type that is implemented differently in different languages. Finally, notice the `in` keyword used with the parameter. This specifies that the value the client sends to the server is "one way." If the server modifies this value, the change will not be visible to the client. The serialized version of the lamp worked roughly this way. It is also possible to specify values as `out` only, meaning that the server does not receive the value from the client but can use it to send a value to the server. Values can also be `inout`, meaning both client and server can see and modify them.

Generating the Stubs

We are now ready to generate Java files from the IDL file. This is accomplished by a program called, not surprisingly, `idltojava`. This program is not included in the JDK, but it is available for free from the Java Developers Connection. `idltojava` takes one argument, the name of the IDL file to convert:

```
idltojava Hello.idl
```

This creates a new directory called `HelloApp`, the name of our package. Within that directory are five files. The following sections look at each of these.

Hello.java

Listing 15.7 shows the interface file, much like the ones we created using RMI. There are only two differences between this interface and the ones used for RMI. The first is the class that is extended: here it is `org.omg.CORBA.Object` instead of `Remote`, as in RMI. The `com.omg.CORBA.Object` interface is implemented by the `org.omg.CORBA.ObjectImpl` class, which defines all the basic behaviors that a CORBA object must provide. The other difference is that the CORBA methods do not throw exceptions. While it is possible for a CORBA method to generate exceptions, the CORBA protocol itself does not.

Listing 15.7   CORBA-ready implementation of "Hello."

```
/*
 * File: ./HelloApp/Hello.java
 * From: Hello.idl
 * Date: Mon Jul 27 17:35:41 1998
 *    By: idltojava Java IDL 1.2 Nov 12 1997 12:23:47
 */
package HelloApp;
public interface Hello
     extends org.omg.CORBA.Object {
     String getMessage(short which);
}
```

HelloHelper.java

The class shown in Listing 15.8 defines some static utility methods that programmers will find useful. We will not discuss all these methods in detail, but take a look at `narrow()`. It takes an arbitrary CORBA object and tries to cast it to a `Hello`. Because most CORBA API calls can return an object of arbitrary type, it is necessary to ensure that the returned object is the right kind of object before using it. This constant checking would get pretty tiresome pretty fast, which is why `idltojava` generates this utility for us.

Listing 15.8 Automatically generated `Helper` class.

```
/*
 * File: ./HelloApp/HelloHelper.java
 * From: Hello.idl
 * Date: Mon Jul 27 17:35:41 1998
 *   By: idltojava Java IDL 1.2 Nov 12 1997 12:23:47
 */
package HelloApp;
public class HelloHelper {
  // It is useless to have instances of this class
  private HelloHelper() { }

  public static void write(
                  org.omg.CORBA.portable.OutputStream out,
                  HelloApp.Hello that)
  {
    out.write_Object(that);
  }
  public static HelloApp.Hello read(
                  org.omg.CORBA.portable.InputStream in)
  {
    return HelloApp.HelloHelper.narrow(in.read_Object());
  }

  public static HelloApp.Hello extract(org.omg.CORBA.Any a) {
    org.omg.CORBA.portable.InputStream in =
      a.create_input_stream();
    return read(in);
  }

  public static void insert(org.omg.CORBA.Any a,
                            HelloApp.Hello that)
  {
    org.omg.CORBA.portable.OutputStream out =
      a.create_output_stream();
    write(out, that);
    a.read_value(out.create_input_stream(), type());
  }
  private static org.omg.CORBA.TypeCode _tc;
```

```
synchronized public static org.omg.CORBA.TypeCode type() {
  if (_tc == null)
    _tc = org.omg.CORBA.ORB.init().create_interface_tc(
                                     id(),
                                     "Hello");
  return _tc;
}
public static String id() {
  return "IDL:HelloApp/Hello:1.0";
}
public static HelloApp.Hello narrow(org.omg.CORBA.Object that)
    throws org.omg.CORBA.BAD_PARAM
{
  if (that == null)
    return null;
  if (that instanceof HelloApp.Hello)
    return (HelloApp.Hello) that;
  if (!that._is_a(id())) {
    throw new org.omg.CORBA.BAD_PARAM();
  }
  org.omg.CORBA.portable.Delegate dup =
    ((org.omg.CORBA.portable.ObjectImpl)that)._get_delegate();
  HelloApp.Hello result = new HelloApp._HelloStub(dup);
  return result;
  }
}
```

_HelloStub.java

This is our old friend the stub! Listing 15.9 shows the class clients use, which in turn talks to the ORB on a program's behalf. As we promised, this extends the ObjectImpl class, providing the default behaviors of a CORBA object. It also provides an implementation of the getMessage() method. Examining this method shows a little about how Java implements the CORBA protocol, but don't get too wrapped up in the details; ultimately they are unimportant. The significant fact is that programs can use the method just as they would a local implementation of Hello.

Listing 15.9   Automatically generated CORBA stub.

```
/*
 * File: ./HelloApp/_HelloStub.java
 * From: Hello.idl
 * Date: Mon Jul 27 17:35:41 1998
 *   By: idltojava Java IDL 1.2 Nov 12 1997 12:23:47
 */
package HelloApp;
public class _HelloStub
        extends org.omg.CORBA.portable.ObjectImpl
        implements HelloApp.Hello
{
```

```
public _HelloStub(org.omg.CORBA.portable.Delegate d) {
  super();
  _set_delegate(d);
}

private static final String _type_ids[] = {
  "IDL:HelloApp/Hello:1.0"
};

public String[] _ids() {
  return (String[]) _type_ids.clone();
}

//   IDL operations
//         Implementation of ::HelloApp::Hello::getMessage
public String getMessage(short which)
{
  org.omg.CORBA.Request r = _request("getMessage");
  r.set_return_type(org.omg.CORBA.ORB.init().
                     get_primitive_tc(org.omg.CORBA.
                                       TCKind.tk_string));
  org.omg.CORBA.Any _which = r.add_in_arg();
  _which.insert_ushort(which);
  r.invoke();
  String __result;
  __result = r.return_value().extract_string();
  return __result;
}
};
```

Writing the Client

Now that all the classes have been defined, we can write a servlet that will use
CORBA to talk to a remote Hello object (Listing 15.10). This servlet allows the
user to select one of four messages, and it returns the message. The init()
method does most of the work here, because most of it only needs to be done
once.

Listing 15.10   Servlet that uses CORBA.

```
import HelloApp.*;
import org.omg.CosNaming.*;
import org.omg.CORBA.*;
import javax.servlet.*;
import javax.servlet.http.*;
import java.util.Hashtable;
import java.io.IOException;
public class HelloServlet extends HttpServlet {
  private Hello helloRef;
  public void init(ServletConfig c) throws ServletException {
    super.init(c);
```

```java
  try {
    // Create and initialize the ORB
    ORB orb = ORB.init((String[]) null, null);

    // Get the root naming context
    org.omg.CORBA.Object objRef =
      orb.resolve_initial_references("NameService");
    NamingContext ncRef = NamingContextHelper.narrow(objRef);

    // Resolve the Object Reference in Naming
    NameComponent nc = new NameComponent("Hello", "");
    NameComponent path[] = {nc};
    helloRef = HelloHelper.narrow(ncRef.resolve(path));
  } catch (Exception e) {
    log("Unable to create ORB");
    throw new UnavailableException(
                      this,
                      "Unable to create ORB");
  }
}
public void doGet(HttpServletRequest req,
                  HttpServletResponse res)
  throws IOException
{
  String URI             = req.getRequestURI();
  String queryString     = req.getQueryString();
  ServletOutputStream out = res.getOutputStream();
  res.setContentType("text/html");
  out.println("<HTML>");
  out.println("<HEAD><TITLE>CORBA demo</TITLE></HEAD>");
  out.println("<BODY>");
  out.println("");

  if(queryString != null) {
    String values[] = req.getParameterValues("which");
    if(values != null && values[0] != null) {
      int which = Integer.parseInt(values[0]);
      try {
        String theMessage =
          helloRef.getMessage((short) which);
        out.println("The Hello object responds: " +
                    theMessage + "<P>");
      } catch (Exception e) {
        log("Unable to get response from CORBA object");
        out.println(
            "Unable to get response from CORBA object");
      }
    }
  }
  out.println("<A HREF=" + URI + "which=0>Message 1<BR>");
  out.println("<A HREF=" + URI + "which=1>Message 2<BR>");
  out.println("<A HREF=" + URI + "which=2>Message 3<BR>");
  out.println("<A HREF=" + URI + "which=3>Message 4<BR>");
```

```
    out.println("</BODY>");
    out.println("</HTML>");
  }
}
```

First an ORB is created. Then the ORB is used to get a naming context. The naming context is a special object that is always present in an ORB; it is used to look up other objects. Note that even the built-in `resolve_initial_references` returns a CORBA object of unknown type, so we use the `narrow()` method in its helper class to cast it to a `NamingContext`. This is then used to look up our `Hello` object, which also must be cast to a `Hello`. Of course we know it is really a `_HelloStub`, but we can treat it as if it were the `Hello` defined in the IDL file. Then, down in the service method, we can use this `Hello` exactly as we would any other object.

Generating the Skeleton

We could now proceed to use the skeleton class that `idltojava` generated and write the `Hello` server in Java. But if we were going to do that, it would make more sense to use RMI and eliminate a lot of the overhead. So instead we will write the server in C++. We will not be saying much about Java or servlets in this section, but it should help show how CORBA works.

The first step in writing a CORBA server is to select an ORB and a development system. In addition to many commercial ORBs, there are an increasing number of quality free ones. We recommend Washington University's TAO or Xerox PARC's ILU, available from these URLs:

http://www.cs.wustl.edu/~schmidt/TAO.html
ftp://ftp.parc.xerox.com/pub/ilu/ilu.html

In addition a free, high-performance ORB, called ORBit, is currently being developed as part of the Gnome project. At the time of this writing it is not quite ready for general use, but it appears very promising. For the most recent updates see one of these

http://www.labs.redhat.com/orbit/
http://www.gnome.org

The next step is to define the class using an IDL. In our case we already have one, class `Hello.idl` used in building the client. It can be used unchanged to define the server—after all, the whole point of the IDL file is to define the class in a language- and implementation-independent way.

Next, the IDL file is used to generate stubs and skeletons. The details on how this is done differ depending on the development system used, but typically it involves running some program on the command line and telling it what language to target. We use a theoretical system that contains a program called `idl2cpp`, which is invoked as `idl2cpp Hello.idl`.

This program generates four files: a header defining the `Hello` class, the code for the stub, a header for the implementation class, and the code for most of the implementation, which a programmer would then need to complete. We may discard the stub code, as we are not writing the client in C++. We now briefly survey the other files (we do not include the full text here). Note that many of the class names and other aspects of this code are specific to the ORB being used. Each ORB vendor has a different way of doing things, and this is right and proper.

`Hello.h` defines the `HelloApp` structure and the `Hello` class. The `Hello` class extends a class called `CORBA::Object`, which, much like Java's `CORBA.Object`, defines the basic behavior of a CORBA object. The skeleton include file, `Hello_skel.h`, defines a base class, which contains a default constructor. `Hello_skel.cpp` contains an implementation of this constructor, which does some ORB-specific initialization and very little else. In particular, it does not have any of the functionality of the `Hello` class and it does not have the `getMessage()` method. That needs to be written by hand.

Writing the Server

Now we are ready to write the implementation class, just as we did for RMI. The class is defined in `Hello_imp.h`, which does not include much more than a constructor and a complete signature for the `getMessage()` method (see Listing 15.11). Next comes the implementation of the classes defined in the header file. It is placed in `Hello_imp.cpp`, as shown in Listing 15.12.

Listing 15.11   Header for a CORBA implementation in C++.

```
// This class implements the 'Hello' interface from the
// IDL file
class Hello_imp : public Hello_skel
{
public:
  Hello_imp (const char *nm);
  ~Hello_imp ();
    CORBA::String getMessage (CORBA::UShort which);
};
```

Listing 15.12   C++ implementation of Hello.

```
#include "Hello_imp.h"
Hello_imp::Hello_imp (const char *nm) : Hello_skel (nm)
{
  // empty
```

```
}
Hello_imp::~Hello_imp ()
{
   // empty
}
CORBA::String
getMessage (CORBA::UShort which)
{
   switch(which) {
     case 0:
       return "Hello World!";
       break;
     case 1:
       return "Oh, hi there";
       break;
     case 2:
       return "This code could have been written in any language!";
       break;
     default:
       return "You asked for a message I don't have";
       break;
   }
}
```

Note that the code in Listing 15.12 extends the skeleton class, which in turn handles the low-level details when the constructor is called. Finally, we need a class with a `main()`, to set everything up and construct a `Hello_imp` for our servlet to use. Again, the details of how this is done depend on the ORB being used, but it should look something like this:

```
// Create a Hello implementation
Hello_imp Hello_impl (argv[1]);
// Let the orb know the object is ready to receive requests
orb->make_object_ready (&Hello_impl, 0);
```

This code constructs a `Hello_impl` and gives it to the system, which then makes it available to handle requests.

Notes on Programming with CORBA

Given how similar RMI and CORBA are, it is natural to wonder if they could somehow be combined. The answer is yes. Currently RMI objects talk to each other via a protocol called Java Remote Method Protocol, but work is currently underway at JavaSoft to allow RMI to talk IIOP. The two are not completely compatible; RMI has some features that are not implementable with CORBA. Sun is defining a subset of RMI, and programmers who write code using this subset will be able to choose IIOP as the transport protocol. Ultimately, programmers will be able to write clients using the somewhat simpler RMI style and still talk to CORBA objects.

NOTE: Despite rumors that have been spread to the contrary, Sun is *not* abandoning RMI in favor of CORBA. RMI is and will continue to be the choice for building distributed systems completely in Java. The CORBA facilities are provided to interface with code written in other languages or code running on systems that do not yet have a port of Java.

The threading and efficiency issues discussed in the RMI section hold in CORBA. It is still necessary to make the implementation class thread safe, and it is still more efficient to cache data where possible instead of making a CORBA call every time data is needed.

What Is DCOM?

By now we should no longer need to sing the praises of distributed object-based programming. Microsoft is a big fan of this style of application programming as well. They started back in Windows 3.1 with OLE, object linking and embedding. This expanded in Windows 95 to COM, the component object model, which has since added facilities for distributed and network-aware objects, becoming DCOM, the distributed component object model. A great deal of the operating system internals, as well as many applications from Microsoft and others, are built as groups of DCOM objects. This means that a programmer equipped with a knowledge of DCOM instantly has access to a huge set of resources and can interface easily with programs like Excel, Word, and Internet Explorer. DCOM is also not limited to Windows—a Solaris implementation has been available since early 1998 and a Macintosh version is in the works.

Unfortunately, there is currently no way to create or access DCOM objects from Java. However, they can be created and accessed from Microsoft J++, which can be described as either a "Java-like" language or "polluted Java," depending on one's political and religious beliefs. In either case, J++ is similar enough to Java that servlet programmers should be comfortable with it.

Conceptually, DCOM is very much like RMI or CORBA, in that programs can retrieve an object by an identifier and then use the object as if it were local to the program even though it may be on the other side of the network. The mechanism for writing a COM object is likewise similar to that for writing other distributed objects. The process starts with a specification written in an interface definition language, although Microsoft's IDL is somewhat different from CORBA's. The IDL file is then put through a translator, in this case `midl.exe`, which creates header files. Programmers then write the code that implements the interface.

DCOM's class hierarchy will seem familiar. All RMI objects extend `RemoteObject`, all CORBA objects extend `CORBA::Object` or something similar, and COM has a base class called `IUnknown` that all COM objects must implement. `IUnknown` has three methods. `AddRef` and `Release` increment and decrement, respectively, the number of users of an object. When the count goes to zero, the object can be freed from memory. The third method `IUnknown` supports is `QueryInterface`. This works like CORBA's `narrow()` operation. When a program asks for an object of a particular type, what is returned is an `IUnknown`. The programs can then call `QueryInterface` to cast the `IUnknown` into the type that was requested.

COM has some interesting differences from other systems. The first is the way objects are created. COM supports the idea of *factories*, classes whose sole job in life is to create instances of other classes. The base factory interface, `IClassFactory`, has two methods. `CreateInstance`, obviously enough, creates a new instance of some class. `LockServer` can be used to hold the factory in memory.

Another unique feature of COM is that there is no equivalent of rmiregistry or the CORBA naming service. The ability to associate names (actually IDs) to objects and connect a program with some object it wants is built into the operating system. All the information necessary to do this is kept in the registry, a very fundamental Windows facility.

The registry also keeps track of what flavor a particular COM object is. There are three distinct kinds of COM objects, although the differences are invisible to programs that use them. *In-process* components are implemented as dlls, and reside inside the client process's memory. *Local* components are implemented as executable exes residing on the same machine as the program that is using them. Finally, *remote* components are created by exes running on some other machine. The registry contains information about which of these a particular object is and necessary additional information, such as the machine name for remote components and a full path for local and in-process components.

We can now see why factories are important; they hide the details of how a COM object is constructed. The program does not need to know whether the object was built by a simple call to new or something including more complex network actions. This effectively hides the difference between remote, local, and in-process objects from programs that use them. As far as clients are concerned, it is all just COM.

Perhaps the most interesting aspect of COM is the way clients get access to objects. It is possible to write clients using the header files generated by midl.exe and some COM API calls, much as other distributed systems use stub classes. However, COM also supports the idea of a *type library*. Type libraries can be thought of as binary representations of the IDL file. The library also lives in the registry. This means that a program armed only with the name of a component can get the type library to determine what interfaces the object supports, then get the class factory to build an instance of the object, then use the object's QueryInterface() method to turn it into the right type, and then use it. All this without knowing anything about the object in advance. As we will see in the following section, this dynamic behavior is important in how J++ uses COM objects.

COM Example

Now that we have gone over the COM internals, we can actually build a COM object. Like the other distributed objects we have written, COM has single method that takes an integer and returns one of several strings.

Writing the IDL File

Before we can create our component, we must have a way to identify it. Because, in principle at least, every COM object in the world could be talking to every other one, names must be globally unique. Sun solves this problem with package-naming conventions; Microsoft solves it through a program that generates IDs that are guaranteed to be unique. This program is called a *guid-gen*. When writing this book, the first ID we were given was 27B69E30-2882-11d2-8874-0008C7008519. We also generated two additional IDs, which we will use shortly, that were identical except for the digit before the first dash, which in one was 1 and in the other 2. Now we can write the IDL description, shown in Listing 15.13, for our component.

Listing 15.13 DCOM definition.

```
import "unknown.idl";
import "wtypes.idl";
[ object, uuid(27B69E30-2882-11d2-8874-0008C7008519), oleautomation ]
interface IHello : IUnknown
{
    HRESULT getMessage([in] int which, [out, string, retval] OLECHAR
    **result);
}
[ uuid(27B69E32-2882-11d2-8874-0008C7008519),
    helpstring("Addison Wesley COM Example"),
    version(1.0) ]
```

```
library Component
{
  importlib("stdole32.tlb");
  interface IHello;
  [ uuid(27B69E31-2882-11d2-8874-0008C7008519) ]
  coclass AWExample
  {
    interface Hello;
  }
};
```

After a few imports, the interface definition begins. It starts with a line specifying what is being defined, in this case an object with our ID. Then comes our method, getMessage(). All methods in COM return an HRESULT, which will be used to determine if the operation succeeded or not. The parameters are specified similar to CORBA, but there are more options than just in and out. Here we use retval, which indicates the value that most calling programs will be interested in, and string, which indicates that the value is a string. In particular, it is a string of OLECHARs, which are 16-bit Unicode characters, just like the ones Java uses.

The next block defines the library, which will turn into the type library. Note that since this library is also accessed through the registry, it also has a guid. The library also has a coclass, again with a guid. The coclass provides the gateway for objects to use the library and, by extension, the component without knowing about its interfaces in advance.

Place the lines in Listing 15.13 in a file called hello.idl, then run midl.exe. This will generate several files, including hello.h, which defines the C++ class that must be implemented.

Writing the Implementation

It almost feels as if we are writing a CORBA object, doesn't it? The concepts are the same, but COM has some slightly different requirements. The place where it changes the least is the implementation of the getMessage() method. The other methods that need to be written are the ones that provide the IUnknown interface. These are fairly straightforward but lengthy, so they are not included here.

The class is almost ready to be compiled, but before we do there is one last fundamental issue we must address. Although COM completely hides the differences between in-process, local, and remote components from client applications, we as the component author must still decide which one we are going to write. As might be expected, an in-process component is the easiest. All that is necessary is to define two additional methods, DllGetClassObject, which returns the class factory, and DllCanUnloadNow, which the operating system uses to determine whether it is safe to free up memory by unloading the DLL. Again, the details are not difficult, but to save a couple of trees we do not include it here.

Finally, now that we have decided on an in-process component, we can write the class factory, which generates instances of our component.

Adding Information to the Registry

Our component has now been built, but before anyone else can find it it must be added to the registry. There are two ways to do this. The best way, which most components do, is to have the component add itself to the registry when it is first run. This makes the process invisible to the user and also makes the component completely self-contained. However, it is also possible to define an auxiliary file that the regedit program can use to add the registry information. Since the code to automatically create the registry entries is complex, we use the second method, as shown here:

```
[HKEY_CLASSES_ROOT\CLSID\{27B69E30-2882-11d2-8874-0008C7008519}]
@="Addison Wesley DCOM example"

[HKEY_CLASSES_ROOT\CLSID\{27B69E30-2882-11d2-8874-0008C7008519}
                        \InprocServer32]
@=C:\\Hello.dll
```

These lines are two name/value pairs. The elements in square brackets are the names.

Note that they include the guid we generated. The @= lines set the values. Also note the hierarchical nature of the registry, which looks very much like the DOS file system. The first line creates an entry under HKEY_CLASSES_ROOT, which is where all COM class IDs are stored. The second entry sets a value for the InprocServer32 name, under the class ID. The presence of this name is what tells the system that this is an in-process object, and the associated value specifies where the DLL file lives.

To add this information to the registry, simply place it in a file called hello.reg and double click on it. Windows responds with a dialog box confirming that the entries have been added.

Using DCOM Objects in J++

As we have seen, our component has an associated type library that completely describes it. J++ includes a *Type Library Wizard* that makes it incredibly easy to go from the type library to a class that can be used directly in a J++ program.

No stubs, no special API calls to request the object, nothing but code that uses the object as if it were local and created in J++ in the beginning.

The wizard is located under the tools menu. Simply select Type Library Wizard and a window containing all the known components will pop up. Look for the Addison Wesley Example, select it, and hit go. True to its name, the wizard has magically created a class that programs can now use. It has also created a file called `hello.txt` describing what it has done. This file contains the following:

```
public class component/AWExample extends java.lang.Object
{
}
public interface component/IHello extends com.ms.com.IUnknown
{
    public abstract int Sum(int, int);
}
```

Note that, despite the superficial resemblance, these are not Java classes. First, the names `component/AWExample` and `component/IHello` are not legal Java identifiers, as slashes are not allowed in names. More important, the `.class` files do no actual work! They have neither Java bytecode nor calls to native methods. Instead, the classes are marked in a special way, and when the virtual machine sees such a class, it does all the underlying work with the factory and `IUnknown`, which ultimately calls the underlying COM object's methods. In a sense, the J++ virtual machine is acting like a cross between a stub and an Object Request Broker.

We can now use our COM object like any other class, like this:

```
public class ComTest {
  public static void main(String argv[]) throws Exception {
    IHello myHello = (IHello) new AWExample();
    String result =
      myHello.getMessage(Integer.parseInt(argv[0]));
    System.out.println("The component said: " + result);
  }
}
```

Unfortunately, that is as far as we can go. We cannot actually write the servlet in J++.

Using DCOM from Servlets

Given the incompatibilities between Java and J++, we cannot just take the code from the preceding example, include it in a servlet, and have it work automatically. Servlets can use COM objects, but doing so is not as straightforward as just writing code. We can write code four ways.

The J++ DCOM class cannot run in a Java virtual machine, but most Java classes can run in the J++ virtual machine. This would seem to suggest that the entire Java Web Server could be run in the J++ environment, and servlets could then use the COM classes directly. In theory, this may be true. In practice, setting up the JWS to do so would be difficult at best, and it would probably produce sporadic results. There are differences in the way J++ implements some of the classes in the core Java packages, and the differences could introduce hard-to-find bugs. On the plus side, the J++ VM is very fast, so server performance would probably improve in this scenario at the cost of reliability.

The second option is using native methods. Native methods provide a sort of escape hatch, allowing a Java class to use code written in any language and compiled to native binaries. In this scenario, the COM portion of our code would be written in C++ and compiled into a DLL, and this DLL would provide a method that the servlet could call. The downside of this approach is that native methods may be dangerous. As we have previously observed, they do not have the robust memory management and thread facilities of Java methods and therefore have the potential to bring down the entire Web server. Plus, programming COM in C++ is harder than doing it in Visual J++.

So we have the Java Web Server and we have J++ running COM code, with no direct way to hook them together. Fortunately, the previous chapters have presented numerous ways for separate applications to communicate.

Chapter 13 discussed sockets, which are a general, flexible, and reliable means for applications to communicate. Sockets are an especially good fit here, because J++ and Java use the same primitive data types and the same representation. This means that both the client and server can use Strings and call writeInt() and readInt() without having to worry about the details of how this information is transmitted. This scheme allows J++ to do what it is good at and Java to do what it is good at, and it keeps both happy.

We first write our server in J++. It is almost identical to the server code in Listing 13.2. Now we have our servlet talk to this server. Again, note the similarity between Listing 15.15 and Listing 13.1. Compile and run the server under J++, and compile the servlet under a Java compiler and install it as usual. The gateway from servlets to the world of COM objects has been thrown open!

Listing 15.14   Socket-based server that uses a COM object.

```
import java.net.*;
import java.io.*;
public class JPPServer {
  public static void main(String argv[]) throws Exception {
    ServerSocket theServerSocket = new ServerSocket(4567);
    Socket        connection;
    IHello        myHello = (IHello) new AWExample();
    DataOutputStream out;
```

```
          DataInputStream  in;
          int             which;
          String          result;
          while(true) {
            // Wait for an incoming connection.  This line will
            // hang until a connection comes in
            connection = theServerSocket.accept();
            // When we get here, we have a connection. Get an
            // output stream, and send some data
            out = new DataOutputStream(connection.getOutputStream());
            in  = new DataInputStream(connection.getInputStream());

            which  = in.readInt();
            result = myHello.getMessage(which);
            out.writeUTF(message);
            in.close();
            out.close();
            connection.close();
          }
        }
      }
```

Listing 15.15 Servlet that talks to the COM server.

```
import javax.servlet.*;
import javax.servlet.http.*;
import java.net.*;
import java.io.*;
import java.util.Hashtable;
public class COMServlet extends HttpServlet {
  public void doGet(HttpServletRequest req,
                    HttpServletResponse res)
       throws IOException
  {
    ServletOutputStream out = res.getOutputStream();
    String queryString      = req.getQueryString();
    String URI              = req.getRequestURI();
    int messageNum          = -1;
    int    which;
    String result;
    if(queryString != null) {
      String values[] = req.getParameterValues("messageNum");
      if(values != null && values.length > 0)
        messageNum = Integer.parseInt(values[0]);
    }
    res.setContentType("text/plain");
    out.println("<HTML>");
    out.println("<HEAD><TITLE>COM Servlet</TITLE></HEAD>");
    out.println("<BODY>");
    // If the user provided a value, get the message from
    // the server, which in turn will get it from the COM object
    if(messageNum != -1) {
```

```
    try {
      // Make the connection to the server
      Socket s = new Socket("localhost",4567);

      // Get data input and output streams from the socket
      DataInputStream  s_in  =
        new DataInputStream(s.getInputStream());
      DataOutputStream s_out =
        new DataOutputStream(s.getOutputStream());

      // Send the requested message number to the server
      s_out.writeInt(messageNum);
      // Get the string back
      result = s_in.readUTF();
      out.println("The component said: " + result + "<P>");
      s_in.close();
      s_out.close();
      s.close();
    } catch(Exception e) {
      out.println("Unable to get data from server");
    }
  }
  out.println("<FORM ACTION=" + URI + " METHOD=GET>");
  out.println("What message would you like?");
  out.println("<INPUT TYPE=TEXT NAME=messageNum>");
  out.println("</FORM>");
  out.println("</BODY>");
  out.println("</HTML>");
  out.close();
  }
}
```

This solution works, but is has the disadvantage that the servlet is now not using the COM object as an object but rather has to go through cumbersome dialog with the server. Hence our fourth solution for bridging the servlet–COM gap. Iona Technologies, a member of the Object Management Group and vendor of the Orbix ORB, has a product called OrbixCOMet that allows CORBA programs to transparently use COM objects as CORBA objects. Using this system, a servlet that uses JDK 1.2's CORBA classes could be written, as shown in Listing 15.10, without needing to know anything about the fact that the object at the other end is really COM. When JavaSoft completes the IIOP/RMI integration, it will even be possible to talk to COM objects using RMI, although the thought of going from RMI to CORBA to COM is enough to make anyone's head spin a little.

Finally, since COM is a binary specification and is ultimately socket based, it should be possible to write a pure Java interface to COM objects. The first step might be to use the COM library files to generate stubs, with each method in the interface turning into a method that makes a socket call and handles the communication. Neither Sun nor Microsoft has announced any intention to build such a system, but a number of public domain projects have been started by a few brave hackers out there. Stay tuned . . .

Conclusion

In many ways distributed objects represent the pinnacle of the object-oriented paradigm. They enable the servlet developer to think only about objects, without having to worry much, if at all, about the fact that some objects really live in an external application.

The issues that programmers do need to concern themselves with are those of performance and choosing the right distributed architecture. Performance simply requires programmers to keep in mind the potential cost of a method invocation. Choosing the architecture is even simpler. When going from one Java program to another, RMI is the obvious choice. When going from Java to a legacy system or a program in another language, use CORBA. When it is necessary to use an object on a Microsoft system, use DCOM on the server side and wrap the application in a socket.

This concludes the survey of methods to communicate with applications outside the Java Web Server. In the next part, we shift gears somewhat to take a look at application programming techniques.

PART IV

Application Development Techniques

CHAPTER 16

Application Design in the Java Web Server

Building a program is a lot like building an apartment complex, and not just because both can be infested with bugs. Both buildings and programs are very complex structures, with many subsystems that must all work together. The old cliché "When the only tool available is a hammer, everything looks like a nail" is equally true in either case.

It has been said that if builders built buildings the way programmers write programs, the first woodpecker that came along would destroy civilization. In this chapter we discuss how to design and build a sturdy Web-based program and offer general pointers that can help steer people away from the worst mistakes.

We start by considering what makes a good design. We then look at how to apply these principles to servlets and related classes. We wrap up by reviewing the tools we introduced in other chapters and considering where each may be appropriate.

Drawing the Blueprints

There is a memorable scene in the film *Witness* in which an Amish community builds a barn in a day. Although it is never explicitly stated, the implication is that no lengthy design process preceded the building. Likewise, it is possible to build a small, simple servlet without a great deal of forethought. In each case, little preparation is needed because the structure is simple and familiar. However, this process does not scale well to either large buildings or large applications. When any endeavor is sufficiently large, whether it is a building or an application, the building process must be broken into three phases: developing a *specification of requirements*, the *design* of the implementation, and the *implementation* itself.

Specification of Requirements Phase

Starting with a well-thought-out and complete specification of requirements is critical: a barn is useless if what is needed is an office building and vice versa. With an application, until it is clear what the application is supposed to do there is no way to come up with a design.

A specification should be as complete and detailed as possible, up to the point where it starts being as granular as code. It is also vital to ensure that everyone involved in the process has the opportunity to contribute and sign off on the specification. Ideally, the design phase does not start until the specification is firm, and conversely, once design does start the specification should not change. If some department or individual does not have the opportunity to weigh in on the design at the beginning, a large portion of the design may need to be scrapped when they later point out some feature or requirement that everyone else overlooked.

Design Phase

Once the specification is final and has been approved by all parties, design can begin. In Java, design primarily means determining which classes are needed and what their roles will be. The bricks of a Java program are objects and the classes that define them. Object-oriented style of programming is a good thing for many reasons such as code reuse. But the principal benefit it offers is a formal way to think about programs. However, there is a good deal more to object-oriented programming than just using an object-oriented language. In the worst case, it would be perfectly possible to reduce Java to a procedural language by defining one class per procedure, each with a single static method. Hopefully, no real Java program out there is quite that bad, but odds are that there are many that could be better.

One of the basic ideas behind object-oriented programming is to model the task as a number of black boxes, where each box provides a set of controls that the other boxes can use to get data, change the first box's state, and so on. Each box also contains other boxes and performs its duties by twiddling the controls on the other boxes. Sometimes the things these boxes represent are quite concrete: a program that models a car probably has a windshield wiper object, a gas tank object, an engine object (which may itself have a fuel injector object and a spark plug object), and so on. In other cases, the classes are fairly abstract. It is hard to find a physical object that acts like a servlet, for example. In either case, the goal is to break down a problem into a set of "things" and the relationships between them.

In addition to defining the set of classes that make up a program, it is important to specify the interactions between classes, which may be significantly more complex than simply calling constructors and invoking methods. For example, the programmer needs to plan what happens if some object is unable to complete its task—probably it should throw an exception—and what other objects need to know that an exception has occurred. In the case of a fatal exception, the user needs to be told that something has gone wrong, and the site administrator needs to know precisely what went wrong. This means that the servlet needs to output an error page and log the exception.

However, not every exception is fatal. Some exceptions only require the object that made the call to wait a bit and try again. Other exceptions mean that a particular operation could not be performed but the application can go on anyway. In each of these cases, a different set of objects in the application needs to know that the exception was thrown.

Implementation Phase

Once a consistent design has been completed and all parties are satisfied that the design satisfies the requirements of the specification, it is time to start implementing. If the design was done properly, it should be easy to go from it to a set of stub classes, that is, classes that contain versions of all members and methods that have complete type signatures but that do not yet do any useful work. The implementation phase then consists of filling in each method.

It is in this phase that the difference between software and buildings becomes apparent. When putting up a building, it is impossible for two or more people to be working on exactly the same girder at exactly the same place and time, due to the pesky laws of physics. On the other hand, if someone makes a mistake that causes the whole building to collapse, it is impossible to just go back to yesterday's version of the building and continue.

Software has neither the first safety net nor the second danger. Fortunately, there are tools available that aid the process of *source control management*. We recommend RCS, a very comprehensive system available free for most major platforms. CVS, a graphical front end to RCS, makes life even easier. Both systems can be downloaded from a variety of locations on the Internet.

RCS, like most other such systems, designates a master copy of the source and allows developers to check out individual files. Files may be checked out for reading, like a library book, but they may also be checked out for modification. Only one person at a time is allowed to check out a file for modification, ensuring that two or more people cannot accidentally overwrite each other's work. This feature is useful even in projects with only a single pro-grammer to help keep track of what is currently being modified and what is stable.

Once a file has been checked out, modified, and tested, it can be checked back in, allowing everyone else to use the new version. At various stages, when the whole project is in a sound, consistent state, the current collection of files can be designated with a version number. For very large systems, where it is im-practical for everyone to recompile the whole system on a regular basis, it is possible to set up jobs that will recompile with the latest checked-in files each night. Later, if something breaks, it is possible to go back to an earlier version of either the project or individual files and trace the harmful change back to its source.

Servlet Class and Good Design

Regardless of how the classes are designed, the one class that is certain to be on the specification list is HttpServlet. But even though the servlet class is proba-bly be the start of the project, it is not the be-all and end-all of it. While it is certainly possible to put all of an application's logic into the service(), doGet(), and doPost() methods, this does not really reflect what kind of "black box" a servlet is. The javadoc page for HttpServlet declares that it "provides a framework for handling the HTTP protocol." Note that this is a very differ-ent concept from "handling an HTTP request." The latter is what the whole application does; the former merely provides a gateway between the applica-tion and the outside world.

From this perspective, there are really only two things a servlet should do: get information about the request from the HttpRequest and send data back through the HttpResponse. In fact, the doGet() method of a real servlet might look very much like Listing 16.1.

Listing 16.1   Generic servlet class structure.

```
public void doGet(HttpRequest req, HttpResponse res) {
  String queryString = req.getQueryString();
  // Step 1, get info from the request
  if(queryString != null) {
    Hashtable queryValues = HttpUtils.parseQueryString(queryString);
    String    values[]   = (String[]) queryValues.get("someValue");
    if(values != null && values.length > 0) {
      someValue = values[0];
    } else {
      error("Needed value not provided");
      return;
    }
```

```
      values[] = (String[]) queryValues.get("someOtherValue");
      if(values != null && values.length > 0) {
        someOtherValue = values[0];
      } else {
        error("Needed value not provided");
        return;
      }
    } else {
      error("Needed value not provided");
      return;
    }
    // Step 2, where all the application stuff happens
    realApplicationClass theApplication =
                    new realApplicationClass(someValue);
    byte results = theApplication.doIt(someOtherValue);
    // Step 3, send data back to the user
    res.setStatus(res.SC_OK);
    res.setContentType("text/html");
    res.setContentLength(results.length);
    res.getOutputStream().write(results);
    res.getOutputStream().close();
}
```

The servlet may not seem to be doing much here. That is because it is not. But it is doing exactly what servlets were meant for. The application class does not need to know anything about how it was called or the details of the protocol. After all, there is no reason why an application such as a game or bulletin board should need to know anything about content types or query strings. Likewise, there is no reason why a servlet should need to know anything about application objects such as players or messages.

Laying out the Rooms

Early in the planning process, good object-oriented design removes most of the work from the servlet class and puts it into other classes. However, there may be occasions where it makes sense to take some of the code and move it even further—out of the JWS entirely and into another process.

Frequently, servlets are written for the express purpose of providing Web access to some other application, such as a database or DCOM object that cannot be completely included within the servlet or perhaps cannot be implemented in Java at all. In these cases there is no decision to be made regarding whether the auxiliary classes will be internal or external. But in other circumstances it may be possible to put the entire application in one place and yet undesirable to do so.

One common reason to place some classes outside the Web server is to isolate native methods. As we have previously observed, native methods may be dangerous, as it is possible for them to conflict with Java's memory or thread management. In these cases it may make sense to put the classes that contain the native code into a separate daemon process. The servlet can then communicate with it via sockets or RMI, as we discussed in Chapters 13 and 15.

It may also make sense to pull classes out of the Java Web Server and into an external application to allow programs other than the JWS to use them. One example of this is if there are two or more Web servers running for the purposes of load balancing. In a load-balanced system, a gateway sits in front of the Web servers and routes each request to whichever server is currently least busy. This means that a user of a servlet may not hit the same Web server each time. One way to make this transition between servers seamless is to make the application a single separate process that both servers use.

There also may be occasions where some completely different process needs access to an application at the same time the server is using it. For example, a servlet might wish to to keep track of user data and generate a summary report for an administrator. One way to do this would be to allow the servlet to generate and send the report when it receives a special query string, but this is a potential security risk. It is much safer to put the application outside the Web server, allow the servlet to write data into the application, and write a separate utility that will talk to the application and retrieve the data. This is an excellent place to use RMI. The classes can reside anywhere on the network, and both the servlet and the utility can use it as if it were local. The servlet might call only some addData() method, and the utility could call generateReport(). Of course, if for some reason the utility is not written in Java, then CORBA can be used to the same effect.

Using the Toolbox

When the only tool available is a hammer, lots of fingers are likely to be hit. Fortunately, servlet programmers have a rich and varied set of tools at their disposal. In this section we briefly review some of the tools we have discussed in this book. Keep in mind that one of the best features of an object-oriented language is that it lends itself very well to code reuse, so any classes written for one application are potential tools for building the next one.

Templating

Templating was discussed extensively in Chapter 6. It is probably the easiest of the Java Web Server (JWS) tools to use, although with simplicity comes a fairly limited applicability. However, when building a site that is going to consist mainly of static pages with common elements on each page, templating is definitely the way to go.

Java Server Pages

Java Server Pages (JSP) is the easiest entry into the world of servlets and can become as complex and sophisticated as is required. If much of the complexity of a page or set of pages is going to be in static HTML, JSP may be the right tool. Note that using JSP does not mean that an object-level design is not needed. JSP pages can contain other classes or derive from another class or call remote methods—everything any other class can do. JSP pages normally occupy the same space in an object diagram that the servlet would; the only difference is that in addition to checking the input values, JSP pages are also responsible for generating the bulk of the output.

Caching

In the broadest sense, caching is merely the act of holding on to something after the first time it is used so that it does not need to be generated or obtained the second time. A *cache* is most often used to hold data that are expensive to obtain. Not every servlet has this property, but anything that requires a database or complex calculations probably does. We illustrate the use of caches several times in this book, including Chapter 14, where the technique was used to store data destined for a database. Caches are also used extensively in the Java Web Server itself for storing things such as HTML pages served out by the `FileServlet`.

Pooling

In a sense, pooling is the other side of caching, where instead of a single repository to hold common data, multiple instances of an object or other resource are available when needed. A *pool* is most often used to hold resources that are expensive to obtain such as a class with a very complex constructor. In Chapter 14, we created a pool of database connections and also provided a general pooling class. Pools, such as the pool of threads that is meant to handle each request, are used extensively in the Java Web Server.

Threads

In Chapter 10, we talked a great deal about how to make servlets thread safe. From this discussion it may seem as if *threads* are just something servlet writers need to react to, but they can also be a powerful tool. There are not that many instances where a servlet needs to create a new thread. However, one common use is to update a cache, as the examples in Chapters 14 and 15 did. A thread can also be used to periodically send information to an administrator and clean out old data, among other things.

Threads are one of the trickier tools to use, especially in the context of the JWS, which handles a large number of threads. One point worth remembering is that most threads a servlet wants to create should be created in the init() method and killed in the destroy() method. There is no reason to create threads in service() or any of the methods it calls, since these methods are always threads of their own anyway. See Chapters 10 and 13 for more information on threads.

Session Tracking

Session tracking can be used to keep track of what a user is doing or to collect information about a user over time. There is nothing built into HTML to connect one request to another, so the issue of *preserving state* comes up repeatedly. A great deal of code out there uses the Perl/CGI model that solves this problem by the use of databases. When converting this code into servlets, session tracking may be a better fit than JDBC, both because it is easier to use and because it has lower overhead. But as discussed in Chapter 8, making session tracking persistent may require using JDBC.

Moving In

Good object-oriented programming practices may not come naturally right away. At first it may seem to be more effort than it is worth. However, all the effort is up front, and in the long run it pays for itself many times over. Also, most programmers find that after a short while they begin to think in terms of objects and develop a feel for the methodology, after which working with class diagrams becomes as second nature as writing code.

Conclusion

Because this chapter skims over a great deal of material that is covered in entire books, it may seem like thin gruel. We strongly felt we needed to include this chapter in the book because in our experience, especially with the advent of the Internet, application development methods are frequently ignored—with drastic consequences. Many are the Internet companies that built applications with no thought to design or scalability and then watched their software drown in a flood of traffic. The message of this chapter is to take the time up front, listen to the client, design first before coding. It will pay great dividends.

CHAPTER 17

Servlet Debugging Techniques

One of the greatest things about Java programming is the scarcity of frustrating bugs like memory leaks and buffer overflows. Some might be tempted to believe that the Golden Age of Programming is almost at hand. Sadly, the bugs will always be with us. Java may protect developers from many memory problems, but by making threads easier to use, it probably increases the frequency of thread-related bugs. And of course Java has no special defense against buggy program logic. This chapter mentions some current debugging tools, especially the freely available ones, but its focus is on underlying debugging techniques. See Chapter 19 to find out how to diagnose performance problems in the Java Web Server itself.

The Java Development Kit (JDK) version 1.1 and earlier ones come with jdb, the Java Debugger—a command line utility that is reminiscent of UNIX debuggers like dbx. Unfortunately, jdb is not very stable and can be frustrating to use. It is tolerable with small stand-alone programs, but in general it should be avoided unless there is no other alternative. This chapter uses it in some of its examples only because it is freely distributed with JDK.

Sun is aware of jdb's shortcomings and is working to improve its stability. Even better, Sun is defining a debugging architecture for the Java platform. The architecture, called jbug, consists of APIs that will expose the inner workings of the Java Runtime Environment (JRE). Once jbug is implemented (in a future release of the JDK), anyone will be able to write a Java debugger. When other Java virtual machine (JVM) implementers adopt jbug, then the same debuggers can be used with different JVM implementations!

Until that happy day, most Java debuggers will depend on integrated development environments (IDEs). These are software packages that tightly tie together editor, compiler, debugger, and sometimes other tools as well. In the past, IDEs have not been useful for servlet developers, since servlets cannot be run (and therefore cannot be debugged) outside the Java Web Server (JWS) or another servlet engine. Loading the mammoth JWS into an IDE is not practical. Fortunately, there are stripped-down servlet engines that can be brought into an IDE without tremendous difficulty. The original one, servletrunner, is free from Sun as part of the Java Servlet Development Kit (JSDK). A commercial product from Live Software, ServletDebugg, is designed to integrate with Borland's JBuilder, and it can serve as a stand-alone debugger with minimal work. Symantec Visual Café has built-in servlet support.

Debugging Servlets with the Java Servlet Development Kit and `jdb`

Developers who want to debug their servlets without commercial tools need to download the free JSDK at

> *http://java.sun.com/products/servlet/index.html*

The kit includes full documentation and a tutorial. It also includes servletrunner, which is like a tiny, no-frills JWS. All it does is run servlets. From a UNIX shell, it can be started with a command line like this:

```
servletrunner -p 8888 -d ~/servlets
```

The -p argument tells servletrunner on what port it should accept connections, and -d tells it where to find servlet class files to run. Web browsers can connect to servletrunner just like they do to the Java Web Server, with URLs like this:

> *http://hostname:8888/servlet/ServletClass*

When servletrunner accepts a connection, it loads the requested servlet class, runs that class's `init()` method, and then calls its `service()` method.

In the JSDK 2.0 distribution for UNIX, servletrunner is a shell script that can easily be modified to work with `jdb`. All that is necessary is to make a copy of the script (call it `servletrunner.debug`) in the same directory (`/bin`) and change the last line of the copied file from

```
$JAVA_HOME/bin/java sun.servlet.http.HttpServer $*
```

to

```
echo "To begin debugging, type"
echo "    run sun.servlet.http.HttpServer $*"
$JAVA_HOME/bin/jdb
```

Then the debug version of servletrunner can be run with the same command-line arguments as the original, but instead of launching the Java servlet engine, it will start jdb. To use jdb on a servlet, that servlet should be compiled with javac's -g option. The -g compiler option puts into the class file extra information that jdb needs to examine local variables, among other things.

Developers who are already familiar with command-line debuggers can safely skip to the Diagnosis and Treatment section. jdb is not much different from any other debugger. It loads a program into its memory and then runs it, all the while keeping it under tight control. jdb always knows what the program is doing and can stop the program whenever it gets to a certain method or even a certain line of code. jdb always knows the contents of the program's memory and can peek inside to see what is in an object's field or a method's variable. jdb is like a good spirit that possesses bad programs, controlling their actions and reading their minds to discover why they went wrong.

Let's look at a sample run of our debug version of servletrunner. Say we have a copy of the Java Web Server's RedirectServlet in the /servlets sub-directory of our home directory. First, we make sure to compile it with javac -g, and second, we make sure that ~/servlets is in our CLASSPATH. (Servletrunner does not need the CLASSPATH setting, but jdb does.) Once everything is ready, we tell servletrunner to start up, looking in ~/servlets for servlet class files and listening on port 8888.

```
~/java/JSDK2.0/bin/servletrunner.debug -d ~/servlets -p 8888
```

servletrunner.debug changes its directory to ~/java/JSDK2.0, sets some environment variables, and starts jdb. It prints this prompt:

```
To begin debugging, type
    run sun.servlet.http.HttpServer -d /home/tsnee/servlets -p 8888
Initializing jdb...
>
```

Before we jump right in, however, let's decide where to start debugging RedirectServlet and set a breakpoint there. Since RedirectServlet does not have an init() method, the logical place to start is service().

```
> stop in RedirectServlet.service
Breakpoint set in RedirectServlet.service
```

Now we can start running the Java code.

```
> run sun.servlet.http.HttpServer -d /home/tsnee/servlets -p 8888
running ...
main[1] servletrunner starting with settings:
  port = 8888
```

```
backlog = 50
max handlers = 100
timeout = 5000
servlet dir = /usr/local/JavaWebServer1.1.1/servlets
document dir = ./examples
servlet propfile = /usr/local/JavaWebServer1.1.1/servlets/servlet.properties
RedirectServlet: init
```

Now the servletrunner is ready to accept a request from a Web browser. From our favorite browser let's try requesting

  *http://hostname:8888/servlet/*RedirectServlet?%2F

This causes servletrunner to execute `RedirectServlet`'s `service()` method, and that triggers the breakpoint we set in `jdb`.

```
Breakpoint hit: RedirectServlet.service (RedirectServlet:46)
Thread-175[1]
```

This means that `jdb` has stopped running the servlet code right before it reached line 46 of `RedirectServlet.java`. It is usually a good idea to have another window open, with the source file in an editor, to look at the source as the bytecode is executed. We can also tell `jdb` to list the source code above and below the line just about to be executed.

```
Thread-175[1] list
42        */
43            public void service(HttpServletRequest req, HttpServletResponse res)
44            throws ServletException, IOException
45            {
46      =>        String location = null;
47            String path;
48            String query;
49            if ((path = req.getPathInfo()) != null) {
50                if ((query = req.getQueryString()) != null)
Thread-175[1]
```

The arrow => indicates the line that is just about to be executed, in this case, a simple assignment. Nothing too interesting here. Let's tell `jdb` to keep running until we get to something more interesting. We can execute the code one line at a time with the `next` and `step` commands. `next` and `step` both execute one simple Java statement at a time, but `next` treats a method call like a simple statement and runs it all at once, while `step` actually steps down into the method and runs it one line at a time.

```
Thread-175[1] next

Breakpoint hit: RedirectServlet.service (RedirectServlet:49)
```

Thread-175[1] Thread-175[1] **next**

Breakpoint hit: RedirectServlet.service (RedirectServlet:54)
Thread-175[1] Thread-175[1] **list**
50   if ((query = req.getQueryString()) != null)
51   location = path + '?' + query;
52   else
53   location = path;
54   =>   } else if ((query = req.getQueryString()) != null) {
55   location = decode(query);
56   }
57   if (location == null) {
58   res.sendError(res.SC_INTERNAL_SERVER_ERROR,
Thread-175[1]

We know that the query string should be %2F, since that is what we typed into our browser window. Let's try to verify it with the print command.

Thread-175[1] print req.getQueryString()
"getQueryString" is not a valid field of (sun.servlet.http.HttpRequest)0x406c08b8

jdb cannot evaluate expressions that include a method call. All it can print are field or local variable values. dump is a little better—it can print out every field in an object—but for now let's just keep going. Line 55 uses the value of getQueryString() in a call to the decode() method, so we can look at it then.

Thread-175[1] **next**

Breakpoint hit: RedirectServlet.service (RedirectServlet:55)
Thread-175[1] Thread-175[1]

Now we are just about ready to run RedirectServlet's decode() method. If we type next again, we will run decode() all at once. Instead, let's step into decode() and run it one line at a time.

Thread-175[1] Thread-175[1] **step**
Breakpoint hit: RedirectServlet.decode (RedirectServlet:81)
Thread-175[1] Thread-175[1] **locals**
Method arguments:
  this = RedirectServlet@80d5ab7
  encoded = %2F
Local variables:
  holdstring is not in scope
  count is not in scope
Thread-175[1]

The **locals** command shows the names and values of all method parameters and local variables in a method. Since decode() does not declare holdstring or count until later on, jdb says they are not in scope. Parameters are always in scope, so we can see that the String parameter encoded, which is the String returned from req.getQueryString(), has the value %2F. Just as we expected!

jdb and servletrunner will get the debugging job done. It won't be done quickly, and in fact several tries may be needed before jdb decides to work properly, but given enough patience, a developer can get an idea of what his or her code is up to.

Diagnosis and Treatment

Any bug that produces an exception is generally easy to find, because exceptions usually generate a stack trace that shows where the problem started. When the program just hangs, on the other hand, the problem can be difficult to track down, since there is no message to indicate where the error is.

The rest of this section will use the Scribble Board servlet as a debugging test case (see Listing 17.1). It is like an extremely simple Web bulletin board. All it does is record and display the last few messages submitted via an HTML form. It is a little too spare to make a good stand-alone bulletin board, but it is fine for a simpler purpose: allowing Web page readers to leave their comments on a Web page. Any static HTML page can use the Java Web Server's server-side include mechanism to add a scribble board. If the servlet is invoked without a servlet path, it assumes that it was called through a server-side include, prints its messages, and then prints an HTML form for submitting new messages. If it is invoked with a servlet path, it assumes that it has been invoked from a form with a new message, records the message, and redirects the browser back to the server-side include page.

Listing 17.1   ScribbleBoard1.java

```
package com.awl.cseng.jws.util;

import javax.servlet.*;
import javax.servlet.http.*;
import java.util.*;
import java.io.*;

/**
 * ScribbleBoard allows users to leave comments on Web pages.
 * It is designed to be used as a server-side include.  It has
 * one initialization parameter, maxMessages, the maximum number
 * of messages to display.
 *
 * service() handles GET and POST requests itself.  Other
 * requests are given to the superclass's service().  service()
```

```
 * tries to determine if it has been invoked as a server-side
 * include; if it has, it invokes handleIncludeRequest().  That
 * method in turn calls printMessages() to print the stored
 * messages and printInputForm() to generate an HTML form for new
 * message submission
 *
 * If service() has not been invoked as a server-side include, it
 * assumes that it has been called with a new message submitted
 * via an HTML form and invokes handleFormSubmission().  That
 * method calls addNewMessage() to actually record the message.
 */
public class ScribbleBoard1 extends HttpServlet {
  // Constants
  /** Number of messages to save, by default              */
  static final int    DEFAULT_MAX_MSGS            = 5;

  /** Init parameter: number of messages to remember        */
  static final String MAX_MSGS_PROPERTY_NAME    = "maxMessages";

  /** initialization parameter: name of this servlet's alias */
  static final String SRVLT_ALIAS_PROPERTY_NAME = "alias";

  /** Name of request parameter                            */
  static final String NEW_MSG_FORM_PARAM_NAME   = "newMessage";


  // Instance fields
  /** Initialization parameter                             */
  int    maxMessages;

  /** Message-storing array                                */
  String messages[];

  /** Index into messages: pos of next message to be added  */
  int    numMessages;

  /** Servlet alias                                        */
  String servletAlias;


  // Methods overridden from HttpServlet

  public String getServletInfo() {
    return "ScribbleBoard version 0.1";
  }


  public void init(ServletConfig config)
  throws ServletException {
    servletAlias = config.getInitParameter(
                           SRVLT_ALIAS_PROPERTY_NAME);
```

```java
      if ( servletAlias == null ) {
        throw new UnavailableException(this,
                                       "Mandatory servlet property \""
                                       + SRVLT_ALIAS_PROPERTY_NAME
                                       + "\" not specified.");
      }

      String messageParam = config.getInitParameter(
                                      MAX_MSGS_PROPERTY_NAME);
      if ( messageParam != null ) {
        try {
          maxMessages = Integer.parseInt(messageParam);
        } catch (NumberFormatException e) {
          log("ScribbleBoard.init: "
              + MAX_MSGS_PROPERTY_NAME
              + " property assigned bad value "
              + messageParam);
          maxMessages = DEFAULT_MAX_MSGS;
        }
      }

      numMessages = 0;
      messages = new String[maxMessages];

      // Use superclass's log() method to to record interesting
      // events.
      log("ScribbleBoard.init: Created array of "
          + maxMessages
          + " strings.");
    }


    public void destroy() {
      messages    = null;
      numMessages = 0;
    }


    public void service(HttpServletRequest req,
                        HttpServletResponse res)
    throws IOException, ServletException {
      String requestMethod = req.getMethod();
      if ( !requestMethod.equals("GET")
      &&   !requestMethod.equals("POST") ) {
        super.service(req, res);
        return;
      }

      if ( req.getServletPath() == null ) {
        // Called as server-side include.
        handleIncludeRequest(req, res);
      } else {
```

```
        // Called directly from browser.
        handleFormSubmission(req, res);
    }
}


// Methods new to this servlet

void handleIncludeRequest(HttpServletRequest req,
                          HttpServletResponse res)
throws IOException, ServletException {
    res.setStatus(HttpServletResponse.SC_OK);
    res.setContentType("text/html");
    ServletOutputStream out = res.getOutputStream();

    printMessages(out);

    // Build a URL for posting new messages directly to this
    // servlet
    String postURL = req.getScheme()
                     + "://"
                     + req.getServerName()
                     + ':'
                     + req.getServerPort()
                     + servletAlias;
    printInputForm(out, res.encodeUrl(postURL));

    out.close();
}


void handleFormSubmission(HttpServletRequest req,
                          HttpServletResponse res)
throws IOException, ServletException {
    String[] newMessage = null;

    // Retrieve NEW_MSG_FORM_PARAM_NAME from POST or GET request

    Hashtable queryParameters = null;
    if ( req.getMethod().equals("POST") ) {
        queryParameters = HttpUtils.parsePostData(
                                        req.getContentLength(),
                                        req.getInputStream());
    } else {  // GET
        queryParameters = HttpUtils.parseQueryString(
                                        req.getQueryString());
    }

    if ( queryParameters != null ) {
        newMessage = (String[])queryParameters.get(
                                        NEW_MSG_FORM_PARAM_NAME);
    }
```

```
    if ( newMessage == null  ||  newMessage[0] == null ) {
      res.sendError(res.SC_INTERNAL_SERVER_ERROR,
            NEW_MSG_FORM_PARAM_NAME + " must be specified.");
      return;
    }

    addNewMessage(newMessage[0]);

    // Now redirect them back so that they can see their message.
    String redirectURL = req.getHeader("Referer");
    if ( redirectURL == null ) {
      res.sendError(res.SC_HTTP_VERSION_NOT_SUPPORTED,
            "Your browser does not supply referer field.");
      return;
    } else {
      res.sendRedirect(res.encodeRedirectUrl(redirectURL));
    }

    res.getOutputStream().close();
}


/**
 * Prints out messages[] in an unordered list
 *
 * @param out Connection to browser
 */
void printMessages(ServletOutputStream out)
throws IOException {
  out.println("<UL>");
  for (int i = 0; i < numMessages; i++) {
    out.println("<LI>" + messages[i] + "</LI>");
  }
  out.println("</UL>");
}


/**
 * Prints out message submission form
 * Example: <PRE>
 * &lt;FORM METHOD="GET" ACTION="http://jeeves/test.shtml"&gt;
 * &lt;INPUT TYPE="TEXTAREA" NAME="newMessage"&gt;
 * &lt;/FORM&gt;
 * </PRE>
 *
 * @param out Connection to browser.
 * @param formAction URL to use in form's ACTION tag.
 */
void printInputForm(ServletOutputStream out, String formAction)
throws IOException {
  out.println("<FORM METHOD=\"GET\" ACTION=\""
              + formAction
              + "\">");
```

```
    out.println("<INPUT TYPE=\"TEXTAREA\" NAME=\""
        + NEW_MSG_FORM_PARAM_NAME
        + "\">");
    out.println("</FORM>");
}


/**
 * Records a new message for future display.
 *
 * @param newMessage Message to record.
 */
void addNewMessage(String newMessage) {
    if ( numMessages == maxMessages ) {
        // Make room for new message--drop topmost (oldest)
        numMessages--;
    }

    // Now shift each element in the array up to make room
    // for a new one
    for (int i = numMessages; i > 0; i--) {
        messages[i] = messages[i - 1];
    }

    messages[0] = newMessage;

    numMessages++;
}
}
```

Chapter 3 discusses the process of loading a servlet into the Java Web Server. `ScribbleBoard` requires an initialization parameter named `alias`, which should be set to whatever `ScribbleBoard`'s servlet alias will be. (As servlets and Beans converge, "initialization parameters" will probably become known as "servlet properties.")

Problems with Loading a Servlet:
`cannot update servlet X: . . .`

Trying to load a new servlet into the server for the first time can be frustrating. It is not so bad if the operation fails with an informative error message, like `Cannot update servlet scribble: Mandatory servlet property "alias" not specified`. However, even after the alias property is set, the administration tool keeps popping up the same dialog box: `Cannot update servlet scribble: .`

Administration tool error messages tend to be terse, but `"."` sets new standards in brevity. What it means is that the Java Web Server caught a runtime exception from the servlet's `init()` method. Since the administration service knows how to handle only ServletExceptions, it cannot deal with things like ArrayIndexOutOfBoundsException or NullPointerException. To find out exactly what happened, check the administration service logs, in <server_root>/ logs/javawebserver/adminservice. In this case, nothing was written to error_log, but look at Listing 17.2 to see what showed up at the end of event_log.

Listing 17.2 event_log.

[Sun Jul 19 18:02:25 EDT 1998] java.lang.NullPointerException:
java.lang.NullPointerException:
    at javax.servlet.GenericServlet.getServletContext(GenericServlet.java:67)
    at javax.servlet.GenericServlet.log(GenericServlet.java:116)
    at com.awl.cseng.jws.util.ScribbleBoard.init(ScribbleBoard.java:83)
    at com.sun.server.ServletState.callInit(ServletState.java:187)
    at com.sun.server.ServletManager.loadServlet(ServletManager.java:735)
    at com.sun.server.ServletManager.loadServlet(ServletManager.java:660)
    at com.sun.server.ServletManager.loadServlet(ServletManager.java:629)
    at com.sun.server.ServletManager.getAndLoadServletState(ServletManager.java:826)
    at com.sun.server.ServletManager.getAndLoadServlet(ServletManager.java:877)
    at com.sun.server.http.admin.ServletAdmin.updateServletProps(ServletAdmin.java:353)
    at com.sun.server.http.admin.ServletAdmin.update(ServletAdmin.java:207)
    at com.sun.server.http.AdminServlet.dispatchRequest(AdminServlet.java:612)
    at com.sun.server.http.AdminServlet.service(AdminServlet.java:349)
    at javax.servlet.http.HttpServlet.service(HttpServlet.java:588)
    at com.sun.server.ServletState.callService(ServletState.java:204)
    at com.sun.server.ServletManager.callServletService(ServletManager.java:940)
    at com.sun.server.http.InvokerServlet.service(InvokerServlet.java:101)
    at javax.servlet.http.HttpServlet.service(HttpServlet.java:588)
    at com.sun.server.ServletState.callService(ServletState.java:204)
    at com.sun.server.ServletManager.callServletService(ServletManager.java:940)
    at com.sun.server.webserver.HttpServiceHandler.handleRequest
                    (HttpServiceHandler.java:416)
    at com.sun.server.webserver.HttpServiceHandler.handleRequest
                    (HttpServiceHandler.java:246)
    at com.sun.server.HandlerThread.run(HandlerThread.java:154)

This is called a *stack trace*. It looks pretty intimidating at first, but it is quite easy to understand. It begins with the exception that caused the problem, a NullPointerException. Then it shows where the exception occurred: in the getServletContext() method of javax.servlet.GenericServlet on line 67 of GenericServlet.java. Since that is part of the server itself, developers cannot do anything about that line of code, but they can figure out what line of their code called the offending line. To see what called getServletContext(), just look at the next line of the stack trace: the log() method of javax.servlet. GenericServlet on line 116 of GenericServlet.java. What called log()? The init() method of ScribbleBoard, line 83! The stack trace continues all the way up, until it gets to the first thing executed by the webpageservice handler thread.

NOTE: With recent versions of the JDK, stack traces do not have line numbers; instead, they print "compiled code," which means that a just-in-time (JIT) compiler has translated the Java bytecode into machine language, losing line number information in the process. To get the line numbers, disable the JIT either with Java's -nojit option or with the command-line argument -Djava.compiler= NONE.

When errors arise from lines the servlet can safely do without, it is tempting to fix the problem simply by removing the lines. However, it is often worth the time to track down mysterious problems just to learn what caused them. In this case, after asking around or posting a question to the Internet (or reading this book), we would discover that the root cause of the problem is that ScribbleBoard's init() method does not call super.init(). This prevents the servlet from keeping track of its ServletConfig object, which means that the servlet's log(), getInitParameter(), getInitParameterNames(), and get-ServletContext() methods will all generate a NullPointerException. So the real solution to this problem is to add the line

```
super.init(config);
```

to the beginning of ScribbleBoard's init() method.

It should be clear by now that it can take quite a bit of detective work to track down servlet bugs. An error message from the server is often only a small first step toward solving the problem. To get better error messages, at least from the servlet loader, wrap the body of each servlet's init() method in a try-catch block, as shown in Listing 17.3.

Listing 17.3 init() method with try-catch block.

```
public void init(ServletConfig config)
  throws ServletException {
    super.init(config);

    try {
      servletAlias = config.getInitParameter(
                                SRVLT_ALIAS_PROPERTY_NAME);

. . .

      // Use superclass's log() method to record interesting
      // events.
```

```
    log("ScribbleBoard.init: Created array of "
        + maxMessages
        + " strings.");
} catch (Exception e) {
    throw new UnavailableException(this, "init() threw " + e);
}
}
```

The try–catch block guarantees that the Java Web Server will never have to deal with any kind of exception besides `ServletException` (of which `UnavailableException` is a subclass). Since Listing 17.3 catches `Exception`, there is no way for any subclass of `Exception` to escape from the method and abnormally terminate `init()`. If an exception is thrown, `init()` catches it and throws an `UnavailableException`, which the Java Web Server can handle gracefully.

If the code with the new `init()` method is compiled and the server restarted, the servlet should load without a problem. It can be invoked from a `.shtml` file like the one in Listing 17.4.

Listing 17.4   `scribble.shtml`.

```
<HTML>
<HEAD>
<TITLE>Scribble Board Test Page</TITLE>
</HEAD>
<BODY>
<P>
Web Page Text
</P>
<servlet name="scribble"></servlet>
</BODY>
</HTML>
```

Problems with Running a Servlet: `500 Internal Server Error`

We load up `/scribble.shtml` in our browser and get an input field. It worked! Now we type something in and press Enter.

`500 Internal Server Error`

The servlet named "**scribble**", at the requested URL
http://localhost:8080/scribble
reported this exception:
0
The administrator of this web server should resolve this problem

Exception 0? That doesn't give us much to go on. Hopefully, there will be more detailed information in the logs. Since the servlet runs in the webpage-service, `<server_root>/logs/javawebserver/webpageservice/error_log` is the place to check first. Sure enough, the last entry in that file is as shown in Listing 17.5.

Listing 17.5 error_log.

[Sun Jul 26 09:53:31 EDT 1998] Exception in servlet scribble
[Sun Jul 26 09:53:31 EDT 1998] java.lang.ArrayIndexOutOfBoundsException: 0
java.lang.ArrayIndexOutOfBoundsException: 0
    at **com.awl.cseng.jws.util.ScribbleBoard.addNewMessage(ScribbleBoard.java:258)**
    at com.awl.cseng.jws.util.ScribbleBoard.handleFormSubmission
                (ScribbleBoard.java:187)
    at com.awl.cseng.jws.util.ScribbleBoard.service(ScribbleBoard.java:129)
    at javax.servlet.http.HttpServlet.service(HttpServlet.java:588)
    at com.sun.server.ServletState.callService(ServletState.java:204)
    at com.sun.server.ServletManager.callServletService(ServletManager.java:940)
    at com.sun.server.webserver.HttpServiceHandler.handleRequest
                (HttpServiceHandler.java:416)
    at com.sun.server.webserver.HttpServiceHandler.handleRequest
                (HttpServiceHandler.java:246)
    at com.sun.server.HandlerThread.run(HandlerThread.java:154)

That's more like it! From the header, we see that it was actually an ArrayIndexOutOfBoundsException that caused the failure. The first line of the stack trace shows that the exception was thrown at line 258 of the servlet code, which is in the addNewMessage() method (see Listing 17.6).

Listing 17.6 ScribbleBoard2.addNewMessage().

```
241      /**
242       * Records a new message for future display
243       *
244       * @param newMessage Message to record
245       */
246      void addNewMessage(String newMessage) {
247          if ( numMessages == maxMessages ) {
248              // make room--drop topmost (oldest)
249              numMessages--;
250          }
251
252          // Now shift each element in the array up to make room
253          // for a new one
254          for (int i = numMessages; i > 0; i--) {
255              messages[i] = messages[i - 1];
256          }
257
258          messages[0] = newMessage;
259
260          numMessages++;
261      }
```

An ArrayIndexOutOfBoundsException means that the servlet tried to use a bad array index. The error log entry shows that index 0 is the culprit. If even index 0 is too big for the array, then it must have been created with length 0, which is the bug here. (Most people think that the expression new String[0] would return null, but in fact it returns an array of type String with length 0. If messages had been null, this line would have thrown a NullPointerException instead.) The array was allocated in init(), so now we turn our attention to Listing 17.7.

Listing 17.7   ScribbleBoard2.init().

```
65    public void init(ServletConfig config)
66    throws ServletException {
67      super.init(config);
68
69      try {
70        servletAlias = config.getInitParameter(
71                                SRVLT_ALIAS_PROPERTY_NAME);
72
73        if ( servletAlias == null ) {
74          throw new UnavailableException(this,
75                            "Mandatory servlet property \""
76                            + SRVLT_ALIAS_PROPERTY_NAME
77                            + "\" not specified.");
78        }
79
80        String messageParam = config.getInitParameter(
81                                MAX_MSGS_PROPERTY_NAME);
82        if ( messageParam != null ) {
83          try {
84            maxMessages = Integer.parseInt(messageParam);
85          } catch (NumberFormatException e) {
86            log("ScribbleBoard.init: "
87                + MAX_MSGS_PROPERTY_NAME
88                + " property assigned bad value "
89                + messageParam);
90            maxMessages = DEFAULT_MAX_MSGS;
91          }
92        }
93
94        numMessages = 0;
95        messages = new String[maxMessages];
96
97        // Use superclass's log() method to record
98        // interesting events.
99        log("ScribbleBoard.init: Created array of "
100            + maxMessages
101            + " strings.");
102      } catch (Exception e) {
103        throw new UnavailableException(this,
104                            "init() threw " + e);
105      }
106    }
```

The hypothesis is that the messages[] field is initialized to a zero-length array. Since the array size is logged on line 99, we can confirm this. Checking <server_root>/logs/javawebserver/webpageservice/event_log proves it.

[Mon Jul 20 23:48:54 EDT 1998] ScribbleBoard.init: Created array of 0 strings.

A master Java programmer could probably find the problem from here just by reading the code. If you can do so, skip ahead to the next subsection. The rest of us would like nothing better than to run this code in a debugger, tracing it line by line, watching the values of local variable messageParam and field maxMessages. That way we could pinpoint the exact line of code at which things began to go wrong. However, if we are willing to exercise our brains a little, we can probably do just as well without any debugging tools. For a small, straight-forward method like this, it might even be faster to solve the problem by inspection rather than taking the time to start up the tool.

When init() is called for the first time, we know that all the fields (maxMessages, messages[], numMessages, and servletAlias) still have their default values. Unless fields are explicitly initialized, Java sets reference fields to null and numeric fields to 0. Therefore messages[] and servletAlias are null, and maxMessages and numMessages are 0.

```
67          super.init(config);
```

The first thing init() does is call the init() method (see Listing 17.8) of its superclass, HttpServlet. Next, it looks up the servlet alias initialization parameter. It assigns this parameter to the servletAlias field. If it was not specified, init() throws an UnavailableException, a subclass of ServletException that tells the Java Web Server that the servlet is not available to accept requests (Listing 17.9).

Listing 17.8 init(), beginning.

```
70          servletAlias = config.getInitParameter(
71                                  SRVLT_ALIAS_PROPERTY_NAME);
72
73          if ( servletAlias == null ) {
74            throw new UnavailableException(this,
75                                  "Mandatory servlet property \""
76                                  + SRVLT_ALIAS_PROPERTY_NAME
77                                  + "\" not specified.");
78          }
```

Listing 17.9 init(), middle.

```
80          String messageParam = config.getInitParameter(
81                                  MAX_MSGS_PROPERTY_NAME);
82          if ( messageParam != null ) {
```

```
83            try {
84              maxMessages = Integer.parseInt(messageParam);
85            } catch (NumberFormatException e) {
86              log("ScribbleBoard.init: "
87                  + MAX_MSGS_PROPERTY_NAME
88                  + " property assigned bad value "
89                  + messageParam);
90              maxMessages = DEFAULT_MAX_MSGS;
91            }
92          }
```

If the mandatory servlet alias property was set, then `init()` checks the optional maximum number of messages property. Since we didn't set that when we loaded the class into the administration tool, `getInitParameter()` will return null at line 80. That means that the body of the `if` block on lines 82 through 92 will be skipped.

```
94          numMessages = 0;
```

So far, the `servletAlias` field has changed its value. Now, at line 94, the `numMessages` field is set to 0. Of course, it was already 0, but it is considered good practice to always explicitly initialize fields, rather than implicitly relying on their default values.

```
95          messages = new String[maxMessages];
```

At last we get to the source of the bug, line 95. This is where our zero-length array is created. Why is `maxMessages` 0? Wasn't it set earlier in the method, on either line 84 or line 90? A cursory reading of the method indicates that `maxMessages` sets one way or another, but after our careful line-by-line review, we know that lines 82 through 92 were skipped. So `maxMessages` kept its default value, 0, all the way through to line 95.

Now that we know exactly what went wrong, it isn't difficult to fix. All the method needs is a check to make sure that `maxMessages` is greater than 0 before allocating the messages array, as shown in Listing 17.10.

Listing 17.10   `ScribbleBoard3.init()`.

```
public void init(ServletConfig config)
  throws ServletException {
    super.init(config);

    try {
      servletAlias = config.getInitParameter(
                                SRVLT_ALIAS_PROPERTY_NAME);

      if ( servletAlias == null ) {
```

```
            throw new UnavailableException(this,
                                "Mandatory servlet property \""
                                + SRVLT_ALIAS_PROPERTY_NAME
                                + "\" not specified.");
        }

        String messageParam = config.getInitParameter(
                                MAX_MSGS_PROPERTY_NAME);
        if ( messageParam != null ) {
          try {
            maxMessages = Integer.parseInt(messageParam);
          } catch (NumberFormatException e) {
            log("ScribbleBoard.init: "
                + MAX_MSGS_PROPERTY_NAME
                + " property assigned bad value "
                + messageParam);
            maxMessages = DEFAULT_MAX_MSGS;
          }
        }

        // Final sanity check
        if ( maxMessages < 1 ) {
          log("ScribbleBoard.init: using default value "
              + DEFAULT_MAX_MSGS
              + " for "
              + MAX_MSGS_PROPERTY_NAME
              + " instead of "
              + maxMessages);
          maxMessages = DEFAULT_MAX_MSGS;
        }

        numMessages = 0;
        messages = new String[maxMessages];

        // Use superclass's log() method to record interesting
        // events
        log("ScribbleBoard.init: Created array of "
            + maxMessages
            + " strings.");
      } catch (Exception e) {
        throw new UnavailableException(this, "init() threw " + e);
      }
    }
```

Now init() correctly handles the cases where (1) the maximum messages parameter wasn't set; (2) the maximum messages parameter was set, but with a value that could not be parsed as a number; and (3) the value of the maximum messages parameter was a number less than 1 (the smallest useful array size).

Problems with Using a Servlet: Garbled Output and Hangs

At this point, the servlet seems to work. A user can type a message into the form, press Enter, and be redirected right back to the page that contains the form, this time with his or her message. The developer can test it all day long without finding a problem. Does that mean that there is no more debugging to be done? Don't bet on it! There is still a whole class of problems left to address: thread bugs! Thread bugs are caused by poor interaction between multiple threads and almost never show up when only one person looks for them. It might be a good idea to review Chapter 10, Writing Thread-Safe Code, before reading the rest of this chapter.

Thread bugs are the most frustrating to combat. For one thing, they don't present themselves until the code is in production, being used by lots of people. For another, they are next to impossible to reproduce in a debugger. However, by simulating a heavy load on (stress testing) the servlet, it is possible to discover them before they sneak into production. Read Chapter 18 to find out how to stress test a servlet. While a servlet is handling lots of requests, watch for two warning signs: garbled output and hangs.

Garbled Output

If the servlet writes out pages with the same bit of HTML repeated two or more times, pages missing some data, or empty pages, there is a good chance that the servlet suffers from resource contention. As Chapter 10 discussed, any resource shared among threads, such as class (static) or instance fields, is a candidate for *race conditions*. For example, the Scribble Board servlet sometimes prints the same message twice in a row.

```
<UL>
<LI>fourth message</LI>
<LI>fourth message</LI>
<LI>third message</LI>
<LI>second message</LI>
<LI>first message</LI>
</UL>
```

Someone could run ScribbleBoard in a debugger for a year and not see the duplication but it will show up the first day it is heavily used. The only way to track it down is to study the code.

Because we know repeated output is a symptom of resource contention, the first thing we should do is look at the class and instance fields. ScribbleBoard's class fields are all constants, so there is no danger that one thread might modify them while another is reading them. That leaves the fields String servletAlias, int maxMessages, int numMessages, and String messages[]. We can eliminate servletAlias because it is only modified once, during init(), which is guaranteed to be run by only one thread at a time. Strings are rarely the object of resource contention anyway, since they cannot be modified once they have been created. ints like maxMessages can be modified at any time, but studying the code reveals that maxMessages, too, is modified only during init().

messages and numMessages, on the other hand, are both read in print-Messages() and changed in addNewMessage() (see Listing 17.11). Different threads can call those two methods at the same time.

Listing 17.11   ScribbleBoard3.addNewMessage().

```
252    /**
253     * Records a new message for future display.
254     *
255     * @param newMessage Message to record.
256     */
257    void addNewMessage(String newMessage) {
258      if ( numMessages == maxMessages ) {
259        // Make room for new message--drop topmost (oldest)
260        numMessages--;
261      }
262
263      // Now shift each element in the array up to make room
264      // for a new one
265      for (int i = numMessages; i > 0; i--) {
266        messages[i] = messages[i - 1];
267      }
268
269      messages[0] = newMessage;
270
271      numMessages++;
272    }
273 }
```

Eureka! If one thread ran printMessages() while another thread was running addNewMessage(), printMessages() might try to use the messages array while it was in an inconsistent state. Let's imagine one possible scenario. Say a thread shows up at line 257 when maxMessages is 5, numMessages is 4, and messages is {"fourth message", "third message", "second message", "first message"}. At line 258, the thread sees that numMessages is less than maxMessages, so it skips lines 259–261 and goes to 265. It then iterates through the for loop, copying each of the first four array elements into the next-higher element. Now messages is {"fourth message", "fourth message", "third message", "second message", "first message"}. If another thread were to run printMessages() right then, it would get the result in Listing 17.11. Race condition!

In this case, the problem is easy to fix. Since `printMessages()` and `addNewMessage()` cannot both be run at the same time, they can both be declared synchronized. All we have to change is the method declaration:

```
void printMessages(ServletOutputStream out)
```

becomes

```
synchronized void printMessages(ServletOutputStream out)
```

and

```
void addNewMessage(String newMessage)
```

becomes

```
synchronized void addNewMessage(String newMessage)
```

Synchronization adds a fair bit of overhead to a Java program, so it is not a good idea to use it willy-nilly. Also, when a program synchronizes on more than one thing at a time, it runs the risk of deadlock.

Hangs

The other symptom of thread problems is hangs. If browsers connect to a server to make a request of a servlet but get no output back, the thread handling the request may be trapped in a deadlock. If we had decided to fix the `ScribbleBoard` problem by creating lock objects and synchronizing on them, it might have been enough to hang the servlet (Listing 17.12).

Listing 17.12 `ScribbleBoard5`.

```
/** messages lock */
Object messagesLock;
/** numMessages lock */
Object numMessagesLock;
...
void printMessages(ServletOutputStream out)
throws IOException {
  synchronized(messagesLock) {
    synchronized(numMessagesLock) {
      out.println("<UL>");
      for (int i = 0; i < numMessages; i++) {
        out.println("<LI>" + messages[i] + "</LI>");
      }
      out.println("</UL>");
    }
  }
}
...
```

```
void addNewMessage(String newMessage) {
  synchronized(numMessagesLock) {
    if ( numMessages == maxMessages ) {
      // Make room for new message--drop topmost (oldest)
      numMessages--;
    }

    synchronized(messagesLock) {
      // Now shift each element in the array up to make room
      // for a new one
      for (int i = numMessages; i > 0; i--) {
        messages[i] = messages[i - 1];
      }
      messages[0] = newMessage;
    }
    numMessages++;
  }
}
```

This kind of thread problem can be much harder to spot just by reading the code, because oversynchronization is even more subtle than undersynchronization. Fortunately, Java provides enough clues to know when a deadlock has occurred.

If a request to a servlet hangs, the first thing to do is figure out what the server is doing. If the server uses Sun's JDK or JRE, it can print out a thread dump. (Some people refer to it as a stack trace, and although it does include stack traces for every thread, it includes other information as well.) Some Java implementations derived from the JDK do the same thing. If the server were started from the command line, pressing Ctrl-\ (UNIX) or Ctrl-Break (Windows NT) in that window would cause the Java interpreter to print a thread dump.

Windows users could get the same effect by clicking on the Window's Close button. If the server were not started in a user's window, UNIX users could cause a dump by running `kill -QUIT <server_process_id>`, but then they would have to find out where the server's output goes. If the server were running as an NT service, there would be no way to get a stack trace from it.

A thread dump contains the full stack trace of every running thread, plus the contents of some internal data structures. One of those structures is the monitor cache (see Chapter 10). Since there tend to be many threads active in the Java Web Server at any one time, the dumps can be hundreds of lines long. However, most of the lines can be safely ignored.

First, look through the stack printouts to see how many threads are executing the servlet. A trace shows what the thread is doing. An individual thread's stack trace looks like the following:

"Thread-45" (TID:0x4066c480, sys_thread_t:0x4152af04, **state:MW**) prio=5
  com.awl.cseng.jws.util.ScribbleBoard.printMessages(ScribbleBoard.java)
  com.awl.cseng.jws.util.ScribbleBoard.handleIncludeRequest(ScribbleBoard.java)
  com.awl.cseng.jws.util.ScribbleBoard.service(ScribbleBoard.java)
  javax.servlet.http.HttpServlet.service(HttpServlet.java)
  com.sun.server.ServletState.callService(ServletState.java)
  com.sun.server.ServletManager.callServletService(ServletManager.java)
  com.sun.server.webserver.HttpServiceHandler.handleRequest(HttpServiceHandler.java)
  com.sun.server.webserver.HttpServiceHandler.handleRequest(HttpServiceHandler.java)
  com.sun.server.HandlerThread.run(HandlerThread.java)

This thread, for example, is running `ScribbleBoard`'s `printMessages()`, which was called from `handleIncludeRequest()`, which was called from `service()`, which in turn was called by JWS methods. Thread dumps include another important piece of data: the state of the thread. State R means that the thread is either running or could be running. MW, on the other hand, means that the thread is waiting to enter a synchronized method or block of code. If at least two threads running the same or related code are in state MW, they could be causing each other to deadlock. This can be verified in the next part of the trace, the `Monitor Cache Dump`.

```
Monitor Cache Dump:
    messagesLock@1080376832/1080782608: owner "Thread-45"
                                        (0x413b5f04, 1 entry)
        Waiting to enter:
        "Thread-28" (0x413d6f04)
    numMessagesLock@1080376816/1080782720: owner "Thread-28"
                                        (0x413d6f04, 1 entry)
        Waiting to enter:
        "Thread-45" (0x413b5f04)
```

Proof positive! The first entry shows that Thread-45 is running code synchronized on `messagesLock` and Thread-28 is waiting to enter the same or other code synchronized on `messagesLock`. The second entry shows that Thread-28 is running code synchronized on `numMessagesLock` and Thread-45 is waiting to enter the same or other code synchronized on `numMessagesLock`. Taken together, these two entries reveal that Thread-45 has `messagesLock` and wants `num-MessagesLock` but Thread-28 has `numMessagesLock` and wants `messagesLock`! Since neither one can move forward until the other moves first, they are stuck in deadlock.

Recognizing a deadlock is one thing; fixing it is another. A thorough discussion is beyond the scope this book; instead, see Doug Lea's definitive *Concurrent Programming in Java* (see Appendix for publication details). All we do here is offer a few tips. For instance, if it is at all possible, try to synchronize on only one object. Synchronized instance methods use the instance itself (`this`), and if they don't ever run code synchronized on anything else, they cannot deadlock. In larger applications, where this is not a practical solution, then at least try to avoid calling one object's synchronized methods from within another object's synchronized method or nesting synchronized blocks, as we saw in `printMessages()` and `addNewMessage()`.

Conclusion

Debugging is not a very glamorous subject, but since it often takes more time than the coding, it is worth thinking about at length. As of the time of this writing, there are not many ways to debug servlets, so developers and quality assurance technicians have to be especially creative. There is no one tool or technique that can diagnose every kind of problem. "Bug squashers" have to be comfortable using debuggers, combing through logs, and generating stack traces before they can hope to identify and correct the problems to which Java programs are prone.

CHAPTER 18

Stress Testing Servlets

Servlets can be like children who are darlings at home but mischievous beasts in public. Just because a servlet behaves well in development does not mean that it will do likewise in production. A developer might test a servlet over and over again without discovering bugs that appear only when many people use it. An analogy is a heart defect that shows up in a person only during exercise. An electrocardiogram will show obvious defects, but only a special test, a stress EKG, can reveal the hidden flaw.

Servlets can be stress tested (or performance tested) by making many requests of them from many different Web clients. Stress tests are the best way to discover thread bugs in a servlet, since multiple threads don't interact within a servlet until multiple clients make requests of it at the same time. Stress tests are also a good way to determine how much load a servlet can handle. (In the latter context, stress testing is often called load testing or volumetric testing.) This chapter discusses how to set up stress tests, how to run them, and how to interpret their results.

Setting up a Stress Test

The first thing to decide is what we want to get out of a stress test: evidence of bugs or performance data. If all we are trying to do is break a servlet, we don't have to design the test as carefully as we do when we want to collect meaningful information about it. This will become clear in the next few pages. Once we know what we want from the test, we can determine what hardware we need to run it and then choose the right software.

Stress Test Goals

A developer's first goal is usually to produce code that works. He or she is primarily interested in testing to find bugs. A programmer's stress test is likely to be pretty simple: hammer the servlet as hard as possible and see how it holds up. Eventually, though, someone will care how fast the code runs and how many people can use it at once. At Time Inc., for example, the management was eager to make sure that the new JWS-based *Money Magazine* Web site could handle as much traffic as the old site. That meant that the servlets had to handle up to 10 requests per second and satisfy each request in less than 2 seconds. Therefore we needed a test that would show two properties: throughput and latency.

For the purposes of this chapter, *throughput* means the number of requests that can be served per unit time, and *latency* means the amount of time a request takes to satisfy. Both these measures are necessary to determine if a servlet is "fast enough." Some people think that average response time (latency) is the only thing they need to worry about, because the faster a servlet runs, the more requests it can handle. Not necessarily! Knowing that the latency of a servlet is 2 seconds, for example, does not mean that it can handle only 30 requests per minute; because the servlet is multithreaded, it might be able to handle 50 simultaneous requests within 2 seconds, for a throughput of 1,500 requests per minute. For the same reason, just because a servlet can handle 1,500 requests per minute does not mean that its latency is 2 seconds. A servlet might take 4 seconds to handle a single request, if it could handle 100 requests at once. Latency and throughput do not affect each other in straightforward ways.

A good way to think about throughput and latency is by imagining a water pipe (Figure 18.1). The wider the pipe, the more water can flow through it. The shorter the pipe, the faster the water will flow. A long, skinny pipe will not let much water through (low throughput) and the water will take a while to get from one end to the other (high latency). A short and wide pipe permits a lot of water to go through it in a short time.

Stress Test Hardware

Whether we are more interested in eliminating bugs from code or measuring its speed, the code should be run in an exact replica of the production environment. If a servlet is tested on a completely different machine from the one it will run on, we cannot be sure that we will find all the bugs that will show up in production. Similarly, performance numbers generated from a single-CPU Wintel box will not accurately predict how a servlet will run on a

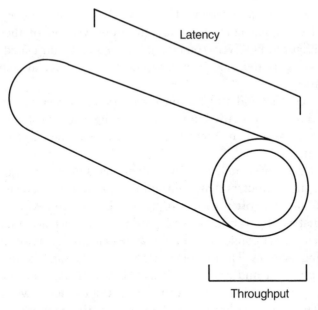

Figure 18.1 Latency and throughput

multiprocessor SGI Onyx. If we are working on a Web site that hasn't launched yet, we can use the production environment itself. Developers writing code for an already running site need a separate testing environment. That is because stress tests can cause a great deal of network traffic and a huge amount of work for the computers involved, so they can easily slow down the site for regular users. Ideally, stress tests should be conducted only on dedicated computers on their own isolated network segment. That way, the normal operation of the Web site won't affect the test, and more important, the test won't slow down the site.

The first thing to think about is setting up the machine that will run the servlet. To best predict how the servlet will run in production, an exact copy of the machine it will use in production should be used. If the servlet is supposed to run on a Sparc Ultra 2 with two CPUs and 128 MB of RAM, that exact hardware profile should be used for the stress test host. It is also good to have the same version of the operating system, with the same patches, on the test host.

There is a big difference between the networking performances of Solaris 2.5 and Solaris 2.6, for example, so servlets tested under 2.6 will probably not perform as well under 2.5. Finally, the servlet execution engine should be the same as the production version. If the Java Web Server is being used, both test and production machines must use the same version of the JWS with the same configuration. Even something as seemingly unrelated to servlets as the server log buffer sizes (see Chapter 4) can have an impact on servlet performance.

Stress tests should still be run if the production environment cannot be duplicated for testing. Any kind of stress testing can reveal bugs in the servlet. It just won't accurately predict how much load the servlet will handle in production.

Client machines make up the second hardware element of stress tests. These are the computers that will run the stress testing Web clients that hit the servlet. While it is often easier to just use one machine for both server and clients, that configuration doesn't produce the most accurate test. For one thing, client-server connections on the same machine use fewer of the machine's networking facilities. The most realistic test uses the same configuration as production: one host and multiple clients. The client machines don't have to be anything special so long as they can run the test client software.

The last stress test hardware component is the network that connects the server and client machines. Most local area networks are divided into segments so that traffic between computers on one network segment doesn't slow down traffic on another segment. For this reason, the stress test host and clients should be isolated on their own network segment for the duration of the test. A stress test can consume a great deal of bandwidth, sometimes enough to render a network useless for any other purpose.

Stress Test Software

The most realistic stress test imaginable would involve scores of people using many different Web browsers to access the servlet. That is not a practical solution for most projects. Also, it would not provide hard data on how long the servlet took to fulfill requests. Luckily, it isn't difficult to write a simple Java program that opens a connection to a servlet and makes a request just as a Web browser would. In fact, there are many such Web clients available on the Internet. One of them, Live™ Software's ServletKiller, can be downloaded to most systems free of charge.

If the goal of the test is uncovering bugs, not collecting performance data, then any stress test client should suffice. If data collection is important, then the best client is one that records the time each servlet request takes (latency). Throughput can be determined from the Java Web Server's access log (see Chapter 21).

Running the Test and Analyzing the Results

Set one or more copies of the stress test client running on each client machine, and then use a browser to connect to the servlet to see if it still produces good output. If the servlet does not work correctly, see Chapter 17 for suggestions on finding the source of the problem. If the bug shows up only under load, chances are that it is thread related (see the Threads section in Chapter 17).

If you glance at the latency figures while the test is underway, they may appear higher than you expected. Don't jump to the conclusion that the servlet is at fault! Many things can cause slow response times. The machine on which the browser runs could be slow or overburdened. The network between the client and the servlet could be saturated. The computer on which the servlet runs could be overloaded. The server within which the servlet runs could be too busy. Of course, the servlet itself could be the culprit, but the other potential causes should be eliminated before spending lots of time optimizing the servlet.

To determine the source of a speed problem, eliminate each possibility, one by one. The following are a few simple procedures that can be carried out while the stress test is underway.

1. *Run a browser from a testing client and hit the servlet.* If it is fast, the stress test client is probably not reporting accurate results. Try the test again with other testing software. If it is slow, then you have eliminated the possibility that the test software is faulty. Go to step 2.

2. *Run a browser from a testing client and hit another servlet running on the same servlet engine.* A good one to try is the Java Web Server's Simple-Servlet, since it doesn't need many server resources and therefore shouldn't be affected by the test. If SimpleServlet is fast, the servlet being tested is the problem. Sorry. If it is slow, then there is still hope that the servlet might not be the problem. Go to step 3.

3. *Try running the stress test clients against the SimpleServlet.* If you get much better results than you did with your servlet, then it is time to admit that your servlet needs work. If the results are the same, then you can cross your servlet off the list of suspects. Hooray! Go to step 4.

4. *Telnet from a testing client to the servlet engine's host.* If everything is fast, the servlet engine is probably the bottleneck. Chapter 19 discusses ways to improve JWS performance. If the telnet session is slow, you have eliminated the servlet engine as a suspect. Go to step 5.

5. *Telnet from one host to another on the same network segment that connects the testing clients and server.* If it is fast, then the network is not the problem—the computer running the servlet engine must be too slow. You will need

a system administrator's help at this point. If the telnet session is slow, the network is the problem, and you will have to refer it to your network administrator. If you do not have a network administrator, then it is time to buy an Addison Wesley Longman networking book.

The stress test client software should generate latency statistics, but if it doesn't, it should at least generate a log of response times, from which latency can be calculated. The math is pretty simple: divide the sum of the response times for each request by the total number of requests. For example, if five requests took 1,200 milliseconds, 1,400 msec, 900 msec, 1,000 msec, and 800 msec, then divide (1,200 + 1,400 + 900 + 1,000 + 800 = 5,300) by 5 to get 1,060 msec. In other words, the latency was 1.06 seconds.

Throughput must be determined by analyzing the access log. Each request will have a corresponding line in the log, and each line will show when the server finished processing the request, to the second. The number of lines between the beginning and end of the test is the total number of requests, and the number of seconds between the time of the first and last request is the total time elapsed. The throughput formula is simply total requests divided by total time. Suppose a test consisted of 3,182 requests between 10:24:32 (32 seconds after 10:24 A.M.) and 10:34:18. You could calculate the throughput by dividing 3,182 requests by (10:34:18 − 10:24:32 = 9 minutes 46 seconds = 586 seconds) to get 5.43 requests per second.

But what do these numbers really mean? What is good and what is bad? It depends. For one company, a latency of 1.06 seconds is acceptable, but a throughput of 5.43 requests per second is woefully inadequate. With that throughput, a servlet could not even handle 20,000 requests an hour. Of course, most sites do not get that much traffic in a day, much less an hour, so this throughput would be more than enough for them.

Solving Servlet Performance Problems

Chapters 11 and 12 discuss ways to speed up Java applications. These techniques often make the code harder to understand and should be applied only to methods that really need them. The way to find these methods is through profiling. A *profile* is a report that shows how much time a program spends in each section of its code.

It is widely believed that most programs spend 80 percent of their time executing only 20 percent of their code. In fact, many programmers refer to this phenomenon as the 80/20 rule. (Some people say that most programs spend 90 percent of their time running 10 percent of their code.) The useful thing that profiling tells us is *which 20 percent* of the code is the time sink. The areas of code that take the most time to run are called hot spots.

Looking at the performance problem analytically, we see another reason to optimize hot spots before anything else: it achieves the greatest benefit for the least amount of work, every programmer's goal. For example, if code can be tweaked to make its hot spots run twice as fast, 40 percent is shaved off the program's total execution time (assuming the 80/20 rule). If the other 80 percent of the code is optimized by the same amount, four times as much work has been done, but the program is only 10 percent faster.

Code profiles are most surprising to the people who wrote the code to begin with. The hot spots are often where we least expect them. One reason is that slow methods that are run only once in a while don't cause nearly as much trouble as so-so methods that are run many, many times.

Memory problems are also likely to show up in unexpected places. When a programmer is done with a big object, he or she might set all the references to it to null, but if the person does not remember to remove() it from every hash table he or she might have put() it into, it stays around all the same. These kinds of memory leaks are almost impossible to find just by reading the code line by line.

The bottom line? Developers who try to improve the performance of code without profiling it doom themselves to hours of fruitless toil.

In-depth Profiling

A good profile of Java code contains lots of different information. For each method in each class, the profile should reveal the number of times the method was called, what other method called it, and how much time it took to execute. For each object on the heap, the profile should show the number of references to it, what other objects held references to it, and how much memory it consumed.

NOTE: By the way, here "time" means wall clock time—the total amount of time that elapses between the instant at which a thread starts executing a method and the instant at which it stops. This is different from CPU time, which is the total amount of time a CPU spends running a method.

Consider two methods, one that generates a simple fractal image and one that records it to a magnetic tape. The generating method probably spends almost all its time running on the CPU, while the recording method spends most of its time waiting for I/O. It would not be surprising for the recording method to use 3 seconds of wall clock time and 3 seconds of CPU time, whereas the recording method might take 5 seconds of wall clock time but less than 1 second of CPU time. In general, Java programmers care more about wall clock time than CPU time. That is because people today don't pay for computer time by the CPU minute as our primitive ancestors did and because interactive response time is more important now than it was in the batch-processing era. (And also because it is easy to find elapsed time in Java but impossible to determine CPU time in a platform-independent way.)

That said, wall clock time isn't so useful by itself. For instance, it would not come as a great shock to find out that a program's `main()` method or a servlet's `service()` method took 100 percent of the execution time. To get any use out of elapsed time figures, you have to know which methods call which other methods. Knowing that a program took 10 seconds to finish and that `main()` began at time index `0` and ended at time index `10` does not do us much good. However, knowing that `main()` called methods `calculate()`, `show()`, and `save()`, which took 3 seconds, 1 second, and 5 seconds, respectively, gives us a much better picture of what is going on inside the program. `main()` itself adds just 1 second of overhead; half of the program's time is spent within `save()`. This means we should focus our optimizing efforts on `save()`.

But where does `save()` spend its time? We also need to know which methods *it* calls. Think of the program as a tree (the computer science kind, not the wooden kind). `main()` is at the root, and it has three children, `calculate()`, `show()`, and `save()`. The methods called by these three methods are their children, `main()`'s grandchildren. When you have followed every single call to every single method and drawn a tree picture with that information, you have written the *call graph*. The nodes are methods and are labeled with their wall clock times. The arcs are method calls and are labeled with the number of times the parent method called the child method. You can often tell where hot spots are just by looking at a call graph (see Figure 18.2).

A similar graph can be built from memory profiling information. Each stack frame of each thread (see Chapter 11) can contain an object that has references to other objects. These objects, in turn, refer to still more objects. The web of references can be described as a graph. The nodes are objects, and the arcs are references from one object to another. If your program contains a memory leak (i.e., objects that should be freed but aren't), all you have to do is locate the bad objects in the graph and trace them back toward a root. At some point, you will find an object that is still being used that contains a reference to an object that is no longer needed. Voilà! You have found your memory leak.

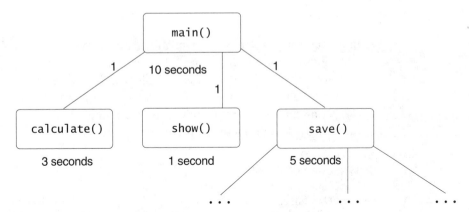

Figure 18.2 Call graph

Profiling Methods

As of this writing, only a few good Java profiling tools are available commercially, and none is free. Profiling tools are not easy to make. Some companies do it by licensing the source code to Sun's Java virtual machine (JVM) implementation and modifying it to collect profiling information. That is a difficult and expensive process, not only doing it the first time but also redoing it every time Sun releases a new version of the JDK. It is also a pain for developers to switch a Java Runtime Environment whenever they want to profile their code. Hopefully, the situation will change after JDK version 1.2 has been around for a while.

JDK 1.2 adheres to Sun's JVM Profiler Interface (JVMPI), an API that third parties can use to develop profiling applications. Once enough independent software vendors (and open source enthusiasts!) write to the JVMPI, other JVM implementers will have a powerful incentive to make their own Java runtimes follow that API as well. Until that happy day, there is no standard way to collect profiling information from a Java application short of putting timing code inside the application itself.

Stack Traces

One profiling trick should work with any Java runtime that can produce stack traces. (See Chapter 17 for more about stack traces.) It sounds silly, but it works, to a degree. Simply do a trace every few seconds and take note of which methods show up. If you notice that some methods appear more often than others (80 percent of the time?), those methods are probably hot spots.

java -prof

A more rigorous way to collect profiling information from Sun's Java implementation is to run programs under Java with the -prof option. This command line option tells the Java runtime to collect CPU and memory usage information about the program it executes. When the program completes, the runtime writes a summary of the information to a machine-parseable ASCII file named java.prof by default. Here are the first few lines of one such file.

```
count callee caller time
540 java/lang/String.<init>(II[C)V <unknown caller> 1
433 java/lang/String.hashCode()I
java/util/Hashtable.put(Ljava/lang/Object;Ljava/lang/Object;)Ljava/lang/Object; 3
411 java/util/Hashtable.put(Ljava/lang/Object;Ljava/lang/Object;)Ljava/lang/Object;
sun/io/CharacterEncoding.<clinit>()V 9
114 java/lang/System.arraycopy(Ljava/lang/Object;ILjava/lang/Object;II)V
java/lang/String.<init>([C)V 0
```

Every method invoked by the program has a corresponding line in the file. The profile information includes the number of times the method was called, which other method called it, and the number of milliseconds of wall clock time spent in the method. This should be enough to build a call graph, but, alas, there are problems with -prof output. Some versions of the JDK produce incorrect information for recursive methods. Some produce bad results for multi-threaded programs! Some of these problems can be fixed by using java_g instead of java.

Another difficulty with java -prof is that the Java program it runs must exit normally or it will not write any profiling output at all. That makes it more difficult to obtain profiling information from servletrunner, since that program does not stop running until someone kills it. The only way to make it stop itself is to run a servlet like the one in Listing 18.1. Please keep in mind that this is the only circumstance in which a servlet should call System.exit()—in general, most people do not want their servlet engines brought to a halt by a servlet.

Listing 18.1   ExitServlet.java.

```java
import javax.servlet.http.*;

public class ExitServlet extends HttpServlet {
    public void service(HttpServletRequest req,
                        HttpServletResponse res) {
        System.exit(0);
    }
}
```

Commercial Profiler Products

One high-quality profiler, called JProbe, is available commercially from KL Group. Another product is available on both the Sun Solaris and Microsoft Windows platforms: Intuitive Systems' OptimizeIt. OptimizeIt does both CPU and memory profiling quickly and easily. It cannot profile servlets directly, but it can profile sun.servlet.http.HttpServer, the Java program invoked by servletrunner, and can therefore generate figures for servlet code indirectly.

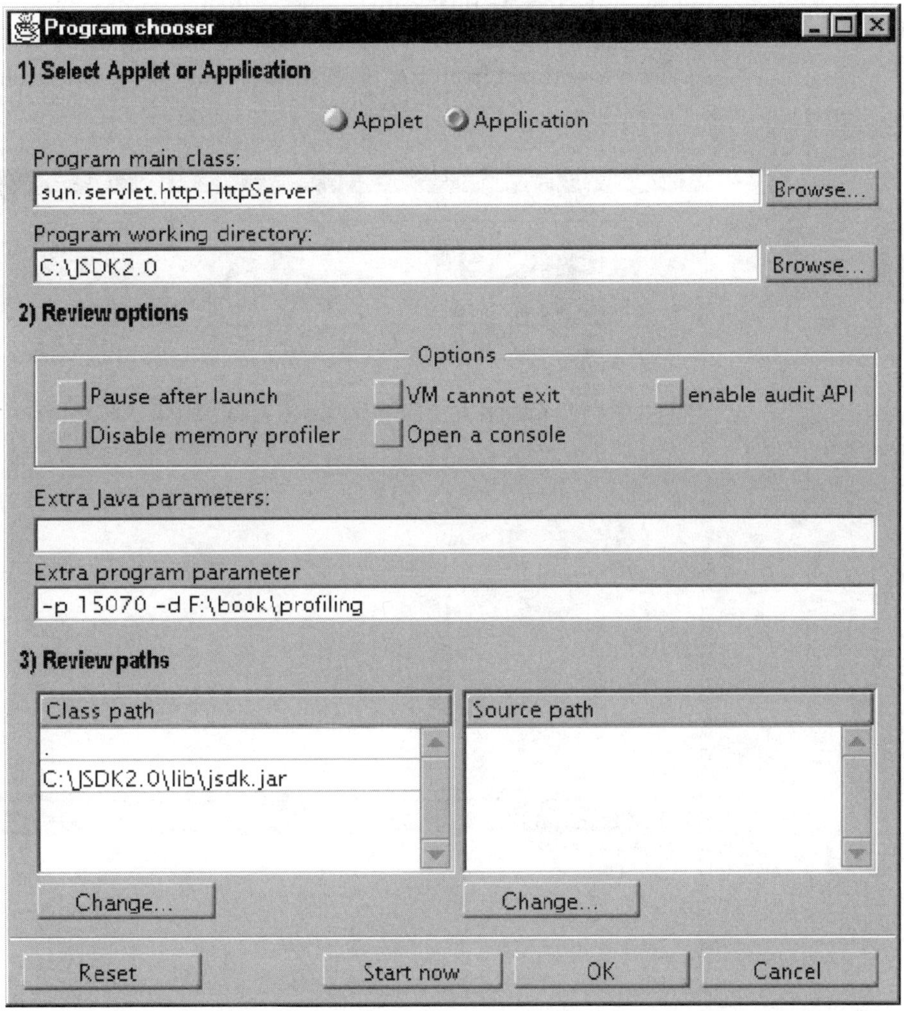

Figure 18.3   OptimizeIt Program chooser

When OptimizeIt starts running, it opens a window called the "Program chooser" (Figure 18.3). To profile a servlet that has been set up to run under servletrunner, click on the Application button in the chooser. The first text input field is for the class whose `main()` method should be run; this should be `sun.servlet.http.HttpServer`. Under "Extra program parameter," you can give OptimizeIt whatever servletrunner command-line options you would normally use. Finally, under "Review paths" at the bottom of the window, click on the class path's Change button to add the `jsdk.jar` file to OptimizeIt's class path.

Now OptimizeIt is ready to run servletrunner. Click on the "Start now" button to begin. At this point, a screen invites you to "`Press the button to start the CPU profiler`" (Figure 18.4). Before starting the profiler, run the servlet a few times from the browser to make sure OptimizeIt has loaded and

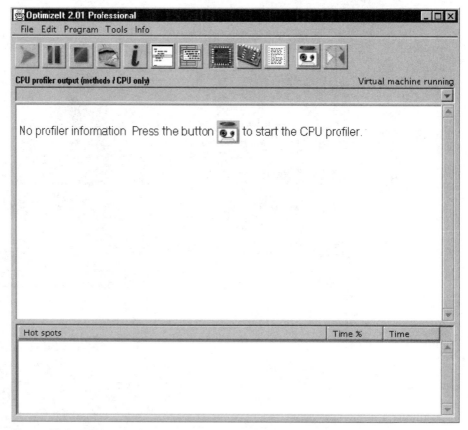

Figure 18.4   CPU profiler

initialized all the relevant classes. That can be quite time-consuming, and it can obscure important hot spots—the ones the servlet encounters once it is up and running.

After starting the profiler, run the servlet a few times, and then stop the profiler. OptimizeIt will show a profile of a thread but probably not an interesting one (Figure 18.5). The main thread, for instance, does not run the servlet code, so its profile does not have any information relevant to your servlet. That information is in a thread in the servletrunner thread group. You can choose one from the dropdown menu under the tool bar.

OptimizeIt shows the methods it has found to be hot spots. You can click in the box to the left of the method to see the part of the call graph that leads to the hot spot. Figure 18.6 shows that one-third of the wall clock time of this

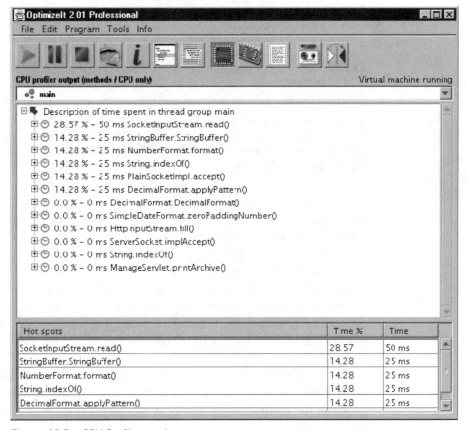

Figure 18.5 CPU Profiler results

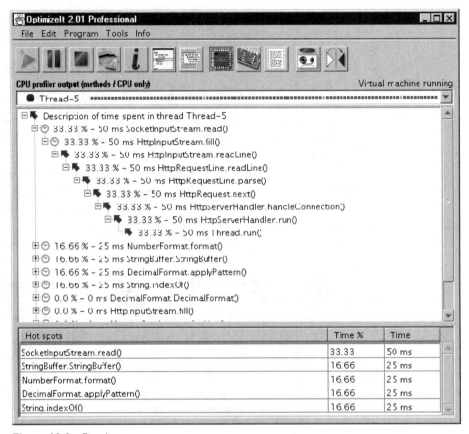

Figure 18.6   First hot spot

thread was spent parsing headers. Since this code is in the servlet engine, not the servlet, there isn't anything we can do about it.

The second hot spot (Figure 18.7), on the other hand, does involve the servlet code. OptimizeIt has singled out the `printArchive()` method of `ManageServlet`. As we know from Chapter 8, the core Java classes that involve internationalization (e.g., parsing and formatting dates) can be quite time-consuming. If `ManageServlet`'s performance needs to be improved, it might be worthwhile to abandon the `Date` class altogether and use `int`s for month, day, and year.

As we mentioned earlier, OptimizeIt also does memory profiling (Figure 18.8). Ctrl-M switches the display from CPU to memory. This screen shows a list of all the classes with instances in memory, from the largest number of instances to the fewest.

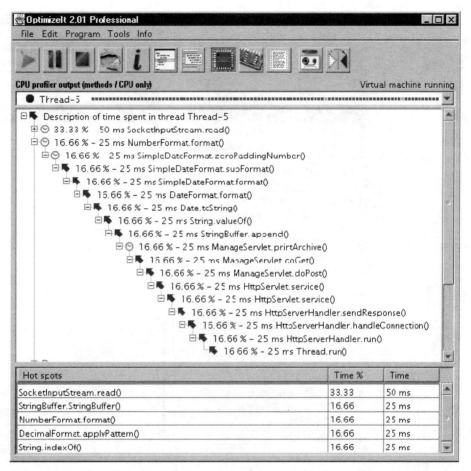

Figure 18.7   Second hot spot

Double clicking on a class shows the part of the call graph that includes methods that allocate instances of the class. This lets you know what parts of the code are allocating objects. If you suspect a memory leak, you will be more interested in what objects are maintaining references to objects that should be garbage collected. OptimizeIt shows that as well, in the Instances display (Figure 18.9).

This window shows what objects contain a reference to an arbitrary object, in this example, a Milestone (from the project management sample application). In this case, we see that it is in a hash table contained within a hash table

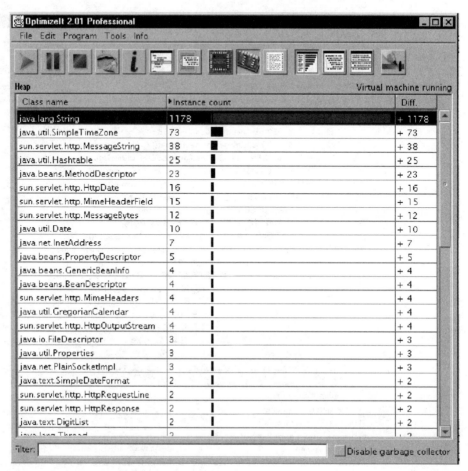

Figure 18.8   Memory profiler

that is itself contained within a third hash table. Trying to find this chain of references without a profiling tool would be a difficult and unrewarding task, to say the least.

Conclusion

Now that the age of the Internet is upon us, anyone can write an application that millions of people might run, so stress testing is an important topic to more people than ever before. It is especially important for Java programs, which

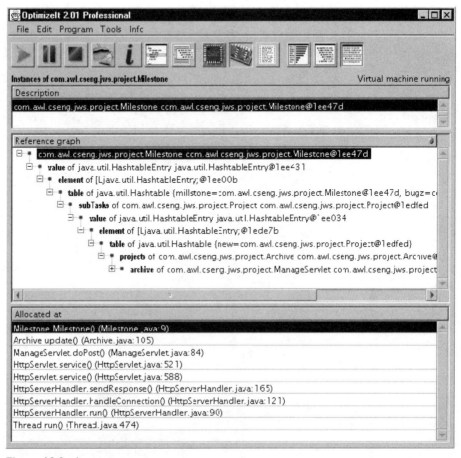

Figure 18.9 Instances

probably employ multiple threads more often than programs in any other language. A lone developer will almost never spot thread problems on his or her own; a stress test is the only way to be sure a multithreaded application will work well in production. Stress testing also shows how much load a program can handle on a particular platform, and it is good for creating profiles of CPU and memory usage.

CHAPTER 19

Performance Tuning for the Java Web Server

If you are like me, then every morning you wake up with the same thought: "What is the bare minimum I have to do to make it through the day?" That may sound like a poor attitude to have, but it's not a bad one for a Web site administrator. All web site administrators should be minimalists. Over the long term, the most successful changes to a Web site are the ones that achieve their aims with the smallest possible tinkering with the original configuration. Why is that? Because any time someone wants to make another change, the person first has to understand every change that was made before. At Time Inc. New Media, the Web server configuration file sizes were measured not in bytes but in megabytes. They were so big and complex that only one person truly understood them, and no one else was willing to change them. That's not good.

Determining and Checking the Minimum Acceptable Performance

Two quantities are important to Web site administrators: the number of hits per day and the amount of time the server takes to serve out a hit, our old friends *throughput* and *latency*. Most people assume that the smaller the latency, the higher the throughput. In other words, if requests take less time to serve, then the server will be able to handle more of them. If the Java Web Server (JWS) handled just one request at a time, that would be true. But since it is multithreaded, the situation is more complicated. Sometimes there is a tradeoff between throughput and latency. That is why we need to determine the minimal requirements for both. Figure out the throughput target by taking the number of hits expected during peak hours and dividing them by the number of seconds in the peak hours. Doing it per day is no good because Web site traffic tends to be extremely inconsistent. For instance, the *Money Magazine* Web site gets most of its 250 million hits per day between 10:00 A.M. and 3:00 P.M., so we knew that the JWS would have to handle 50,000 hits per hour, or 15 hits per second. If we just divided 250,000 by the number of seconds in a day, we would have come up with 3 hits per second, which was not accurate at all.

Determining the maximum latency, on the other hand, is pretty subjective. How long should users have to wait to view a Web page? A maximum of 3 or 4 seconds isn't bad, but if Web pages have lots of nested HTML tables, the browser might take a second or two just to render them, so in that case there should be a maximum latency of 2 seconds.

Now that you have your goals, you need to know if the server meets them or not. How do you find out if your server can handle 15 hits per second with a latency of 2 seconds? Stress testing! Chapter 18 talks about how to stress test servlets, and you can do exactly the same thing to see if your server meets the minimum requirements.

Improving the Performance of the Server

There are five ways to improve the performance of the Java Web Server: upgrade its Java Runtime Environment (JRE), upgrade or reconfigure the computer it runs on, use the Service Tuning screen of the JWS administration tool, increase the log file buffer sizes in the JWS administration tool, and rewrite the most-used servlets to be more efficient.

Upgrading the Java Runtime Environment

The improvement that has the biggest impact on performance is changing the Java Runtime Environment used by the Java Web Server. JWS version 1.1 is shipped with JRE derived from Sun's Java Development Kit (JDK), version 1.1.4. By default, JWS uses this JRE. Since that is the JRE Sun used to test the JWS, there is always the possibility that using another JRE will have unforeseen consequences. Stick with the default for as long as you can. When it just isn't fast enough, switching to JDK version 1.1.7 can more than double throughput.

Here is something to watch out for. The JRE and the JDK can be downloaded from the Sun Web site. The JRE is a stripped-down version of the JDK, meant for people who want to just run Java programs, not write them. The JRE does not have a Java compiler, so the JRE cannot be used with the Java Web Server if Page Compilation is to keep working; the JDK must be used.

It's pretty easy to switch from the default JRE to the JDK. First, make sure your JAVA_HOME environment variable is set to the directory that contains the JDK. Second, make sure that your CLASSPATH environment variable contains everything the JDK needs. That's it! Now the Java Web Server is ready to run with `<server_root>/bin/httpd.nojre` instead of `httpd` (UNIX) or `<server_root>\bin\httpdnojre.exe` instead of `httpd.exe` (Windows).

Upgrading or Reconfiguring the Server Machine

If you are using the fastest available JRE but you still need better performance from the JWS, try running it on a faster machine. Before you spend a lot of money on new equipment, though, make sure it will help. The JWS does not need much memory, so chances are that going from 64 MB to 128 MB of RAM will not make a big difference. If possible, get a system administrator to study the computer that hosts the JWS while it is under load to see what the limiting factor is. If the disk is too slow, for instance, getting a faster CPU will not help.

At Time Inc. New Media, we spent quite a bit of time optimizing the *Money Magazine* host, a Sparc Ultra 2 originally running Solaris 2.5.1. The first thing we did was upgrade the operating system to version 2.6, which has much more efficient networking code. That was the easy part—beyond that, we needed expert assistance from Sun. The rest of this section covers some of the things we learned.

By default, Solaris 2.6 is not configured to handle a very large number of connections. For one thing, the hash table that the kernel uses to store TCP/IP connections is not very big. It can be made bigger by adding

```
set tcp:tcp_conn_hash_size=262144
```

to the /etc/system file and rebooting.

Other changes don't require rebooting. (In fact, these commands have to be run every time the machine comes up.)

```
/usr/sbin/ndd -set /dev/tcp tcp_conn_req_max_q0 4096
```

creates a larger queue for the kernel to use for keeping track of new connections.

```
/usr/sbin/ndd -set /dev/tcp tcp_close_wait_interval 60000
```

reduces the time spent in the TIME_WAIT state to 60 seconds, which allows the kernel to more quickly reclaim ports after their connections have ended.

```
/usr/sbin/ndd -set /dev/tcp tcp_smallest_anon_port 2048
```

increases the number of available ports to 63000.

Using JWS Service Tuning

The only direct parameters that Web administrators can control are the three tabs of the Service Tuning screen of the administration tool. The first tab allows them to set the file cache size of the `FileServlet` and set the maximum number of concurrent client connections. The default file cache size is only one megabyte; a site that serves much HTML or other static content needs as large a cache as possible.

The second tab sets the minimum and maximum number of handler threads and the maximum amount of time a handler thread should remain idle before being stopped. If you are using native threads, keep in mind that each thread can take up a significant number of operating system resources, so you don't want to leave many threads lying around idle.

The third tab defines how the server treats clients that request keep-alive connections. A keep-alive connection is one that remains open after the initial request is finished, allowing a Web browser to make multiple HTTP requests without going through the time-consuming process of opening and closing a socket for each request. A little-known benefit of long-lived TCP/IP connections is that they handle larger volumes of data more efficiently than short ones do. Clearly, keep-alive is a good thing. The only sites that might want to cut down on it are those whose users sometimes get "connection refused" messages. Such errors can be an indication that the server machine has run out of room for new connections.

Increasing JWS Log File Buffers

This improvement is not very obvious, but it could have a significant impact on server performance. Since the server is constantly writing to its logs, larger log buffers enable the server to perform less disk I/O. Development servers often have a buffer size of 0, so log messages are sent to the disk as soon as they are generated, which is better for development. For production, though, larger buffer sizes are better. This issue is discussed in detail in Chapter 21.

Rewriting Servlets

Servlets running on the same server are like families living in the same house. When faced with finite resources (like bathroom time or JVM heap space), one must be considerate of others. A servlet that makes many memory requests or uses lots of thread synchronization can make it difficult for other servlets to get what they need. Chapter 11 explains this phenomenon. If some servlets are taking a disproportionate share of Java virtual machine resources, rewriting them to be more efficient will speed up every servlet on the server. Chapter 18 discusses useful techniques for finding out which pieces of code use the lion's share of CPU time and memory.

Conclusion

The Java Web Server took many person-years to optimize, and the authors saw it deliver around 200 (cached) pages per second. That's about three-quarters of a million pages an hour. In other words, there isn't much room for improvement. It will be fast enough for almost any use "out of the box," and more speed can be gained by changing its environment (upgrading its JRE or host machine) than by reconfiguring the server itself. However, there are server parameters that do have an effect on performance, like the service tuning options and log buffer sizes. Finally, performance can be improved by optimizing servlets that take too many memory or thread resources.

PART V

Java™ Web Server™ Internals

CHAPTER 20

Security and Custom Realms

Back in Chapter 3, we discussed the administrator's view of security. In that chapter we showed how the administration tool can be used to manipulate users, groups of users, and access control lists that associate permissions with users and groups. We also discussed the various realms that are accessible, including the `defaultRealm`, which includes the administrator account, and the operating system-specific realm, which contains users on the local system.

In this chapter, we go under the hood of the Java Web Server (JWS) security system. We discuss the classes that are used to represent realms, users, and access control lists (ACLs) and show how these classes can be used to create custom realms and ACLs, giving a great deal of flexibility to how system resources can be protected. Before diving into the details, however, we provide an overview of how security works in the Java Web Server.

URLs served by the JWS are not protected unless the user specifically configures the server to protect them. The administration tool is the vehicle used to protect a URL. After the user uses the administration tool to protect a URL, the URL is put on a list of protected URLs. Each time a request for a URL arrives at the Java Web Server, the list is scanned to see if the URL is on it. If the URL is not found on the secured list, the request is fulfilled. If it is found, then the request header is examined to see if the requesting user has permission to access the URL. If the user has already logged in to the JWS, then the HTTP authentication information that identifies the user is checked against the list of users who are allowed access. If the user is on the list, access is granted. If not, access is denied. If the user has not logged in, the user is asked to log in and the checking is done after they have logged in.

The diagram in Figure 20.1 provides a summary of the process, and it describes how most Web servers implement security. The one quirk of the Java Web Server is the concept of a realm. When a URL is protected in the JWS, the

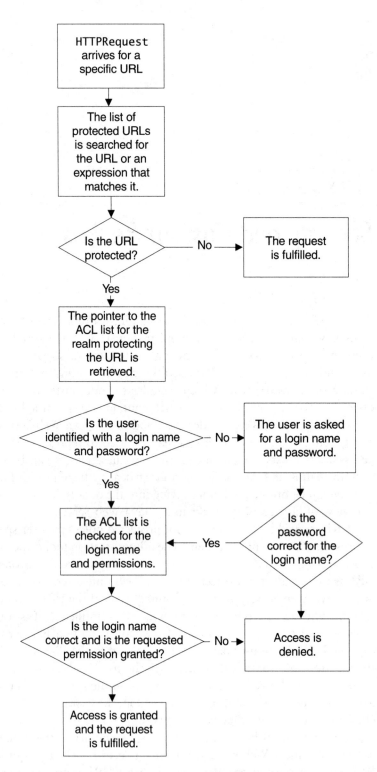

Figure 20.1 Flowchart of security in the JWS

protection exists within a realm. A realm is simply a domain of security. Realms to handle the fact that security is generally a platform-specific feature exist in the Java Web Server. Realms exist in the JWS for NT, UNIX, SSL security, and signed servlets and also for demonstration purposes. Realms provide for the needs of most users. The purpose of this chapter is to explain how a realm is built so that if the need arises you can build your own.

When might you want to make your own realm? Say user information were stored in an existing database and the users recorded in that database needed to have access to a URL on the Java Web Server. It would be a shame and an administrative nightmare to enter all those users into the JWS through the administration tool. A better solution would be to protect the URLs in question with a custom realm that could query the database for user information and then grant access if users properly identified themselves. This chapter explains how to create such a custom realm.

Security and Access Control Lists

Security in the Java Web Server is built on top of the security features of the Java programming language. In particular, users, groups, and ACLS are built on top of interfaces in the `java.security.acl` package. We therefore start our exploration with a look at these interfaces. The core Java language interfaces and the classes that implement the interfaces are summarized in Table 20.1. The last entry in the table is the class that implements the realm, the Java Web Server container for different security domains.

The classes that are used for security are related as shown in Figure 20.2. Note how the `Acl` class and the `AclEntry` class are the center of the structure.

The `java.security.acl` *Package*

Now that we have a general picture of how the security classes work together, we can proceed to the details of each of the classes and then to an example of how a custom realm would be built. The custom realm we build implements the kind of realm mentioned in the introduction, one that allows the Java Web Server to use a space of users that is stored in a database.

`java.security.Principal`

The `javadoc` page for this interface describes a principal as "anything that can have an identity." In JWS terms, this means an entity that may have access to some resource or pages on the server. We concern ourselves only with users as

Table 20.1   Java Web Server Security Interfaces

Java Language Interface	Description	JWS implementation class
java.security.Principal	Any entity that can have permissions or rights. An instance of this interface is the entity that is granted permissions.	com.sun.security.acl. PrincipalImpl
java.security.acl.Group	A group of principals.	com.sun.server.security. acl.GroupImpl
java.security.acl.Permission	An interface that contains permissions for a resource.	com.sun.server.security. acl.PermissionImpl
java.security.acl.AclEntry	A mapping between a principal and a permission. This interface contains what permissions have been granted or denied a principal.	com.sun.server.security. acl.AclEntryImpl
java.security.acl.Acl	A collection of ACL entries.	com.sun.server.realm.util. FileAcl com.sun.server.realm.Realm

principals, although it is possible for a machine or portion of a network to be a principal as well.

Principals do not have a great deal of functionality; they may be thought of as little more than a wrapper around a name. In particular, there is no built-in notion of "proving" that a principal is really who it claims to be.

The JWS implements the Principal interface in the com.sun.security. acl.PrincipalImpl class. As we will see shortly, classes that represent users can extend this class and provide methods that enable principals to authenticate themselves.

java.security.acl.Group

This interface defines a group of principals and provides methods to add and remove principals from a group. It is interesting to note that Group extends Principal, meaning that Groups themselves have an identity and may be added to other Groups.

In the JWS, the Group interface is implemented by the com.sun.server. security.acl.GroupImpl class, which other classes can extend to provide spe-

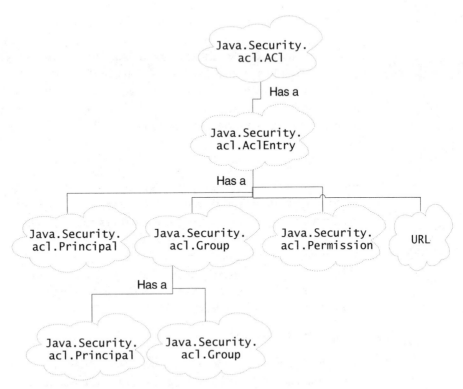

Figure 20.2   Class structure of the JWS security classes

cialized group functionality. We do not cover Group functionality in depth, but like other aspects of the JWS security API, it is possible to create custom groups.

java.security.acl.Permission

This interface represents a permission, such as access to a resource. As with Principal, Permission is little more than a wrapper around the name of the permission.

   The Java Web Server contains a class called com.sun.server.security.acl.PermissionImpl that implements the Permission interface. Typical permissions are the ones that show up in the administration tool: GET, POST, HEAD, and PUT.

java.security.acl.AclEntry

This interface associates a Principal with one or more Permissions. Permissions can either be denied or granted. If a Permission is marked as negative with a minus sign in the properties file or FileAcl class controlling the permission, that indicates that the `Principal` does not have the specified `Permissions`, which implies that the `Principal` does have all unnamed `Permissions`. More commonly, an `AclEntry` can be marked as positive with a plus sign, indicating that `Principal` has the named `Permissions`, and no others.

The JWS provides the `com.sun.server.security.acl.AclEntryImpl` class to implement the `AclEntry` interface. We do not need to concern ourselves with this class, but we mention it for completeness.

java.security.acl.Acl

Here is where it all comes together. An `ACL` contains a set of `AclEntries` and provides methods to add or remove a `Permission` to or from a `Principal` and check whether a `Principal` has a given `Permission`.

There are several classes within the JWS that implement `Acls`, but the most common is `com.sun.server.realm.util.FileAcl`. This class stores the ACL as a file under the `<server_root>/realms/data` directory. For example, in `<server_root>/realms/data/defaultRealm` is a file called `defaultAcl.acl`, which should contain something like

```
+User.jeeves=GET,POST
```

This line indicates that the user named `jeeves` has `GET` and `POST` permission. Note the plus sign, which indicates that the permissions are being granted. A minus sign would indicate that these permissions were being denied.

These interfaces and the JWS classes that implement them form a major part of the JWS security. Every protected resource has an associated `ACL`. The `AclEntries` in that `ACL` will map `Principals` to permissions like `GET` and `POST`. When a user comes in and requests such a resource, the user is represented as a `Principal`, and the `Acl` is checked to see if the user has that permission.

To boil all this down, an `Acl` simply says what users may do. `Acls` do not ensure that users are really who they say they are. That job is handled by the `Realm` classes.

Realms

Realms may be thought of as simply collections of users and ACLs and a means for verifying that users are who they say they are. The list of users may come from anywhere, such as a file, the operating system, or a database. The means of verification are somewhat more limited; currently only password and certificate verification are available in the Java Web Server. Passwords may themselves be stored in files, the operating system, a database, or anywhere else.

One useful method of authentication, cookies, is not supported in the Java Web Server. In some cases it would be useful for the JWS to read a cookie that was created by another security system. The Java Web Server would decrypt the cookie and use it to map to a space of users available to the server or to identify tokens that could be used to grant access to various URLs. Unfortunately, the JWS's security mechanism is tightly bound to the HTTP authentication headers, which makes the use of cookies difficult.

We can now complete the picture of how JWS security works. When a request comes in, the JWS checks to see if the relevant URL is protected by an `Acl` and, if so, what `Realm` that `Acl` is in. If it is protected, it sends information back to the browser indicating that it is protected and naming the realm. The browser responds by popping up a window asking for a name and password. This information is then passed back to the server. The `Realm` sees if the given password matches the given name. If it does, the `Realm` builds a `Principal` representing the user and then asks the `Acl` whether this `Principal` has the right `Permissions`. If so, access to the resource is granted. If not, it responds with an error code and the user may be prompted to log in again.

Custom Realms

The JWS comes with classes that handle both file-based realms, which can be used only to add users who already have accounts on the local network, and operating system-based realms, which may become unwieldy when there are a lot of users. A logical thought is to store usernames and passwords in a database.

Implementing a custom realm is not difficult; it is just necessary to extend the `com.sun.server.realm.Realm` class and provide methods to get users, groups, and ACLs. In our example, we get users out of a database. We do not support groups, although it would not be too complicated to get groups out of the database as well. Finally, we use the same file-based ACLs as the `defaultRealm`. Listing 20.1 shows the code.

Listing 20.1 `DBRealm.java`, a database-based realm.

```
import java.io.*;
import java.security.*;
import java.security.acl.*;
import java.util.*;
import java.sql.*;
import com.sun.server.realm.*;
import com.sun.server.realm.util.*;
public class DBRealm extends Realm
{
```

```
private EveryoneOkAcl theAcl = new EveryoneOkAcl();
private String dbUser        = "dbuser";
private String dbPasswd      = "dbuser";
private String dbUrl         = "jdbc:postgresql:testdb";
/**
 * Constructor. No special processing here--
 * it's all done in init()
 */
public DBRealm()
{
  super();
}
/**
 * Set up the realm
 */
public synchronized void init(Properties props)
      throws BadRealmException, NoSuchRealmException
{
  try {
    super.init(props);
    // Load the class that will talk to the database
    Class.forName("postgresql.Driver");
  } catch(Exception e) {
    throw new BadRealmException(e.getMessage());
  }
}

public Acl getAcl() throws BadRealmException
{
  return theAcl;
}

public Enumeration getAclNames() throws BadRealmException
{
  Vector n = new Vector()
  n.addElement("EveryoneOkAcl");
  return n.elements();
}

public Acl getAcl(String name)
      throws NoSuchAclException,BadRealmException
{
  return theAcl;
}

public Acl addAcl(String name, Principal owner)
      throws BadRealmException
{
  throw new BadRealmException("Unable to add new acls");
}

public void removeAcl(String name)
      throws NoSuchAclException, BadRealmException
```

```
{
   throw new BadRealmException("Unable to add new acls");
}

public Enumeration getGroupNames() throws BadRealmException
{
   // Our simple Realm doesn't support groups.
   // We indicate this to the system
   // by throwing this exception
   throw new BadRealmException(
            "Groups not implemented in DBRealm.");
}

public Group getGroup(String name)
      throws NoSuchGroupException, BadRealmException
{
   // Our simple Realm doesn't support groups.
   // We indicate this to the system
   // by throwing this exception
   throw new BadRealmException(
            "Groups not implemented in DBRealm.");
}

public Group addGroup(String name)
      throws InUseException, BadRealmException
{
   // Our simple Realm doesn't support groups.
   // We indicate this to the system
   // by throwing this exception
   throw new BadRealmException(
            "Groups not implemented in DBRealm.");
}

public boolean removeGroup(String name)
      throws InUseException,
         BadRealmException,
         NoSuchGroupException
{
   // Our simple Realm doesn't support groups.
   // We indicate this to the system
   // by throwing this exception
   throw new BadRealmException(
            "Groups not implemented in DBRealm.");
}

public Enumeration getUserNames() throws BadRealmException
{
   // Get usernames from the database
   try {
      Class.forName("postgresql.Driver");
      Connection db  =
         DriverManager.getConnection(dbUrl, dbUser, dbPasswd);
```

```
        Statement  st  = db.createStatement();
        Vector results = new Vector(10);

        // Get all the data from the test database
        ResultSet rs =
          st.executeQuery("select username from dbrealm");

        while(rs.next()) {
          results.addElement(
              new String(rs.getBytes("username")).trim());
        }
        return results.elements();
      } catch (ClassNotFoundException e1) {
        throw new BadRealmException("SQL Error: " +
                                      e1.getMessage());
      } catch (SQLException e) {
        e.printStackTrace();
        throw new BadRealmException("SQL Error: " +
                                      e.getMessage());
      }
    }

    public User getUser(String name)
          throws NoSuchUserException, BadRealmException
    {
      // Look in the database for this user
      try {
        Class.forName("postgresql.Driver");
        Connection db =
          DriverManager.getConnection(dbUrl, dbUser, dbPasswd);
        Statement  st = db.createStatement();

        // Get all the data from the test database
        ResultSet rs = st.executeQuery(
          "select * from dbrealm where userName = '" +
          name + "'");
        // Does the user exist?  If not, throw an exception
        if(!rs.next()) {
          throw new NoSuchUserException("No such user as " +
                                          name);
        }
        // We have a user. Return a User object representing her
        return new DBRealmUser(
                    new String(rs.getBytes("userName")).trim(),
                    new String(rs.getBytes("password")).trim(),
                    this);
      } catch (ClassNotFoundException e1) {
        throw new BadRealmException("SQL Error: " +
                                      e1.getMessage());
```

```
      } catch (SQLException e) {
        e.printStackTrace();
        throw new BadRealmException("SQL Error: " +
                                   e.getMessage());
      }
    }

    public void deleteUser(String name)
        throws InUseException,
          BadRealmException,
          NoSuchUserException
    {
      try {
        Class.forName("postgresql.Driver");
        Connection db =
          DriverManager.getConnection(dbUrl, dbUser, dbPasswd);
        Statement  st = db.createStatement();

        // Get all the data from the test database
        st.executeUpdate(
              "delete from dbrealm where userName = '" +
              name + "'");
      } catch (SQLException e) {
        e.printStackTrace();
        throw new BadRealmException("SQL Error: " +
                                   e.getMessage());
      }
    }

    public Principal getDefaultAclOwner()
        throws BadRealmException
    {
      try {
        // Change this to reflect the default ACL owner in your
        // realm.
        return getUser("admin");
      } catch(NoSuchUserException e) {
        e.printStackTrace();
        throw new BadRealmException(
                        "Default Owner does not exist.");
      }
    }
    protected void setDefaultPolicies() throws BadRealmException
    {
      // Add default policies within this realm;
      // For example:
      // Existance of a user called "root" etc.
    }
}
```

Note that this is not the most efficient code. In particular, it reopens the connection to the database and creates a new statement each time. This significantly slows down performance, but it is the easiest way of ensuring that the database use is thread safe. See Chapter 14 for more on JDBC and efficiency.

Now that we have our realm, Listing 20.2 shows a class representing users within it. The most interesting method here is authenticate. It entirely captures the way users sign in to a particular realm. Here we just check the password against the one that came out of the database. We could also have done the database lookup here, instead of in DBRealm.getUser, but doing it this way keeps all the database-related code in one class.

Listing 20.2   DBRealmUser.java, a user in our database-based realm.

```java
import java.util.*;
import com.sun.server.realm.*;
import com.sun.server.realm.util.*;
public class DBRealmUser
               extends sun.security.acl.PrincipalImpl
               implements User, PassphraseAuth
{
  private DBRealm theRealm;
  private String username;
  private String password;
  /**
   * Constructor, sets the fields
   */
  DBRealmUser(String username,
              String password,
              DBRealm theRealm)
  {
    super(username);
    this.username = username;
    this.password = password;
    this.theRealm = theRealm;
  }

  /**
   * Get a particular attribute of this user.  We have none
   */
  public Object getAttribute(String name) {
    return null;
  }

  /**
   * Get the realm this user lives in
   */
  public Realm getRealm() {
    return theRealm;
  }
  /**
   * Get a list of the attributes associated with this user.
```

```
     * We have none
     */
    public Enumeration getAttributeNames() {
      return null;
    }

    /**
     * Can this user be authenticated?  Yes!
     */
    public boolean isAuthenticationEnabled() {
      return true;
    }
    /**
     * Did the user provide the correct password?
     */
    public boolean authenticate(String providedPassword)
         throws NoSuchUserException
    {
      return password.equals(providedPassword);
    }
}
```

There are many other things that could be done in this method. If it was desired to have users only identify themselves, not password-protect resources, this method could just return true. Some sites prefer passwords to be case insensitive, in which case it would just be necessary to replace `password.equals` with `password.equalsIgnoreCase`.

Using Custom Realms

Once the two classes in Listings 20.1 and 20.2 have been compiled and placed in the JWS's class path, using them is quite easy. First, of course, the database should be created and some users stored in it. Because we indicated that the realm owner was named `admin`, that account must be present in the database.

Now the JWS must be told about the new realm. This is done by adding a file under `<server_root>/realms`. It may be called anything, but keep in mind that whatever it is called will be the name presented to users in the popup when they log in. For our example we will just call it `DBRealm`. The file should contain the following:

```
classname=DBRealm
directory=realms/data/DBRealm
```

The first line specifies the class that will be used for this realm, and the second indicates where the `FileAcl` should read and store its data. Note that this is a property file, and if a custom realm needs any other information, it can be stored here and passed to the `Realm`'s `init()` method.

After this file has been created, the JWS should be restarted. After that, the administration tool will see `DBRealm` and users can be placed into ACLs, and ACLs can be used to protect resources.

Custom ACLs

In the last section we showed how to create a custom realm to handle authenticating users. It is also possible to create a custom ACL that uses a different method of determining what permissions a user has. This kind of ACL might be desired for many reasons, but the most common is to create a system that automatically allows all users to GET and POST so that an administrator does not need to manually add every new user to an ACL. It can be particularly useful on sites where anyone can get a free account but must still log in.

One example of this kind of site is the Java Developer's Connection, although it uses a different scheme. Listing 20.3 shows a servlet that will allow any user to join a special site.

Listing 20.3   `SignUpServlet.java`, a servlet through which users can sign themselves up for the datbase realm.

```
import java.io.*;
import java.sql.*;
import java.text.*;
import javax.servlet.*;
import javax.servlet.http.*;
public class SignUpServlet extends HttpServlet
{
   // Replace these with values for your system
   private String dbUser       = "dbuser";
   private String dbPasswd     = "dbuser";
   private String dbUrl        = "jdbc:postgresql:testdb";
   public void doGet(HttpServletRequest req,
                     HttpServletResponse res)
       throws IOException
   {
     PrintWriter out = res.getWriter();
     String values[];
     String name    = null;
     String passwd  = null;
     res.setContentType("text/html");
     out.println("<HTML>");
     out.println("<HEAD><TITLE>Sign-up Servlet</TITLE></HEAD>");
     out.println("<BODY>");
     // Did the user provide a name and password?
     values = req.getParameterValues("name");
     if(values.length == 0) {
       printForm(out);
       return;
     } else {
```

```
        name = values[0];
    }
    values = req.getParameterValues("passwd");
    if(values.length == 0) {
      printForm(out);
      return;
    } else {
      passwd = values[0];
    }
    try {
      Connection db;     // The connection to the database
      Statement  st;     // Our statement to run queries with
      ResultSet rs;
      // Load the driver
      Class.forName("postgresql.Driver");

      // Connect to database
      db = DriverManager.getConnection(dbUrl, dbUser, dbPasswd);
      // Create a statement to use to send queries
      st = db.createStatement();

      // Is this name already in use?
      rs = st.executeQuery(
          "select * from dbrealm where userName = '" +
          name + "'");
      if(rs.next()) {
        out.println("That name is already in use - ");
        out.println("please choose another<P>");
        printForm(out);
        rs.close();
        st.close();
        db.close();
        return;
      }
      // Add the user
      st.executeUpdate(
            "insert into dbrealm values('" +
            name +
            "','" +
            passwd + "')");
      st.close();
      db.close();
      out.println("Thank you for joining!");
      out.println("</BODY>");
      out.println("</HTML>");
    } catch (Exception e) {
      out.println("Unable to get data: " + e);
    }
  }
  void printForm(PrintWriter out) {
    out.println("Thank you for your interest!");
    out.println("To sign up, just provide a ");
    out.println("username and password.");
```

```
        out.println("<FORM ACTION=/servlet/SignUpServlet " +
                "METHOD=GET>");
        out.println("Name: ");
        out.println("<INPUT TYPE=TEXT NAME=name><BR>");
        out.println("Password: ");
        out.println("<INPUT TYPE=TEXT NAME=passwd><BR>");
        out.println("<INPUT TYPE=SUBMIT NAME=Go!>");
        out.println("</FORM>");
        out.println("</BODY>");
        out.println("</HTML>");
    }
}
```

To automatically grant GET and POST access to all users, we just need to
write a custom ACL. Listing 20.4 shows the code.

Listing 20.4   EveryoneOkAcl.java, an ACL that allows every user GET
and POST access.

```
import java.security.*;
import java.security.acl.*;
import java.util.*;
public class EveryoneOkAcl implements Acl {
    /**
     * We're never going to change this ACL's name, so
     * just ignore this
     */
    public void setName(Principal caller, String name)
        throws NotOwnerException
    {
    }
    /**
     * Return the name of this ACL
     */
    public String getName()
    {
        return "EveryoneOkAcl";
    }
    /**
     * Add an entry to this ACL.  Since we don't really
     * keep track of entries, we just acknowledge the
     * request and move on
     */
    public boolean addEntry(Principal caller, AclEntry entry)
        throws NotOwnerException
    {
        return true;
    }
    /**
     * Remove an entry from this ACL.  Again, since we are
     * not really keeping track of entries, we ignore this
     */
```

```
    public boolean removeEntry(Principal caller,AclEntry entry)
        throws NotOwnerException
{
    return true;
}
/**
 * Get the permissions for the given user specified
 * by this ACL.  We'll  just allow GET and POST
 */
public Enumeration getPermissions(Principal user)
{
    Vector v = new Vector(2);
    v.addElement(
        new com.sun.server.security.acl.PermissionImpl("GET"));
    v.addElement(
        new com.sun.server.security.acl.PermissionImpl("POST"));
    return v.elements();
}

/**
 * Get the entries representing principal/permission pairs.
 * Since we don't actually have any entries, just return an
 * empty enumeration.
 */
public Enumeration entries() {
    Vector v = new Vector();
    return v.elements();
}

/**
 * Determine whether the specified principal has the specified
 * permission.  We're letting everyone through, so we just
 * need to determine if the requested permission is
 * GET or POST.
 */
public boolean checkPermission(Principal principal,
                                  Permission permission)
{
    return (permission.toString().equals("GET") ||
            permission.toString().equals("POST"));
}
/**
 * Add an owner to this ACL.  We won't allow that
 */
public boolean addOwner(Principal a, Principal b) {
    return false;
}
/**
 * Delete an owner from this ACL.  We won't allow that
 */
public boolean deleteOwner(Principal a, Principal b) {
    return false;
}
```

```
/**
 * Determine if the given principal is an owner.
 * Since this ACL doesn't have an owner, return false
 */
public boolean isOwner(Principal a) {
  return false;
}
}
```

The interesting method here is checkPermissions. Normally an ACL would look through its AclEntries to see if the permission should be granted, but in this case we just automatically answer true to any GET or POST request. Now we can modify our realm to use this ACL by removing references to FileAclInfo, as shown in Listing 20.5.

Listing 20.5   DBRealm.java, a variation of DBRealm that uses EveryoneOkAcl.

```
import java.io.*;
import java.security.*;
import java.security.acl.*;
import java.util.*;
import java.sql.*;
import com.sun.server.realm.*;
import com.sun.server.realm.util.*;
public class DBRealm extends Realm
{
  // Even though usernames and passwords are in a database,
  // the ACL info will still come from files
  private FileAclInfo aclInfo = null;
  // Replace these with values for your system
  private String dbUser      = "dbuser";
  private String dbPasswd    = "dbuser";
  private String dbUrl       = "jdbc:postgresql:testdb";
  /**
   * Constructor. No special processing here--
   * it's all done in init()
   */
  public DBRealm()
  {
    super();
  }
  /**
   * Set up the realm
   */
  public synchronized void init(Properties props)
        throws BadRealmException, NoSuchRealmException
  {
    System.out.println("Initing db realm");
    // Set up the ACL
    aclInfo = new FileAclInfo(this);
    try {
      super.init(props);
```

```
            // Load the class that will talk to the database
            Class.forName("postgresql.Driver");
        } catch(Exception e) {
            e.printStackTrace();
            throw new BadRealmException(e.getMessage());
        }
    }
    /**
     * Get the default ACL for this realm
     */
    public Acl getAcl() throws BadRealmException
    {
        return aclInfo.getAcl();
    }

    /**
     * Get the names of ACLs within this realm
     */
    public Enumeration getAclNames() throws BadRealmException
    {
        return aclInfo.getAclNames();
    }

    /**
     * Get a particular ACL
     */
    public Acl getAcl(String name)
            throws NoSuchAclException,BadRealmException
    {
        return aclInfo.getAcl(name);
    }

    /**
     * Add a new ACL to this realm
     */
    public Acl addAcl(String name, Principal owner)
            throws BadRealmException
    {
        return aclInfo.makeAcl(name, owner);
    }

    /**
     * Remove an ACL from this realm
     */
    public void removeAcl(String name)
            throws NoSuchAclException, BadRealmException
    {
        aclInfo.deleteAcl(name);
    }

    public Enumeration getGroupNames() throws BadRealmException
    {
```

```
        // Our simple realm doesn't support groups.
        // We indicate this to the system
        // by throwing this exception
        throw new BadRealmException(
                  "Groups not implemented in DBRealm.");
    }

    public Group getGroup(String name)
          throws NoSuchGroupException, BadRealmException
    {
        // Our simple realm doesn't support groups.
        // We indicate this to the system
        // by throwing this exception
        throw new BadRealmException(
                  "Groups not implemented in DBRealm.");
    }

    public Group addGroup(String name)
          throws InUseException, BadRealmException
    {
        // Our simple realm doesn't support groups.
        // We indicate this to the system
        // by throwing this exception
        throw new BadRealmException(
                  "Groups not implemented in DBRealm.");
    }

    public boolean removeGroup(String name)
          throws InUseException, BadRealmException,
                NoSuchGroupException
    {
        // Our simple realm doesn't support groups.
        // We indicate this to the system
        // by throwing this exception
        throw new BadRealmException(
                  "Groups not implemented in DBRealm.");
    }
    /**
     * Get the users in this realm.  This info will come from
     * the database
     */
    public Enumeration getUserNames() throws BadRealmException
    {
        // Get usernames from the database
        try {
            Connection db =
                DriverManager.getConnection(dbUrl, dbUser, dbPasswd);
            Statement  st  = db.createStatement();
            Vector results = new Vector(10);

            ResultSet rs =
                st.executeQuery("select username from dbrealm");
```

```
      while(rs.next()) {
        results.addElement(
              new String(rs.getBytes("username")).trim());
      }
      rs.close();
      db.close();
      return results.elements();
    } catch (SQLException e) {
      e.printStackTrace();
      throw new BadRealmException("SQL Error: " +
                                      e.getMessage());
    }
  }

/**
 * Get a particular user.  Note that the object returned
 * is actually an instance of DBRealmUser, which implements
 * Principal.
 */
public User getUser(String name)
      throws NoSuchUserException, BadRealmException
{
  // Look in the database for this user...
  try {
    Connection db =
      DriverManager.getConnection(dbUrl, dbUser, dbPasswd);
    Statement  st = db.createStatement();

    ResultSet rs = st.executeQuery(
                "select * from dbrealm where userName = '" +
                name + "'");
    // Does the user exist?  If not, throw an exception
    if(!rs.next()) {
      rs.close();
      db.close();
      throw new NoSuchUserException("No such user as " +
                                      name);
    }
    rs.close();
    db.close();
    // We have a user. Return a User object representing
    // the user
    return new DBRealmUser(
                new String(rs.getBytes("userName")).trim(),
                new String(rs.getBytes("password")).trim(),
                this);
  } catch (SQLException e) {
    e.printStackTrace();
    throw new BadRealmException("SQL Error: " +
                                    e.getMessage());
  }
}
```

```
/**
 * Remove a user by deleting the user from the database
 */
public void deleteUser(String name)
      throws InUseException,
         BadRealmException,
         NoSuchUserException
{
  try {
    Connection db =
      DriverManager.getConnection(dbUrl, dbUser, dbPasswd);
    Statement   st = db.createStatement();

    // Get all the data from the test database
    st.executeUpdate(
          "delete from dbrealm where userName = '" +
          name + "'");
    db.close();
  } catch (SQLException e) {
    e.printStackTrace();
    throw new BadRealmException("SQL Error: " +
                                   e.getMessage());
  }
}
/**
 * Get the ACL owner, a user named admin
 */
public Principal getDefaultAclOwner() throws BadRealmException
{
  try {
    // Change this to reflect the default ACL owner in your
    // realm
    return getUser("admin");
  } catch(NoSuchUserException e) {
    e.printStackTrace();
    throw new BadRealmException(
              "Default Owner does not exist.");
  }
}
/**
 * Here is where we can set special policies, but our example
 * doesn't have any
 */
protected void setDefaultPolicies() throws BadRealmException
{
}
}
```

Compile and install these classes as before. Installing a class is just a matter of creating the file and directory under <server_root>/realms. Then use the administration tool to create an ACL called EveryOkAcl. This must be done because it sets an entry in a property file called <server_root>/properties/

server/javawebserver/webpageservice/acl.properties that must be present for authentication to work. Finally, the administration tool can be used to protect resources in this realm.

Conclusion

In this chapter we not only look under the hood of the Java Web Server's security implementation, we take the engine apart. We examine the classes used to implement security and show how they can be customized for special purposes.

For this chapter and for all three chapters in Part V, it is important to note that these classes and interfaces are specific to the 1.x releases of the Java Web Server. In future versions, these classes will probably be implemented differently. That said, although custom realms are not implemented every day, it is comforting to have the capability of creating them when they are needed.

CHAPTER 21

Logging in the Java Web Server

Running a successful Web site is like running a hotel for invisible people. It is not evident who the visitors are, where they come from, who sent them, or what rooms they prefer. A concierge who wants to get to know her guests has to do so indirectly. She can't talk to them or even see them, but she can read the hotel's sign-in book, measure its electricity consumption, and count the number of times its doors open and close.

Web administrators never see their visitors, either, but each visit leaves traces in the server log files, and that is where Web administrators look for clues. This chapter discusses what kind of information the Java Web Server (JWS) keeps in its logs, how to change the format of the logs, and how servlets can keep logs of their own. We explain what logs are and why they are important. Then we go into the details of how the JWS uses logs, how administrators can configure them, and how programmers can override them altogether. Logging within individual servlets is discussed at the end of this chapter.

Basics of Logging: Definition, Purpose, Location

The Java Web Server keeps track of pretty much everything it does in files called logs. Every time it handles a browser request or loads a servlet, the server makes a note in the form of a log entry. A log is just a flat text file with one entry following another. The administration tool provides a nice log-viewing GUI, but it is not strictly necessary; log files can be examined with more or Notepad. Listing 21.1 shows some lines from the access log, which records Web browser requests.

Listing 21.1   `access_log`.

```
127.0.0.1 - - [19/Jun/1998:23:12:14 -0400] "GET /system/doc/release_notes.html HTTP/
      1.0" 200 43162
127.0.0.1 - - [19/Jun/1998:23:12:15 -0400] "GET /system/doc/images/banner.gif HTTP/
      1.0" 200 4422
127.0.0.1 - - [19/Jun/1998:23:12:15 -0400] "GET /system/doc/images/duke.gif HTTP/
      1.0" 200 1457
127.0.0.1 - - [19/Jun/1998:23:47:20 -0400] "HEAD / HTTP/1.0" 200 1999
127.0.0.1 - - [19/Jun/1998:23:53:15 -0400] "GET /pservlet.html HTTP/1.0" 401 321
127.0.0.1 - admin [19/Jun/1998:23:53:33 -0400] "GET /pservlet.html HTTP/1.0" 401 321
127.0.0.1 - jeeves [19/Jun/1998:23:54:14 -0400] "GET /pservlet.html HTTP/1.0" 200 148
127.0.0.1 - - [19/Jun/1998:23:54:26 -0400] "GET /pservlet.shtml HTTP/1.0" 404 385
```

This format, called Common Logfile Format, is a compromise between human and computer readability. It is ASCII, so humans can read it, but it has enough structure to make it possible for reporting tools to parse. It is the same log format used by many other Web servers, including Apache, Netscape, and NCSA. The JWS also allows developers to use their own log formats.

Logs can show how many visits a site receives, where the visitors are from, what links they followed to the site, and which Web browsers they used, among other things. The administration tool has a few useful log analysis functions, and there are scores of reporting tools on the Internet that can condense logs into specialized reports. At Time Inc. New Media, a whole team of people collects and analyzes log data to produce charts showing where browsers are coming from and tables showing who referred them. Managers and advertisers use the reports to determine how good a job we are doing.

Logs are also one of the best diagnostic tools for server administrators and servlet developers. They are the first thing to check when the server is misbehaving. If a servlet throws an exception, a full stack trace will show up in a log, usually giving enough information to track down the source of the problem immediately.

By default, the Java Web Server puts the logs in a directory called logs under the server root. Under the Logs directory, each server has its own directory, and under those directories, each service has its own directory, as shown in Figure 21.1.

Every directory has at least two logs: `error_log` and `event_log`. The server directories (`adminserver` and `javawebserver`) generally have empty log files—since services do most of the work in the JWS, services, not servers, generate the log output. Usually, the only reason a server writes to its log files is if it is having trouble with its services. Services, on the other hand, can be quite wordy. Their logs, especially access logs on busy sites, may become quite large.

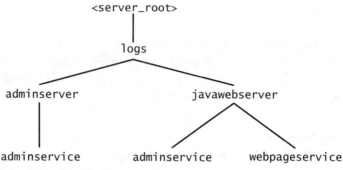

Figure 21.1   Log directory structure

Java Web Server Logs

The Java Web Server produces five kinds of logs: access, agent, referer, error, and event. Access logs record browser requests. Agent logs record the type of browser that made the requests. Referer logs record the URL of the page that led a browser to a page on the server. (Yes, it should be spelled "referrer," but since it was misspelled in early WWW standards documents, the misspelling has now become the standard.) Error logs record errors, either from servlets or from the server itself. Event logs can contain just about everything a server does.

Each log serves a separate purpose, so most of them have different formats. The developers of the Java Web Server could have decided to write separate classes to produce each type, but since they are smart, they chose to separate the formatting from the other aspects of the code. The log formats are determined by format classes, and other aspects of log management are handled by other classes. That means that a new format can be introduced simply and easily—all that is necessary is a new format class, which is fairly simple to code. In general, the only method it needs to have is write().

Log format classes come in two varieties: per-request and per-event. Per-request classes are meant to be called for each Web request. Their write() methods take ServletRequest and ServletResponse objects as parameters. These classes can be turned on or off: in other words, they log either every request or no requests. The access, agent, and referer logs are all per-request.

Per-event format classes are meant to be called only when certain things happen (such as an error). They each have two write() methods, one that takes a String and one that takes an int and a String. This is because these classes support logging levels. A logging level is a nonnegative integer that corresponds to some level of importance. Usually, level 0 is the highest priority, level 2 (the default) is the lowest priority, and level 1 is in between. Most of the time, these logs ignore everything less important than level 0, although this threshold can be changed.

The following sections discuss each of the Java Web Server's five log types. For each type we list its format class, explain its rationale, describe the format of its output, tell what logging levels it supports, and, finally, describe how it can be used in Web site administration.

Access Log: Format Class
`com.sun.server.log.http.HttpLog`

This log answers the questions "Where are my visitors coming from? Who are they? When are they coming? What are they looking for? Are they successful?" Every request to a Web server has an entry in the access log, unless the Web designer has disabled it from the administration tool. The access log is enabled by default. It uses the simple and popular Common Logfile Format.

Format

Every entry in the access log has seven fields, all on one line:

127.0.0.1 - tsnee [01/Mar/1998:17:50:41 -0500] "GET /index.html HTTP/1.0" 200 1999

If the server does not have enough information to fill in a field properly, it just writes -. The first field is the address of the machine from which the request came. By default, it is the machine-friendly numeric IP address, not the human-friendly hostname. When a request comes in, all the server knows is the IP address, and it can take as long as several seconds to use this address to look up the hostname through the domain name service (DNS). If a busy server on the Internet tried to look up the hostname for every request, it would slow to a crawl.

Most reporting tools perform the name lookup when they read the log. However, administrators of low-traffic intranet sites could probably configure the server to do the DNS lookup without incurring a huge performance penalty. The way to do this is to change the value of the `log.access.options` property in `<server_root>/properties/server/javawebserver/webpageservice/systemDefaults.properties` from `nodns` to `dns` and then restart the server.

The second field of an access log entry is supposed to be the name of the user who made the request. The name should be determined using a little-known Internet protocol called the Identification protocol. However, few hosts support it, and those that do tend to do it very slowly, so the Java Web Server does not even try to look up the user's name. In all versions up to 1.1.2 (and perhaps beyond), this field is always -.

The third field is also for usernames, in this case the names users give to authenticate themselves to the server. As Chapter 20 revealed, every page a server's administrator has protected with an ACL can be shown only to users with proper names and passwords, and these names are recorded here. Requests for pages that do not require authentication have - in this field.

The fourth field is the time of the request, in square brackets, using the format [DD/Mmm/YYYY:HH:MM:SS +/-GGGG], where DD is the two-digit day of the month; Mmm is the three-letter month, first letter uppercase, following letters lowercase; YYYY is the four-digit year (Y2K compliant!); HH is the two-digit hour in military format (00-23); MM is the two-digit minute; and SS is the two-digit second. Finally comes a space, either a plus or a minus sign, and a four-digit number (GGGG). This number is the difference between the server's local time and Greenwich Mean Time. For instance, the East Coast is five hours behind GMT (–0500) during Daylight Savings Time, so 5:50 P.M. EDT on March 1, 1998 is written

[01/Mar/1998:17:50:41 -0500]

The fifth field is the request from the browser, in double quotes. When a user types in a URL or clicks on a link containing a URL, the browser breaks down the URL into its component parts to find out the protocol (HTTP), hostname, port number, and path. Then it contacts the host and requests the path. For instance, when a Web browser is given a URL like

http://www.money.com/money/plus/index.oft

it decides to use HTTP to contact the machine named www.money.com at the default HTTP port and request /money/plus/index.oft. It does this by opening a connection to port 80 of www.money.com and writing GET /money/plus/index.oft HTTP/1.0 over it. This request is what the server writes to the log.

NOTE: HTTP version 1.1, which is still not used by the majority of browsers as of this writing, allows the whole URL to be sent, as in GET *http://www.money.com/plus/index.oft* HTTP/1.1.

The sixth field contains the status code of the server's response. Most requests have status code 200, which means "OK." Status code 404 means "Not found" (i.e., someone requested a page that doesn't exist). Code 500 means an internal server error, perhaps caused by a malfunctioning servlet. The World Wide Web Consortium maintains a complete list of HTTP 1.0 status codes at *http://www.w3.org/Protocols/HTTP/HTRESP.html*

The seventh and last field is the size of the server's response to the browser's request, not counting headers. For instance, if the request was for a file, then this is where the server records the size of the file.

Levels

All or None, default All.

Use

This log shows how many successful requests a site served, when they were served, and, for pages that require authentication, to whom they were served. It shows which requests caused server errors.

Agent Log: Format Class
`com.sun.server.webserver.AgentLog`

We go from one of the most interesting logs to one of the least interesting. All the agent log does is record which browsers have visited a site.

Format

This log records whichever string a browser uses to identify itself in the User-Agent field of the HTTP request header. Browsers are supposed to write "productname/version," perhaps followed by whitespace and extra information. For example,

Mozilla/4.05 [en] (X11; U; Linux 2.0.30 i586)

Levels

All or None, default None.

Use

There is no way to match entries in the agent log to entries in any other log, so there is no way to tell which browser initiated a particular request. The only useful information this log produces is a summary showing what percentage of a site's visitors use which browser.

Referrer Log: Format Class
com.sun.server.webserver.RefererLog

This log answers the question "What kinds of Web browsers are my visitors using?" The referer log is turned off by default. When a browser requests an image embedded in a page with the IMG element or when a user clicks on a link (to an image or anything else) in a page, that page is said to "refer" to the image. When the browser requests the image, it can send the URL of that referring page in the HTTP Referer header.

Format

The referer log uses the format "referringURL – request," where "referring-URL" is the page that generated the request. For example,

http://mammon.money.com:8080/system/admin.shtml - /system/images/banner.gif

shows that someone followed a link from the /system/admin.shtml page of the Web server running on port 8080 of mammon.money.com to /system/images/banner.gif on the local server.

Levels

All or None, default None.

Use

This log is useful for tracking down the source of broken links and for finding out how Web traffic flows through a site.

Error Log: Format Class
com.sun.server.log.TraceLog

This log answers the questions "Are visitors encountering any problems on my site? Where are the problems coming from?" Servlet developers care more about this log than any other, especially while they are debugging their code. After a servlet has been deployed in production, it should not be heard from again via the error log, but Web administrators still need to check the log every day.

Format

Error log entries tend to come in pairs. First comes a single line with the date in square brackets followed by a general description of the error.

[Mon Jul 20 23:37:09 EDT 1998] Exception in servlet scribble

On the next line is the same date but a more detailed description, including a stack trace, as shown in Listing 21.2.

Listing 21.2   `error_log.`

```
[Mon Jul 20 23:37:09 EDT 1998] java.lang.ArrayIndexOutOfBoundsException: 0
java.lang.ArrayIndexOutOfBoundsException: 0
        at com.awl.cseng.jws.util.ScribbleBoard.addNewMessage(ScribbleBoard.java:158)
        at com.awl.cseng.jws.util.ScribbleBoard.service(ScribbleBoard.java:93)
        at javax.servlet.http.HttpServlet.service(HttpServlet.java:588)
        at com.sun.server.ServletState.callService(ServletState.java:204)
        at com.sun.server.ServletManager.callServletService(ServletManager.java:940)
        at com.sun.server.webserver.HttpServiceHandler.handleRequest
                        (HttpServiceHandler.java:416)
        at com.sun.server.webserver.HttpServiceHandler.handleRequest
                        (HttpServiceHandler.java:246)
        at com.sun.server.HandlerThread.run(HandlerThread.java:154)
```

Levels

This log can record All Problems, Major and Minor Problems, Major Problems, or None. Major and Minor Problems are the default. Errors are categorized as major or minor based on the judgment of the Java Web Server design team.

Use

This log is enormously useful to servlet developers and maintainers. It is also the first place a Webmaster should look if his server starts to misbehave. Keep in mind that some error messages end up in the event log.

Event Log: Format Class
`com.sun.server.log.TraceLog`

This log answers the question "What is my server doing behind the curtains?" The event log records practically everything imaginable—every time the server starts or stops, every step of the process. This is also where most servlets write their log information.

Format

Event logs use the same format class (and therefore the same basic format) as error logs—a time stamp in square brackets followed by a message. Unlike error logs, event logs rarely contain stack traces.

[Sun Jul 19 08:42:02 EDT 1998] ServletManager.instantiateServlet: Loaded local class
   class com.sun.server.webserver.CgiServlet
[Sun Jul 19 08:42:02 EDT 1998] com.sun.server.webserver.CgiServlet: init
[Sun Jul 19 08:42:02 EDT 1998] ServletManager.loadServlet: cgi: class = com.sun.server.
   webserver.CgiServlet, class URL = , arguments = {bindir=cgi-bin}

Levels

This log can record All Events, Detailed Events, Start/Stop Events, or None. By
default, "Detailed Events" are recorded. If the level is changed to Start/Stop
Events or None, then servlet log() output will not be recorded.

Use

Some people glance through the referer or agent logs out of sheer curiosity, but
the event log is about as interesting as the phone book. However, it is the best
way to find out what a Web server is up to. For instance, if a servlet that is supposed to maintain state seems to forget it after every request, the event log reveals whether the server is reloading or reinitializing it unexpectedly.

Log Management

The administration tool allows a good deal of flexibility to Web developers
who want to adjust the default behavior of their logs. (The administration tool
is discussed in Chapter 3.) The most important logging administration decision
to make is buffer size. Larger buffer sizes increase performance of the whole
server. Unfortunately, some versions of the Java Web Server (including 1.1.1)
do not flush their log buffers before they shut down, so any data that hasn't
been written out by then is simply lost. Also, logs with large buffers are not updated so often, which is inconvenient for developers who want to see log output as soon as possible. Selecting a buffer size of 0 guarantees that every log
message will be written immediately. However, smaller buffer sizes hurt performance, because the more often the server has to write to disk, the less time
it has to respond to browser requests. A server used exclusively for development should probably set its log buffers to 0, and even a production server
should not use the maximum buffer size unless its performance requirements
demand it.

Customizing Server Log Formats

A site that needs a different format for any of the server logs can replace the default format classes with locally written classes. However, as of version 1.1.1,

the Java Web Server does not officially support this. The JWS team made that decision because writing custom classes requires using some of Sun's internal, lightly documented classes and because poorly written format classes can hurt server performance or even cause the server to hang.

Those bold enough to disregard Sun's warnings can read on for step-by-step instructions. Note that they apply only to JWS 1.1.1 and 1.1.2. Earlier versions either do not allow custom logs at all or contain a bug that prevents customization from working properly. Future versions will probably have a slightly different interface for better internationalization.

1. *Choose which log to replace.* Most people want to override the access log, whose format class is com.sun.server.log.http.HttpLog.

2. *Write the format class.* The new format class needs to extend the existing class for that log and override one or two methods, according to Table 21.1. Remember that the code must be thread safe, just like a servlet (see Chapter 10). Also, the code must be highly efficient (see Chapter 12). A slow format class will degrade the performance of the entire server. A buggy class might cause errors in the data sent back to the Web browser.

3. *Put the format class into the server's* CLASSPATH. The server needs to be able to load the new class, so put it somewhere the server can see it. A good place to consider is <server_root>/classes.

4. *Tell the server to start using the new format class.* The server uses properties files to determine which format classes to use for which logs. Every JWS service has a systemDefaults.properties file, and this is the file that needs to change (by hand—the administration tool doesn't support this). To change the Web page service's access log, edit <server_root>/properties/server/

Table 21.1   Log Types and Format Classes

Log type	Log class to extend	Method to override
Access	com.sun.server.log.http.HttpLog	write(sun.servlet.http.HttpRequest, sun.servlet.http.HttpResponse)
Agent	com.sun.server.webserver.AgentLog	write(sun.servlet.http.HttpRequest, sun.servlet.http.HttpResponse)
Error	com.sun.server.log.TraceLog	write(String) or write(int, String)
Event	com.sun.server.log.TraceLog	write(String) or write(int, String)
Referer	com.sun.server.webserver.RefererLog	write(sun.servlet.http.HttpRequest, sun.servlet.http.HttpResponse)

javawebserver/webpageservice/systemDefaults.properties and change the line that begins with log.access.formatclass= to log.access.formatclass= newclassname. The Error log uses the line log.error.formatclass, the Referrer log uses log.referer.formatclass, and so on.

5. *Restart the server.* The server needs to be restarted after any of its properties files have been changed with an editor. (Only changes made through the administration tool take place immediately.) When it comes back up, it will be using the new class.

Examples of Custom Format Classes

Of the two different examples of custom format classes, one changes the file format, and one writes to a database instead of a file. They are available on the accompanying CD. The file example should work for all but the highest-volume Web sites. The speed of the database example greatly depends on the choice of JDBC driver and database.

Text Log

To change the file format, use the following steps.

Step 1. Choose which log to replace.

In this example, we replace the access log. This means extending com.sun. server.log.http.HttpLog and overriding its write() method.

Step 2. Write the format class.

Say we want to change the format of the access log to Request /index.html from 127.0.0.1. A naive implementation would look like Listing 21.3. Unfortunately, it is neither fast nor thread safe. Operations on Strings tend to be slow, especially string concatenation. Using separate calls to the log's print() and println() methods means that log entries could become mixed together if different threads ran this method at the same time.

Listing 21.3   JWSlog1.java.

```
package com.awl.cseng.jws.log;

import sun.servlet.http.*;
import java.io.*;
```

```
public class JWSlog1 extends com.sun.server.log.http.HttpLog {

  public void write(HttpRequest req, HttpResponse res) {
    try {
      // Use print() and println() inherited from
      // com.sun.server.log.Log
      print("Request ");
      print(req.getRequestURI());
      print(" from ");
      println(req.getRemoteHost());
    } catch (IOException e) {
      e.printStackTrace();
    }
  }
}
```

For example, if requests for /system/doc/index.html and /index.html happened to complete simultaneously, the two threads could enter the method together and produce the following output:

Request /system/doc/index.htmlRequest /index.html from 127.0.0.1
 from 152.2.22.81

The first thread managed to run the first two print() statements, writing Request /system/doc/index.html to the log. Then it was preempted by the second thread, which ran through the whole method, writing Request /index.html from 127.0.0.1. Only then could the first thread get to the last print() and println() and write from 152.2.22.81. (For more on thread safety issues, see Chapter 10.)

A better implementation of the JWSlog class is as shown in Listing 21.4. This version uses byte arrays instead of Strings. As we note in Chapter 10, this avoids a good deal of overhead. We can't avoid Strings entirely, however: the HttpRequest methods don't return byte arrays, so we still have to do two String conversions per request.

Listing 21.4 JWSlog2.java.

```
package com.awl.cseng.jws.log;

import sun.servlet.http.*;
import java.io.*;

public class JWSlog2 extends com.sun.server.log.http.HttpLog {

  // Constants
  protected static final byte request[] = "Request ".getBytes();
  protected static final byte from[]    = " from ".getBytes();
  protected static final byte lineSep[] =
          System.getProperty("line.separator", "\n").getBytes();
```

```
    // Methods
    public synchronized void write(HttpRequest req,
                                   HttpResponse res) {
      // Use OutputStream inherited from com.sun.server.log.Log
      OutputStream out = getOutputStream();
      try {
        out.write(request);
        out.write(req.getRequestURI().getBytes());
        out.write(from);
        out.write(req.getRemoteHost().getBytes());
        out.write(lineSep);
      } catch (IOException e) {
        e.printStackTrace();
      }
    }
  }
}
```

This version is also thread safe because `write()` is synchronized. However, this will be a significant performance drag on the server. The only reason to use synchronization is to make sure that the thread won't be preempted between calls to the `OutputStream`'s `write()`. If all those `write()`s could be consolidated into one `write()`, then this method would not need to be synchronized (see Listing 21.5). Since there is only one call to `write()`, we can rely on the `OutputStream` to keep log entries from running into each other.

Listing 21.5 JWSlog3.java.

```
package com.awl.cseng.jws.log;

import sun.servlet.http.*;
import java.io.*;

public class JWSlog3 extends com.sun.server.log.http.HttpLog {

  protected static final byte request[] = "Request ".getBytes();
  protected static final byte from[]    = " from ".getBytes();
  protected static final byte lineSep[] =
         System.getProperty("line.separator", "\n").getBytes();

  public void write(HttpRequest req, HttpResponse res) {
    byte requestURI[] = req.getRequestURI().getBytes();
    byte remoteHost[] = req.getRemoteHost().getBytes();

    byte buf[] = new byte[request.length
                + requestURI.length
                + from.length
                + remoteHost.length
                + lineSep.length];
    int index   = 0;

    System.arraycopy(request,  0, buf, index, request.length);
    index += request.length;
```

```
        System.arraycopy(requestURI, 0, buf, index,
                           requestURI.length);
        index += requestURI.length;

        System.arraycopy(from, 0, buf, index, from.length);
        index += from.length;

        System.arraycopy(remoteHost, 0, buf, index,
                           remoteHost.length);
        index += remoteHost.length;

        System.arraycopy(lineSep, 0, buf, index, lineSep.length);
        index += lineSep.length;

        try {
          getOutputStream().write(buf, 0, index);
        } catch (IOException e) {
          e.printStackTrace();
        }
      }
    }
  }
```

To compile a custom log class, make sure that <server_root>/lib/jws.jar is in the CLASSPATH.

Step 3. Put the compiled class into the server's CLASSPATH.

Since the example belongs to the com.awl.cseng.jws.log package, simply copying it into the server's classes directory isn't enough. It can either be put into a JAR file that is then added to the server's CLASSPATH, or it can go into a subdirectory of <server_root>/classes, specifically <server_root>/classes/com/awl/cseng/jws/log.

Step 4. Tell the server to start using the new format class.

Edit   <server_root>/properties/server/javawebserver/webpageservice/systemDefaults.properties and change the line that begins with log.access.formatclass= to

```
log.access.formatclass=com.awl.cseng.jws.log.JWSlog
```

Step 5. Restart the server.

When the server comes back up, try requesting some pages from it. When the new format class has written enough data to its OutputStream, the Output-Stream will flush the data (in the new format) to the access log file. The size of the format class's OutputStream buffer is defined in the administration tool.

Database Log

Most Web sites probably use Perl scripts to parse their logs and produce more useful summaries. However, sites that required a number of reports from different sets of logs would have a difficult time using only Perl. Time Inc. New Media, for instance, condenses gigabytes of log data into about 50 different reports every week. To do this, the reporting group has to move logs from every server to a central machine and load them into a SQL database, which is a difficult and error-prone operation.

The Java Web Server can write logs directly to a database with JDBC. The JWS team hopes to make that a configurable option one day. Today, database log classes must be written by hand—or copied out of this book (Listing 21.6).

Listing 21.6 DBlog.java.

```
package com.awl.cseng.jws.log;

import sun.servlet.http.*;
import java.io.*;
import java.sql.*;
import java.util.Vector;
import java.util.Enumeration;

/**
 * An object of this class writes to a database table instead of
 * a text file.  For efficiency, the write() method caches log
 * entries, and a single thread (created by the constructor)
 * periodically flushes the cache to the database.  This also
 * takes care of any JDBC thread-safety issues.
 *
 * This class uses dual caches: the write() method writes to one
 * while the db update thread flushes the other.  When the update
 * thread has finished flushing its cache, it swaps caches and
 * starts on the other.
 *
 * Servers with moderate traffic should decrease the update
 * interval.  Heavily loaded servers will probably need to modify
 * this class to use multiple update threads, each with its own
 * Connection and PreparedStatement.
 *
 * The driver class name (postgresql.Driver), database name
 * (jws), table name (access), username (test), password (test),
 * and schema information (columns "urlPath" and "remoteHost")
 * are all hard-coded.
 */
public class DBlog
    extends com.sun.server.log.http.HttpLog
    implements Runnable
{
```

```
// Constants

/** Name of db table to hold log entries                    */
protected final static String TABLE_NAME = "access";

/** Name of JDBC driver                                      */
protected final static String DRIVER_CLASS_NAME
                        = "postgresql.Driver";

/** JDBC URL                                                 */
protected final static String DB_URL
                        = "jdbc:postgresql:jws?auth=password";

/** Login name JDBC will use to log in to the database       */
protected final static String USERNAME   = "test";

/** Password JDBC will use to log in to the database         */
protected final static String PASSWORD   = "test";

/** Number of milliseconds to wait between database updates */
protected final static int   INTERVAL    = 30000;

// Fields

/** Reference to current cache                               */
Vector    cache;

/** First of two caches                                      */
Vector    alpha_cache;

/** Second of two caches                                     */
Vector    beta_cache;

/** Controls access to current cache                         */
Object    cache_lock;

/** Controls access to database                              */
Object    db_lock;

/** Thread that controls all database access                 */
Thread    dbUpdater;

/** Persistent connection to the database (not thread safe) */
Connection conn;

/** Persistent SQL statement object (not thread safe)        */
PreparedStatement stmt;

// Constructors

/**
```

```
 * This constructor calls the default constructor to initialize
 * the DBlog, then closes its argument, since DBlogs don't use
 * flat files.
 */
public DBlog(OutputStream os) {
  this();

  try {
    os.close();
  } catch (IOException e) {
    // doesn't matter
  }
}


/**
 * Creates the dual caches, loads the JDBC driver specified in
 * the properties file, and opens a connection to the database.
 *
 * Unfortunately, there is no documented way for a format class
 * constructor to signal an unrecoverable error.  There isn't
 * even a way to log it.  So all this constructor can do is
 * write to System.err.
 */
public DBlog() {
  try {
    // Create dual caches, locks
    alpha_cache = new Vector(100, 100);
    beta_cache  = new Vector(100, 100);
    cache       = alpha_cache;
    cache_lock  = new Object();
    db_lock     = new Object();

    // Initialize JDBC
    Class.forName(DRIVER_CLASS_NAME);
    conn = DriverManager.getConnection(DB_URL,
                                       USERNAME,
                                       PASSWORD);
    // If the following statement is changed, both write() and
    // flush_cache() must be updated to reflect the change.
    stmt = conn.prepareStatement("INSERT INTO "
                  + TABLE_NAME
                  + "(urlPath,remoteHost) VALUES(?,?)"
                  );
    // Start JDBC access thread.
    dbUpdater = new Thread(this, "Log db updater");
    dbUpdater.start();
  } catch (Exception e) {
    e.printStackTrace();
  }
}
```

```
// Methods


/**
 * Adds an entry to the current log cache.
 *
 * Handles errors the only way it can--by writing their
 * stack traces to System.err.
 */
public void write(HttpRequest req, HttpResponse res) {
  try {
    String[] entry = new String[2];
    entry[0] = req.getRequestURI();
    entry[1] = req.getRemoteHost();

    synchronized(cache_lock)
    {
      cache.addElement(entry);
    }
  } catch (Exception e) {
    e.printStackTrace();
  }
}

/**
 * Stops the dbUpdater thread and closes the database
 * connection.
 */
public void finalize() {
  try {
    // Stop dbUpdater thread before closing the connection.
    dbUpdater = null;

    // Make sure the dbUpdater thread isn't still writing
    // to the db.
    synchronized(db_lock)
    {
      stmt.close();
      conn.close();
    }
  } catch (SQLException e) {
    e.printStackTrace();
  }
}

/**
 * Main body of dbUpdater thread sleeps and flushes the current
 * cache to the database.
 */
public void run() {
  while(true) {
    try {
      Thread.sleep(INTERVAL);
```

```
            } catch (InterruptedException e) {
                // Ignore
            }

            flush_cache();
        }
    }

    /**
     * Swaps caches and flushes the old one to the database with
     * stmt.  An instance of this method should not be called by
     * more than one thread at a time.
     *
     * Handles errors the only way it can--by writing their
     * stack traces to System.err.
     */
    public void flush_cache() {
        Vector working_cache;   // reference to cache to be flushed

        synchronized(cache_lock) {
            if ( cache.size() < 1 )
            {
                // Nothing to flush
                return;
            }

            // Swap caches
            if ( cache == alpha_cache )
            {
                working_cache = alpha_cache;
                cache         = beta_cache;
            }
            else
            {
                working_cache = beta_cache;
                cache         = alpha_cache;
            }
        }

        // Flush old cache to database.
        Enumeration e = working_cache.elements();
        synchronized(db_lock) {
            while (e.hasMoreElements()) {
                String[] entry = (String[])e.nextElement();
                try {
                    stmt.setString(1, entry[0]);
                    stmt.setString(2, entry[1]);
                    stmt.executeUpdate();
                } catch (SQLException ex) {
                    ex.printStackTrace();
                }
            }
        }
    }
```

```
      // Done--empty the cache
      working_cache.removeAllElements();
    }
  }
```

Chapter 14 discusses JDBC and the Java Web Server. Pay close attention to the parts about thread safety: some JDBC drivers might not allow different threads to share the same Connection object, even if they take turns using it! Because this example just uses one Connection object, which is opened, used, and closed by one thread, it should work with any driver.

Logging for Servlets

If a servlet throws an exception, the Java Web Server catches it and prints a stack trace in an Error log (for Web page service servlets, logs/javaweb-server/webpageservice/error_log). Developers can use information to figure out what went wrong with the servlet. Unfortunately, end users will see a "500 Server Error" page. A more polished servlet would catch its own exceptions, log them, and then either try to recover or just write a nice error message back to the browser. Unfortunately, the Servlet API does not address the logging issue very thoroughly. In fact, all it says is that servlets inherit a method named log from GenericServlet (superclass of HttpServlet).

Sun's javadoc for GenericServlet tells us that the log method "writes the class name of the servlet and the given message to the servlet log." What is the servlet log? The API doesn't say: it is "implementation dependent." In the JWS, log() output goes to <server_root>/logs/javawebserver/webpageservice/event_log, and for Sun's servletrunner, it goes to the terminal where servletrunner was started.

Most stand-alone Java programs don't bother with log files. They simply write to System.out or System.err. Programs that act as servers need to exercise more care. UNIX servers started at boot time often have their output sent to the system console, where few if any people see it. On NT, this output simply disappears. In general, programs that aren't meant to be run from the command line should not use System.out or System.err.

Simple Logging

Using the servlet's log() method is by far the easiest way to record errors or any other events. However, there is a common bug associated with it. Servlets that override init(ServletConfig) *but do not invoke their superclass's* init(ServletConfig) *method* generate a NullPointerException the first time they try to use their log() method. We raise this point because many servlets override init(), but not all take the trouble to call super.init().

For example, consider this `HelloWorld`-style servlet, which takes a file-name as an initialization parameter and prints it to the browser, as shown in Listing 21.7. It can be modified to log its errors with only minimal changes (see Listing 21.8).

Listing 21.7 `MessageOfTheDay.java`.

```java
package com.awl.cseng.jws.util;

import java.io.*;
import javax.servlet.*;
import javax.servlet.http.*;

public class MessageOfTheDay extends HttpServlet {
  byte[] message;

  public void init(ServletConfig config)
  throws ServletException {
    super.init(config);

    String filename = config.getInitParameter("filename");
    if ( filename == null ) {
      throw new UnavailableException(this,
            "Init parameter \"filename\" not found.");
    }

    try {
      // Allocate array big enough to hold the file
      File file = new File(filename);
      int len = (int)file.length();
      message = new byte[len];

      // Read the file into the array
      FileInputStream in = new FileInputStream(file);
      in.read(message);
      in.close();
    } catch (IOException e) {
      throw new UnavailableException(this,
                                "Cannot read " + filename);
    }
  }

  public void doGet(HttpServletRequest req,
                  HttpServletResponse res)
  throws java.io.IOException {
    res.setStatus(HttpServletResponse.SC_OK);
    res.setContentType("text/plain");
    OutputStream out = res.getOutputStream();
    out.write(message);
    out.close();
  }
}
```

Listing 21.8 MessageOfTheDayLog.java.

```java
package com.awl.cseng.jws.util;

import java.io.*;
import javax.servlet.*;
import javax.servlet.http.*;

public class MessageOfTheDayLog extends HttpServlet {
  byte[] message;

  public void init(ServletConfig config)
  throws ServletException {
    super.init(config);

    String filename = config.getInitParameter("filename");
    if ( filename == null ) {
      log(
      "MessageOfTheDay.init: Init parm \"filename\" not found.");
      throw new UnavailableException(this,
                     "Init parameter \"filename\" not found.");
    }

    try {
      // Allocate array big enough to hold the file
      File file = new File(filename);
      int len = (int)file.length();
      message = new byte[len];

      // Read the file into the array
      FileInputStream in = new FileInputStream(file);
      in.read(message);
      in.close();
    } catch (IOException e) {
      log("MessageOfTheDay.init: Cannot read " + filename);
      throw new UnavailableException(this,
            "Cannot read " + filename);
    }
  }

  public void doGet(HttpServletRequest req,
                    HttpServletResponse res)
  throws java.io.IOException {
    try {
      res.setStatus(HttpServletResponse.SC_OK);
      res.setContentType("text/plain");
      OutputStream out = res.getOutputStream();
      out.write(message);
      out.close();
    } catch (Exception e) {
      log("MessageOfTheDay.doGet: " + e);
    }
  }
}
```

Advanced Logging

The common servlet log is fine for simple logging needs. Servlets that require more functionality, for instance separate logs or conditional logging, need something a little more powerful. The class in Listing 21.9, loosely based on Sun's `TraceLog`, is an example of such a log.

Listing 21.9 `Log.java`.

```java
package com.awl.cseng.jws.log;

import java.io.IOException;
import java.io.OutputStream;
import java.io.FileOutputStream;
import java.io.BufferedOutputStream;
import java.util.Date;
import java.text.DateFormat;
import com.awl.cseng.jws.util.SeverityLevel;

/**
 * Highly optimized general-purpose logging class.  Uses fast
 * byte arrays instead of slow Strings.  Tightly coupled with
 * SeverityLevel class.
 *
 * @see SeverityLevel
 * @author Tom Snee
 */
public class Log {

  // Constants
  static final SeverityLevel DEFAULT_THRESHOLD
                              = SeverityLevel.ERROR;

  // Instance fields
  BufferedOutputStream out;
  DateFormat           formatter;
  SeverityLevel        threshold;

  // Constructors
  /**
   * Creates a log object with default severity threshold.
   *
   * @see SeverityLevel
   * @param filename Name of the log file.
   * @param append True: append to log file; False: overwrite
   * log file.
   * @exception IOException If the specified file cannot be
   * opened.
   */
  public Log(String filename, boolean append)
  throws IOException {
    FileOutputStream raw = new FileOutputStream(filename,
                                                append);
```

```
        out         = new BufferedOutputStream(raw);
        formatter   = DateFormat.getDateTimeInstance();
        threshold   = DEFAULT_THRESHOLD;
    }

    /**
     * Creates a log object with default severity threshold.
     *
     * @see SeverityLevel
     * @param out OutputStream to which log entries should be
     * written.
     */
    public Log(OutputStream raw) {

            if ( raw instanceof BufferedOutputStream ) {
                out = (BufferedOutputStream)raw;
            } else {
            out = new BufferedOutputStream(raw);
            }

        formatter   = DateFormat.getDateTimeInstance();
        threshold   = DEFAULT_THRESHOLD;
    }

    // Methods
    /**
     * This method writes messages to a log file, if their severity
     * levels are above the threshold.  The file format is
     * <PRE>[date] severity: message</PRE>.
     *
     * WARNING: This method contains hidden synchronization.
     *
     * As a design decision, this method returns an IOException
     * instead of throwing one.  This is because callers should not
     * have to put calls to write() within a try-catch block.
     * That is important because
     * 1. this method will probably be called from within "catch"
     * statements to begin with, and nested try-catches can be hard
     * to read;
     * 2. few callers of this method will ever care if it threw an
     * exception or not.
     *
     * @see #setThreshold
     * @see #getThreshold
     * @param severity The severity level of the message.
     * @param msg Message to be written, if its severity exceeds
     * the current threshold.
     * @returns An IOException if one were encountered in writing
     * the log, otherwise null.
     */
    public IOException write(SeverityLevel severity,
                             byte[] message) {
```

```
// Implementation note: This method does everything possible
// to avoid calling a synchronized method (out.write()) more
// than once.  If in the future synchronization becomes less
// expensive than array copying, this should be changed.

if ( !severity.asSevereAs(threshold) )
  return null;

try {
  String dateString = formatter.format(new Date());
  byte[] dateBytes  = dateString.getBytes();
  int dateLen       = dateBytes.length;

  byte[] severityBytes = severity.getBytes();
  int severityLen      = severityBytes.length;

  String lineSeparator
                = System.getProperty("line.separator");
  byte[] lineSepBytes  = lineSeparator.getBytes();

  byte buffer[] = new byte[dateLen
                + severityLen
                + message.length
                + lineSepBytes.length
                + 5];
  // 5?  Overhead from extra bytes '[', ']', ':', ' '.

  int index = 0;

  // [date] ...
  buffer[index++] = '[';
  System.arraycopy(dateBytes, 0, buffer, index, dateLen);
  index += dateLen;
  buffer[index++] = ']';
  buffer[index++] = ' ';

  // ...severity: ...
  System.arraycopy(severityBytes, 0, buffer, index,
                   severityLen);
  index += severityLen;
  buffer[index++] = ':';
  buffer[index++] = ' ';

  // ...message...
  System.arraycopy(message, 0, buffer, index,
                   message.length);
  index += message.length;

  // ...<eol>
  System.arraycopy(lineSepBytes, 0, buffer, index,
                   lineSepBytes.length);
```

```
      out.write(buffer);
    } catch (IOException e) {
      return e;
    }

    return null;
}

/**
 * Gets the bytes from the message String and calls
 * <A HREF="#write(com.awl.cseng.jws.util.SeverityLevel,
 * byte[])">write(SeverityLevel, byte[])</A>.
 */
public IOException write(SeverityLevel severity,
                         String message) {
  return write(severity, message.getBytes());
}

/**
 * Sets the severity threshold.  No messages less severe than
 * this will be printed.
 *
 * @param severity The severity threshold.
 */
public void setThreshold(SeverityLevel severity) {
  threshold = severity;
}

/**
 * Returns the severity threshold.  No messages that fall under
 * it will be printed.
 *
 * @return The severity threshold.
 */
public SeverityLevel getThreshold() {
  return threshold;
}

/**
 * Flushes any log output that might be buffered.
 *
 * @return IOException if there is a problem flushing the log.
 */
public IOException flush() {
  try {
    out.flush();
  } catch (IOException e) {
    return e;
  }
  return null;
}
```

```
/**
 * Closes the log.
 *
 * @return IOException if there is a problem closing the log.
 */
public IOException close() {
  try {
    out.close();
  } catch (IOException e) {
    return e;
  }
  return null;
}
}
```

Messages written to this log, like UNIX syslog messages, must have a severity level. Instead of using an `int`, the `Log` class uses a special type called `SeverityLevel` (see Listing 21.10). It would be less work to just use `int`s, but then the `write()` method would have to throw an illegal argument exception if it were called with anything outside the range it expected. With a special type, that kind of error becomes almost impossible to make, and if it is made, it is caught at compile time, not runtime. How would a servlet use these classes? Let's use the message of the day servlet shown in Listing 21.11 as an example.

Listing 21.10 `SeverityLevel.java`.

```
package com.awl.cseng.jws.util;

/**
 * SeverityLevel is a parameterized type of seven log message
 * severity levels.  They are, in decreasing order, EMERGENCY,
 * ALERT, CRITICAL, ERROR, WARNING, NOTICE, INFO, and DEBUG.
 */
public class SeverityLevel {

  public static final SeverityLevel EMERGENCY
                                = new SeverityLevel(0);
  public static final SeverityLevel ALERT
                                = new SeverityLevel(1);
  public static final SeverityLevel CRITICAL
                                = new SeverityLevel(2);
  public static final SeverityLevel ERROR
                                = new SeverityLevel(3);
  public static final SeverityLevel WARNING
                                = new SeverityLevel(4);
  public static final SeverityLevel NOTICE
                                = new SeverityLevel(5);
  public static final SeverityLevel INFO
                                = new SeverityLevel(6);
  public static final SeverityLevel DEBUG
                                = new SeverityLevel(7);
```

```java
private int     severity;
private String str;
private byte[] b;

/**
 * Private constructor--this class wouldn't be type safe
 * otherwise.
 */
private SeverityLevel(int severity) {
  this.severity = severity;
  switch (severity) {
  case 0:
    str = "EMERGENCY";
    b   = str.getBytes();
    break;
  case 1:
    str = "ALERT";
    b   = str.getBytes();
    break;
  case 2:
    str = "CRITICAL";
    b   = str.getBytes();
    break;
  case 3:
    str = "ERROR";
    b   = str.getBytes();
    break;
  case 4:
    str = "WARNING";
    b   = str.getBytes();
    break;
  case 5:
    str = "NOTICE";
    b   = str.getBytes();
    break;
  case 6:
    str = "INFO";
    b   = str.getBytes();
    break;
  case 7:
    str = "DEBUG";
    b   = str.getBytes();
  }
}

/**
 * Compares severity levels.
 *
 * @param level Severity level to compare.
 * @return False if level is less severe.
 */
public boolean asSevereAs(SeverityLevel level) {
  return (this.severity <= level.severity);
}
```

```
/**
 * @return String representation of severity level.
 */
public String toString() {
  return str;
}

/**
 * @return Copy of byte-array representation of severity level.
 */
public byte[] getBytes() {
  // Don't send a reference to the original array!  It might be
  // changed.
  byte[] copy = new byte[b.length];
  System.arraycopy(b, 0, copy, 0, b.length);
  return copy;
}
}
```

Listing 21.11 MessageOfTheDayFinal.java.

```
package com.awl.cseng.jws.util;

import java.io.*;
import javax.servlet.*;
import javax.servlet.http.*;
import com.awl.cseng.jws.log.Log;
import com.awl.cseng.jws.util.SeverityLevel;

public class MessageOfTheDayFinal extends HttpServlet {
  byte[] message;
  Log logger;

  public void init(ServletConfig config)
  throws ServletException {
    super.init(config);

    String logfile = config.getInitParameter("logfile");
    if ( logfile == null ) {
      logfile = "/tmp/ExampleServlet.log";
    }
    try {
      logger = new Log(logfile, true);
    } catch (IOException e) {
      throw new UnavailableException(this,
                      "ExampleServlet.init: Cannot open "
                      + logfile
                      + ": "
                      + e);
    }

    String filename = config.getInitParameter("filename");
    if ( filename == null ) {
      logger.write(SeverityLevel.ERROR,
```

```
        "MessageOfTheDay.init: Init parm \"filename\" not found.");
      throw new UnavailableException(this,
                        "Init parameter \"filename\" not found.");
    }

    try {
      // Allocate array big enough to hold the file
      File file = new File(filename);
      int len = (int)file.length();
      message = new byte[len];

      // Read the file into the array
      FileInputStream in = new FileInputStream(file);
      in.read(message);
      in.close();
    } catch (IOException e) {
      logger.write(SeverityLevel.ERROR,
        "MessageOfTheDay.init: cannot read " + filename);
      throw new UnavailableException(this,
          "Cannot read " + filename);
    }
  }

  public void doGet(HttpServletRequest req,
                    HttpServletResponse res)
  throws java.io.IOException {
    try {
      res.setStatus(HttpServletResponse.SC_OK);
      res.setContentType("text/plain");
      OutputStream out = res.getOutputStream();
      out.write(message);
      out.close();
      logger.write(SeverityLevel.INFO,
        "MessageOfTheDay.doGet: successfully wrote response to "
        + req.getRemoteUser());
    } catch (Exception e) {
      logger.write(SeverityLevel.ERROR, "Caught "
                                        + e
                                        + " in doGet");
    }
  }
}
```

MessageOfTheDayFinal's init() method constructs an instance of the com.awl.cseng.jws.log.Log class, which is referred to by the new instance field logger. This reference can be used to log errors or just record interesting pieces of information.

Conclusion

In our experience, poor logging is the biggest complaint end users have about server-side software (aside from poor documentation). Developers have little motivation to make their programs more verbose than is absolutely necessary for their own debugging purposes. Once the programs go into production, though, developers often find themselves spending more time supporting the code than they did writing it. In the long run, we are all better off when programs tell their maintainers about every request, response, and state transition they encounter. System operators usually relish the chance to play detective, so if programmers give them the information they need to debug and fix problems themselves, the programmers have to deal with fewer vaguely worded problem reports (e.g., "The server isn't responding" or, our favorite, "Your program is messed up.").

CHAPTER 22

Services and the Java Server Infrastructure

Throughout this book we have occasionally referred to the `webpageservice` and the `securepageservice`, the "boxes" in which servlets run. At this point these services may seem nothing short of magical. They do things like thread management, logging, talking to the administration interface, and other things no mere mortal servlet is able to do. Fortunately, this is magic that anyone can learn. It is even possible to create new services that have nothing to do with the Web or HTTP and run them in the same engine where now-familiar portions of the Java Web Server run.

In this chapter we explain when it is appropriate to use a service instead of a servlet, what makes up a service, how they interact with the overall architecture of the Java Web Server (JWS), and their life cycle. We present a very simple service that does some simple text manipulation, and we show how to extend it to handle a custom log format, interact with the administration tool, and even how to allow a service to use servlets.

But first, a word of precaution. Although the magic of services is open to anyone, it is not supported by Sun or JavaSoft in any official capacity. The code presented in this chapter works with the Java Web Server version 1.1.1 and will probably continue to work through the next few revisions; however, at the time of this writing, plans are afoot to completely rewrite the internals of the Java Web Server. While that version will probably support something like services, the APIs may not remain the same.

The `webpageservice` and `securepageservice` are something like restaurants—places where people go to buy all sorts of delicious items. These services run in a larger system that can be called the Java Server Infrastructure (JSI), which is something like a huge mall. In addition to these two restaurants, it has many other shops, each of which runs pretty much independently. Just as the shops in a mall share certain resources, such as water and electricity, all services share a common heap and virtual machine. And just as a mall is convenient because everything is in one place, the JSI puts all the network resources under the single roof of the administration tool.

Services versus Servlets

No, it is not the death match of the century. Servlets and services are the best of friends, and neither would think of harming the other. However, when starting a new project, the programmer must decide which of them is the most appropriate for the task.

Almost always, the decision falls on the side of servlets. There is not a lot that a service can do that a servlet running in the `webpageservice` or `securepageservice` cannot. Both handle network requests and can send out arbitrary kinds of data as a response. Writing servlets is generally easier. Since all the hard work of handling the connection and the protocol is already done, the servlet needs to deal with only the application logic.

That said, a servlet cannot be used in some cases, most notably, if the connection needs to be persistent. A persistent connection occurs if the communication between a client and the back end consists of more than a single request followed by a single response. For example, the client and server may need to negotiate a number of parameters before starting to communicate, as telnet does. This kind of communication can, in principle, be handled by a servlet. Each step of the communication would require opening a new connection, and the servlet would need to manage multiple simultaneous conversations using the session tracking mechanism. However, building a new connection at each step may be very time consuming.

Similarly, a servlet cannot be used if an existing protocol is being replicated. If a programmer wishes to reimplement FTP or SMTP in Java, it has to be in a service.

Finally, a service is necessary if the developer wants more sophisticated control in the administration tool than the simple name/value pairs provided for servlets. A service can specify a very wide range of controls to the administration tool for both setting parameters and monitoring performance.

Inside a Service

Each service contains two major components. The first handles the low-level details, such as logging, servlet management, managing the connection, and so on. The second handles the details of the protocol and either generating the responses or delegating the work to a servlet that will do so.

com.sun.server.Service *Class*

The com.sun.server.Service class, or another class that extends it, does all the hard work. It listens for new connections, possibly at multiple ports, and manages threads, servlets, security, and logs. In the webpageservice, this is the class com.sun.service.http.HttpService. It is this class that the administration tool affects when a new realm or servlet is added or the number of active threads is changed. Most services use the provided com.sun.server.Service class and do not worry about the details. However, some services, in particular those that need servlets, logging, or security realms, must extend this class to provide the additional functionality.

com.sun.server.EndpointHandler *Interface*

When a service gets a connection, it encapsulates it in an Endpoint object and passes it to a class that implements the EndpointHandler interface. This class is expected to implement the communication protocol. No default class that implements EndpointHandler is provided.

The interface does not specify much. It has an init() method, which is called once for each thread in the JWS (i.e., the number of threads specified in the administration tool), The init() method is passed a Service and a ServiceEndpoint. The ServiceEndpoint contains information about the connection: whether it is TCP or UDP, what the timeout on the socket is, and so on. Most EndpointHandlers do not need to worry about the details.

EndpointHandler also has a handleRequest method that gets an Endpoint object. This object can be used to get an input and output stream. The simplest EndpointHandler simply does a bunch of reads and writes. Note that there is no destroy() method or any equivalent. init() should not allocate any static resources; only the service should do this.

In the webpageservice, the interface is implemented by a class called sun.server.http.HttpServiceHandler. This is the class that worries about mapping filename extensions to content types, mapping URLs to servlets, implementing servlet chaining, and so on.

A Simple Service

It is possible to write many useful services by doing nothing other than implementing the EndpointHandler interface. Most of the common network services, such as FTP, NNTP, and SMTP, could be written this way. Listing 22.1 is a simple service written this way. It is yet another variation on "Hello, world."

Listing 22.1   `ServiceHandler` for a simple service.

```
import java.io.*;
import java.net.*;
import com.sun.server.*;

public class HelloServiceHandler implements EndpointHandler {
  /**
   * This service is so simple, it doesn't need any
   * information from the service or ServiceEndpoint.
   * We still need to provide the init method
   * to satisfy the interface requirements
   */
  public void init(Service s, ServiceEndpoint se) {
  }

  /**
   * This gets called for each request
   */
  public void handleRequest(Endpoint e) throws IOException {
    TcpEndpoint tcpEndpoint = (TcpEndpoint) e;
    Socket s             = tcpEndpoint.getSocket();
    byte[] buf           = new byte[512];
    InputStream   ins    = s.getInputStream();
    OutputStream outs    = s.getOutputStream();
    PrintWriter   outp   = new PrintWriter(outs);
    int len;

    while(true) {
      len        = ins.read(buf,0,buf.length);
      String tmp = new String(buf,0,len);
      // When we see an exclamation point, we close
      // the connection
      if(tmp.indexOf("!") != -1) {
        outs.close();
        ins.close();
        s.close();
        return;
      }

      outp.println("Hello, world!  You said: " + tmp);
      outp.flush();
    }
  }
}
```

Notice the `com.sun.server` package that is imported at the top. Unlike the servlet API, which is defined as a standard extension to the Java language, the classes used to build services are components of the commercial Java Web Server.

Installing `HelloService`

This class can be compiled like any other; it only needs the `<server_root>/lib/jws.jar` file to be added to the class path. Once it has been compiled, there are only a few things that need to be done to install it. First and most important, make sure that the `HelloService.class` file is somewhere in the JWS's class path. Then create a new directory called `<server_root>/properties/server/javaserver/HelloService`.

The directory should contain three files that the JWS will use to figure out various things about the service. These files are `endpoint.properties`, which defines the endpoint behavior of the service, `service.properties`, which defines various things about the underlying service, and `adminUI.properties`, which describes what information should be available and modifiable from the administration applet. Finally, the administration service needs to be told to manage the new service. This is done by adding an entry to `properties/server/javaserver/administer_services.properies`.

`endpoint.properties` File

This file should contain the lines shown in Listing 22.2, including information about the endpoint. The first line states that this endpoint will use TCP. Endpoints can also communicate over UDP. The second line states that the `HelloService` class should be used as the interface. The next two lines state that the service should listen on all active interfaces, on port 4000. The remainder of the file sets up properties that the JWS will use to determine how many threads to start up, how long to allow a client to wait for a connection, and so on.

Listing 22.2   Contents of the `endpoint.properties` file.

```
endpoint.main.class=com.sun.server.TcpServiceEndpoint
endpoint.main.handler=HelloServiceHandler
endpoint.main.interface=*
endpoint.main.port=4000

endpoint.main.backlog=50
endpoint.main.min.threads=3
endpoint.main.max.threads=10

# handler expire timeout in seconds
endpoint.main.timeout=300
```

```
# service shutdown grace period in seconds.
endpoint.main.grace=30
```

service.properties File

This file should contain the lines shown in Listing 22.3. The first four lines contain information that will be presented through the administration tool. The last line defines the class that will provide the underlying service functionality. We discuss this file in more detail in the next section; for the moment, the only important thing to note is that when the init() method is called, the service object that is passed in will be of this type.

Listing 22.3   Contents of the service.properties file.

```
service.name=HelloService
service.description=Hello World
service.vendor=Addison Wesley Longman
service.version=1.0
service.class=com.sun.server.Service
```

adminUI.properties File

This file should contain the following lines:

```
# Categories
admin.ui.Category.1.config.Setup=images/SetupIcon.gif

# Sections
admin.ui.config.1.Basic=

com.sun.server.admin.toolkit.BasicEndpoint
admin.ui.config.2.Tuning=

com.sun.server.admin.toolkit.EndpointTuning
```

administer_services.properties File

This file contains a simple list of services to administer. It is not necessary to add a new service to this file in order for it to run; creating the directory with the first three files will do that. However, one of the benefits of the JWS is the ease of administration, so why not use it? All that is needed is to add HelloService to the administer property, making the file look something like this:

```
server.service.administer=webpageservice securepageservice
HelloService adminservice
```

NOTE: The adminservice must be the last one listed so that it will be able to administer all the others.

Using HelloService

Once these four files have been created and HelloService.class placed in CLASSPATH, the service is ready to be used. Restart the service, then bring up the administration applet. HelloService should now be listed along with the now-familiar webpage and securepage. Initially HelloService will not be running, but it can be started by highlighting its entry and clicking Start. Double clicking its entry brings up a control panel similar to the others, although with only a single screen. This screen allows the port and interfaces to be changed, as well as the number of threads and the time-out period. Note that these are the editable properties specified in the adminUI.properties file.

Once everything is up and running, telnet to port 4000, and type something. It may be necessary to hit Return before the data is actually sent. Each line that is sent will be echoed back preceded by Hello, world! You said:. Enter a line with an exclamation point to exit.

Extending the com.sun.server.Service Class

The com.sun.server.Service class that does all the underlying work—it listens to the main socket; dispatches to an EndpointHandler; and handles logging, servlets, and communicating with the administration interface. It implements Runnable. The run() method listens at the port, when a connection comes in obtains or creates an EndpointHandler, creates an Endpoint, and calls handle-Request.

If a custom service needs servlets, custom logs, or an administration tool, programmers extend this class and override one or more methods. No one should override run()!

Service has an init() method, which can be used to allocate static resources. init() is called once when the JWS starts up and once each time the service is restarted via the administration tool. init() is passed a Properties object. The value of the properties comes from the properties/server/javaserver/<service_name> directory, and many (but not all) can be modified with the administration tool.

Changing the service class that Service should use is quite easy. Here is quite possibly the most boring class ever contained in a Java book:

```
import com.sun.server.*;
public class HelloService extends Service {
}
```

Compile this code and put it in the JWS's class path. Then change the `service.class` line in the `service.properties` file to

```
service.class=com.sun.server.HelloService
```

Restart the server. Nothing will have changed, which is not surprising considering that the class does nothing new. In the next few sections we show how to override `Service()` methods in `HelloService` to do a number of interesting things.

Adding Custom Properties and Administration Screens

While the service we have created follows in the proud tradition of "Hello, world" programs throughout the ages, perhaps it should be given some more personality by changing the way it echos text. Maybe instead of responding to each line with "`Hello, world! You said: `" it could say something like "`Whoa dude! You exclaimed: `".

Unfortunately, the way things stand right now, it would be necessary to edit and recompile `HelloWorldHandler` to make this change. And when the boss sees the result and writes a memo disallowing cutesy behavior in production code, it would be necessary to do so again. It would be great if there were some way to change this in some configuration file or even better use the administration applet. Rejoice; there is! And best of all, it is very simple.

First, it is necessary to create a file to hold the service-specific properties. This file can have any name, as long as it has a suffix of `.properties` and is present in the `<server_root>/properties/server/javawebserver/HelloService` directory. In fact, the properties listed in all files within that directory will be sent to the service. We will call our file `hello.properties` and put the following line in it:

```
HelloService.prefix=Hello World!  You said:
```

Of course, to use these properties, some changes have to be made to the `Service` and `Endpoint` classes. The `Service` class will need to get the property in its `init()` method, as shown in Listing 22.4. Likewise, the `Handler` will need to get the property from the service in its endpoint, as shown in Listing 22.5.

Listing 22.4 Implementation of the service.

```
import com.sun.server.*;
public class HelloService extends Service {
    private String prefix = "";

    public void init(PropertyConfig p) throws ConfigException {
        super.init(p);
        String tmp = p.getProperty("HelloService.prefix");
        if (tmp != null) prefix = tmp;
    }

    public String getPrefix() {return prefix;}
}
```

Listing 22.5 Version of ServiceHandler with an external property.

```
import java.io.*;
import java.net.*;
import com.sun.server.*;

public class HelloServiceHandler implements EndpointHandler {
    private String prefix = "";

    /**
     * Get the prefix from the service
     */
    public void init(Service s, ServiceEndpoint se) {
        HelloService hs = (HelloService) s;
        prefix          = hs.getPrefix();
    }

    /**
     * This is called for each request
     */
    public void handleRequest(Endpoint e) throws IOException {
        TcpEndpoint tcpEndpoint = (TcpEndpoint) e;
        Socket s                = tcpEndpoint.getSocket();
        byte[] buf              = new byte[512];
        InputStream   ins       = s.getInputStream();
        OutputStream outs       = s.getOutputStream();
        PrintWriter   outp      = new PrintWriter(outs);
        int len;

        while(true) {
            len         = ins.read(buf,0,buf.length);
            String tmp = new String(buf,0,len);
            // When we see an exclamation point, we close
            // the connection
            if(tmp.indexOf("!") != -1) {
                outs.close();
                ins.close();
                s.close();
                return;
            }
```

```
                outp.println(prefix + tmp);
                outp.flush();
            }
        }
}
```

That is all that is necessary to separate out the properties from the code. Restart the JWS, and `HelloService` will use the prefix value specified in `hello.properties`. Now for the real fun part. In order to export this property to the administration applet, it is necessary to just add a single line to `adminUI.properties`:

```
admin.ui.config.3.Properties=
/com.sun.server.admin.toolkit.PropertyValueEditor file=hello
```

Now restart the JWS, and there will be a new option on the setup menu called Properties. Double clicking on it will bring up a screen reminiscent of the servlet properties screen, with a single property called Prefix. Prefix can be edited, and the `hello.properties` file updates accordingly.

If there are lots of properties, they can be grouped into several sections. For each group it will be necessary to create a new file and add a new entry to the `adminUI.properties` file.

It is possible to do much more sophisticated things, like having a slider that can be used to set a property from a range, like the "Number of threads" slider in the basic properties screen. While doing so is not that difficult, it is beyond the scope of this book—and it's not presently documented or supported by JavaSoft. The interested reader can investigate the properties files of the web-pageservice and delve into the underlying classes with javap.

Adding Logging

In order to have services write to log files, it is necessary only to override the `getlog` method in the service, shown in Listing 22.6. Now that the service is capable of logging, `serviceHandler` can be modified to use the log, as shown in Listing 22.7.

Listing 22.6   Version of the service that supports logging.

```
import java.io.*;
import java.net.*;
import com.sun.server.*;
import com.sun.server.log.*;
public class HelloService extends Service {
    /**
     * The log object.  We start with a NullTraceLog,
     * which will discard any data.  If we cannot create
```

```
 * a real log, at least this will ensure that we do not get
 * any NullPointerExceptions
 */
private TraceLog helloLog    = new NullTraceLog();
private boolean  createdLog = false;

/**
 * The endpoint handler calls this method to get the log.  We
 * currently have only one and will return that one for all
 * requests
 */
public synchronized Log getLog(String name)
     throws IOException
{
  if(!createdLog) {
    File f  = new File(getDefaultLogDirectory() +
                          File.separator + "hello.log");
    FileOutputStream o = new FileOutputStream(f);
    helloLog           = new TraceLog(o);
    createdLog         = true;
  }

  return helloLog;
  }
}
```

Listing 22.7   Version of ServiceHandler that uses the log.

```
import java.io.*;
import java.net.*;
import com.sun.server.*;
import com.sun.server.log.*;
public class HelloServiceHandler implements EndpointHandler {
  private TraceLog helloLog = null;

  /**
   * Get the log from the service
   */
  public void init(Service s, ServiceEndpoint se) {
    try {
      helloLog = (TraceLog) s.getLog("Hello");
    } catch (IOException exc) {}
  }

  /**
   * This is called for each request
   */
  public void handleRequest(Endpoint e) throws IOException {
    TcpEndpoint tcpEndpoint = (TcpEndpoint) e;
    Socket s                = tcpEndpoint.getSocket();
    byte[] buf              = new byte[80];
    InputStream  ins        = s.getInputStream();
    OutputStream outs       = s.getOutputStream();
```

```
    PrintWriter  outp        = new PrintWriter(outs);
    int len;

    while(true) {
      len       = ins.read(buf,0,buf.length);
      String tmp = new String(buf,0,len);
      // When we see an exclamation point, we close
      // the connection
      if(tmp.indexOf("!") != -1) {
        outp.close();
        outs.close();
        ins.close();
        s.close();
        return;
      }

      outp.println("Hello, world!  You said: " + tmp);
      outp.flush();

      // Log this request
      if(helloLog != null) {
        helloLog.print(tmp);
        helloLog.flush();
      }
    }
  }
}
```

This code is a little uglier than it needs to be, because now the handler's init() method needs to get information from the service. This overhead can be eliminated by making Service and EndpointHandler the same class, which can be done because one is a class and the other is an interface. However, this may needlessly complicate matters, since there would now be one class with two init() methods that are called under different circumstances. In order to avoid this confusion, we recommend using two separate classes.

Adding Servlets

We now have a service that makes it fairly easy to change the text that is printed, but what if we would like to be able to print out many different prefixes? Perhaps under some circumstances we would like to prefix the output with "Hello, world" and at other times we would want the Spanish "Hola, mundo." Of course all this could be done with something like a big case statement in the service handler, but what if tomorrow it also becomes necessary to support the French "Bonjour, monde"? Thanks to servlets, we can dynamically extend our service with code to handle specific kinds of requests without having to go in and change the service each time.

Extending a service to use servlets is not difficult, but it does require a lot of classes. As we discussed in Chapter 9, much of the servlet API is expressed in interfaces, for example ServletRequest and ServletResponse. When writing servlets for the JWS this is not really a concern, as JavaSoft has provided classes that implement the interfaces for us. Service writers do not have this luxury to fall back on and must do all the hard work themselves. In addition, there are other classes related to how the service manages and communicates with servlets that must be written.

HelloServlet

Rather than jump straight into all these classes, it makes more sense to start with something familiar and work backward. With that in mind, the first thing we define is the base servlet class that all the application-specific servlets will extend. This is exactly analogous to the HttpServlet class that all Java Web Server servlets extend. Listing 22.8 shows the code for our base class, HelloServlet.

Listing 22.8   Base class for Hello servlets.

```
import java.io.*;
import java.util.*;
import javax.servlet.*;
public class HelloServlet extends GenericServlet {
   private ServletConfig theServletConfig = null;
   private ServletContext theServletContext = null;

   public ServletContext getServletContext() {
      return theServletContext;
   }

   public String getInitParameter(String name) {
      return theServletConfig.getInitParameter(name);
   }

   public Enumeration getInitParameterNames() {
      return theServletConfig.getInitParameterNames();
   }

   public void log(String msg) {
      System.err.println(msg);
      theServletContext.log(msg);
   }

   public ServletConfig getServletConfig() {
      return theServletConfig;
   }
```

```
  public String getServletInfo() {
    return "Base HelloServlet class";
  }

  public void init(ServletConfig config)
        throws ServletException
  {
    super.init(config);
    theServletConfig = config;
    theServletContext = config.getServletContext();
  }

  public void service(ServletRequest req, ServletResponse res)
    throws ServletException, IOException
  {
    int len;

    echoLoop(req.getInputStream(),
             res.getOutputStream(),
             "Default:");
  }

  public void echoLoop(ServletInputStream ins,
                       ServletOutputStream outs,
                       String prefix)
    throws IOException
  {
    int len;
    byte buf[] = new byte[1024];

    while(true) {
      len          = ins.read(buf,0,buf.length);
      String tmp = new String(buf,0,len);
      // When we see an exclamation point,
      // we close the connection
      if(tmp.indexOf("!") != -1) {
        return;
      }

      outs.println(prefix + tmp);
      outs.flush();
    }
  }

  public void destroy() {}
}
```

Most of this code was written to satisfy the ServletContext interface, which GenericServlet implements to make life easier for servlet writers so that code can simply call things like log() instead of having to call getServlet-Context().log().

This class has introduced several other classes that we must now implement. The following sections review each in turn.

HelloServletRequest and HelloServletResponse

Request and response classes can be quite complicated and can allow a great deal of information to be passed to and from the client, as Http-ServletRequest and HttpServletResponse do. Ours can be much simpler, since we do not need much more than simple wrappers around the input and output streams, as shown in Listing 22.9. The response is even simpler, as shown in Listing 22.10.

Listing 22.9   Request class for Hello servlets.

```
import java.io.InputStream;
import java.io.OutputStream;
import java.io.IOException;
import java.net.Socket;
import javax.servlet.*;
import com.sun.server.*;

public class HelloServletRequest implements ServletRequest {
  private ServletInputStream in;

  HelloServletRequest(ServletInputStream in) {
    this.in = in;
  }

  public ServletInputStream getInputStream()
      throws IOException
  {
    return in;
  }

  public int getContentLength() {
    return -1;
  }

  public String getContentType() {
    return null;
  }

  public String getProtocol() {
    return "Echo 1.0";
  }

  public String getScheme() {
    return null;
  }
```

```java
  public String getServerName() {
    return "echo";
  }

  public int getServerPort() {
    return 0;
  }

  public String getRemoteAddr() {
    return null;
  }

  public String getRemoteHost() {
    return null;
  }

  public String getRealPath(String path) {
    return null;
  }

  public String getParameter(String name) {
    return null;
  }

  public String[] getParameterValues(String name) {
    return null;
  }

  public java.util.Enumeration getParameterNames() {
    return null;
  }

  public Object getAttribute(String name) {
    return null;
  }

  public java.io.BufferedReader getReader() {return null;}
  public java.lang.String getCharacterEncoding() {return null;}
  public java.io.PrintWriter getWriter() {return null;}
}
```

Listing 22.10   Response class for Hello servlets.

```java
import java.io.InputStream;
import java.io.OutputStream;
import java.io.IOException;
import java.net.Socket;
import javax.servlet.*;
import com.sun.server.*;
public class HelloServletResponse implements ServletResponse {
  private ServletOutputStream out;
```

```
HelloServletResponse(ServletOutputStream out) {
    this.out = out;
}

public ServletOutputStream getOutputStream()
    throws IOException
{
    return out;
}

public void setContentLength(int len) {}
public void setContentType(String type) {}

public java.lang.String getCharacterEncoding() {return null;}
public java.io.PrintWriter getWriter() {return null;}
}
```

HelloInputStream and HelloOutputStream

Just as HttpServlets need to be able to get an instance of OutputStream to send results, so will HelloServlets. In addition, we need to provide an InputStream, although it is currently not used. These two classes are presented in Listings 22.11 and 22.12.

Listing 22.11   Input stream for Hello servlets.

```
import java.io.InputStream;
import java.io.OutputStream;
import java.io.IOException;
import java.net.Socket;
import javax.servlet.*;
import com.sun.server.*;
public class HelloInputStream extends ServletInputStream {
    protected InputStream in;

    public HelloInputStream(InputStream in) {
        this.in = in;
    }

    public int read() throws IOException {
        return in.read();
    }
}
```

Listing 22.12   Output stream for Hello servlets.

```
import java.io.InputStream;
import java.io.OutputStream;
import java.io.IOException;
import java.net.Socket;
import javax.servlet.*;
import com.sun.server.*;
```

```
public class HelloOutputStream extends ServletOutputStream {
  protected OutputStream out;

  public HelloOutputStream(OutputStream out) {
    this.out = out;
  }

  public void write(int b) throws IOException {
    out.write(b);
  }

  public void flush() throws IOException {
    out.flush();
  }

  public void close() throws IOException {
    out.close();
  }
}
```

HelloServletConfig

We now need to create a ServletConfig class, which the servlets will use to obtain configuration information passed to them through the administration tool. It too is pretty simple; it only provides a means for servlets to request properties and the ServletContext. (Listing 22.13).

Listing 22.13   ServletConfig class for Hello servlets.

```
import javax.servlet.*;
import java.util.Properties;
import java.util.Enumeration;
import com.sun.server.*;
public class HelloServletConfig implements ServletConfig {
    private ServletManager theServletManager = null;
    private Properties theProperties        = null;

    public HelloServletConfig(ServletManager m,Properties p) {
       theServletManager = m;
       theProperties     = p;
    }

    public ServletContext getServletContext() {
       return new HelloServletContext(theServletManager);
    }

    public String getInitParameter(String name) {
       return theProperties.getProperty(name);
    }
```

```
     public  Enumeration getInitParameterNames() {
        return theProperties.propertyNames();
     }
}
```

HelloServletContext

Again think back to the classes that HttpServlets use. It is possible for servlets to get a ServletContext object, which describes all the servlets currently in the system and provides access to them. We need to provide a similiar class, although again in the current architecture no one will use it (Listing 22.14). Note the use of a ServletManager to actually get servlet names, which is discussed in more detail next.

Listing 22.14 ServletContext class for Hello servlets.

```java
import javax.servlet.*;
import com.sun.server.*;
import java.util.Enumeration;
public class HelloServletContext implements ServletContext {
   private HelloServletManager theServletManager = null;

   public HelloServletContext(ServletManager m) {
      theServletManager = (HelloServletManager) m;
   }

   public String getRealPath(String path) {
      return "/";
   }

   public String getMimeType(String file) {
      return "text/plain";
   }

   public String getServerInfo() {
      return "Hello service";
   }

   ServiceParameters getParameters() {
      return null;
   }

   public Object getAttribute(String name) {
      return null;
   }

   public Enumeration getServletNames() {
      return theServletManager.getLoadedServletNames();
   }
```

```
public Servlet getServlet(String name) {
  return theServletManager.getServlet(name);
}

public void log(Exception e, String message) {
  theServletManager.logEvent(0,message);
  theServletManager.logError(e);
}

public void log(String message) {
  theServletManager.logEvent(0,message);
}

public Enumeration getServlets() {
  return theServletManager.getLoadedServlets();
}
}
```

HelloServletManager

Here is the code for `HelloServletManager`. This is the class that actually tracks servlets and is responsible for loading, initializing, retrieving, and ultimately destroying them. Most of this work is handled in the base class, so we just need to provide code to map servlet names to classes and handle logging, as shown in Listing 22.15.

Listing 22.15   `ServletManager` class for the hello service.

```
import java.io.*;
import java.net.Socket;
import javax.servlet.*;
import com.sun.server.*;
import com.sun.server.log.*;
import com.sun.server.security.*;
class HelloServletManager extends ServletManager {
  private Service service;

  public HelloServletManager(Service s) throws IOException {
    super(s);
    service = s;
  }

  /**
   * Allows a servlet to write an exception to the log.
   * This is one of the abstract methods implementers
   * must provide
   */
  public void logError(Throwable e) {
    try {
      TraceLog l = (TraceLog) service.getLog("log");
      l.write(e);
```

```
      } catch (Exception exc) {}
    }

    /**
     * Allows a servlet to log a message at a priority level.
     * This is one of the abstract methods implementers
     * must provide
     */
    public void logEvent(int level,String message) {
      try {
        TraceLog l = (TraceLog) service.getLog("log");
        l.write(message);
      } catch (Exception exc) {}
    }

    /**
     * Return a servlet config.
     * This is one of the abstract methods implementers
     * must provide
     */
    public ServletConfig getServletConfig(java.util.Properties p)
    {
      return new HelloServletConfig(this,p);
    }
}
```

Modifying HelloService *and* HelloServiceHandler *to Use Servlets*

Whew! That's a lot of classes, but we are finally ready to make HelloService handle servlets. First the service must create and install a servlet manager, as shown in Listing 22.16.

Listing 22.16   Version of the HelloService that supports servlets.

```
import com.sun.server.*;
public class HelloService extends Service {
  private String prefix = "";
  private static HelloServletManager theServletManager = null;

  public void init(PropertyConfig p) throws ConfigException {
    super.init(p);
    String tmp = p.getProperty("HelloService.prefix");
    if (tmp != null) prefix = tmp;
    if(theServletManager == null) initServletManager();
  }

  private void initServletManager() {
    System.err.println("Initializing servlet manager");
    try {
      theServletManager = new HelloServletManager(this);
    } catch (Exception e) {
```

```
      System.err.println("Couldn't create servlet manager: " +
                          e);
      e.printStackTrace(System.err);
    }
  }

  public String getPrefix() {return prefix;}
  public void setServletManager(ServletManager s) {
    super.setServletManager(s);
    theServletManager = (HelloServletManager) s;
  }

  public ServletManager getServletManager() {
    if(theServletManager == null) initServletManager();
    return theServletManager;
  }
}
```

ServiceHandler now uses the service to get the servlet manager and then calls the callServletService method to pass control to the servlet's service() method. Each request that comes in must be mapped to a servlet. We do this by looking at the first line of input. If it is, for example, "French," we dispatch to a servlet called frenchServlet, as shown in Listing 22.17.

Listing 22.17   Version of the service handler that uses servlets.

```
import java.io.*;
import java.net.*;
import com.sun.server.*;
public class HelloServiceHandler implements EndpointHandler {
  private Service theService = null;
  private String prefix = "";

  /**
    * Get the prefix from the service
    */
  public void init(Service s, ServiceEndpoint se) {
    theService      = s;
    HelloService hs = (HelloService) s;
    prefix          = hs.getPrefix();
  }

  /**
    * This gets called for each request
    */
  public void handleRequest(Endpoint e) throws IOException {
    TcpEndpoint tcpEndpoint = (TcpEndpoint) e;
    Socket s                = tcpEndpoint.getSocket();
    InputStream   ins       = s.getInputStream();
    OutputStream outs       = s.getOutputStream();
    String servletName      = "";
```

```
        // Determine the name of the servlet the user really wants
        byte data[] = new byte[1];
        // Read one byte at a time until we get to the end of the
        // first line
        while(ins.read(data) > 0) {
           if(data[0] == '') break;
           servletName = servletName + new String(data,0,1);
        }

        // Try to get the servlet to handle this request
        try {
           HelloInputStream in   = new HelloInputStream(ins);
           HelloOutputStream out = new HelloOutputStream(outs);

           HelloServletRequest  req = new HelloServletRequest(in);
           HelloServletResponse res = new HelloServletResponse(out);

           // Here's where the real magic happens.  The
           // servletManager will look for the servlet
           // by name, load and init() it if it has not
           // yet been initialized, and then call its
           // service method
           theService.getServletManager().callServletService(
                                             servletName,
                                             req,
                                             res);
        } catch (Exception e2) {
           String stmp = "Couldn't kick off the servlet: " +
              e2 + "\n";
           outs.write(stmp.getBytes());

           ByteArrayOutputStream tmp = new ByteArrayOutputStream();
           PrintWriter p             = new PrintWriter(tmp);
           e2.printStackTrace(p);

           e2.printStackTrace(System.err);

           outs.write(tmp.toString().getBytes());
        }
     }
  }
}
```

The last thing that needs to be done to enable servlets is to create a servlets.properties file in the same directory as the rest of the service properties. This can initially be empty; the JWS will write configuration information to this file. As constructed, hello servlets have no parameters that need to be stored, but the HelloService administration tool can have screens to handle passing parameters to servlets, just as is done for HttpServlets in the Java Web Server. As might be expected, enabling this functionality is as simple as adding a few more lines to the adminUI.properties file. Properties added are stored in servlets.properties and will be available to init() methods through the properties argument.

Conclusion

Well, we said that would be a lot of work, and we were not lying! Still, the power and flexibility of services can be worth the effort of writing all those classes. But more often than not, it is far better to confine application development to HttpServlets, which can do nearly everything custom services can do and do it a great deal more easily.

APPENDIX

Developer Resources

The Internet is a fountain of useful information for software developers. This is especially true for Java-based technology. With Sun Microsystems leading the way and hundreds of thousands of developers helping each other through the network, it is amazing how quickly you can find information about a specific problem or get advice from an experienced programmer. This appendix provides a brief guide to information available through the Internet and other sources that may be helpful to beginning and advanced programmers who want to learn about the Java™ Web Server™ (JWS).

Following are the different categories of information available, the best resources in each category, and a list of every resource in the category known to us, including brief annotations.

FAQs

FAQs are documents that answer and explain frequently asked questions. They are a staple of the Internet. Almost every topic has a well-maintained FAQ file. The best FAQs for the Java Web Server follow.

Sun's Java Web Server FAQ

Sun has a Java Web Server FAQ at

http://jserv.java.sun.com/products/webserver/faq/

that provides a comprehensive introduction to the Java Web Server and explains many frequently encountered problems and confusing issues. This FAQ is a great way to get started.

547

Java Programmer's FAQ at the Café au Lait Site

For a central repository of information on all Java-based technology, the hard-to-top FAQ site can be found at

http://metalab.unc.edu/javafaq/

It has links to most major sources of information about the Java programming language and is updated frequently. This FAQ document is great for beginners and advanced programmers alike.

Java Programmer's FAQ

Java author Peter Van Der Linden's explanation of Java technology can be found at

http://www.afu.com/javafaq.html

More than 100 pages of information on a wide variety of topics.

Web Pages and Sites

A tremendous variety of Web sites exists for Java Web Server enthusiasts (see list that follows). The official word from Sun is available at

http://jserv.java.sun.com/

It contains all the JWS documentation, API descriptions, White Papers, FAQs, new versions, and a store in which to buy the Java Web Server over the Web.

Another great site for Java Web Server developers is the Java Developer's Connection (JDC) at

http://developer.java.sun.com/

This is the place for Java developers! Download advanced versions of the JDK and other Java software, report bugs and vote for the most important, read technical White Papers, and so on.

Be sure to check out the toolbar, a collection of applets that lets developers communicate with other. They include a chat application, a bulletin board, a way to find other people currently on the site with related interests, and so on.

To encourage people to share information, the JDC has introduced an idea called Duke Dollars. Every visit to the site earns $1, and new members start with $10. When asking a question on the boards you can specify how many Duke Dollars the answer is worth, and pay the person who provides the answer. At last year's JavaOne conference, the person with the most Duke Dollars got a rather nice jacket. This site is powered by the JWS.

Draft Java Coding Standard

http://gee.cs.oswego.edu/dl/html/javaCodingStd.html

Doug Lea, author of the book, *Concurrent Programming in Java*, proposes some Java coding standards. At the end of the Web page is a great related documents list that focuses on coding standards.

Java-Linux

http://www.blackdown.org/java-linux.html

Information on the port of the Java virtual machine for Linux.

Java Design: Building Better Apps and Applets

http://www.oi.com/java/

Peter Coad's speech on building Java applications.

Java Developer's Connection

http://developer.java.sun.com/

Sun's Web site for the developer community. Full of interesting tips, tricks, and downloads.

ServletCentral

http://www.servletcentral.com/

A grass-roots magazine called *ServletCentral* is one of the best places on the net for servlet and Java Web Server information. This magazine contains articles about servlets and other information that gives a picture of where the Servlet API and the Java Web Server are headed.

JavaWorld

http://www.javaworld.com/

JavaWorld is a commercial magazine with a sophisticated approach to Java technology. It is a good source for news about Java and in-depth articles on current topics.

Richard Baldwin's Scoop on Java

http://www.phrantic.com/scoop/onjava.html

Nicely written tutorials for Java and JavaScript.

Search Engines

http://www.infoseek.com/
http://altavista.digital.com/
http://www.dejanews.com/

It is probably worth the effort to periodically check for "servlet" and "Java Web Server" and see what pops up. We use the three listed here often.

Other Information

http://www.developer.com/

A repository of lots of different developers' resources, including Gamelan; it is an Earth Web Inc. site. A good place to find code or just see what others are doing.

Tools

http://www.livesoftware.com/

Live™ Software produces a wide range of tools, including ServletDebugger and ServletKiller.

Mailing Lists

The Java Web Server mailing lists provide an ongoing conversation about current topics of interest to developers. The only warning here is that it is best to have some sort of e-mail filter program to sort the incoming mail from a mailing list into a separate folder. The volume of mail from lists can get rather large.

The best mailing list for the Java Web Server is called *jserv-interest*. It can be subscribed to from

http://jserv.java.sun.com/products/java-server/lists.html

Although this is a tremendous source of information, be warned that it leads to a pretty tremendous volume of mail. There is also a *servlet-interest* mailing list run by Sun. A comprehensive list of Java mailing lists is available at

http://metalab.unc.edu/javafaq/mailinglists.html

jserv-interest Mailing List

http://jserv.java.sun.com/products/java-server/lists.html

Mailing list for JWS developers. Closely monitored by the Java Web Server development team.

jserv-interest Mailing List Archives

http://archives.java.sun.com/archives/jserv-interest.html

Archives for the jserv-interest list.

Newsgroups

Back in the 1980s, the ancient days before the Web, Usenet newsgroups were where all the *real* fun on the Internet was. Usenet is now something like the old part of town—the buildings are not as flashy as they once were and a lot of disreputable businesses have moved in. But there are still some excellent night spots for those who know where to look.

Most of the groups in the `comp.lang.java` hierarchy have some degree of useful information and are worth scanning periodically, if not reading completely. A good newsreader will make time spent on Usenet even more profitable. Sadly, the newsreaders built into Web browsers are not good ones. Modern newsreaders can provide sophisticated filtering and grouping of messages.

For example, they allow automatic deletion of all messages with "FAST CASH!!!" in the title or messages posted by particularly tedious individuals. It is also possible to put all messages that contain the word "servlet" at the top of a list or highlight them in a special color. We recommend `strn` or `slrn` for users on UNIX; the latter is also available for Windows. `slrn` can be obtained from

http://space.mit.edu/~davis/slrn.html

Before starting to read any of the information at the Java newsgroups, or indeed any other groups on Usenet, it is worth becoming familiar with the rules of "netiquette," which are posted often to *new.announce.newusers*. Nettiquete is really nothing more than the rules of polite society. Adhering to the rules when posting makes it much more likely that messages are read and received well, and lead to helpful answers.

In particular, before posting to a group take the time to read it for a while and look up the group's list of FAQs. Many questions, especially on technical groups, come up repeatedly, and answers to such questions are better obtained from the FAQs than by irritating the other readers of the group by asking the questions again.

Here is a short list of groups that servlet developers may find useful. Note that there are no groups about servlets per se, but there are lots of groups that discuss related issues that servlet developers may find interesting.

- *comp.lang.java.announce:* Announcements of commercial or free Java products. Moderated, which means someone is making sure questions get answered and everyone behaves. Worth keeping an eye on.
- *comp.lang.java.programmer:* General issues around programming in Java.
- *comp.lang.java.help:* Help for beginning users of Java—how to get programs to compile and so on.
- *comp.infosystems.www.servers.misc:* A place to talk about server technology in general, including the JWS.

comp.lang.java.corba

Discussions of Java and CORBA, covering both the official ORB in 1.2 and existing commercial ORBs under 1.1.

comp.lang.java.advocacy

Perpetual Java Sux/Java Rules flamewars. Avoid.

comp.lang.java.announce

Announcements of commercial or free Java products. Moderated. Worth keeping an eye on.

comp.java.programmer

General issues relative to programming in Java.

comp.lang.java.security

Security and Java. Note that this refers not to HTTP security in the Java Web Server but rather to issues of how secure Java systems are, the new security features in 1.2, and so on.

comp.lang.java.databases

JDBC and related issues.

comp.lang.java.beans

The Bean and related APIs. A good place to talk about servlet Beans.

comp.lang.java.machine

Java virtual machine

comp.lang.java.help

Help for beginning users of Java—how to get programs to compile and so on.

comp.lang.java.gui

Discussions of AWT and Swing.

comp.lang.java.softwaretools

Discussions and comparisons of commercial and free development tools.

comp.infosystems.www.authoring.cgi

Writing CGIs. Could potentially have some servlet-related information.

comp.infosystems.www.servers.misc

Server technology in general, including the JWS.

comp.infosystems.www.servers.unix
Web servers on UNIX (there is no corresponding *www.servers.nt*).

comp.infosystems.www.misc
General discussion about the Web.

Professional Organizations and Conferences

Java Lobby

The mission of the Java Lobby at

http://javalobby.com/

is as follows: "The main purpose of the Java Lobby is to represent the needs and concerns of the Java developer and user community to the companies and organizations who have influence in the evolution of Java."

JavaOne

JavaOne every spring is the best source of information about Java technology. One day, we hope, there will be a Java Web Server conference.

Books

There are so many good books about the Java programming language that it is hard to pick favorites. Here is a list of the books we found helpful while writing this book.

Concurrent Programming in Java: Design Principles and Patterns by Doug Lea (Reading, MA: Addison Wesley Longman, 1997).
This is an authoritative book on threads in Java, a confounding topic.

Java Threads, Second Edition, by Scott Oaks and Henry Wong (Sebastopol, CA: O'Reilly, 1999).
A comprehensive book about threads.

The Java Virtual Machine Specification, Second Edition, by Tim Lindholm and Frank Yellin (Reading, MA: Addison Wesley Longman, 1999).
The canonical description of the Java virtual machine. This book is particularly useful for getting a deeper understanding of how to write high-performance code.

The Java Language Specification by James Gosling, Bill Joy, and Guy Steele
(Reading, MA: Addison Wesley Longman, 1996).
  The definition of the language.

The Java Programming Language, Second Edition, by Ken Arnold and
James Gosling (Reading, MA: Addison Wesley Longman, 1998).
  A readable introduction to Java. This book would be valuable to beginners.

JDBC Database Access with Java: A Tutorial and Annotated Reference by
Graham Hamilton, R.G.G. Cattell, and Maydene Fisher (Reading, MA:
Addison Wesley Longman, 1997).
  A comprehensive look at the JDBC API.

Java Network Programming by Elliotte Harold (Sebastopol, CA: O'Reilly,
1997).
  An excellent introduction to network communications and how Java supports
  such programming.

INDEX

Binary Software Evaluation Agreement

READ THE TERMS OF THIS AGREEMENT AND ANY PROVIDED EVALUATION TERMS AND/OR SUPPLEMENTAL LICENSE TERMS (COLLECTIVELY "AGREEMENT") CAREFULLY BEFORE OPENING THE SOFTWARE MEDIA PACKAGE. BY OPENING THE SOFTWARE MEDIA PACKAGE, YOU AGREE TO THE TERMS OF THIS AGREEMENT. IF YOU ARE ACCESSING THE SOFTWARE ELECTRONICALLY, INDICATE YOUR ACCEPTANCE OF THESE TERMS BY SELECTING THE "ACCEPT" BUTTON AT THE END OF THIS AGREEMENT. IF YOU DO NOT AGREE TO ALL THESE TERMS, PROMPTLY RETURN THE UNUSED SOFTWARE TO YOUR PLACE OF PURCHASE FOR A REFUND OR, IF THE SOFTWARE IS ACCESSED ELECTRONICALLY, SELECT THE "DECLINE" BUTTON AT THE END OF THIS AGREEMENT.

Evaluation Terms

These Evaluation terms, the terms of the attached Binary Code License Agreement, and any Supplemental terms constitute the "Evaluation Agreement." Capitalized terms not defined herein shall have the same meanings ascribed to them in the Agreement. These Evaluation terms shall supersede any inconsistent or conflicting terms in the Agreement.

1. Notwithstanding Section 1, You may use Software for internal evaluation purposes only. You shall have no right to use Software for productive or commercial uses. No license is granted for any other purpose. You may not transfer Software in whole or in part to any third party.

2. Software may contain a timebomb mechanism. You agree to hold Sun harmless from any claims based on your use of Software for any purposes other than those of internal evaluation.

3. This Evaluation Agreement commences on the date on which you receive Software (the "Effective Date") and will expire thirty (30) days from the Effective Date, unless terminated as provided herein. Upon expiration, You agree to immediately cease use of and destroy Software.

4. Sun is under no obligation to support Software or to provide upgrades or error corrections ("Updates") to the Software. If Sun, at its sole option, supplies Software Updates to You, the Software Updates will be considered part of Software, and subject to the terms of this Evaluation Agreement.

Sun Microsystems, Inc.

Binary Code License Agreement

1. LICENSE TO USE. Sun grants you a nonexclusive and nontransferable license for the internal use only of the accompanying software and documentation and any error corrections provided by Sun (collectively "Software"), by the number of users and the class of computer hardware for which the corresponding fee has been paid.

2. RESTRICTIONS. Software is confidential and copyrighted. Title to Software and all associated intellectual property rights is retained by Sun and/or its licensors. Except as specifically authorized in any Supplemental License Terms, you may not make copies of Software, other than a single copy of Software for archival purposes. Unless enforcement is prohibited by applicable law, you may not modify, decompile, reverse engineer Software. Software is not designed or licensed for use in on-line control of aircraft, air traffic, aircraft navigation or aircraft communications; or in the design, construction, operation or maintenance of any nuclear facility. You warrant that you will not use Software for these purposes. You may not publish or provide the results of any benchmark or comparison tests run on Software to any third party without the prior written consent of Sun. No right, title or interest in or to any trademark, service mark, logo or trade name of Sun or its licensors is granted under this Agreement.

3. LIMITED WARRANTY. Sun warrants to you that for a period of ninety (90) days from the date of purchase, as evidenced by a copy of the receipt, the media on which Software is furnished (if any) will be free of defects in materials and workmanship under normal use. Except for the foregoing, Software is provided "AS IS". Your exclusive remedy and Sun's entire liability under this limited warranty will be at Sun's option to replace Software media or refund the fee paid for Software.

4. DISCLAIMER OF WARRANTY. UNLESS SPECIFIED IN THIS AGREEMENT, ALL EXPRESS OR IMPLIED CONDITIONS, REPRESENTATIONS AND WARRANTIES, INCLUDING ANY IMPLIED WARRANTY OF MERCHANTABILITY, FITNESS FOR A PARTICULAR PURPOSE, OR NONINFRINGEMENT, ARE DISCLAIMED, EXCEPT TO THE EXTENT THAT THESE DISCLAIMERS ARE HELD TO BE LEGALLY INVALID.

5. LIMITATION OF LIABILITY. TO THE EXTENT NOT PROHIBITED BY LAW, IN NO EVENT WILL SUN OR ITS LICENSORS BE LIABLE FOR ANY LOST REVENUE, PROFIT OR DATA, OR FOR SPECIAL, INDIRECT, CONSEQUENTIAL, INCIDENTAL OR PUNITIVE DAMAGES, HOWEVER CAUSED REGARDLESS OF THE THEORY OF LIABILITY, ARISING OUT OF OR RELATED TO THE USE OF OR INABILITY TO USE

SOFTWARE, EVEN IF SUN HAS BEEN ADVISED OF THE POSSIBILITY OF SUCH DAMAGES. In no event will Sun's liability to you, whether in contract, tort (including negligence), or otherwise, exceed the amount paid by you for Software under this Agreement. The foregoing limitations will apply even if the above-stated warranty fails of its essential purpose.

6. Termination. This Agreement is effective until terminated. You may terminate this Agreement at any time by destroying all copies of Software. This Agreement will terminate immediately without notice from Sun if you fail to comply with any provision of this Agreement. Upon Termination, you must destroy all copies of Software.

7. Export Regulations. All Software and technical data delivered under this Agreement are subject to U.S. export control laws and may be subject to export or import regulations in other countries. You agree to comply strictly with all such laws and regulations and acknowledge that you have the responsibility to obtain such licenses to export, reexport, or import as may be required after delivery to you.

8. U.S. Government Restricted Rights. Use, duplication, or disclosure by the U.S. Government is subject to restrictions set forth in this Agreement and as provided in DFARS 227.7202-1(a) and 227.7202-3(a) (1995), DFARS 252.227-7013(c)(1)(ii) (Oct 1988), FAR 12.212(a) (1995), FAR 52.227-19 (June 1987), or FAR 52.227-14(ALT III) (June 1987), as applicable.

9. Governing Law. Any action related to this Agreement will be governed by California law and controlling U.S. federal law. No choice of law rules of any jurisdiction will apply.

10. Severability. If any provision of this Agreement is held to be unenforceable, this Agreement will remain in effect with the provision omitted, unless omission would frustrate the intent of the parties, in which case this Agreement will immediately terminate.

11. Integration. This Agreement is the entire agreement between you and Sun relating to its subject matter. It supersedes all prior or contemporaneous oral or written communications, proposals, representations and warranties and prevails over any conflicting or additional terms of any quote, order, acknowledgment, or other communication between the parties relating to its subject matter during the term of this Agreement. No modification of this Agreement will be binding, unless in writing and signed by an authorized representative of each party.

For inquiries, please contact Sun Microsystems, Inc., 901 San Antonio Road, Palo Alto, California 94303.

Java™ Technology from Addison-Wesley

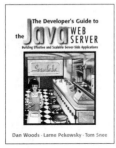

ISBN 0-201-37949-X

ISBN 0-201-37963-5

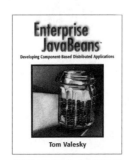

ISBN 0-201-60446-9

ISBN 0-201-43329-X

ISBN 0-201-48543-5

ISBN 0-201-61563-0

ISBN 0-201-30972-6

ISBN 0-201-18393-5

ISBN 0-201-32573-X

ISBN 0-201-32582-9

http://www.awl.com/cseng
◆◆ Addison-Wesley

Addison-Wesley Computer and Engineering Publishing Group

How to Register Your Book

Register this Book

Visit: **http://www.awl.com/cseng/register**

Enter this unique code: **csng-xeaq-glgx-gfcy**

Then you will receive:

- Online updates about *The Developers Guide to the Java™ Web Server*
- Exclusive offers on other Addison-Wesley books
- Access to our online book contest*

Visit our Web site

http://www.awl.com/cseng

When you think you've read enough, there's always more content for you at Addison-Wesley's web site. Our web site contains a directory of complete product information including:

- Chapters
- Exclusive author interviews
- Links to authors' pages
- Tables of contents
- Source code

You can also discover what tradeshows and conferences Addison-Wesley will be attending, read what others are saying about our titles, and find out where and when you can meet our authors and have them sign your book.

We encourage you to patronize the many fine retailers who stock Addison-Wesley titles. Visit our online directory to find stores near you or visit our online store: **http://store.awl.com/** or call **800-824-7799**.

Contact Us via Email

cepubprof@awl.com
Ask general questions about our books.
Sign up for our electronic mailing lists.
Submit corrections for our web site.

bexpress@awl.com
Request an Addison-Wesley catalog.
Get answers to questions regarding
your order or our products.

innovations@awl.com
Request a current Innovations Newsletter.

webmaster@awl.com
Send comments about our web site.

mary.obrien@awl.com
Submit a book proposal.
Send errata for an Addison-Wesley book.

cepubpublicity@awl.com
Request a review copy for a member of the media
interested in reviewing new Addison-Wesley titles.

Addison Wesley Longman
Computer and Engineering Publishing Group
One Jacob Way, Reading, Massachusetts 01867 USA
TEL 781-944-3700 • FAX 781-942-3076

*See web site for contest rules and duration

CD-ROM WARRANTY

Addison Wesley Longman, Inc., warrants the enclosed disc to be free of defects in materials and faulty workmanship under normal use for a period of ninety days after purchase. If a defect is discovered in the disc during this warranty period, a replacement disc can be obtained at no charge by sending the defective disc, postage prepaid, with proof of purchase to:

Addison Wesley Longman
Editorial Department
One Jacob Way
Reading, MA 01867

After the ninety-day period, a replacement disc will be sent upon receipt of the defective disc and a check or money order for $10.00, payable to Addison Wesley Longman, Inc.

Addison Wesley Longman, Inc., makes no warranty or representation, either expressed or implied, with respect to this software, its quality, performance, merchantability, or fitness for a particular purpose. In no event will Addison Wesley Longman, its distributors, or dealers be liable for direct, indirect, special, incidental, or consequential damages arising out of the use or inability to use the software. The exclusion of implied warranties is not permitted in some states. Therefore, the above exclusion may not apply to you. This warranty provides you with specific legal rights. There may be other rights that you may have that vary from state to state.

> More information and updates are available at
> *http://www.awl.com/cseng/titles/0-201-37949-X/*

Use of this software is subject to the Binary Code License terms and conditions on pages 575–577. Read the License carefully. By opening the package, you are agreeing to be bound by the terms and conditions of this License from Sun Microsystems, Inc.